D0969295

PSYCHOLOGICAL PROBLEMS OF AGEING

The Wiley Series in

CLINICAL PSYCHOLOGY

J. Mark G. Williams *School of Psychology, University*
(Series Editor) *of Wales, Bangor, UK*

Robert T. Woods *(Editor)*	Psychological Problems of Ageing: Assessment, Treatment and Care
William Yule *(Editor)*	Post-Traumatic Stress Disorders: Concepts and Therapy
Nicholas Tarrier *Adrian Wells* *Gillian Haddock* *(Editors)*	Treating Complex Cases: The Cognitive Behavioural Therapy Approach
Michael Bruch *Frank W. Bond* *(Editors)*	Beyond Diagnosis: Case Formulation Approaches in CBT
Martin Herbert	Clinical Child Psychology: Social Learning, Development and Behaviour (second edition)
Eric Emerson *Chris Hatton* *Jo Bromley* *Amanda Caine* *(Editors)*	Clinical Psychology and People with Intellectual Disabilities
J. Mark G. Williams *Fraser N. Watts* *Colin MacLeod* *Andrew Mathews*	Cognitive Psychology and Emotional Disorders (second edition)
Phil Mollon	Multiple Selves, Multiple Voices: Working with Trauma, Violation and Dissociation

Further titles in preparation: *A list of
earlier titles in the series follows the index*

PSYCHOLOGICAL PROBLEMS OF AGEING

Assessment, Treatment and Care

Edited by
Robert T. Woods
University of Wales, Bangor, UK

JOHN WILEY & SONS, LTD

Chichester · New York · Weinheim · Brisbane · Singapore · Toronto

Copyright © 1999 by John Wiley & Sons Ltd,
Baffins Lane, Chichester,
West Sussex PO19 1UD, England

National   01243 779777
International   (+44) 1243 779777
e-mail (for orders and customer service enquiries):
cs-books@wiley.co.uk
Visit our Home Page on http://www.wiley.co.uk
or http://www.wiley.com

Other Wiley Editorial Offices

John Wiley & Sons, Inc., 605 Third Avenue,
New York, NY 10158-0012, USA

WILEY-VCH Verlag GmbH, Pappelallee 3,
D-69469 Weinheim, Germany

Jacaranda Wiley Ltd, 33 Park Road, Milton,
Queensland 4064, Australia

John Wiley & Sons (Asia) Pte Ltd, 2 Clementi Loop #02-01,
Jin Xing Distripark, Singapore 129809

John Wiley & Sons (Canada) Ltd, 22 Worcester Road,
Rexdale, Ontario M9W 1L1, Canada

Library of Congress Cataloging-in-Publication Data

Psychological problems of ageing : assessment, treatment and care /
edited by Robert T. Woods.
    p.   cm. — (The Wiley series in clinical psychology)
Includes bibliographical references and index.
ISBN 0-471-97434-X (pbk.)
1. Aged—Mental health.   2. Aging—Psychological aspects.
3. Psychotherapy for the aged.   4. Geriatric psychiatry.   I. Woods,
Robert T.   II. Series.
    [DNLM: 1. Mental Disorders—in old age.   2. Aging—psychology.
3. Psychotherapy—in old age.   WT 150 P97375 1999]
RC451.4.A5P7774   1999
618.97'689—dc21
DNLM/DLC
for Library of Congress   98-46227
                                                               CIP

British Library Cataloguing in Publication Data

A catalogue record for this book is available from the British Library

ISBN 0-471-97434-X

Typeset in 10/12pt Palatino by Dorwyn Ltd, Rowlands Castle, Hants.
Printed and bound in Great Britain by Bookcraft (Bath) Ltd, Midsomer Norton, Somerset
This book is printed on acid-free paper responsibly manufactured from sustainable forestry, in which at least two trees are planted for each one used for paper production.

CONTENTS

ABOUT THE EDITOR

Bob Woods has been practising as a clinical psychologist with older people for over 20 years. His interest was activated prior to clinical training by his experience working for a few months as a nursing assistant in a psychogeriatric ward for people with dementia. He trained and worked initially as a clinical psychologist in Newcastle upon Tyne, where there is a strong tradition of old age research. Subsequently he has combined extensive clinical work with older people with academic appointments at the Institute of Psychiatry and latterly at University College, London. In both settings he was heavily involved in training clinical psychologists in work with older people. His previous books include the first British text-book in the area *Clinical Psychology with the Elderly*, with P. G. Britton, and with Una Holden, *Reality Orientation*, now in its third edition as *Positive Approaches to Dementia Care*. He is a member of the Medical and Scientific Advisory Panel of the Alzheimer's Disease Society and co-authored the Society's guide for caregivers. His published research has included studies on both depression and dementia, on assessment and therapeutic approaches, and on family caregivers. He holds the first Chair in Clinical Psychology with the Elderly in the UK, at the University of Wales, Bangor, where he is Associate Director of the Institute of Medical & Social Care Research.

LIST OF CONTRIBUTORS

Peter G. Britton

Senior Lecturer in Applied Psychology, 4th Floor, Ridley Building, University of Newcastle upon Tyne, Claremont Place, Newcastle upon Tyne NE1 7RU, UK

Peter G. Coleman

Professor of Psychogerontology, Centre for Research into Psychological Development, University of Southampton, Highfield, Southampton SO17 1BJ, UK

Leah P. Dick

Formerly of Geriatric Research, Educational and Clinical Center, VA Palo Alto Health Care System, Palo Alto, CA, and Stanford University School of Medicine, Stanford, CA, USA

Anne B. Edwards

Department of Human Development and Family Studies, The Pennsylvania State University, University Park, PA 16802, USA

Dolores Gallagher-Thompson

Geriatric Research, Education and Clinical Center, VA Palo Alto Health Care System, Palo Alto, CA, and Stanford University School of Medicine, Stanford, CA 94025, USA

Chris Gilleard

Director of Psychology, Springfield Hospital, Tooting, London SW17 7DJ, UK

Bob G. Knight

Merle H. Bensinger Associate Professor, Leonard Davis School of Gerontology, Ethel Percy Andrus Gerontology Center, University of Southern California, Los Angeles, CA 90089-0191, USA

Robin G. Morris — *Reader in Neuropsychology, Institute of Psychiatry, De Crespigny Park, London SE5 8AF, UK*

Ian Stuart-Hamilton — *Principal Lecturer in Psychology, University College Worcester, Henwick Grove, Worcester, WR2 6AJ, UK*

Larry W. Thompson — *Geriatric Research, Education and Clinical Center, VA Palo Alto Health Care System, Palo Alto, CA, and Stanford University School of Medicine, Stanford, CA 94025, USA*

Robert T. Woods — *Professor of Clinical Psychology of the Elderly, Institute of Medical & Social Care Research, University of Wales, Wheldon Building, Bangor, Gwynedd LL57 2UW, UK*

Steven H. Zarit — *Professor of Human Development, Department of Human Development and Family Studies, and Assistant Director for Behavioural Sciences, Gerontology Center, Henderson S-105, Pennsylvania State University, University Park, PA 16802, USA*

SERIES PREFACE

The Wiley Series in Clinical Psychology aims to provide a comprehensive set of texts covering the application of psychological science to the problems of mental health and disability. In 1996, Wiley published a large 29-chapter *Handbook of the Clinical Psychology of Ageing*, edited by Professor Bob Woods, a comprehensive volume addressing all aspects of the psychology of older adults. It remains the standard reference work in this area. However, because of the need continually to update the research evidence, and to communicate to health and care professionals what is essential to their practice, the Wiley Series in Clinical Psychology asked Bob Woods to update and distil the wisdom from the Handbook into a shorter, more focused form that would tell practitioners what they need to know.

In this volume, then, we have the essentials: about cognitive and emotional changes in later life; about the issues that arise for those who care for older adults, especially those who suffer dementia; about what psychological treatments may address such emotional and identity problems that arise. Including authors from the UK and the USA, the book takes a broad but evidence-based perspective, and will be an invaluable resource not only for psychologists, but for all professionals involved with the care of older people.

J. Mark G. Williams
Series Editor

PREFACE

In the Preface to the *Handbook of the Clinical Psychology of Ageing* (John Wiley & Sons, 1996), I suggested that that volume was intended to be a celebration of the maturity of clinical psychology with older people, reflecting the coming of age of the specialism. I am delighted that it has also proved to be a valuable training resource, primarily for clinical psychologists in training, but for other professional groups also. This volume is more directly geared to such training needs, a day-to-day resource for those gaining experience in psychological work with older adults, considerably less weighty than the *Handbook*.

This book largely comprises chapters from the *Handbook*, updated where necessary by the original authors, covering three main areas. These provide, first, an introduction to normal ageing; second, an examination of the clinical context, both in terms of the psychology of the major clinical disorders encountered and the settings for the work undertaken; and finally, clinical psychological assessment and therapy is discussed.

Deciding which chapters to include was a difficult task, as each of the 29 chapters in the *Handbook* covers a key area, and a case could be made for the inclusion of each one. However, by substantially adapting and revising my own contributions to the book, I have sought to ensure that the reader is introduced to as many as possible of the key issues, and is directed to further reading where further detail is required. If the Handbook were intended to be comprehensive, almost everything that a trainee might need to know, this book is more focused, covering what the trainee really needs to know.

It has proved possible to retain the international perspective of the book, with three chapters from authors in the USA, reflecting some of the important clinical psychology developments there. Recent years have seen increasing international collaborations in this field, a welcome development in a field where sharing of research, knowledge and expertise is vital to the progress that is still required to benefit current and future generations of older people.

Much has been achieved over the past 20 years or so; the growth in the number of psychologists working with older people has been great, but many challenges remain:

- Residential care in many places leaves much to be desired.
- Community care struggles to find effective ways of supporting people with dementia at home.
- The increasing emphasis on primary care as a focus for service delivery raises many issues for clinical psychology—not least in terms of manpower.
- Legal and ethical frameworks are challenged by the complexity of the problems encountered by some older people and their caregivers.
- Ageism in health and social care remains, although often disguised.
- Models of service delivery often seem to allow insufficient scope for rehabilitation; assessing how much improvement an individual might show given the opportunity is a difficult task.
- Future generations of older people may well have quite different expectations of psychological support and interventions in late life.

The agenda for the new millennium is demanding, but there is much that clinical psychological approaches and perspectives may contribute to these and other areas that must be addressed.

Once again I am grateful to all the contributors; to Michael Coombs and all at John Wiley and Sons Ltd for their encouragement to produce this volume; to my colleagues for continued support; and to Brenda Ellis for all her help with this and other projects.

Bob Woods

Chapter 1

INTRODUCTION

Peter G. Britton* and Robert T. Woods**

INTRODUCTION

The application of psychological knowledge to the needs of older people has provided both challenge and opportunity in the second half of the twentieth century. As a new millennium approaches, it is timely to review the response of clinical psychology to these demands and to anticipate future developments. The knowledge base relating to the psychological processes of normal ageing and to abnormalities arising has grown almost exponentially in this period. Combined with a greater sophistication in techniques of application and intervention, this has provided the basis for a far more powerful and effective contribution to the maintenance and improvement of the quality of life of older people. In the UK, and in many other countries, much has been achieved. However, the potential has often not been fulfilled, largely because on both a national and international basis the funding of posts and training and recruitment has not been able to keep pace with the demand for psychological inputs to a wide range of services for older people.

OLDER PEOPLE

As we consider the development of clinical psychology with older people, the starting point must be to acknowledge that the target population has changed and will continue to change considerably. Our very language has to develop with a growing recognition of the stigmatizing effects of

* University of Newcastle upon Tyne, Newcastle upon Tyne, UK; ** University of Wales, Bangor, UK

Psychological Problems of Ageing: Assessment, Treatment and Care. Edited by R.T. Woods.
© 1999 John Wiley & Sons Ltd.

language on potentially devalued groups in society. Ten years ago, this section would have been entitled "The Elderly", 20 years ago "The Aged". Some might simply see political correctness at work here, or assume a merely cosmetic relabelling to protect sensitivities. However, there are certainly clear signs of current cohorts of older people making inroads into some of the disempowering forces that surround them, particularly in the roles of consumer and campaigner. Each generation of older people will bring to late life their own history and values, and will accordingly influence and be influenced by the social culture of the time. A clinical psychology of ageing must be responsive to the dynamic tapestry produced by the interaction of cohort effects, temporal changes and the myriad of processes occurring to the individual over time, which are conveniently subsumed under the umbrella term "ageing".

A continuing issue has been the definition of the older person, couched more traditionally as "When does old age begin?". The term "older person" is vague enough, of course, to include virtually the entire population! The usual arbitrary cut-off point for many purposes, including psychological research and practice, is 65 (or sometimes 60). Some of the more dramatic predictions of a decade or two ago, which seemed to imply that most Western societies were about to be overwhelmed by a flood ("a rising tide") of older people, have been tempered by reality. In the UK, the figures provided by the Office of National Statistics (Social Trends,1997) suggest that overall the population over 65 has stabilized, following dramatic growth in the 1960s and 1970s. The current trend is for there to be fewer 65–70-year-olds but an increasing number in their late 70s and 80s (see also Chapter 7, this volume).

In the UK, almost half of Department of Health and local authority social services expenditure is accounted for by the 16% of the population over 65 (Audit Commission, 1997). As it is the over-75 year-old age group who are most likely to use care services, the current demographic trends are exercising greatly those responsible for planning the future pattern of health and social care and its financial sustainability. Over-75s have an increasing need for health and social care resources as physical and mental health problems arise more frequently, and social networks change.

More older people will have spouses living with them and have children and grandchildren. However, increased social mobility and changes in family structure mean that far fewer will live close enough to their children for them to provide care and support (Grundy,1996) There remain some concerns that politicians and planners have not reacted adequately to the projected increases in the proportion of the population aged over 75 and, particularly, over 85. The next century, with the post-war "baby boom" generation reaching 65 in the years from 2011, promises once again an increase in the overall elderly population in Western countries. For example, this predicted increase is expected to lead to a population of 6.8 million over-75's in the UK by the year 2034, compared with 4 million in 1994.

An implication of the shifting demography of late life is that the imbalance in life expectancy between the sexes becomes all the more apparent. In general, the slight excess of women (5:4) in the "younger-old" has changed by the age of 80+ to a situation where the greater majority of survivors are women (3:1 at 85; 10:1 at 100), usually living on their own. Most older people in Europe and North America are women, who have lived through times of dramatic change in the role and position of women in society.

International perspectives and cross-cultural comparisons are fraught with pitfalls concerning the reliability of statistics and predictions. However, there is broad agreement that the improvements in neonatal care and childcare of the twentieth century will continue to lead to increases in the proportions of older people on a worldwide basis. Thus, there is likely to be a substantial increase in the proportion of older people as reductions in infant mortality are achieved in India, other parts of Asia and Africa. In 1997 life expectancy in North America and the UK is in the late 70s; in Africa it is in the late 50s. The biggest impact initially is likely to be in countries such as Japan and China, where previously the proportion of older people was less. In China, where family size has been regulated in recent years, the rate of proportional increase is likely to be particularly steep.

These demographic shifts must be seen in the context of rapid change in the economic and social structure of many countries. The past 30 years in the UK have seen significant transformation from a mainly industrial to a post-industrial society. The political and economic conditions of the past decade have led to very significant alterations in the expectancies people have of stability of employment and provision for economic support in old age. "Retirement" age has become much more fluid, as many over 50, let alone the over-55s, take advantage of early retirement schemes offered by firms to avoid compulsory redundancies. Financial privation and old age no longer go hand in hand, but rather the gap between the "haves" and the "have-nots" continues to widen. The potential costs of care for older people have significantly influenced planning and provision as the 1990s have advanced; in the UK, long-standing expectations that the state would finance care if needed in late life have rapidly been dispelled, with state help increasingly available only when the bulk of the person's own resources has been expended. Concerns regarding the funding of long-term care in 20 or so years' time, when the next major increase in the number of older people is expected, led in 1998 to the establishment of a Royal Commission on Long-term Care.

Patterns of service delivery in the UK have increasingly reflected these changes. Previously there was a relatively stable model of service provision which combined support from Local Authority-based Social Services and National Health Service-based resources. These services were often less than ideal, with a tendency for community care provision to be patchy and hospital-based resources often equally so. Typically, buildings used had been asylums and workhouses built a century or more before, and were known as such to their elderly clientele. Often poorly maintained and located away from centres of population, they communicated a message of devaluation and social death, despite the efforts of caring and committed staff.

Much has now changed. Community care legislation and the impact on health care of the most radical NHS re-organization to date have had a dramatic effect in a very short time. The pace and volume of change have often seemed to outrun the ability of managers to cope with the pressures of delivering services. Professional staff have been left unsure of their roles and responsibilities. More importantly, older people have been confused about where their services were to be obtained and exactly who was responsible. Hopefully, much of this uncertainty is transitory, but to many who have attempted to provide a service through the period there is a clear suspicion that great efforts will continue to be needed to ensure that the end results will be beneficial in terms of service provision at an individual level.

Partnership between the public and private (or independent) sectors is now the order of the day, with the former providing much of the professional input. Much of the longer-term care of older people with physical or mental health problems in residential settings has passed into the private sector. The resulting greater disaggregation of long-term care poses a considerable challenge to society in ensuring the adequate monitoring of the standards of quality of care.

This UK perspective is mirrored in Europe and North America, where patterns of service delivery are altering and developing in a variety of ways as adaptation occurs to similar demographic and economic pressures. The key point here is that no part of the overall picture is static: older people, the social, historical, political and economic context, the pattern of services—all are dynamically interrelated; mismatches between expectations and reality are inevitable when so much change occurs so quickly. A good example of the interaction between social expectations and psychological function was provided by Levy & Langer

(1994). In a cross-cultural study involving groups from the USA and China, it was shown that memory performance in later life was related to positive views of ageing. In cultures where older people were respected and valued, there was less apparent decline in cognitive function with age. The older person cannot and must not be studied in isolation from his/her context; he/she is enmeshed in a presumptive world order, rich in accumulated experiences and expectancies.

The clinical psychology of ageing has to respond to this moving picture, but must be careful not to lose sight of those aspects that show continuity over time, or those that have a tendency to repeat themselves with some regularity. Roles may change, the place of work may be different, but the challenge remains: to apply psychological knowledge and principles to assist older persons in need most effectively to fulfil their potential.

CLINICAL PSYCHOLOGY WITH OLDER PEOPLE

Moving on from psychometric assessment

Psychological knowledge is rapidly increasing and our understanding of how to apply this knowledge to practical situations has improved markedly. If we look back to the early 1970s, psychologists' work with older people was almost totally confined to assessment. An overview of publications of the time suggests that basic psychometrics as an aid to diagnosis formed the core of this work. There was little intervention and even less involvement with organizations providing services or the wider political context of care for the elderly. In the late 1970s an increasing interest in intervention models and their application was evident (Woods & Britton, 1977; Miller, 1977a). A UK survey (Cooper, 1983) seemed to indicate that the increasing number of specialist psychologists in this sector were still continuing to emphasize aspects of individual assessment and counselling in their work. The 1980s saw the emergence of publications in the US and UK of specialized texts for psychological work with the elderly (Hussian, 1981; Hanley & Hodge, 1984; Woods & Britton, 1985) which reflected an increasing range of applications.

It would seem that something of a threshold was reached at this point, with an increasing knowledge and skills base interacting with increased numbers of psychologists working with the elderly to produce a sudden upsurge in activity and interest. Other professions in care settings were starting to seek psychological insights for their own practice and managers were becoming aware of the potential of psychological support to an increased extent.

Content of training

This developing role is apparent in reflecting on the evolving content of training in work with older people on one UK clinical psychology training course, with which one of us has been involved for 30 years. Most such courses were initially based around the core areas of adult mental illness, work with children and the "mentally handicapped" (in the terminology of the time). The 1960s saw no specific teaching on older people, although some sessions were given on contemporary psychological research with the elderly. Placement records suggest, however, that assessment of the older person in in-patient and out-patient settings formed a significant component of practical experience.

By the late 1970s there was still no identifiable separate component of teaching, but clear evidence that application of psychological skills and techniques to this age group was quickly evolving. Some teaching sessions contained specific material on the use of therapeutic techniques such as behavioural therapies in individual problems such as challenging behaviours in older people. The mid-1970s appointment of the first psychologists with full-time posts for work in this area started to lead to an increasing use of specific elderly placements (often split at that time with neuropsychology).

The 1980s saw the development of a separate and specific component of teaching related to older adults and strenuous efforts to ensure that the teaching of a broad range of therapeutic skills extended to cover this age group. This was in response to professional pressures nationally and locally, as by then a competent and vociferous group of psychologists working in settings for older people had developed. In 1980, a UK special-interest group (PSIGE, Psychologists' Special Interest Group—Elderly) was formed, later to become a subsystem of the British Psychological Society, Clinical Division. Its regional groups have been an important influence in developing teaching on work with older people on many training courses. Teaching was a combination of material on normal psychological development, assessment and intervention. More specific "elderly" placements appeared as options for elective choice.

Larner's (1986) comments on training issues are of interest. Ten core areas are highlighted:

1. The need to be aware of current research on normal ageing.
2. Theories of ageing, making reference to the "new" concepts of life-span development.
3. Avoiding mythology and stereotyping.
4. The need to effectively "tailor' interventions for older adults.

5. Awareness of service planning and staff training models.
6. Ability to work in a range of settings.
7. Ability to relate to multidisciplinary others.
8. The problems of secondary referral (often with little awareness by the client of referral).
9. Possible staff burnout and demoralization.
10. The impact of death and its anticipation on the practitioner, carers and client.

Current training courses address many of these issues. Professional expectancies have significantly increased in the 1990s and are reflected in training. All UK training courses now have a specific component on work with older people, in many cases comparable in length to input relating to the "longer established" client groups. Pressures over many years resulted in the early 1990s in "compulsory" placements in work with older people or, as an alternative, a clear and specific training component of a wide range of practical work with this client group.

This range of inputs and experiences reflects the vastly increased extent of activities which psychologists working with older people now perform. The core skills of psychometric assessment are still essential, increasingly supplemented by advances in neuropsychological testing. Assessment techniques for other areas—mood, behaviour and quality of life—have a more prominent role. A wide range of interventions for individuals, groups and families are introduced in training. Systemic and family approaches are used, especially in relation to the complexities of caregiving. The stresses and strains of caregiving for both family and professional caregivers are explored, as are the intricacies and eccentricities of evolving care delivery systems.

All of this seems a long way from the constrained roles of 30 years before. The development of a UK Curriculum in Clinical Psychology (Powell, 1994) has given much needed impetus to a life-span approach as the underlying perspective for a generic clinical psychology course. This is an interesting and rapid development less than a decade after the pleas from Larner, quoted earlier, that the fledgling life-span models be recognized in training. This new curriculum also covers many of the themes in input described above and should have a marked positive effect on training in work with older people.

Diversity of roles

What marks out clinical psychology with older people from other specialities is the multiplicity of roles which are likely to arise. A major role continues to be that of an organized and systematic contribution to assessment. This is a primary focus of effective psychological help, for without soundly based, reliable, valid assessment, adequate formulation and intervention are impossible. Assessment ranges over the whole spectrum from the characteristics of the individual to their interaction with the social and physical environments. Psychometric assessment still figures strongly. Defining a specific strengths/needs profile of, say, cognitive abilities may make an important impact on the person's care. Books edited by Wattis & Hindmarch (1988) and Beech & Harding (1990) provide helpful overviews of assessment models and methods.

The traditional base of psychometric cognitive assessment in the global tests of intelligence and memory which predominated in the past has increasingly been supplemented by much more specific measures from current cognitive neuropsychology. These can enable a more explicit definition of current problems of, say, memory and attention, which can assist care planning or be used to monitor the effects of treatment or illness. The potential of these techniques will be evident later in this volume (see Chapters 5 and 9).

At other levels of assessment the use of psychological techniques can guide intervention. The use of analogue situations—much more extensively employed with people with learning disabilities—has brought a degree of systematization and more adequate definition to handling challenging behaviours in dementia settings (Sabin, 1994). The ability to innovate in such ways is a core part of the contribution of psychologists to care.

The definition and assessment of "quality of life" and "adjustment" is a further area to which psychologists have contributed in a variety of ways. What are the needs in various groups? How can they be defined and systematized? Current models of service provision increasingly require that the individual is assessed in these respects with the preparation of an individual care plan or similar document which outlines needs, individual, environmental and social, and equates these with resources available. The paper by Harding, Baldwin & Baser (1987) emphasized the need for client-focused needs assessment, and many since have developed scales from these and similar ideas; the work of Kitwood and associates has been particularly valuable (Kitwood and Bredin, 1992).

The psychologist brings skills in designing and applying observational methods and other information-gathering techniques which enable these assessments to have credible reliability and validity. All too often techniques developed by committed research teams seem to fail to deliver in the reality of day-to-day use.

At the heart of the psychological approach to care is an effective formulation. Psychologists often grossly under-represent this skill when evaluating their contribution to care. Psychologists are trained to formulate and to adapt that formulation on a hypothetico-deductive basis and are scientist-practitioners to a far more significant extent than is often conveyed. The MPAG report (MPAG, 1990) on psychological contributions to, and structures in, the NHS emphasized these approaches as a central component. Psychologists have the potential to be major contributors to the formulation of care plans and packages. Of course, with the diversification of care providers, skills in infiltrating the care system in such a way as to be able to influence the care-planning process are equally important; here, and elsewhere, there is much to learn from colleagues working in learning disabilities, who have been tackling such challenges for some time.

Beyond formulation, clinical psychology can contribute a number of intervention approaches to the care process. Early work tended to be specifically focused on problems such as memory deficits and the application of behavioural techniques in institutional settings (Woods & Britton, 1977). There was some reluctance to grasp that the range of techniques applicable to adult work could with care be extended to work with older adults. Recent years have seen an upsurge in the use of a wide variety of procedures, from behavioural to psychoanalytic, for individuals, families and groups, more closely reflecting practice with younger people. A review of the effectiveness of these approaches (Woods & Roth, 1996) suggests that in areas such as depression, outcomes are as positive with older adults as with younger people. While there are many areas for further research and development, there are no grounds for therapeutic pessimism on the basis of age. Chapters 7, 10, 11 and 12 reflect some of the progress already achieved in the application of psychological therapies to the problems of older people and their supporters.

These chapters discuss approaches that might be used with any age group, e.g. psychotherapy and cognitive-behavioural therapy, as well as those which are thought of as more specific to older people, usually because of their application to people with cognitive impairment, e.g. reality orientation and reminiscence. There has also been increasing interest in systemic approaches (Richardson et al., 1994; Roper-Hall, 1993), although little in the way of outcome research is yet available.Although often characterized as "Family Therapy" these techniques can be applied whenever there is an individual within a "system", whether that system be his/her own family, or a residential setting, or a network of service providers in the community. Inability to gather all the members of the system together does not preclude the use of systemic principles and methods, which are of use even when simply seeing an individual (Walker,1996). The holistic themes surrounding systemic approaches are seen as particularly relevant to handling the multifactorial problems of older people with complex problems of biological, social and psychological change. Walker stresses that the techniques can be useful even when family or carers are unwilling or unable to be available, in that the core methodology of circularity and reflexivity can make a substantial contribution to formulation and intervention. Awareness of family relationships and dynamics, an appreciation of the family life-cycle and recognition of the interconnected nature of many of the problems encountered are essentials of the clinical psychologist's work with older people. Gilleard (1996) provides a useful overview of family therapy approaches in work with older adults, and their applicability to families where one member has a dementia is described by Benbow et al. (1993).

Broader horizons

We have described a number of potential roles in the application of assessment, formulation and treatment models of clinical psychology to the older person. There is, however, a great deal of scope for further development. In recent years there have been many advances in psychological theories and methods applied to health care. A powerful influence has been the increasing integration of interdisciplinary research, contributing to more effective care. For example, Rabbitt (1988) made a plea for increased involvement by a range of psychological specialities and other disciplines in collaborative work to assist in a broader understanding of the ageing process.These themes are reflected in the recent developments of multi-disciplinary Institutes or Centres for the Elderly in major University settings.

Theoretical as well as practical developments are important, since the (clinical) psychology of ageing lacks effective models. Models of adjustment have come and gone, and attempts have been made to extend some of the classical theories of behavioural, cognitive, systemic and psychoanalytic schools to encompass the older person, but very little of this work is based on evidence from studies of older people. Erickson's theory is among the very few to provide at least some attempt at an integrated model of life-span development, and the more recent compensatory models of Baltes & Baltes (1990) show promise as their potential is explored. The absence of the life-span developmental perspective from mainstream psychology should be acknowledged. The body of knowledge on which clinical psychology purports to be built has been described as largely reflecting the psychological features of young undergraduates; even in clinical psychology, research studies often exclude the over-65s from consideration. Bender (1986) demonstrated that older people were under-represented in published psychological studies; what is required is not simply more studies specifically on older people, or comparisons of older and younger people on yet more aspects of cognition, but rather studies that reflect the psychological functioning of people across the life span, and which seek to make sense of individual differences.

The area of health psychology may well prove a fruitful source of models which could be applied more generally to the older person. Within the health belief models of Becker (1974) and Moos (1992) lies an approach integrating the characteristics of individuals with their environmental and social context as influences on their attitudes to health. They provide a potential avenue to better understanding of preventative care as well as effective care following disease onset. They emphasize the importance of personality and cognitive characteristics of the individual, as well as a supportive social context and appropriate environment. Developments in locus of health control models (Wallston, Wallston & De Vellis, 1978) are also useful in helping to understand the balances between internal and external factors and influences on health behaviour. Concepts of "hardiness" (e.g. Kobasa & Maddi, 1985) also give some insights into characteristics which could be important in effective care. An implication of the behavioural medicine models may be for the individual to be educated throughout life to provide increased cognitive coping resources to match his/her increased vulnerability to health problems in the later years.

Also relevant to older people is work on communication and compliance. Many studies, of course, reflect the low level of effective communication in the "consultation" within health care contexts (Ley, 1988). This problem is accentuated with the older person, who may well have decreased sensory acuity to add to other difficulties in giving and receiving information in the health care context. Whilst there is solid experimental evidence to reinforce the need for supporting "advice cards" for regularly occurring problems, these do not yet seem to have become routine practice in clinical settings. A typical example might be the use of self-test techniques for those with late-onset diabetes. Some clinics give both practical training and clear guidelines, but others simply prescribe a set of test equipment and, presumably, hope that effective testing emerges. This area is a clear example of one in which the psychological and behavioural components of good practice have been known for many years, but their implementation remains the problem (Yates, 1990).

Psychological approaches need to keep pace with advances in knowledge regarding problems of mental health in older people. Attempts have been made to be much more specific about the definition and nature of depression in late life, which may present in subtly different ways from those of younger onset. For example, there are different trajectories of recovery which may potentially occur in the older person; an improvement in mood and interaction, for instance, might be associated with a much slower recovery in some of the specific components of cognitive performance necessary for effective adaptation (Austin et al., 1992).

In the dementias, change has been quite dramatic as improvements in neuropathology have combined to produce an increasingly sophisticated classification (Neary & Snowden, 1990). These developments have already given some clarity to previously opaque findings; some psychological functions which appeared to be idiosyncratically different in "demented" clients were differentiated substantially when a more accurate definition of the "dementia" was used. We have moved a long way from the "senile and pre-senile" categorizations of the early 1980s to the very explicit definitions and descriptions of the "new dementias", such as Lewy body dementia. A more specific and sophisticated knowledge base has already had its effect on medical treatment in avoiding inappropriate medication (McKeith et al., 1994). These developments provide new opportunities for psychological investigations which will lead to more effectively targeted psychological support to provide amelioration for specific deficits or general management of the clients.

The substantial increase in the number of people with learning disabilities who are presenting to care settings in older age groups provides a new challenge. The increase seems to be a product both of improvements in medical care, which are leading to increased life expectancies in some groups (e.g. Down's syndrome) and of the policies of community care, which mean that older persons with learning disabilities are no longer living their concluding years in an institutional setting. In many cases these clients have a combination of physical health problems and adjustment difficulties which are an immense challenge to carers and supporting professionals. We urgently need some directed and effective research on the psychological needs and resources of this group of people which relates to their specific problems. Particular issues arise for the ageing parents of people with learning disabilities, many of whom struggle to continue to provide support despite their own failing health, and fear what will happen to their child after their death.

A similar problem of lack of specific knowledge of effects and incidence in older people arises in the areas of addiction, dependency and substance abuse. The major psychological research in these problems seems to clearly target the adolescent and young adult age group. However, there is increasing evidence of problems extending into old age. The ageing drinker on city streets is a familiar sight, and the potentially damaging links between an ageing brain and excessive alcohol are well known. There remain many gaps in what is known of the overall picture of alcohol abuse by older people. Similarly, very little is known about the effects of drugs or substance abuse in the older person. Again, this seems to be an area which would merit more specific research.

PROFESSIONAL ISSUES

Ageism in clinical psychology

Butler (1969) drew attention to "ageism", described as reflecting "a deep-seated uneasiness on the part of the young and the middle-aged—a personal revulsion to and distaste for growing old, disease, disability, and fear of powerlessness, uselessness and death". Ageism is now often more broadly defined, to include discrimination on the basis of age at any point in the life span (Bytheway, 1995), but the original sense of devaluing and distancing from older people remains of relevance, and raises personal as well as professional issues.

Personal issues are discussed below; the key professional issue is whether clinical psychology services are equitably distributed across age groups. Statistics in the UK on the work of clinical psychologists in the National Health Service indicate that older people are under-represented amongst the clients of clinical psychology services, on the basis of the age distribution of the general population. Figures for 1991/1992 are presented by Skelton-Robinson (1995), and the 1992/1993 figures are referred to by Gilleard et al. (1995). A consistent pattern is evident: less than 10% of clinical psychologists' referrals are 65 and over, compared with 16% of the total population. Children up to the age of 15 are referred in proportion to their numbers in the overall population; the excess of referrals are seen in the 16–64 age group. If the increased health needs and service use of older people as a group are taken into account, this proportionally low frequency of contact may be seen as virtually a neglect of the needs of older people for the services provided by clinical psychology.

These figures do not prove, of course, that clinical psychologists are ageist; rather, they indicate that the profession has yet to develop to the point where it is adequately meeting the needs of older people. Partly, this reflects that there are not enough posts, and indeed not enough trained clinical psychologists to fill those posts which are available. Where a service has developed and a critical mass has been established, then referral patterns will change, and the proportion of older patients rise (Skelton-Robinson, 1995). However, it appears that direct referral rates from general practitioners (GPs) remain low. Some GPs have suggested that older people are less likely to be seeking a psychological approach; they are certainly more likely to receive benzodiazepines as an anxiolytic or hypnotic (Sullivan et al., 1988), despite warnings about the raised side-effect risk in older people (Higgitt, 1992). It is unclear to what extent GPs could encourage more referrals for psychological help rather than continuing to offer medication as a first line of treatment.

Training developments

Real progress has been achieved in the training of clinical psychologists in the UK, all of whom are required under current British Psychological Society training accreditation criteria to gain a range of experience with older adults. Although working with older people is often a less popular choice initially, surveys have shown that there is nothing as effective as a good placement experience in persuading a trainee that this area is worth a second look in terms of career choices (Thomas and Cook, 1995). However, providing sufficient placements for the current numbers in training in the UK is proving difficult. In fact, many more training places are required to meet the anticipated demand for qualified clinical psychologists in all specialties. The limited number of placements with older people is seen as a major obstacle to this expansion. A 1995 survey of training courses suggested that for 21 of the 23 courses, difficulty in finding older-adult placements would limit any expansion; in comparison, 13 courses cite learning disabilities and child/adolescent placements as being in short supply, while only three have difficulties in the adult mental health area. The pressure to expand is great: the large proportion of vacant posts across all client groups, but affecting older-people posts as much as any, is a source of embarrassment and frustration to the profession. In this context, compulsory elderly experience may be vulnerable; removing this requirement would go some way to allowing greater throughput of trainees. However, there are other client areas where difficulties are also encountered; existing placements could be used more effectively, and more use made of shared placements to maximize use of scarce supervisor resources. It would be a retrograde step to allow a clinical psychologist to qualify without ever working with an older person; however, more than just token experience is required. The variety and challenge of work with older people cannot be perceived in working with just one or two cases. Flexible ways are increasingly being found to ensure that clinical psychologists in training receive a positive exposure to older people, their variety of needs and the potential for clinical psychology to make a significant contribution in this area. Knight et al. (1995) provide a detailed overview of training issues in the USA, which reflects similar pressures on supervisory resources and the same difficulties in ensuring that a meaningful experience in work with older people is obtained. The development in 1993 of a specialist group—a Section on Clinical Geropsychology (Section II) of the Clinical Psychology Division of the American Psychological Association—has given a focus to initiatives to develop specialist training in this area.

Recruitment and retention

In the UK, vacant posts are commonplace in clinical psychology, because training output has not kept pace with the ever-increasing demands. The essential difficulty has been at the level of entry to the profession; retention rates within the profession are now fairly high, and in a still young profession retirement is not yet a significant source of loss.

Across all specialisms, this leads to a credibility gap: there is the rhetoric of what may be achieved with a psychological approach; there is the reality of a difficulty in delivering the goods. There are simply too few appropriately trained care agents with the psychological skills to apply the techniques. Under-recruitment to work with older people has been a recurrent problem. This leads often to single-handed psychologists, working without the support of like-minded colleagues; retention within the speciality is not helped by the pressures of working alone in this way, feeling overwhelmed by the apparently never-ending demands. The near certainty of not filling the post eventually means that no-one considers it worthwhile to respond to clinical need by even creating a specialist post.

Recruitment and retention are greatly helped by the enthusiastic and supportive network of psychologists working in this area, through the Special Interest Group of the British Psychological Society's Division of Clinical Psychology (PSIGE, formed in 1980) and its local groups: they provide much of the academic teaching on older people on many courses; they provide the placements; and they provide a realistic but innovative model of practice. It is also necessary to ensure that those attracted to work with this client group are adequately motivated and rewarded so that their services are retained. In the past it has been one of the areas of employment in which relatively early promotion to a high grade has been possible. Flexible working arrangements, the option of a post split with another speciality and encouragement of continuing professional development are needed in any package to attract newly qualified staff.

Immediately after qualifying, an established department with several psychologists already working with older people is often preferred. In the USA, increasing difficulty in securing funding to work with other client groups has begun to increase interest in older adult work, where some limited funding is available (Knight, 1998, personal communication).

Other models

If there are simply not enough qualified clinical psychologists, are there other ways in which the service might be provided? The availability in many countries including the UK of a large number of psychology graduates, on the wrong side of the training bottleneck, has led to the creation of many entry level posts, for example, Assistant Psychologist posts in the UK, again particularly in hard-to-recruit areas. Aspiring candidates for clinical psychology training vie for such posts, which are seen as an excellent way of obtaining the relevant experience required by most courses. From another perspective, they might be viewed as cheap labour. Such assistants often contribute a great deal to a service, are highly motivated and learn rapidly. By and large, the development of assistant posts has been on an *ad hoc*, short-term basis, with the implicit assumption that if a qualified person were available this would be preferable. However, the question must be raised of whether there are certain relatively routine tasks that might be better fulfilled by a technician/assistant under supervision by a qualified person. This is an issue for the profession and employers which might require a substantial rethink of career patterns.

Another model that has yet to attract serious attention in the UK, but is very common in some countries (e.g. The Netherlands), is that of a specialist rather than a generic training. The end result is a specialist "geropsychologist", who is not qualified to work with, say, people with learning difficulties or children. There would be similarly specific training for other specialities, such as neuropsychology. This model has some advantages at a superficial level, allowing a deeper basic training in the special needs of a client group. However, few are sure which area they wish to specialize in prior to training; preferences form and evolve from exposure to a range of client groups. It would be important for specialists in older people to have a good grounding in work with adults of all ages, as we firmly believe there are as many similarities to as differences from general adult work.

An alternative approach might be to replace the current single qualification in clinical psychology by a range of developing qualifications which would reward the incoming "assistant" by a Diploma, develop skills and knowledge in a generic Masters' degree and focus the potential of the subject and individual in a professional Doctorate linked to their speciality. This would ensure a generic basic training, but recognize the increasing extent of post-qualification specialization. It seems unlikely that the profession will be able to resist for long the demands it currently does not satisfy, both from purchasers of and clients for services and also from an increasing number of committed graduates in psychology for further training.

ETHICAL ISSUES

The central ethical issue arising in work with older people relates to power; older people, especially those who are physically frail or have dementia, are devalued and disempowered. It is difficult for the professional to resist the role of taking decisions for the person, of using more or less subtle persuasion to pursue the professional's agenda, of not even attempting to listen to the person's own views. This leads, for example, to people with dementia often having their rights arbitrarily removed, without the benefit of any legal framework to protect their interests. The door of the ward is locked: it is for the good of the patients, who otherwise would only wander off, get lost and perhaps come to harm. There is a small band of dedicated patients who stand by the door, periodically trying to open it. Those entering the ward have to carefully ensure the door is locked without anyone escaping. The patients are imprisoned, for the best of motives. There is no need to develop alternative ways of providing care, of monitoring patients' safety, of offering more constructive activities while the door remains (illegally) locked. Often such actions are taken outside the law simply because the existing legal framework seems unwieldy, and not designed for such scenarios. A recent challenge in the UK courts to the practice of interpreting compliance with remaining in hospital to indicate consent to remain, despite the person having insufficient cognitive capacity to give informed consent, ultimately failed (the so-called Bournewood judgement, House of Lords Judgments, 1998). However, the case and legal arguments made transparently clear the inadequacies of the current framework, which provides few safeguards for "compliant incapacitated patients". People with dementia do not campaign, do not complain articulately, and so the situation continues. The power of the professional is symbolized in this example by the carrying of keys, like the warder in a jail. Psychological tests may similarly be the means of power: they may be used to give a diagnosis that is used to "explain" actions and behaviours that will then never be understood (see Gilhooly, 1986).

Many examples might be given of ethical issues arising in psychological work with older people. Barrowclough & Fleming (1991) describe how behaviour therapy and environmental modification have often been applied without any consultation with the older people involved regarding the targets for change. The all-powerful therapist knows best, once again. Reality orientation and activity groups have on occasions used materials more appropriate for children than for adults, further devaluing those participating. Woods (Chapter 12, this volume) emphasizes the primacy of values and attitudes to prevent devaluation and dehumanization of the older patient.

The second major ethical issue relates to possible conflicts of interest between patients and their families. Given the relatively ready availability of institutional care as a complete "solution" to a complex situation, issues often arise over whose needs should have precedence—the patient's or the carer's? Generally in society there is a perception that older people's needs take second place to those of younger adults and children. If health care resources are limited, questions are asked about the value of an operation, say to replace a hip, in an older person, who will "after all have only a few years to live". Similarly, the welcome focus on carers' needs over recent years seems to have resulted in carers' needs automatically having priority. There can be no hard and fast rules about such competing demands; balanced and negotiated compromises must be sought, rather than a quick-fix solution which rides roughshod over one party's needs. The King's Fund (1986) document, "Living Well into Old Age", recommends advocacy schemes, so that someone may articulate the perspective of the person with dementia; family and professionals cannot always fulfil this role, in view of their potentially conflicting interests.Work with families also raises issues of confidentiality. It is disturbing how often an older person's case is discussed in some detail with his/ her adult child, without the permission of the older person, perhaps even in his/her presence! It sometimes appears that because a person is over 65, the proper boundaries no longer need to be observed. In reality, greater attention is needed to such matters, not less.

Woods (1997) has drawn attention to the tendency of family care-givers to be viewed by services as "saints", whereas of course human fraility is only too apparent in most families. Professionals need to be aware of the risks of abusive situations developing within the family context, often in the context of long-standing difficult relationships, mental health and alcohol problems in the carer, and the carer being dependent on the victim for finance or accomodation (Homer & Gilleard, 1990; Kingston & Reay, 1996). Guidelines for the detection and response to elder abuse are being developed and implemented in many areas currently.

In research with (and sometimes in the treatment of) people with dementia, issues of consent arise. Even if the person agrees to participate in a project, is he/she competent to make that decision? Another adult can not consent for the person with dementia, although it is wise to have the approval of relatives before proceeding. Kitwood (1995) draws attention to the issue of how invasive or intrusive the procedures to be used may be; drug trials and unpleasant and uncomfortable procedures require fuller consent than, say, dementia care interventions where, it might be argued, a person who is "not unwilling" might be included. There is also a duty on researchers to carry out the study on a day-to-day basis in a way which does not devalue or intimidate the person further.

Issues of life and death abound in work with older people, and have major ethical implications. Increasingly, euthanasia is being discussed, by older and younger people, and many are considering making "advance directives" indicating their wishes for medical intervention if a time comes when they are unable to speak for themselves. Some older people who kill themselves are thought to have made a rational decision to end their life, not being in a depressed mood at the time. The search for control over what has always been seen as ultimately inevitable, but always capricious and uncontrollable, is a powerful one. Confronted with a frail woman in her late 80s, tormented by pain, terminally ill, who begs staff to help her die, it is difficult to retain simple views on these challenging issues.

PERSONAL ISSUES

Work with older people raises a multitude of personal issues for those who are involved. As with any specialty there are clear positives in the successful pursuit of the care plan which gives a new lease of life to someone, where a clear difference is made to a person's life. There are also the challenging aspects, perhaps most prominent of which is the increased contact with issues of bereavement and death, alluded to in Butler's description of ageism, quoted earlier. These issues are worthy of some exploration, since they relate to the quality of professional life in work with this population and therefore to the ability of the practitioner to sustain his/her input.

Much has been written on stress and coping in the psychological workplace (Cormack, Nichols & Walsh, 1991; Cushway, 1992). This literature examines the links between the individual's background and experiences and the nature of the professional situation. There is a clear expectation that, by becoming aware of his/her own development and coping styles, the psychologist can help to ameliorate the effects of stressors and remain efficient. However, we often are seen to attempt to ignore our emotional reactions and experiences, taking refuge in a "superpsychologist" myth which renders us professionally and personally vulnerable (Mollon, 1989).

Consider some of the potential sources of problems for the trainee, supervisor and practising psychologist. At the trainee level, work with older people is often seen as a significant challenge. Trainees bring to their courses their own versions of the common stereotypy and mythology surrounding the older person. Our own experiences of teaching incoming trainees has shown this, as initial quizzes and role plays continue to reveal these misconceptions. Most trainees have had little contact with older people, except grandparents. Those contacts which have occurred tend to be on a superficial level, even within the nuclear family. It is evident that, whilst individuals may visit their elders, they rarely know them, how they really think and feel. It is extremely rare to have close friends and confidants who are 50 years older. Meeting "normal" older people can be a helpful preparation for an older adult placement. Being able to put into context the often-reported findings of decline on tests of cognitive function is helpful; older people are able to learn, to successfully graduate from the Open University (Cohen, 1996), to develop new skills and interests. Decline in memory with age "is neither universal nor inevitable . . . there is considerable variation, so that some aspects of memory are less adversely affected than others . . . some individuals are less adversely affected than others" (Maylor, 1996). Recognizing that most voluntary organizations and charities would cease to function if the over 65s withdrew also emphasizes the positive attributes of many older people, and their positive contribution to society.

This, then, necessitates some very basic education on the personal and psychological characteristics of older people before exposure to clinical placements. Many supervisors have experienced the trainee who seems to suffer from a form of "client shock" or "setting shock" in the initial weeks of a placement. The roots of this shock may be in the individual's poor awareness of the realities of older persons and their care settings, of their potential and their needs.

A particular stress on the trainee may be the extensive range of skills and competencies required in working with this age group. Perhaps more than in any other setting, there is a need for competence across a wide range of skills from detailed neuropsychological assessment to supportive psychotherapy. Interpersonal and organizational abilities are stretched as the need to work with a range of carers and care-providing structures emerges. These features of the work can again come as something of a surprise to a trainee who has, perhaps, worked in more constrained systems in previous attachments. There seems to be a clear need to address issues of this nature in the preparation of trainees and in the training of supervisors.

An important and recurrent area of difficulty and concern for all involved with older people is the continued presence of issues surrounding loss and death. For many trainees there is an initial shock at the closeness of death to their clinical practice. This may be one of the few settings where clients may die during a trainee's involvement with them. They need to be prepared with adequate support strategies for themselves, families and carers. As this was being written, one of our trainees arrived for a community visit to a client only hours after the client's death from a heart attack. The likelihood of this situation arising means that the trainee must be briefed and aware of appropriate strategies and have access to active personal support and counselling.

There is a clear need for there to be specific training on bereavement and loss, and care of the dying and bereaved, in initial training and in continuing professional development. This training needs to be spread throughout courses, so that an initial sensitization to issues and awareness of models can be built on by discussions of incidents and experiences. Professionals can have considerable problems as they face their own mortality and vulnerability in reflecting upon their work with others.

The impact and influence of religion on the client arises in work with older people to an extent which seems much greater than with other groups. This is emphasized in studies such as the work of Reid et al. (1978). Very few training courses address the role of religious belief and thought in the life of the client in either formal or informal sessions. It is much more likely that issues of religion will arise in work with older people. Those involved in psychological care must be aware of the core structures and beliefs of the major religions of the cultural groups they serve in order to be optimally effective in maintaining the quality of life of the client (Koenig, Smiley & Gonzales, 1988). Work with older people and the proximity of mortality can also be a major challenge to the personal belief system of the psychologist and carer. This topic area is one which is very difficult to introduce to psychological training or practice, and hard to justify to management and appraisers, but we ignore it at our peril if we are concerned to give a "holistic" service to our clients and maintain our own personal integrity.

Sexuality in older people often appears to be a taboo topic; the professional perhaps finds it difficult to raise the issue with an older person, even perhaps dropping the item regarding change in sexual interest from a standard questionnaire. Gibson (1996) discusses a number of the myths that have developed about sexuality in later life; individual differences are great and it is important that the psychologist working with older people is both well-informed regarding the changes that do occur and comfortable in discussing these topics with older people.

A further challenge to the personal skills of the therapist is emerging as awareness grows of the influence of earlier disaster or trauma on the development of mental illness in later life. A primary example of this seems to be the increasing reports of phenomena arising from the wars of the 1940s and 1950s as influences on current problems (Zeiss & Dickman, 1989). Handling the recall of intensely traumatic memories buried for 50 years can place considerable demands on the skills of the therapist. Many of the national events surrounding the marking of the 50th anniversary of World War II have involved media images which have awoken memories of events and trauma in those involved which have required intervention.

The danger of those working with older people losing sensitivity to individual needs—even while being enthusiastic advocates for the "client group"—reflects, perhaps, the relative isolation of those working in this area, and the real pressures and personal challenges involved day by day. The need for support and supervision is evident; psychologists are not immune to the fears and apprehensions identified by Butler as underlying the use of ageism as a defensive manoeuvre. Working with older people confronts us with fantasy and reality regarding our own ageing and that of family members and others close to us; practitioners require supervision to enable them to be aware of, and reflect on, the impact of their personal issues on their work, and vice versa. Whilst we live, we age, and we cannot—and should not—profess detachment from the universal process of growing older.

However, the challenge and opportunity of using our psychological knowledge to "add life to the years" remains our goal and gives us reward and motivation.

REFERENCES

Audit Commission (1997). The coming of age: improving care services for older people. London: Audit Commission.

Austin, M.P., Ross, M., Murray, C., O'Carroll, R.E., Ebmeir, K.P. & Goodwin, G.M. (1992). Cognitive functioning in major depression. *Journal of Affective Disorders*, **25**, 21–31.

Baltes, P. B. & Baltes, M. M. (1990). Psychological perspectives on successful aging: the model of selective optimization with compensation. In P. B. Baltes & M. M. Baltes (Eds), *Successful Aging: Perspectives from the Behavioral Sciences* (pp. 1–34). Cambridge: Cambridge University Press.

Barrowclough, C. & Fleming, I. (1991). Ethical issues in work with older people. In P.J. Barker & S. Baldwin (Eds), *Ethical Issues in Mental Health* (pp. 68–83). London: Chapman and Hall.

Becker, M.H. (1974). The health belief model and personal health behaviour. *Health Education Monographs*, **2**, 324–508.

Beech, J.R. & Harding, L. (Eds) (1990). *Assessment of the Elderly*. Windsor: NFER-Nelson.

Benbow, S. M., Marriott, A., Morley, M. & Walsh, S. (1993). Family therapy and dementia: review and clinical experience. *International Journal of Geriatric Psychiatry*, **8**, 717–725.

Bender, M.P. (1986). The neglect of the elderly by British psychologists. *Bulletin of British Psychological Society*, **39**, 414–416.

Butler, R.N. (1969). Age-ism: another form of bigotry. *Gerontologist*, **9**, 243–246.

Bytheway, B. (1995). *Ageism*. Buckingham: Open University Press.

Cohen, G. (1996). Memory and learning in normal ageing. In R. T. Woods (Ed.), *Handbook of the Clinical Psychology of Ageing* (pp. 43–58). Chichester: Wiley.

Cooper, A. (1983). Working with the elderly: a survey. *PSIGE Newsletter*, **8**, 9–16.

Cormack, M., Nichols, K. & Walsh, S. (1991). Creating a system for personal development and professional support. *Clinical Psychology Forum*, **37**, 8–10.

Cushway, D. (1992). Stress in clinical psychology trainees. *British Journal of Clinical Psychology*, **31**, 169–179.

Gibson, H.B. (1996). Sexual functioning in later life. In R.T. Woods (Ed.), *Handbook of the Clinical Psychology of Ageing* (pp. 183–193). Chichester: Wiley.

Gilhooly, M. (1986). Ethical and legal issues in therapy with the elderly. In I. Hanley & M. Gilhooly (Eds), *Psychological Therapies for the Elderly* (pp. 173–197). Beckenham: Croom Helm.

Gilleard, C. J. (1996). Family therapy with older clients. In R. T. Woods (Ed.), *Handbook of the Clinical Psychology of Ageing* (pp. 561–573). Chichester: Wiley.

Gilleard, C., Askham, J., Biggs, S., Gibson, H.B. & Woods, R. (1995). Psychology, ageism and health care: a DCP symposium. *Clinical Psychology Forum*, **85**, 14–15.

Grundy, E.M.D. (1996). Population Reviews: (5) The population aged 60 and over. *Population Trends*, **84**, 14–20.

Hanley, I. & Hodge, J. (eds) (1984). *Psychological Approaches to the Care of the Elderly*. Beckenham: Croom Helm.

Harding, K., Baldwin, S. & Baser, C. (1987). Towards multi-level needs assessment. *Behavioural Psychotherapy*, **15**, 134–143.

Higgitt, A. (1992). Dependency on prescribed drugs. *Reviews in Clinical Gerontology*, **2**, 151–155.

Homer, A.C. & Gilleard, C.J. (1990). Abuse of elderly people by their carers. *British Medical Journal*, **301**, 1359–1362.

House of Lords. (1998). In re L (by his next friend GE). Judgements, 25th June.

Hussian, R.A. (1981). *Geriatric Psychology: A Behavioral Perspective*. New York: Van Nostrand Reinholt.

King's Fund (1986). Living well into old age: applying principles of good practice to services for people with dementia. Project Paper 63. London: King's Fund.

Kingston, P. & Reay, A. (1996). Elder abuse and neglect. In R. T. Woods (Ed.), *Handbook of the Clinical Psychology of Ageing* (pp. 423–438). Chichester: Wiley.

Kitwood, T. (1995). Exploring the ethics of dementia research: a response to Berghmans and ter Meulen. *International Journal of Geriatric Psychiatry*, **10**, 655–657.

Kitwood, T. & Bredin, K. (1992). A new approach to the evaluation of dementia care. *Journal of Advances in Health & Nursing Care*, **1**, 41–60.

Knight, B.G., Teri, L., Wohlford, P. & Santos, J. (Eds) (1995). *Mental Health Services for Older Adults: Implications for Training and Practice in Geropsychology*. Washington, DC: American Psychological Association.

Kobasa, S.C. & Maddi, S. (1985). Effectiveness of hardiness: exercise and social support as resources against illness. *Journal of Psychosomatic Research*, **29**(5), 525–533.

Koenig, H.G., Smiley, M. & Gonzales, J.A.P. (1988). *Religion, Health and Ageing*. New York: Greenwood.

Larner, S. (1986). Training issues in working with the elderly. *PSIGE Newsletter*, **20**, 405.

Levy, B. & Langer, E. (1994). Aging free from negative stereotypes: successful memory in China and among the American deaf. *Journal of Personality and Social Psychology*, **66**, 989–997.

Ley, P. (1988). *Communication with Patients: Improving Communication, Satisfaction and Compliance*. London: Croom Helm.

McKeith, I.G., Fairbairn, A.F., Perry, R.H. & Thompson, P. (1994). The clinical diagnosis and misdiagnosis of senile dementia of Lewy body type (SDLT). *British Journal of Psychiatry*, **165**, 324–332.

Maylor, E. A. (1996). Older people's memory for the past and the future. *Psychologist*, **9**(10), 456–459.

Miller, E. (1977a). *Abnormal Ageing: The Psychology of Senile and Presenile Dementia*. Chichester: Wiley.

Miller, E. (1977b). The management of dementia: a review of some possibilities. *British Journal of Social and Clinical Psychology*, **16**, 77–83.

Mollon, P. (1989). Narcissus, Oedipus and the psychologist's fraudulent identity. *Clinical Psychology Forum*, **23**, 7–11.

Moos, R.H. (1992). *Coping Responses Inventory: Adult Form Manual*. Stanford, CT: Centre for Health Care Evaluation, Stanford University.

MPAG (1990). *Clinical Psychology Project: Full Report*. Manpower Planning Advisory Group, London: Department of Health.

Neary, D. & Snowden, J.S. (1990). The differential diagnosis of the dementias caused by neurodegenerative disease. *Neurosciences*, **2**, 81–88.

Powell, G. (1994). *Curriculum in Clinical Psychology*. Leicester: BPsS Books.

Rabbitt, P. (1988). Social psychology, neurosciences and cognitive psychology need each other (and gerontology needs all three of them). *Psychologist*, **12**, 500–506.

Reid, W.S., Gilmore, A.J.J., Andrews, G.R. & Caird, F.I. (1978). A study of religious attitudes of the elderly. *Age and Ageing*, **7**, 40–45.

Richardson, C.A., Gilleard, C.J., Lieberman, S. & Peeler, R. (1994). Working with older adults and their families—a review. *Journal of Family Therapy*, **16**, 225–240.

Roper-Hall, A. (1993). Developing family therapy services with older adults. In J. Carpenter & A. Treacher (Eds), *Using Family Therapy in the Nineties* (pp. 185–203). Oxford: Blackwell.

Sabin, N. (1994). Video analogues: a novel way to start addressing the challenging needs and challenging environments of confused older people. *PSIGE Newsletter*, **49**, 23–27.

Skelton-Robinson, M. (1995). Access to clinical psychology services for older adults. *PSIGE Newsletter*, **53**, 6–8.

Social Trends (1997). 27, Office for National Statistics. London: HMSO.

Sullivan, C.F., Copeland, J.R.M., Dewey, M.E., Davidson, I.A., McWilliam, C., Saunders, P., Sharma, V.K. & Voruganti, L.N.P. (1988). Benzodiazepine usage amongst the elderly: findings of the Liverpool community survey. *International Journal of Geriatric Psychiatry*, **3**, 289–292.

Thomas, C. & Cook, F. (1995) An investigation into the factors determining the choice of specialism in Clinical Psychology. *Clinical Psychology Forum*, **78**, 13–17.

Walker, J. (1996) Using systemic ideas with individuals. *PSIGE Newsletter*, **55**, 19–22.

Wallston, K.A., Wallston, B.S. & De Vellis, R. (1978). Development of the multi-dimensional health locus of control scales. *Health Education Monographs*, **6**, 160–170.

Wattis, J.P. & Hindmarch, I. (1988). *Psychological Assessment of the Elderly*. Edinburgh: Churchill-Livingstone.

Woods, R. T. (1997). Why should family caregivers feel guilty? In M. Marshall (Ed.), *State of the Art in Dementia Care* (pp. 39–44). London: Centre for Policy on Ageing.

Woods, R.T. & Britton, P.G. (1977). Psychological approaches to the treatment of the elderly. *Age and Ageing*, **6**, 104–112.

Woods, R.T. & Britton, P.G. (1985). *Clinical Psychology with the Elderly*. Beckenham: Croom Helm/Chapman & Hall.

Woods, R. T. & Roth, A. (1996). Effectiveness of psychological interventions with older people. In A. Roth & P. Fonagy (Eds), *What Works for Whom? A Critical Review of Psychotherapy Research* (pp. 321–340). New York: Guilford.

Yates, A. (1990). A review on drug compliance. *PSIGE Newsletter*, **34**, 13–16.

Zeiss, R.A. & Dickman, H.R. (1989). PTSD 40 years later: incidence and person–situation correlates in former POWs. *Journal of Clinical Psychology*, **45**(1), 80–87.

Chapter 2

INTELLECTUAL CHANGES IN LATE LIFE

*Ian Stuart-Hamilton**

INTRODUCTION

Psychologists have found that old age is associated with a decline in intellectual skills.

This is a statement which, if it appeared as a newspaper headline, would rival (the probably apocryphal) "no-one hurt in small earthquake" for blandness. However, if one were asked to summarize the findings on ageing and intelligence in one brief sentence, it would be hard not to derive a permutation of the above. Researchers and received wisdom agree on this point, as a casual perusal of specialist textbooks or a straw poll of public opinion would quickly confirm. For those requiring more empirical evidence, any general textbook on ageing will provide ample references on the statistically significant age-related decline in intellectual skills. It should also be noted that cross-sectional studies tend to find that the difference emerges earlier in life than do longitudinal studies, because of experimental artifacts. The latter tend to identify intellectual decline as a significant trend in the mid-60s or later (see e.g. Birren & Schaie, 1990; Bromley, 1988; Craik & Salthouse, 1992; Perlmutter & Hall, 1992; Salthouse, 1991a; Stuart-Hamilton, 1994).

Such a statement of fact is in itself too general to be of much value. Although on average there are changes associated with ageing, these shifts in ability are not uniformly true of all ageing people, neither can we be certain that we are measuring and describing them in the best possible

* University College Worcester, Worcester, UK

Psychological Problems of Ageing: Assessment, Treatment and Care. Edited by R.T. Woods.
© 1999 John Wiley & Sons Ltd.

manner. For example, it is worth noting that the picture is muddied by the consideration that inter-individual variability increases with age. In other words, there is more variability between old than between young adults (Morse, 1993; Rabbitt, 1993). In this chapter, I wish to look at how ageing change is measured, some of the potential pitfalls which may be produced, and the caveats which have to be added to our general statement about change.

We shall begin with a brief survey of the nature of intellectual change in old age, before considering possible experimental artifacts.

MEASURING INTELLECTUAL CHANGE IN OLD AGE

The majority of studies on intellectual change in old age concentrate upon cognition and psychometrics. This in itself creates potential problems, because cognition paradigms have usually been designed for young people (often undergraduate "volunteers") and are primarily interested in finding models which exclude the possibility of individual differences. Conversely, psychometrics usually ignores models and concentrates on describing differences (see Rabbitt, 1988). This means that descriptions of age-related changes and models of how these occur are often drawn from separate and often incompatible backgrounds. In this chapter, we are concentrating upon intellectual change *per se*, rather than models of it, but the reader should be alerted to the fact that the field of study is weakened by the lack of an integrated model.

Crystallized and fluid intelligence

Once one moves beyond the description of general intellectual change in old age, the issue becomes less clear-cut. Certainly, not all intellectual skills decline; some are preserved or may even slightly improve. The most familiar description, and still perhaps the "industry standard" is to divide the intellect into fluid and crystallized intelligence (Horn & Cattell, 1967) and observe the relative age effects on these. "Crystallized skills", as the name suggests, are relatively fixed and unaffected by the ageing process. Essentially, they are skills involving a high degree of pre-learnt knowledge, and a convenient (if not absolutely accurate) synonym is "general knowledge". Tests of crystallized intelligence typically ask subjects to provide definitions of esoteric words or to answer rather recondite questions. As has often been observed, these tests usually tacitly assume a white, middle-class knowledge base as the measure of all things. One may have a superb knowledge of beer mats or whippet racing, for example, but this is not counted as "intelligence" in the same league as, for example, knowledge of Mozart's operas or Western political history. Allowing for this, however, studies have, practically without exception, found that ageing does not alter the level of crystallized intelligence, which may in fact increase slightly.

"Fluid intelligence", however, shows a general decline once subjects pass the age of 60. (Studies differ on the onset age, but a figure of 65 is not unreasonable.) Fluid intelligence is the measure of "the ability to solve problems for which there are no solutions derivable from formal training or cultural practices" (Stuart-Hamilton, 1995b). It roughly corresponds to the lay person's concept of "native wit", and is tested by the standard format of IQ test questions ("What is the next number in the sequence?", "Which is the odd one out?", etc.). There is no doubt that elderly people display a decline on these sorts of tasks, and may in some instances display an average group performance which is more than two standard deviations below that of young adults (e.g. Raven's Matrices IQ test—Clayton & Overton, 1976; Panek & Stoner, 1980). To assess the impact of this, these data should be placed in context. An intelligence test score more than two standard deviations below the mean is taken by most authorities as the definition of mental retardation. Although many studies have found less extreme results, the average intellectual status of elderly people is, on the basis of psychometric test evidence alone, very poor. For example, summarizing Salthouse's (1992) analysis, elderly people are on average 1.75 standard deviations below the young adults' mean on tests of reasoning ability (extrapolated from Salthouse, 1992, pp. 175–176).

Clearly, everyday experience informs us that, functionally, elderly people are performing well above the level of mentally disadvantaged adults. A host of reasons can be cited, not least that crystallized skills can compensate for some of the effects of fluid intellectual decline. For example, there are the often-cited studies by Charness (1979, 1981) which demonstrated that elderly chess and bridge players, although lacking the memory and basic processing efficiency of younger players, could maintain parity through having access to a greater range of strategies acquired through more years of experience. Salthouse (1984) and Bosman (1993) similarly found that elderly typists could compensate for lower typing speeds by, for example, being able to plan further ahead. Morrow et al. (1994) studied the ability of older and younger aeroplane pilots to remember verbal information. There was an age difference, but this was either removed (for visual materials) or diminished (for spoken materials) when the verbal information was in the form of air traffic control commands. Such methods of compensation may mean that although elderly people are "really" much less efficient at processing information, they can cover up many of their "failings" by having a greater range of pre-learnt strategies to support them. To this end, it can also be observed that training can often remove at least the worst excesses of age differences on a task (e.g. Baltes & Willis, 1982), although such training may be applicable only to the task in question and does not necessarily transfer to other tasks (e.g. Herrmann, Rea & Andrzejewski, 1988).

However, although there are possible explanations for why changes in psychometric tests are not directly reflected in changes in everyday performance, the fact remains that these changes do occur, and that they reflect a radical change in the efficiency of processing. This is compounded by the observation made by Rabbitt (1984) and many other researchers that, if one partials out fluid intelligence from studies of age differences, then the age difference usually disappears. Furthermore, the supposed preservation of crystallized intelligence may be in part an experimental artifact: tests of this skill usually have no time limit, but if one is imposed, or if more rigid criteria for accepting a correct answer are applied, then an age deficit becomes apparent (Core, unpublished, cited Rabbitt, 1984; Botwinick & Storandt, 1974). Again, Stuart-Hamilton and Rabbitt (unpublished) found that there was a slight but significant age decline on the National Adult Reading Test (NART) if group comparisons were made rather than (more conventionally) correlating the subjects' ages with their test scores. (The relative stasis of the younger adults tended to mask the decline in the older subjects.) Conversely, experimental artifacts associated with fluid intelligence tests (e.g. that elderly people cannot write down their answers as quickly for purely physical reasons), when controlled for, reduce the size of the age deficit, but typically they do not completely remove it (e.g. Storandt, 1976).

The search for causes of ageing decline

Researchers have long acknowledged that studies of age differences may be contaminated by cohort effects, which will be considered in greater detail below. These assume that any age group differences which are attributable to differences in lifestyle, method of upbringing, etc., must be excluded as experimental artifacts. As we shall see below, this is a debatable assumption. However, in this section we shall take this argument at face value and concentrate upon "intrinsic" aspects of ageing which might influence intellectual change.

The most striking candidate is the physical decline of the ageing body. There is overwhelming evidence that ageing is associated with a reduction in the efficiency of just about every physical process in the body (see Birren & Schaie, 1990; Corso, 1981, 1987; Bromley, 1988; Perlmutter & Hall, 1992; Stuart-Hamilton, 1994). The fact that the body is slower to respond means that at the very least the brain cannot enact its commands as quickly (as indeed has been seen in the work of Storandt, cited above). The fact that the senses are in decline means that the information the brain receives is compromised. For example, Lindenberger & Baltes (1994) demonstrated that there is a very strong correlation between sensory functioning integrity and intellectual skills (accounting for over 90% of age-related variability on tests of intellectual ability). Finally, the fact that the metabolic and cardiovascular systems are declining means that, put simplistically, the brain's source of energy is waning. For these reasons alone, it would be surprising if there were not a decline in intellectual functioning. In addition, however, it should be noted that the central nervous system is also heir to its share of natural shocks, with a notable decline in the speed of neural transmission, an irreplaceable loss of cells (circa 10% by some estimates) and an increase in neural noise. On *a priori* grounds, one would expect these deleterious changes in brain functioning to have a negative effect upon intellectual performance.

The general consensus is that general intellectual decline can be linked to physical decline. This can be demonstrated at a very general level. For example, in training studies, Hawkins, Kramer & Capaldi (1992) and Powell (1974) demonstrated that older people's state of physical fitness could be related to intellectual state. Another illustration is provided by the terminal drop theory (Kleemeier, 1962; Riegel & Riegel, 1972). This argues that prior to death, an older person's intelligence experiences a relatively sudden calamitous drop. This is held to be linked to an equivalent decline in the physical processes underpinning it, and indicates an imminent and fatal failure of a bodily process. White & Cunningham (1988) demonstrated that a sudden intellectual drop predicted death with reasonable accuracy only in subjects aged under 70. It can be argued that death in young old age is likely to be attributable to a relatively sudden calamitous physical change, whilst in older elderly people, death is likely to be attributable to a steady decline, which will not therefore manifest itself in a sudden change in intellect. There is some debate over what aspects of intellectual functioning are involved in the terminal drop (see Stuart-Hamilton, 1994; White & Cunningham, 1988). However, of interest here is that for some elderly people, intellectual change may be strongly associated with physical state.

It should also be noted that the theory of fluid and crystallized intelligence cited above (Horn & Cattell, 1967; Horn, 1982) is explicitly linked to physical functioning. It is held that fluid intelligence is dependent upon the body's physical state, and specifically the condition of the central nervous system. (Crystallized intelligence is felt to be relatively unaffected by physical state, unless there is a catastrophic failure.) This is most conveniently illustrated by the strong correlation between fluid intelligence scores and reaction times (amongst other things, a convenient measure of "neural efficiency"). For example, if older and younger adults are matched for fluid intelligence, then they will also be matched for speed of reaction times and vice versa (e.g. Hertzog, 1991; Rabbitt & Goward, 1986; Salthouse, 1991b; Schaie, 1989). The speed hypothesis (also known as the general slowing hypothesis) argues that the speed and efficiency of neural processing underpin fluid intellectual abilities (e.g. Eysenck, 1985). The concept is intuitively reasonable: it is clear that physical health and intellectual functioning must have some link, and the correlation between neural efficiency and intelligence is a direct and plausible one. However, some words of caution need to be sounded. The first is that if there is a decline in neural efficiency, the effect is not uniform across individuals. For example, Rabbitt (1993) demonstrated that there are significant differences between individuals in the degree of preservation of specific intellectual skills. For example, one elderly person may have a well-preserved skill A, whilst skill B is in serious decline; whilst for another individual, the opposite pattern may apply. Again, the work cited above on bridge and chess players and typists indicates that declines in fluid skills can be offset by experience and/or practice, and that performance on fluid intelligence tasks can be restored by training. This argument is further supported by the current debate on Brinley plots. Several meta-analyses of studies of young-old differences in reaction times on similar tasks have found that when the young and old mean scores are plotted against each other, a linear relationship is found (the Brinley plot). It is tempting to assume that this indicates a uniform slowing. However, Perfect (1994) demonstrated that the linear relationships may be a statistical artifact, and can be generated using unrelated sets of data, whilst Lindenberger, Mayr & Kliegl (1993) note that comparing old and young subjects on single tasks may be overly simplistic and may ignore considerations of other key factors, such as compensatory strategies.

Therefore, although fluid intelligence may be linked to physical changes, and in particular to neural processing, it cannot be assumed that the decline in physical factors is met by a general and uniform decline in fluid intelligence.

The pattern of age-related change

As may be surmised from the work on terminal drop cited in the previous section, the curve plotting the decline of an elderly individual's intellectual performance may display a sudden and precipitous decline. However, an age group as a whole will display a relatively gentle decline, which is what one would intuitively expect when individual people's performances are averaged out. If one considers the distribution of intelligence test scores, one finds a normal distribution which, over time, becomes skewed towards a lower average, although the extremes of the distribution remain unaffected (see e.g. Rabbitt, 1984). From this it can be surmised that some elderly people retain their youthful levels of performance and that, on an individual basis, decline is not inevitable.

The magnitude of the age decline can also be determined by the intrinsic nature of the task set. (This is aside from artifactual considerations, such as speed of written response, sensory modality used to receive information, etc., discussed below.) For example, it has often been noted that the magnitude of the age deficit increases disproportionately with increased processing load—the so-called age × complexity effect. For example, Botwinick, Robbin & Brinley (1960) gave subjects a card-sorting task, and found that the age difference increased the more sets the cards had to be sorted into. Although Salthouse (1985) raises several cautionary points regarding the age × complexity effect (notably that it is difficult objectively to measure "complexity"), the phenomenon is a reasonably robust one.

Performance on traditional developmental psychology measures

The changes described above might be interpreted as simply a regression, but essentially the young and old adults belong on the same continuum. The relevance of this is not hard to detect. If we assume that older adults are essentially less efficient versions of younger adults, then the same models of mental functioning can be applied to both groups. However, there is a body of evidence which suggests that for many older adults, there is a qualitative as well as a quantitative change in functioning. This refers to the debate, common in developmental psychology, but less often aired in the psychology of ageing, between the continuous progress and stage theories of development. The debate is of some antiquity, but in modern times traces its roots to the dichotomy established by the contrasting theories of Locke and Rousseau. The former argued that children are born essentially as "immature adults", and function in roughly the same manner. The principal difference between child and adult was that the former had less knowledge of the world, and had to acquire this through experience. In contrast, Rousseau argued that the child enters the world with a radically different set of values and methods of experiencing their surroundings. The child progresses through several stages in which he/she has an outlook and way of thinking considerably at variance with those of an adult, before acquiring a mature perspective during adolescence. Whether one believes that children gradually acquire knowledge, but essentially think like adults, or that they pass through distinct stages, has become an article of faith in developmental psychology. The most noted proponent of the stage theory has been Piaget, and (echoing Locke's and Rousseau's nationalities) some of his most noted opponents have been native English speakers. However, it has been tacitly assumed by both camps that, to all intent and purposes, the adult level of thinking is attained more or less complete by the late teens, and that thereafter, methods of thinking remain more or less intact. Perhaps the only major critique of this approach has come from some of the "neo-Piagetians", who have argued that a further refinement of thinking occurs in adulthood, in which people become better able to cope with abstract problems (e.g. they become more adept at using the dialectic approach—see Kramer, Kalbaugh & Goldston, 1992; Labouvie-Vief, 1992; Pratt & Norris, 1994). However, few have supposed that in old age there might be a regression to earlier stages of reasoning (indeed, Piaget rejected this concept in his writings).

However, there is now a considerable body of evidence that an appreciable proportion of elderly people demonstrate just such a regression on tasks which are routinely performed correctly by pre-teens children. For example, Papalia (1972) demonstrated that older subjects tended to make more errors on Piagetian conservation tasks. There are several versions of the task, but the best known involves the subject observing two balls of modelling clay of equal size. One ball is rolled out by the experimenter into a sausage shape, and the subject is asked if the two pieces still contain the same quantities of clay. (The correct answer is, of course, "yes".) Other qualities of the clay which remain unaffected by the transformation in appearance can also be tested (e.g. whether the two pieces will still displace the same volume of water). Typically, children under the age of about seven years fail these tests, since they erroneously assume that there has been a change in the property of the reshaped piece of clay. Various explanations have been advanced. One suggestion is that the child fails to integrate information about all the dimensions of the clay pieces. For example, when the piece is rolled flat, he/she may observe that the piece has increased along the horizontal axis, and so think that it is bigger, whilst ignoring the fact that the increase in width has been met by a corresponding decrease in height. Other researchers have noted that failure on the task may be due to a misunderstanding of the experimenter's intent. For example, the child may see that the piece has retained the same quantity of clay, but from experience of teachers asking leading questions, may feel that because the experimenter has asked if it has changed, a heavy hint has been dropped that it has changed. Accordingly, critics of Piaget have noted that by altering the presentation of the task, a significantly greater proportion of children will give the correct answer (see Donaldson, 1978). Regardless of the cause of the children's performance, the fact remains that children as young as seven years can successfully perform the Piagetian conservation task, and certainly by the teenage years, the success rate amongst non-mentally handicapped children is complete. It is therefore very surprising to find that an appreciable proportion of elderly, non-dementing adults perform the task incorrectly. The phenomenon has been observed in several independent studies (see Blackburn & Papalia, 1992). The phenomenon is not confined to Piagetian studies, but is apparent in other traditional tests of childhood psychological functioning. For example, Stuart-Hamilton (1993) gave subjects the task of drawing an apple pierced through by a knitting needle. The younger adult controls drew the apple with only the external features of the needle visible (a technique called "perceptual realism"). However, about 10% of the elderly (and non-dementing) volunteers made an "intellectual realism" error, namely, they drew the apple as if it were transparent (i.e. all of the needle was shown). This drawing error is usually encountered only in pre-teenage children.

Why should these errors occur? The most obvious explanation is that they are symptomatic of a general intellectual decline. It has already been noted that on some measures, average performance in older age groups falls to a level normally classified as severely mentally disadvantaged. Perhaps failure at such childhood tasks is a very striking manifestation of this phenomenon. However, this explanation is too simplistic. The most obvious rebuttal is that older people can easily be trained to perform such tasks correctly (see Blackburn & Papalia 1992). It seems more likely that the proportion of older people in question have simply forgotten rather than lost the capacity. This is indicated by the finding that if people's education levels are partialled out of the equation or controlled for, then the age group difference is abolished (e.g. Blackburn, 1984; Rebok, 1987). Blackburn & Papalia (1992) argue that age-related changes in concepts may reflect the rejection or forgetting of methods of formal analysis taught in schools, and the adoption of other, perhaps simpler, methods used in childhood. If this is so, then a "failure" in traditional developmental tasks may reflect a change in lifestyle (and associated cognitive demands) rather than a cognitive decline. Labouvie-Vief (1992) suggests that an aspect of post-formal thought may be a move away from purely abstract thought to an integration of logical and emotional considerations. It is possible that intellectual tasks may be viewed with a different scale of priorities by older people. However, this argument requires more empirical investigation before firm conclusions can be drawn. It is worth noting, however, that a qualitative shift in performance on traditional developmental tasks may also be characteristic of non-cognitive development. For example, McDonald & Stuart-Hamilton (1996) found an age shift in reactions to Piagetian moral reasoning tasks (Piaget, 1932). Since these place very low mnemonic and cognitive demands upon the subject (they are designed for use on young children), it is unlikely that age-related changes can be attributed to changing processing capacity.

THE SEARCH FOR A PURE AGEING EFFECT

To illustrate the arguments advanced in the following sections, let us take the following hypothetical (but entirely plausible) example. Suppose we take two groups of people in their 20s and 70s and test them on a battery of intelligence tests. It can be reliably predicted that the younger group will out-perform the older. However, there are problems in interpreting this result, and as good gerontologists, one of the first questions we would wish to ask is whether the difference we have found is due to ageing or to a cohort effect.

Cross-sectional studies

It is logical that, if we wish to demonstrate an age difference, then we should satisfy ourselves that a difference between two age groups is due to differences in their ages, rather than to other experimental artifacts. In much of developmental psychology, this is not a problem. For example, in comparing groups of four- and six-year-old children drawn from the same culture, it is improbable that the two groups have been raised in dramatically different ways or have had very different life experiences, and therefore one would be prepared to accept that group differences are due to differences in level of maturation. However, the same cannot be said for comparisons of younger and older adults. The life experiences of older people and younger people are usually drastically different. For example, in the current epoch, adults in their 20s have generally led fairly relaxed, materially comfortable lives. The experiences from the first 20 years of people in their 70s will almost certainly be of privation, rationing and war, and generally, older people have been raised in more constricted circumstances, both financially and in terms of social and emotional expression. A full description of generational differences in upbringing is more properly the preserve of a sociological work, but the point needs to be made that the experiences of different generations form a cultural divide.

It might be supposed that such differences may be of relatively little importance in studies of intellectual change, since the latter is a fairly "objective" measure. However, this is not necessarily the case. Associated with the societal changes has been an increase in the length and variety of compulsory education. In the UK at least, the minimum school leaving age has increased through this century from 12 to 16 years, with the majority of school leavers who do not immediately find employment undertaking further training of some description. Today, approximately one in five school leavers will enter some form of higher education, compared with a relative handful 50 years ago. This means that the average individual of today is likely to have received a longer period of education than an older person. Furthermore, the average school curriculum has changed with, typically, a breaking away from rigid patterns of learning to more exploratory approaches to gathering and interpreting information. Whether these changes have necessarily been for the better is not of concern here. What matters is that older and younger adults have typically been prepared and trained to deal with intellectual problems in different ways. When we say that older and younger adults display differences in intellectual ability, part of this difference may be due to differences in educational upbringing. Unfortunately, such an assumption cannot be easily tested. It can be demonstrated that length of education can have an effect on performance (e.g. Blackburn & Papalia, 1992, demonstrated that performance on Piagetian reasoning tasks was in part determined by length of education). However, it would be practically impossible to quantify the effects of differing educational and life experiences of two groups raised 50 years apart. This raises a serious problem for the measurement of age differences. Once one admits on *a priori* grounds the possibility of a cohort effect which cannot be adequately quantified and hence accurately analysed, then this opens the floodgates for any number of other cohort effects to be cited as experimental contaminants.

The problem is further compounded by another consideration, namely, if we decide to look for cohort effects, then there is no statistical law to tell us when to stop. Suppose one decides to examine the difference between our hypothetical groups of younger and older adults. It is decided that measures of length of education, state of health and material well-being will be considered and their effects partialled out of the equation. Suppose that after the variables have been accounted for, there is still an age difference, although it has diminished in size. There is nothing to stop the determined experimenter taking a further trawl of possible confounding factors (number of toys owned when a child, number of siblings, etc.) to see if the age difference can be reduced still further. Mercifully, researchers in "real life" do not do this, but in theory, one could throw any number of cohort effects into the equation to reduce the size of the age difference. Therefore, the comparison of age groups is attacked on two fronts by the cohort effect. First, it may not be possible to quantify, and hence measure, the effects of some influences, and second, there is no rule to determine how many cohort effects can be considered. The result of this is that although one might demonstrate an age difference, the "true" size of this difference is hard to determine.

Longitudinal studies

Two possible solutions to this problem are: to tolerate some contamination, or to remove the problem of the cohort effect altogether by running a longitudinal study. The first option is the one which is usually (tacitly) adopted. This may be acceptable, because most studies which have removed contaminating variables have still found an age difference, albeit reduced in size (see Salthouse, 1991a). However, the issue is muddied by the fact that researchers differ in the number of confounding variables they identify for removal, making cross-study comparisons more difficult. An "industry standard" list of confounding variables whose effects all researchers would guarantee to remove from the equation is the sort of idea easy to propose on paper but difficult, if not impossible, to enact. The second proposed option—the longitudinal study—is also not without criticism. At its most basic, this necessitates following a single set of subjects through their lifespan and comparing their performances at different times. It will yield measures of age change, and escapes the problem of the cohort effect, since because only one cohort is being studied, any changes can be attributed only to ageing. However, aside from any other considerations, the longitudinal method is very expensive to run; for this reason alone, only a handful of studies have been performed. There is the added consideration that it takes decades to complete experiments. For example, a longitudinal study assessing differences between the 20 and 70 year-old adults will (obviously) take 50 years to run. Since much of psychology relies upon sequences of original experiments and increasingly esoteric follow-up studies, it should be readily obvious that the longitudinal method is not feasible for widespread use. Neither should it be assumed that the longitudinal method is immune from contamination. An often-cited problem is the "drop-out effect": subjects performing less well in a study (especially one assessing intellectual skills) tend to withdraw from the study with greater frequency than more intellectually gifted subjects (e.g. Riegel & Riegel, 1972). Accordingly, unless adjustments are made to the analysis, there is a danger that the longitudinal method paints an overly optimistic picture of ageing change. There are other often-cited criticisms, for example, that a longitudinal study tells one about the lifespan development only of a particular age cohort; it is possible that other generations might have different patterns of development. Again, one must be certain that the measures with which one begins the study are the right ones. Changing the tests and methods of assessment part way through a longitudinal study will seriously compromise the ability to compare performance before and after the change.

To a certain extent these criticisms can be met by more sophisticated designs. For example, Schaie (1983, 1994) has designed the Seattle Longitudinal Study to incorporate the testing of several different age cohorts at once. This enables cross-checks to be carried out between the performance of the different cohorts as they reach the same age at different points in time. This enables any cohort differences to be controlled for, since in effect generational differences in the pattern of change across the lifespan can be observed and then controlled for, for comparative purposes. However, studies such as Schaie's are rare, if only because of the considerable expense. Short of inventing a time machine, there is no manner in which the longitudinal study can be made a practical option for more than a handful of researchers.

It follows from the above arguments that there is no such thing as a "perfect" measure of ageing. Whether we choose a cross-sectional or longitudinal methodology, and no matter how carefully we guard against cohort and drop-out effects, we cannot completely "cleanse" our findings of "impurities". (For further discussion, see e.g. Salthouse, 1991a; Stuart-Hamilton, 1995a.)

Controlling for physical and sensory changes

The problem is further compounded by considerations of the testing procedures employed with elderly research subjects. For example, one must consider the effect of physical age-related changes on performance. We have already noted that Storandt (1976) found that approximately half of the age difference on some intelligence tests was attributable to the older subjects having slower handwriting. Again, Rabbitt (1989) demonstrated that elderly people with relatively mild hearing loss were severely disadvantaged in recalling spoken word lists (although their recall was equivalent to normal-hearing controls on visually presented lists). Without a full screening of physical state, it is possible that age-related deficits may in part be an artifact of physical decline. This argument can be developed further. Without wishing to sound facetious, what consideration does one wish to give to age-related changes in mental functioning? For a proportion of people, old age is the harbinger of a catastrophic deterioration in practically all aspects of intellectual performance because they develop a dementing illness. Dementia is not exclusively a disease of old age (for example, there are demented patients in their 40s), but it increases markedly in frequency the older one becomes. (White et al., 1986 provide the heuristic that 1% of 60 year-old people have dementia, and this proportion doubles with every five years of extra age.) Other chapters in this volume address the issue of dementia in greater detail, but it is worth noting here that calculations of "typical" elderly performance exclude considerations of dementia. In a truly demographically representative sample, an age-appropriate proportion of dementing patients would be included in the sample. By excluding such people, the sample is being biased, and the older the sample one takes, the greater this bias becomes. Since, by the above calculations, about a quarter of people aged over 80 have at least some symptoms of dementing illness, such selectivity is making a major statement about what is "normal" ageing. This is not intended to be tendentious. However, if one excludes an appreciable proportion of a group because they are deemed "abnormal", why should other negative and reasonably typical aspects of ageing which also have an effect on performance be ignored by most researchers? For example, rheumatism and arthritis will almost certainly affect writing speed, whilst cardiovascular problems possibly exert a double effect from the condition and from the drug treatment. However, subjects are rarely excluded from studies on these grounds.

Although it is not of course couched in these terms, in effect researchers choose to consider some aspects of health as a cohort effect to be excluded, whilst others are often taken as part and parcel of typical ageing. However, arthritis and rheumatism are not an inevitable part of ageing (indeed, they are a young person's disease as well), so, strictly speaking, patients suffering from these illnesses should be excluded. However, this is surely stretching a point beyond reasonable tolerance: reaction times can be enhanced by exercise or drinking a cup of strong coffee; should we therefore assess somebody's reaction time only after they have exercised and drunk a cup of coffee? Any description of ageing must surely take into account the typical experiences of older people. If some people lack the physical problems of others, then this makes them exceptional (and fortunate), not typical. It is worth noting that Anstey, Stankov & Lord

(1993) found that primary ageing is a significantly better predictor of fluid intelligence than measures of "health" (measured in terms of number of drugs currently being taken, self-rating and number of identified illnesses). Unfortunately, this evidence is less helpful than it first appears, since the researchers' measures of primary ageing comprised tests of "sensory, motor, and central nervous system functioning" (p. 563), which are arguably assessing "health" by another name.

However, whichever solution an experimenter adopts, there is a paradox which ensures that not all parties will be satisfied. One can veer towards being demographically correct by including subjects with physical ailments, in which case one is including contaminants which hide the "pure" ageing effect. Conversely, one might try to compensate by matching old and young subjects on physical health, in which case the sample becomes demographically incorrect. Accordingly, any sampling is inevitably a compromise.

Test conditions

The manner in which subjects are tested may also yield cohort effects. Some effects may act against older subjects. For example, test situations often resemble formal examinations or a visit to the doctor. Such an environment may be less off-putting for younger people, who have more recently experienced the school and higher education system (or indeed, may still be in it). In other instances, conditions may disproportionately favour older subjects. For example, it has often been observed that under exam-like conditions, stimuli are presented with a clarity which does not resemble the everyday world. An absence of distractions, extraneous noise, etc., may favour elderly people with impaired senses and reduced processing capacity.

Recruitment

Another problem with volunteers is that, excluding considerations of health, they are often not demographically representative. A casual study of journal abstracts will reveal that most studies use groups of volunteers recruited through advertisements and participation in general health programmes. Such people are not usually typical of all of the elderly population, but only of active, community resident (and usually middle-class) older people. Amongst subsections not likely to be represented are the physically frail, the socially withdrawn, the semi-literate (about 20% of adults are only functionally literate at best) and the mildly demented. This means that many studies may be veering towards studying the "best preserved" rather than the truly representative.

Conclusions

The evidence and arguments presented indicate that any methodology is likely to colour the results. Principally, this may occur by introducing cohort effects which make it difficult to determine how much of a discovered age difference is actually due to "pure" ageing. Unfortunately, it is difficult to control for cohort effects, for two principal reasons. First, some cohort effects can plausibly be argued to exist, but they are difficult or impossible to measure, and therefore the true extent of their influence cannot be assessed. Second, controlling for some cohort effects may have the effect of making the sample demographically unrepresentative, as well as questioning whether very typical (though not inevitable) aspects of ageing, such as sensory and motor skill decline, should be ignored. Ultimately, it is unlikely that these experimental artifacts are distorting the major findings on change. The same phenomena have been discovered across too many studies of people from a wide variety of cultures for an alternative case to have any validity. However, the problem does become a serious one in another two respects. First, because of the potential biases in many studies, it is difficult to extrapolate such predictions as the proportion of the full population who will behave in the same manner as the experimental subjects. Second, because of the same biases, it is difficult to provide accurate figures of the proportion of an age effect which is attributable to "pure" ageing as opposed to cohort effects, general experimental artifacts, etc. One now needs to ask whether these criticisms are of importance.

The search for a demographically representative finding is obviously important if one wishes to make predictions about the population as a whole. However, within the context of theoretical studies, the issue is of interest but not necessarily of central importance. It might be argued that if demographic concerns did become of importance (e.g. if a test was found which accurately predicted the onset of dementia) then a study could be repeated using a carefully selected sample of people. However, usually the time and expense required to perform this task would outweigh the advantages. Another problem with demographic sampling is that it is only representative of a particular epoch. As was observed earlier in this chapter, performance parameters are likely to change with successive cohorts, so the demographically representative data of today will relatively quickly become outdated. A final consideration is that a demographically representative sample of older people would include some variability induced by people in the early stages of dementia. The question of whether such data should be included in the main body of findings is debatable.

Similarly, the debate about searching for a "pure" ageing effect is not clear-cut. It seems intuitively obvious that we should wish to be sure that a difference between old and young adults is due purely to ageing and not to, for example, cohort effects. However, there are problems with this approach. First, there is the oft-repeated observation that the traditional measure of age—namely, chronological age—is essentially arbitrary. Other measures of ageing, such as physiological age, psychological age and social age, are often rather more accurate predictors of state and performance; chronological age is essentially a useful but basically coincidental general guide to the likely state of an average person (see Stuart-Hamilton, 1994). This means that taking a group of people of the same chronological age and expecting them to display a uniform pattern of behaviour solely attributable to their "age" is at best problematic. People age at different rates, so a lack of uniformity in what is found is practically guaranteed. A method of sidestepping this issue might be to devise a more accurate measure of ageing, based upon social, psychological and physical ageing factors which could be agreed upon, but unfortunately the issue is too complex for an easy solution to be reached.

A further problem concerns what is meant by "pure" ageing. The tacit assumption is that it is an effect free from cohort effects. As has been noted elsewhere, it is practically impossible to remove cohort effects, since many of them can be posited but are sufficiently intangible for their effects to be statistically or experimentally controlled for. However, if such effects could be removed, then it is debatable that what would be left would be meaningful. It is a truism that development does not take place in a vacuum, as the tragic (but mercifully rare) evidence of attic children testifies. Pratt & Norris (1994) provide strong evidence of the role of social development and environment in the intellectual lives of elderly people. To remove such effects over a whole lifetime may be in effect to deny an integral part of the intellect which can only develop through social interaction. Since this by definition is unique, we cannot attain a measure of ageing which does not include cohort influences. Stated another way, can we attain a measure of an older person's intellect which can ignore the effects of a lifetime's experience? In attempting to minimize cohort effects, this may be what we are doing. In many ways the issue resembles a replaying of the nature–nurture debate, in that it addresses the question of how much of the ageing effect is attributable to growing old *per se*, and how much is due to environmental factors. If we adopt an extreme view that "pure" ageing is purely a measure of genetically controlled factors, then the measure becomes almost impossible.

An additional consideration is that if one concentrates upon inherited aspects of ageing, then one is implicitly assuming that there are evolutionary mechanisms at work (e.g. Lorenz, 1965; see Johnson, 1993). However, the debate over the evolutionary purpose of ageing is far from resolved. Although it is popularly conceived that ageing is a method of culling individuals who can no longer breed or work efficiently, in their natural habitat the majority of animals die or are killed before they display signs of ageing (which in most species are found only in zoo animals and pets). This indicates that ageing need not have evolved as a "self-culling" mechanism. Indeed, if it is designed as one, then it is a remarkably inefficient process. Progressively weakening an individual, making them more forgetful and less bright, seems like adding a liability to the rest of the group, rather than aiding it. If evolutionary pressure had designed a "switch-off" mechanism, surely a very rapid degenerative illness, such as a complete failure of the immune system (which could easily be genetically programmed) would be more appropriate. Other explanations, such as the disposable soma theory (Kirkwood, 1988), explain ageing as an incidental product of other processes. This indicates that ageing may not have an evolutionary purpose, which in turn casts doubt on whether a search for a "pure" genetic component to ageing has much relevance.

Therefore the majority of studies of ageing may be neither measures of "pure" ageing nor demographically representative. However, under most circumstances, it is doubtful if these are desirable goals. At one level, this can be interpreted as "studies of ageing contain errors, but they do not matter", which in its way is as enthralling as the earthquake headline cited at the start of this chapter. However, viewed from another angle, such criticisms are important, because they question whether the goals which researchers set (usually tacitly) are necessarily the right ones.

Therefore, it can be taken as read that there is a general decline in intellectual ability in old age. It can also be taken as read that for any individual or any task, this is probably an inaccurate statement.

REFERENCES

Anstey, K., Stankov, L. & Lord, S. (1993). Primary aging, secondary aging, and intelligence. *Psychology and Aging*, **8**, 562–570.

Baltes, P. & Willis, S.L. (1982). Plasticity and enhancement of intellectual functioning in old age. In F.M. Craik & A.S. Trehub (Eds), *Aging and Cognitive Processes*. New York: Plenum.

Birren, J.E. & Schaie, K.W. (Eds) (1990). *Handbook of the Psychology of Aging*, 3rd edn. San Diego, CA: Academic Press.

Blackburn, J.A. (1984). The influence of personality, curriculum, and memory correlates on formal reasoning in young adults and elderly persons. *Journal of Gerontology*, **39**, 207–209.

Blackburn, J.A. & Papalia, D.E. (1992). The study of adult cognition from a Piagetian perspective. In R.J. Sternberg & C.A. Berg (Eds), *Intellectual Development*. Cambridge: Cambridge University Press.

Bosman, E.A. (1993). Age-related differences in the motoric aspects of transcription typing skill. *Psychology and Aging*, **8**, 87–102.

Botwinick, J., Robbin, J.S. & Brinley, J.F. (1960). Age differences in card sorting performance in relation to task difficulty, task set and practice. *Journal of Experimental Psychology*, **59**, 10–18.

Botwinick, J. & Storandt, M. (1974). Vocabulary ability in later life. *Journal of Genetic Psychology*, **125**, 303–308.

Bromley, D.B. (1988) *Human Ageing. An Introduction to Gerontology*, 3rd edn. Bungay: Penguin.

Charness, N. (1979). Components of skill in bridge. *Canadian Journal of Psychology*, **133**, 1–16.

Charness, N. (1981). Aging and skilled problem solving. *Journal of Experimental Psychology: General*, **110**, 21–38.

Clayton, V. & Overton, W.F. (1976). Concrete and formal operational thought processes in young adulthood and old age. *International Journal of Human Ageing and Human Development*, **7**, 237–246.

Corso, J.F. (1981). *Aging Sensory Systems and Perception*. New York: Praeger.

Corso, J.F. (1987). Sensory-perceptual processes and aging. *Annual Review of Gerontology and Geriatrics*, **7**, 29–55.

Craik, F.I.M. & Salthouse, T.A. (Eds) (1992). *The Handbook of Aging and Cognition*. Hillsdale, NJ: Erlbaum.

Donaldson, M. (1978). *Children's Minds*. London: Fontana.

Eysenck, H.J. (1985). The theory of intelligence and the psychophysiology of cognition. In R.J. Steinberg (Ed.), *Advances in Research in Intelligence*, vol. 3. Hillsdale, NJ: Erlbaum.

Hawkins, H.L., Kramer, A.F. & Capaldi, D. (1992). Aging, exercise, and attention. *Psychology and Aging*, **7**, 643–653.

Herrmann, D.J., Rea, A. & Andrzejewski, S. (1988). The need for a new approach to memory training. In M.M. Gruneberg, P.E. Morris & R.N. Sykes (Eds), *Practical Aspects of Memory: Current Research and Issues*. Chichester: Wiley.

Hertzog, C. (1991). Aging, information processing speed, and intelligence. *Annual Review of Gerontology and Geriatrics*, **11**, 55–79.

Horn, J.L. (1982). The theory of fluid and crystallised intelligence in relation to concepts of cognitive psychology and aging in adulthood. In F.I.M. Craik & S. Trehub (Eds), *Aging and Cognitive Processes*. New York: Plenum.

Horn, J.L. & Cattell, R.B. (1967). Age differences in fluid and crystallised intelligence. *Acta Psychologica*, **26**, 107–129.

Johnson, M.H. (Ed.) (1993). *Brain Development and Cognition: A Reader*. Cambridge, MA: Blackwell.

Kirkwood, T.B.L. (1988). The nature and causes of ageing. In *Research and the Ageing Population*. CIBA Foundation Symposium, No. 134 (pp. 193–207). Chichester: Wiley.

Kleemeier, R.W. (1962). Intellectual changes in the senium. *Proceedings of the Social Statistics Section of the American Statistical Association*, **1**, 290–295.

Kramer, D.A., Kalbaugh, P. & Goldston, R. (1992). A measure of paradigm beliefs about the social world. *Journal of Gerontology*, **47**, 180–189.

Labouvie-Vief, G. (1992). A neo-Piagetian perspective on adult cognitive development. In R.J. Sternberg & C.A. Berg (Eds), *Intellectual Development*. Cambridge: Cambridge University Press.

Lindenberger, U. & Baltes, P.B. (1994). Sensory functioning and intelligence in old age: a strong connection. *Psychology and Aging*, **9**, 339–355.

Lindenberger, U., Mayr, U. & Kliegl, R. (1993). Speed and intelligence in old age. *Psychology and Aging*, **8**, 207–220.

Lorenz, K. (1965). *Evolution and the Modification of Behaviour*. Chicago: University of Chicago Press.

McDonald, L. & Stuart-Hamilton, I.A. (1996). Changes in performance of Piaget's moral reasoning tasks in later life. *Age & Ageing*, **25**, 402–404.

Morrow, D., Leirer, V., Altieri, P. & Fitzsimmons, C. (1994). When expertise reduces age differences in performance. *Psychology and Aging*, **9**, 134–148.

Morse, C.K. (1993). Does variability increase with age? An archival study of cognitive measures. *Psychology and Aging*, **8**, 156–164.

Panek, P.E. & Stoner, S.B. (1980). Age differences on Raven's Coloured Progressive Matrices. *Perceptual and Motor Skills*, **50**, 977–978.

Papalia, D.E. (1972). The status of several conservation abilities across the lifespan. *Human Development*, **15**, 229–243.

Perfect, T.J. (1994). What can Brinley plots tell us about cognitive aging? *Journal of Gerontology: Psychological Sciences*, **49**, 60–64.

Perlmutter, M. & Hall, E. (1992). *Adult Development and Aging*. New York: Wiley.

Piaget, J. (1932). *The Moral Judgement of the Child*. London: Penguin.

Powell, R.R. (1974). Psychological effects of exercise therapy upon institutionalized geriatric mental patients. *Journal of Gerontology*, **29**, 157–161.

Pratt, M.W. & Norris, J.E. (1994). *The Social Psychology of Aging*. Cambridge MA: Blackwell.

Rabbitt, P.M.A. (1984). Memory impairment in the elderly. In P.E. Bebbington & R. Jacoby (Eds), *Psychiatric Disorders in the Elderly* (pp. 101–119). London: Mental Health Foundation.

Rabbitt, P.M.A. (1988). Human intelligence (critical notice of R.J. Sternberg's work). *Quarterly Journal of Experimental Psychology*, **40A**, 167–187.

Rabbitt, P.M.A. (1989). Secondary central effects on memory and attention of mild hearing loss in the elderly. *Acta Psychologica Scandinavica*, **27**, 284–299.

Rabbitt, P. (1993). Does it all go together when it goes? *Quarterly Journal of Experimental Psychology*, **46A**, 385–434.

Rabbitt, P.M.A. & Goward, L. (1986). Effects of age and raw IQ test scores on mean correct and mean error reaction times in serial choice tasks: a reply to Smith and Brewer. *British Journal of Psychology*, **77**, 69–73.

Rebok, G.W. (1987). *Life-span Cognitive Development*. New York: Holt, Rinehart & Winston.

Riegel, K.F. & Riegel, R.M. (1972). Development, drop, and death. *Developmental Psychology*, **6**, 306–319.

Salthouse, T.A. (1984). Effects of age and skill in typing. *Journal of Experimental Psychology: General*, **13**, 345–371.

Salthouse, T. (1985). *A Theory of Cognitive Aging*. Amsterdam: Elsevier North-Holland.

Salthouse, T.A. (1991a). *Theoretical Perspectives on Cognitive Aging*. Hillsdale, NJ: Erlbaum.

Salthouse, T.A. (1991b). Mediation of age differences in cognition by reductions in working memory and speed of processing. *Psychological Science*, **2**, 179–183.

Salthouse, T.A. (1992). Reasoning and spatial abilities. In F.I.M. Craik & T.A. Salthouse (Eds), *The Handbook of Aging and Cognition*. Hillsdale, NJ: Erlbaum.

Schaie, K.W. (1983). The Seattle Longitudinal Study: a 21-year exploration of psychometric intelligence in adulthood. In K.W. Schaie (Ed.), *Longitudinal Studies of Adult Psychological Development* (pp. 64–135). New York: Guilford.

Schaie, K.W. (1989). Perceptual speed in adulthood: cross-sectional studies and longitudinal studies. *Psychology and Aging*, **4**, 443–453.

Schaie, K.W. (1994). The course of adult intellectual development. *American Psychologist*, **49**, 304–313.

Storandt, M. (1976). Speed and coding effects in relation to age and ability level. *Developmental Psychology*, **12**, 177–178.

Stuart-Hamilton, I.A. (1993). Intellectual realism in the drawings of elderly people. *Journal of Educational Gerontology*, **8**, 110–114.

Stuart-Hamilton, I.A. (1994). *The Psychology of Ageing: An Introduction*, 2nd edn. London: Jessica Kingsley.

Stuart-Hamilton, I.A. (1995a). Problems with the assessment of intellectual change in elderly people. In F. Glendenning & I.A. Stuart-Hamilton (Eds), *Learning and Cognition in Later Life*. Aldershot: Avebury Press.

Stuart-Hamilton, I.A. (1995b). *Dictionary of Psychological Testing, Assessment and Treatment*. London: Jessica Kingsley Publishers.

White, L.R., Cartwright, W.S., Cornoni-Huntley, J. & Brock, D.B. (1986). Geriatric epidemiology. In C. Eisdorfer (Ed.), *Annual Review of Gerontology and Geriatrics*, No. 6. New York: Springer.

White, N. & Cunningham, W.R. (1988). Is terminal drop pervasive or specific? *Journal of Gerontology*, **43**, 141–144.

Chapter 3

IDENTITY MANAGEMENT IN LATER LIFE

*Peter G. Coleman**

INTRODUCTION: THE SELF AND AGEING

This review of recent theoretical and methodological advances made by personality and social psychologists in the study of ageing focuses on the self. In this it reflects a dominant mode of thinking within gerontology, one that emphasizes the importance of subjective experience, and in particular the self-concept, as opposed to objective indicators (e.g. Atchley, 1991; Markus & Herzog, 1991).

Since the 1960s, subjective indicators such as life satisfaction, self-esteem and, more recently, perceived control of life, have received pride of place in the assessment of adjustment. This is justified by the consistent body of evidence, including longitudinal research findings, which show that elders' "perception and evaluation of situations are more relevant for determining behaviour and feelings, such as well-being and satisfaction, than the objective situations" (Rudinger & Thomae, 1990, pp. 291–292). One cannot judge quality of life on the basis of externally assessed health or environmental parameters without taking into account people's own individual evaluations, which in turn reflect their goals, commitments and meaning systems.

This view is not without its critics. In presenting his own, recently republished, normative developmental view of ageing based on cross-cultural studies, Gutmann (1994) is scathing in his comments on the individualistic accounts which predominate in current gerontology:

* University of Southampton, Southampton, UK

Psychological Problems of Ageing: Assessment, Treatment and Care. Edited by R.T. Woods.
© 1999 John Wiley & Sons Ltd.

> . . . the tragic sense of life is denied, and the study of development is con-
> founded with the study of "whatever works" or "whatever feels good" to the
> isolated individual. Consequently, the "life satisfaction" scale becomes the
> ultimate measure of developmental achievement in later adult life.

Gutmann observes that in traditional societies older people have important social and cultural functions, and argues that psychological changes
with age, including greater assertiveness in women and detachment in
men, equip them to play new roles, but that these are increasingly denied
them in modern societies.

The developmental tradition Gutmann represents has been in decline in
gerontology since the discrediting of "disengagement theory" (Cumming
& Henry, 1961). In retrospect, this appears as an over-ambitious attempt
to provide a functional theory of changes with age which were observed
in a large cross-sectional study of elderly people living in Kansas City.
The subsequent debate focused on the problems in separating genuine
age changes from generational changes, and in establishing the voluntary
character of the disengagement observable in the data (see Coleman,
1993). As will be noted later, the term "disengagement" has recently
resurfaced in studies of the very old (Johnson & Barer, 1992). However,
the debate which dominated social gerontology in the 1960s, between
"disengagement" theory and the rival "activity" theory of "successful
ageing", was eventually resolved in favour of a model of social and
psychological ageing which emphasized the importance of continuity of
different types of lifestyle over age. A unitary model of social and psychological ageing was rejected.

This view was consistent with results from longitudinal studies of personality traits, which have continued to indicate considerable stability in
the profile individuals show over time (McCrae & Costa, 1990). However,
systematic differences between older and younger people do emerge
from studies of motivational attitudes, showing, for example, a different
temporal basis to older people's identity (they emphasize the past more)
and the pursuit of maintenance of present positive conditions rather than
change and development (Dittmann-Kohli, 1990). These differences will
be discussed in greater depth later, but it is important to stress at the
outset that the evidence from self-report statements illustrates how well
older people adapt to their changing circumstances. In fact, a succession
of claims have been made for adaptivity itself, the potential and pre-
paredness for dealing with change, as a criterion of successful ageing.

These have taken a variety of forms, but recently Baltes & Baltes (1990)
have elaborated a more precise model of selective optimization with compensation as a prototype strategy of successful ageing. "Selection" refers

to the adaptive task of the person and society to concentrate on those domains that are of high priority and which suit their skills and situation. "Optimization" reflects the view that people will have become skilled at maximizing their chosen life courses with regard to quantity and quality. "Compensation", like selection, results from restrictions in the range of adaptive potentials, and involves aspects of both the mind (e.g. the use of new mnemonic strategies) and technology (e.g. the use of a hearing aid). An interview with the pianist Arthur Rubinstein provides an apt illustration of the principles in question. His own account of the ways in which he overcame his weaknesses with ageing in piano playing included playing a smaller number of pieces (selection), practising these more often (optimization), and slowing down his speed of playing before fast movements, thereby producing a contrast that enhanced the impression of speed in the fast movements (compensation).

Researchers active in the study of "successful ageing" have also identified a danger in relying solely on subjective viewpoints to judge adaptation (Baltes & Baltes, 1990; Ryff & Essex, 1992). Individuals adapt to adversity even to the point of distorting and denying reality. Elderly people will often express satisfaction with poor living conditions, for example. As a result, over-reliance on such measures leads to the underestimation and neglect of genuine behavioural and ecological deficiencies. Moreover, some people may be generally positive construers of everything. Subjective indicators therefore need to be supplemented with objective criteria. Nevertheless, these observations in themselves serve to highlight the immense power of transformation which the perceiving self is able to wield.

In Western culture perception of the self by the self assumes overwhelming importance:

> [the] conception of person as a bounded, unique, more or less integrated motivational and cognitive universe, a dynamic center of awareness, emotion, judgment, and action organized into a distinctive whole and set contrastively both against other such wholes and against a social and natural background (Geertz, 1979, p. 229).

As Freeman (1993) notes, the fact that such a mode of perception is culture-bound does not make it a less essential part of our nature. It is not that we "merely" believe that we are such beings: we are them. These beliefs are implicated in virtually everything we think and everything we do. We cannot step outside them.

Claims for the importance of self-esteem, the evaluative component of self-conception, in the processes of adjustment to ageing have been made regularly over the last 30 years. Research in the 1960s and 1970s showed high self-esteem to be predictive of survival and successful adaptation in difficult circumstances, such as relocation to new housing or to an institutional setting. More recently, detailed longitudinal studies on older spouses have confirmed self-esteem to be one of the best predictors of successful resolution of bereavement (Lund, 1989). The beneficial effects of social support on older people in stressful circumstances appear to be due substantially to the bolstering of self-esteem (Krause, 1987).

Since the early Duke University studies, low self-esteem has also been implicated in the onset of late-life depression (Busse & Reckless, 1961; Busse, 1985). Of course, the central importance given to self-esteem in human adjustment is not peculiar to late life, and the role of loss of self-esteem in the origins of depression has had strong advocates for some time (Robson, 1988). It is difficult, however, to demonstrate that low self-esteem predates the onset of depression and is not simply an early manifestation of the clinical disorder. This problem is exacerbated by the fact that measures of self-esteem and depression usually contain common items.

There is an extensive literature on the formation and development of self-conception through the life course (e.g. McAdams, 1990). A particular source of inspiration has been Erik Erikson's life-stage model of identity, which views the self as being formed in adolescence and early adulthood, but subsequently transformed in mid-life through the development of "generativity" (the capacity to give to the next generation) and in late life by "integrity" (the acceptance of the gift of one's life) (Erikson, Erikson & Kivnick, 1986). There is evidence for change in self-conceptions in adulthood in the way that Erikson suggests, for example towards greater self-acceptance (Kogan, 1990).

However, what has emerged most clearly from empirical research is the considerable stability of self-conception with age (Bengtson, Reedy & Gordon, 1985; Baltes & Baltes, 1990). The resilience of self-esteem in particular, in the face of both physical and social changes, runs counter to common expectations. Increased awareness of this stability has led to a greater interest in the particular factors that may be associated with loss of self-esteem in old age, since this is certainly not a feature of ageing itself. Until the 1970s there had been little research on the processes by which the self is regulated in later life. In recent years, however, there have been considerable conceptual, theoretical and methodological advances.

Many studies on the self have turned away from the passive representation typical within traditional scientific procedures. It recognizes that individuals are active agents who seek ways of maintaining and developing their self-image even in disadvantageous circumstances. The very term "adjustment", which for so long has played a central part in the study of ageing, has been superseded by such terms as "coping" and "management", which are less suggestive of passivity and do not overemphasize the problematic nature of ageing. The study of intentional processes relating to identity has become an important new theme in gerontological research. At the same time it is acknowledged that human identities are constructions in a certain cultural environment at a particular historical time (Sarbin, 1986).

Another key feature of recent theorizing about the self is the emphasis on "narrative". Culture provides us with language and a mastery of narrative form through which we construct the self stories that we tell ourselves and others. The conception of self as story has provided a rich basis for reformulating questions about continuity and change with age in self-conceptions (Munnichs, 1992; McAdams, 1993; Marshall, 1993).

In the following section some of these key conceptual issues about identity and ageing are examined further: the nature of the links between personality and identity, the structure of the self and the various forms of self-conceptions it contains, the intentional nature of the self and the interpretive skills necessary to discern its actions, the self's motivations and techniques for achieving the goals it sets, and the choice of appropriate research methods for studying the self. This is followed by a survey of recent research on stability of and change in the self over the life span and particularly in the course of ageing. Emphasis is given to work carried out within the framework of a life story model of identity. Particular attention is paid to self processes in circumstances of physical and mental frailty. Consideration is also given to the importance to the self of individual and cultural perceptions of ageing, and in conclusion some implications are derived for practice.

NEW THINKING ABOUT THE SELF AND AGEING

One way of relating self-concept to personality is to see the former as a subset of the latter, as comprising "those motivations, attitudes and behaviours which are relevant to self-definition and the meaning of one's life" (McAdams, 1993, p. 266). However, it is also possible to define personality in a way that does not overlap with self-concept, "as the set of characteristic dispositions that determine emotional, interpersonal, experiential, attitudinal and motivational styles" (McCrae & Costa, 1988, p. 177).

McCrae & Costa go on to note both the logical and the theoretical reasons for interrelation: personality traits form part of the content of self-concept, and personality is most often measured through self-report; evidence supports the hypotheses that neurotics are more dissatisfied with their lives and that extraverts are more optimistic (although these links are not high). But an important indicator of functional difference is the growing consensus that personality traits tend to be stable with age, whereas key aspects of self, such as goals, values, coping styles and control beliefs, are more amenable to change (Dittmann-Kohli, 1994; Filipp & Klauer, 1986; Ryff, 1991).

As far as the structure of the self is concerned, the distinction articulated by William James (1890) between "I" and "me", the self as awareness and the self as object in awareness, has been commonly repeated. However, as Sherman & Webb (1994) note, James did not refer to two separate things, but to separate aspects of the same process constantly in interplay. It is the objective self that can be thought of in terms of structure and can be analysed. James referred to the material Me, the social Me and the spiritual Me, the former two being most accessible to objective study, whereas the spiritual Me is more subjective and closer to the primary consciousness of the I. The significance of James's conception of the spiritual Me and his dialectical I–Me conception of the self for the process of ageing will be referred to later.

The objective self has been traditionally differentiated in terms of the concepts actual self, ideal self and social (image of) self. Self-esteem is conceptualized in terms of the gap between the ideal self and the actual self, and self-efficacy in terms of the gap between the ideal self and the social image of self. These are the concepts most often utilized in the earlier studies cited by Bengtson, Reedy & Gordon (1985). However, a far greater variety of present actual and future possible self-referent conceptions are now being utilized, including the good, the bad, the hoped-for, the feared, the not-me and the ought-to selves (Markus & Nurius, 1986). Greater attention is also paid to domain-specific self-concepts. For example, it has been demonstrated that age differences in locus of control may vary across domains such as health and intellectual functioning (Lachman, 1986). There has also been much interest in the way self-perceptions coalesce to form higher-order constructs, for example in studies on life "themes" (Kaufman, 1986) and "stories" (McAdams, 1993), which will be the focus of consideration later in the chapter.

By far the most significant change of the last 10 years is the emphasis on the self as active, competent and creative in response to the challenges it faces, rather than passive, dependent and reactive (Breytspraak, 1991;

Marshall, 1993). Such developments within the study of ageing owe much to Atchley's work on management of identity and the achievement of continuity through the role changes, stigmas and threats of later life (Atchley, 1989). Of continuing importance is the framework which Rosenberg (1979) devised to integrate a variety of social psychological theories to explicate how events are interpreted so as to have a favourable impact on the self. He delineated four principles: comparisons with others; reflected appraisals by others; observation of (change in) own behaviour; centrality/peripherality of self-aspects involved. In addition, current thinking acknowledges the importance of goal setting through reconsideration and revision of previous history and future plans. Although responses from others are essential to these processes, it is the active searching self who chooses what to select and to attend to.

Contemporary critique of the passive and deterministic model of development of the self resulting from societal and organismic processes is represented most strongly in the field of ageing studies by the writings of Dannefer (e.g. Dannefer, 1984, 1989; Dannefer & Perlmutter, 1990). He emphasizes how "cognitive generativity" makes possible developmental processes, quite distinct from physical ontogeny and habituation, "that are the source and expression of the human self, and that give humans personhood" (Dannefer & Perlmutter, 1990, p. 144). Cognitive generativity allows the individual to interpret the past and present, as well as to envision alternative lives and alternative futures. He notes that not only is ageing sensitive to processes that are at least partially under the control of or mediated by the self, such as values, beliefs and intentional decisions, but that the self is also active in the "production and reproduction of social institutions and practices from which the social forces that impact individual aging derive" (Dannefer, 1989, p. 3). From this perspective, the life course itself can be seen not as part of the "natural order" but of the "humanly produced order". It constitutes not a closed "text", but a text that is open to revision and reinterpretation (Dannefer, 1989, pp. 12–13).

Dannefer's critique of the way the concept of development has been used in psychology to deny the importance of intentional action is echoed by other scholars. Freeman & Robinson (1990) have argued that development may be better conceived of "within" individuals than "across" them, and in terms of the progressive transformation of the "ends" that individuals seek in their lives. In his later book, Freeman (1993) analyses the way individuals reconstruct the meaning and significance of their past lives, a theme very familiar to gerontologists, but now perceived as central to the study of the self. He stresses the importance of hermeneutics at two levels. Individuals create their own selves in the way they interpret and make sense of their past and present experience. But to understand the constructive processes involved also requires careful interpretation on the part of the observer, for humans are not following mechanistic patterns but are beings "housed in language, culture and history" (Freeman, 1993, p. 5).

Emphasis on an active, intentional and interpretive self also helps make more understandable the resilience of the self through the processes of ageing. But, although the stability of the self with ageing has been established for some time (Bengtson, Reedy & Gordon, 1985), the implications have taken longer to be accepted. Earlier theoretical reviews (e.g. Breytspraak, 1984; Kuypers & Bengtson, 1973) now seem excessively negative. Interpretive processes as social comparisons and reflected appraisals, far from being less significant factors in maintenance of the self in old age, appear to be of considerable importance (Baltes & Baltes, 1990).

At the same time, questions have been raised about an excessive theoretical concern with stability, consistency and continuity with age. Much of the literature on ageing depicts an embattled self warding off threats (Lieberman & Tobin, 1983; Kaufman, 1986). But, as will be noted later, the results of recent studies on late life have led to a questioning of whether there is an over-emphasis in the ageing literature on continuity and self-preservation (Johnson & Barer, 1996). The oldest-old may gain benefit from adapting by accepting change. Control over circumstances may become less important, internal controls over meaning more so. It is significant, perhaps, that Ryff (1989) has found that middle-aged people stressed the importance of self-acceptance (and positive relations with others) as important to well-being, but that older people stressed accepting change (and positive relations with others).

Atchley (1991) summarizes the important methodological issues related to the study of the ageing self. Rating scales provide only limited information on the self. What is required are models of analysis which integrate a complex array of information into a whole. The growing emphasis on self as process requires more descriptive, ethnographic studies of spontaneous messages about the self in everyday life, and qualitative analysis of stories told about the self in social interaction.

Because one is dealing with personal constructions, longitudinal studies which take the person's earlier self as baseline are essential. With some exceptions (e.g. Field & Millsap, 1991; Coleman, Ivani-Chalian & Robinson, 1993), reported research has continued to be cross-sectional in nature. This raises difficulties for interpreting differences in self-representation that have been found as cohort or age effects. A rare example of research on the self employing cross-sectional, longitudinal and sequential analytic strategies is provided by Gatz & Karel's (1993) study of perceived control over 20 years. For all groups, mean levels became more internal over time, suggestive of cultural change. There were also developmental changes towards greater internality as young adults progressed into middle age. The oldest generation of women remained the most external, providing evidence for a striking historical shift in women's experience. The greater clarity that can be provided by such research designs is evident, and it is important to seize opportunities both to analyse already collected longitudinal material and to invest in laying down data for future study.

STABILITY AND CHANGE IN THE SELF WITH AGEING

Studies using subjective rating scales and content analysis of responses to self-completion stems have continued to present a picture of relative stability of self-concept and self-esteem with ageing (Baltes & Baltes, 1990; Atchley, 1991; Dittmann-Kohli, 1990; McCrae & Costa, 1988; Coleman, Ivani-Chalian & Robinson, 1993). More important have been the advances made in elucidating the dynamic processes underlying stability. There is now a considerable literature on how adults maintain continuity and positive self-evaluation in the face of threats, e.g. attributing failures to external causes, de-emphasizing certain goals for those more attainable, making social comparisons with those doing less well (Whitbourne, 1986; Atchley, 1989; Dittmann-Kohli, 1990; Ryff & Essex, 1992; Heidrich & Ryff, 1993; Sherrard, 1994).

On the basis of her studies of development in adult identity, Whitbourne (1986) argued that adults of all ages wish to see themselves as loving, competent and good. They find ways to evaluate their role performance favourably, or, cast in a role they cannot perform well, they are likely to devalue its importance and focus attention on areas of life that are more consistent with high self-esteem. Ryff & Essex (1992) investigated older women undergoing relocation. Those women who felt that they compared favourably with others in their new environments and who perceived that their families and friends had positive assessments of how they were doing had higher levels of well-being. As the authors observed, change in self-conception in later life can be positive as well as negative.

Systematic differences in the way older and younger people think about themselves have also been noted. It is to older people's advantage that they show increased self-acceptance (Ryff, 1991), a more realistic ideal self and lowered expectations (Dittmann-Kohli, 1990). In a series of projects comparing older and younger people's responses to sentence completion stems, Dittmann-Kohli (1990, 1994) has demonstrated how simply carrying on in the same way can be a sufficient and satisfying goal for many older people. Their identity is based largely on their past self and life. By contrast, younger people's depends more on the goals they have set themselves and as a consequence they show more anxiety regarding whether they will reach them. Older adults seem to suppress former dreams and desires, and many are aware of the necessity to find new goals. They refer more often to wanting peace and quiet. Fulfillment is spoken of in terms of satisfaction or contentment, implying acceptance of life conditions, rather than of happiness as a state of feeling consequent upon achievement. Of particular significance in Dittmann-Kohli's work is the demonstration that cognitions about the self and life make up a rich, complex and interrelated network of knowledge and thinking ranging from everyday matters to existential issues.

Longitudinal study of older people's illustrations of positive self-esteem ascriptions over a 10-year period has shown considerable stability in terms both of inter-individual comparisons and of group mean scores (Coleman, Ivani-Chalian & Robinson, 1993). The only major change observed was an increased mention of leisure activities as the majority of the sample passed from their 70s to their 80s. It was also noted that greater initial mention of others (apart from family members) was related to maintained high self-esteem over this length of time. This suggests that the resilience of self-esteem may vary in discernible ways.

In his review of the subject, Atchley (1991) articulates a theoretical position in which the experiences of normal ageing influence the self in many ways, mostly for good, until the point of frailty. Older people, he argues, could be expected to have a more tested, stable set of processes for managing the self, as well as more robust self-concepts.

APPLICATION OF THE LIFE STORY MODEL OF IDENTITY

The study of the ageing self has been strongly influenced by the growing interest in the importance of life story to identity. A number of theoreticians, beginning with Cohler (1982), have postulated an increasing coherence of life story with age (Whitbourne, 1985; Munnichs, 1992; McAdams, 1993; Freeman, 1993).

The process of socialization, at least in Western cultures (Geertz, 1979; Freeman, 1993), requires the formation of distinctive identities. This happens in stages, first through the "scenario" of expectations about the future that we begin to set for ourselves in childhood and adolescence, and secondly through the "story" of our already lived lives that we start to construct by early adulthood (Whitbourne, 1985). According to Munnichs (1992), it takes a definite form in mid-life with a growing awareness of finitude. McAdams (1990, 1993) elaborates Erikson's concept of generativity as continuous with identity:

> Once the individual becomes a historian of the self, the history and the history making expand to encompass as much as they can. Generativity therefore becomes part of identity. In order to know who I am, I must have some inkling of what I have done and what I am going to do in the future in order to be generative. (McAdams, 1990, pp. 184–185).

His subsequent studies on generativity in narrative accounts are the first attempt to operationalize this concept (McAdams & de St Aubin, 1992; McAdams, de St Aubin & Logan, 1993). By late life the life history report is a significant indicator of well-being (Coleman, 1986; Hagberg, 1995; Sherman, 1994), as would be predicted by Erikson's (1950) theory of ego integrity and Butler's (1963) concept of life review.

Adaptation has to take place following events that are not consistent with either the "scenario" or the "story". Reminiscence is the means by which the life story is further elaborated, kept in good order and made more coherent, clear and memorable. Reminiscence work has been taken up enthusiastically by professional workers for the contribution it can make to assessment, diversionary activity and therapy with older people (Bornat, 1994). But it is important to recognize that the past itself can be a source of disturbance and that "life review" counselling needs to be carried out sensitively, usually on a one-to-one basis and over a period of time (Haight, Coleman & Lord, 1995).

A satisfactory life story guarantees meaning so long as the link with the past is maintained. But what if present experience is dissonant? Various studies have illustrated how older people are able to transform present experience in ways that confirm important themes in their lives (Kaufman, 1986; Tobin, 1991). It is the theme, for example, of being the loved mother of a united family, that provides the persistent sense of meaning even when the "reality" fails to match. The capacity to make the past vivid, to draw it to others' attention by creating stories in which the important people and events become "bigger and better", also helps enhance the sense of continuity. Anthropological studies within residential settings have demonstrated how, if the need arises, reality may be much more malleable than we imagine and that this transformation can occur at the level of the group, and not only the individual (Hazan, 1980; 1992).

Particularly within a fast-changing society, however, challenges to the values an old persons's story expresses are likely to be more insistent. These can result in disturbed questioning of norms previously taken for granted (Coleman & McCulloch, 1990). Within older people's groups these norms and values are naturally defended (Jerrome, 1992), but isolated individuals are more at risk. Opportunities may need to be provided to help older persons re-assert their sense of integrity. There is evidence that many old people in our society lack the encouragement they need and the audience to whom to tell their story (Coleman, 1994).

Within this theoretical framework of identity construction, "I" can be seen as a storyteller who tries to integrate various life events into a coherent story. But success is not necessarily guaranteed. Ruth & Oberg (1992) report an analysis of elderly women's life histories, based on the major structural, thematic and evaluative elements they contain. They note that the narrating self in women's stories is more contradictory and less integrated, as well as being anecdotal. The women described their own lives more in relation to those of significant others, perceived events with the latters' eyes, and more often used "we" rather than "I". Their accounts reflect a view of themselves more as objects (of men's feelings) than as subjects in their own lives. Their achievements were underplayed and they often used the passive tense.

This analysis provides an important corrective to much of the theoretical writing in this field, which seems to assume that people have little difficulty in seeing their life as a story, and as something continuous and coherent. Both clinical and non-clinical observation suggests, rather, that some older people do not have a sense of having lived a "life", but rather feel confused, hurt or depressed about what has happened to them. A satisfactory identity has not yet been constructed. Older as well as younger people may still need to find out who they are, and to begin composing a story that they can call their own. Greater sensitivity to the problems surrounding narrative reconstruction has resulted from recognition of the long-term trauma caused by child abuse (e.g. Byrd, 1994).

The adequacy of story as a model of identity for the whole of adult life has also been questioned by others. McAdams (1990) himself has suggested that old people may finally move beyond story making. Having accepted the gift of their life, they come to live in the present moment, the "eternal now". A number of gerontological authors refer to the possibilities of a shift from a materialistic-rational to a transcendent perspective on self and life (Tornstam, 1994; Reker & Wong, 1988).

William James (1890) described the material and social Me as strongly appropriative (i.e. not only my body, my possessions, but also my family, my friends), whereas the spiritual Me is constituted by my states of consciousness, with at its core "the more active-feeling states". Sherman & Webb (1994) comment that these are useful concepts for describing a spiritual process in which some older people are able to live without the more appropriative aspects of the self and engage in an inward journey in which the duality of subject and object is transcended. In so doing, they reach a state which Fromm (1976), drawing on Meister Eckhart, referred to as "being" rather than "having". It is important to note, too, that in Fromm's terms "being" implies change, i.e. "being" is "becoming". In this context it is worth commenting on the increased research on the significance of religious belief and practice in older people's lives (Koenig, 1993; Levin, 1994), as well as increased theological reflections on the process of ageing (e.g. Gerkin, 1989).

THE SELF IN CIRCUMSTANCES OF PHYSICAL AND MENTAL FRAILTY

It is when ageing reaches the point of frailty that more serious challenges are posed to the self. Older people are not by virtue of their age expert at dealing with problems of disability. Atchley (1991) elucidates some of the negative consequences: interrupted continuity in way of life, more need for more extreme coping methods, reduced capacity to use defences such as selective interaction, difficulty in identifying new possible selves, depersonalization of the social environment, changes in reference groups, rusty skills in using feedback from others to fashion new self-conceptions. The very stability and long continuity of the self that has been achieved and preserved through the processes of ageing make adjustment more difficult now that real change is required. Self characteristics which are particularly highly valued in Western societies, such as competence and self-reliance, may be less easy to maintain than interpersonal skills such as warmth and humour.

Many use the past to reinforce the old image of the self (Lieberman & Tobin, 1983; Tobin, 1991), but this becomes more difficult as family and friends die who could help reaffirm this past self. Changing the reference group to incorporate other frail and disabled older people is in itself a big step to take. The crisis of sudden and unexpected disability may provoke autobiographical work (Kaufman, 1988), in which people question their past life, reaffirm and/or set new goals.

One very important form of self-perception is that of being in control of events. Increasing frailty is often accompanied by growing constraints and the need for greater efforts to maintain a sense of control. Most impressive is the evidence from research in institutional settings that relatively minor interventions designed to increase perceived control can have beneficial outcomes. For example, improvements in mental alertness and increased involvement in activities, as well as high adjustment levels, have been reported from controlled studies where residents have been encouraged to take initiatives for themselves (Rodin, 1986; Langer, 1989).

There has been comparatively little research on the self in very old age and in frailty, but early reports from a major ongoing longitudinal study of over-85s in San Francisco give reason to question some aspects of the picture just presented (Johnson & Barer, 1992; 1996). In the very old the sense of aloneness resulting from multiple bereavements is counterbalanced by their special status as long-term survivors. Cultural differences were also evident in the way long life was evaluated. The African-Americans who were interviewed saw their long lives most positively and tended to attribute to them religious and supernatural significance. Moreover, in both black and white members of the sample, change was accepted more readily than might be imagined, not only in the outside world but also in the self. People conveyed the sense of having lived beyond their old lives and selves.

In harmony with the results of other ethnographic studies of late life (Hazan, 1980; 1992; Jerrome, 1992), Johnson emphasizes that time is malleable, and that for very old people the past and future are de-emphasized and life is lived in the present. In a re-evaluation of the resonant (for gerontologists) concept of disengagement, she also argues that the evidence also points to a growing interiority and detachment and a welcoming of increased disengagement from potentially bothersome or stressful roles and relationships. Control also is given up and, again contrary to the results of studies already cited (Rodin, 1986; Langer, 1989), the oldest old appear to gain benefit from so doing, whites referring more to a belief in fate, African-Americans more to the Lord as having control. These studies suggest that continuity may not be as desirable a goal as we have thought and that accommodation to change may be the most adaptive course in late life. A similar perspective has emerged from recent German studies (Brandstädter & Greve, 1994).What remains important is internal control over meanings and interpretation. This may take the form of emphasizing previous life themes, sometimes by manipulating perception of present reality (Kaufman, 1986; Tobin, 1991), but it can also mean absorption into overarching religious and other modes of thought and feeling that lead towards an acceptance of one's place in the scheme of things (Sherman, 1981).

An important distinction in studies of self-evaluation is that between judgements of competence and judgements of value (Bengtson, Reedy & Gordon, 1985; Freden, 1982). It is quite possible for someone to accept a declining sense of the former while maintaining that life has not lost any of its meaning or value. Any change, even perhaps physical and mental decline with age, can be accepted so long as it can be made meaningful. The capacity to attach meaning to disruptive events is a remarkable human capacity, but as yet little studied within the social sciences. As already stated, researchers are now giving more consideration to the role of religious beliefs and practices in adjustment to ageing. But greater attention is also needed to all forms of philosophy of life that have enduring psychological influence on people's cognitive and emotional responses to change (Sherman, 1981; Reker & Wong, 1988).

Both Atchley (1991) and Breytspraak (1991), in their separate reviews of the field, note that new forces can emerge from physical disability (Breytspraak cites Yeats's newfound ability to convey emotions) and that we should seek more to investigate previously recorded (e.g. Scott-Maxwell, 1968; Newton, 1980) and new examples of vital inner life in the midst of disability.

Of all the disabilities of ageing, dementia poses the greatest challenges for the self. In fact, the gradual memory losses incurred are often described in terms of loss of identity (Breytspraak, 1991; Sabat & Harré, 1992). Because of the nature of the condition, it is more difficult to investigate the self in dementia by standard approaches of question and answer, but the use of sensitive observation can deliver much. In recent years a number of noteworthy attempts have been made to describe both the experience of becoming demented and its psychosocial consequences (Kitwood, 1997; Kitwood & Bredin, 1992; Gubrium, 1986).

Besides stimulating attempts to monitor and improve dementia care (Jones & Miesen, 1992), this growing interest will hopefully lead to fresh understanding of the nature of the self. The self is particularly threatened by dementia because, unlike other memory disorders, it attacks long past as well as recent memories. Even early memories are not spared (Fromholt & Larsen, 1991). However, it is also typically a gradual process and much can be done to preserve a more coherent sense of self by sensitive counselling and repeated encouragement of individuals to recall their story (Mills & Coleman, 1994). There comes a point when a person's story must be sustained by others if it is to be kept alive, but this is more likely to occur if efforts have already been made to encourage and keep active the person's own account of his/her story.

THE INFLUENCE OF PERCEPTIONS OF AGEING

A potentially important negative influence on the experience of self in later life is the individual's own attitude to the ageing process, which is itself shaped by societal perceptions of old age. Within Western culture in particular, there is a strong tradition of seeing old age as burdensome (Warnes, 1993). The dominant modern meaning of ageing is a biological process with medical aspects of illness and incapacitation (Frank, 1993). Consistent with this, Dittmann-Kohli's research on elicited self-conceptions shows that the number of thoughts dealing with the ageing body and its physical status increases in later life (Dittmann-Kohli, 1990; 1994).

Although age identification is not a pronounced feature of the spontaneous self-concept (McCrae & Costa, 1988), perhaps because one's age is always changing, fear of the future self is a significant factor in adjustment to ageing. Negative attitudes to old age are correlated with low self-esteem (Bengtson, Reedy & Gordon 1985). Moreover, there is evidence from longitudinal studies that fear of dependency and a negative attitude to ageing are predictive of loss of self-esteem and depression in subsequent years as frailty and dependency increase (Mertens & Wimmers, 1987; Coleman et al., 1993).

Ryff's study (1991), already referred to, in which she demonstrated older people's greater self-acceptance, showed anticipated decline in all dimensions of well-being with further ageing. This appears more a reflection of a cultural stereotype than a realistic view. Average decline in well-being with advanced age is in fact relatively small (Smith & Baltes, 1993; Wenger, 1992), but where there is consciousness of actual decline in physical and mental competence, it is likely that the social stigma attached to age will exacerbate the negative effect on self-confidence, in what has been called the cycle of social breakdown (Kuypers & Bengtson, 1973).

Social psychological studies of ageing have benefited from recent advances in discourse analysis being applied. Investigators have been led to explore how certain images, models and assumptions about the nature of ageing lie behind everyday speech, and how the very language we use may restrict and inhibit older people and even promote their decline (Coupland, Coupland & Giles, 1991; Giles, 1991). For it is not just that younger people's communications about old age are riddled with negative ageist assumptions about mental decline, incompetence and loss of well-being: older people also stereotype themselves. They take on characteristics they believe (rightly or wrongly) to be typical of the social group to which they belong. When age is made salient in social encounters, "older people will, compared to a non-age-salient condition, look, move, sound and talk 'older' " (Giles, 1991, p. 104).

The only adequate answer is a major cultural re-evaluation of ageing of the kind Gutmann (1994) argues for. In former times, only few individuals reached a great age. As Dannefer (1989) points out, this selective phenomenon in itself gave older people some authority. He notes that in colonial America, octogenarians would dispense advice on successful ageing to younger people. This provided older people with a greater sense of agency. Now whole cohorts age, but our culture has not yet found the means to address this issue purposefully. Older people need to be provided with more incentive to take charge of their own ageing process, but also to perceive new potentials—physical, psychological, social and spiritual—in that process. Society, in turn, needs to recognize the value of older people's continuing contributions.

Nonetheless, it would be wrong to exaggerate the impact of negative cultural perceptions of age in Western societies. Most older people refuse to wear the label "old" (Thompson, Itzin & Abendstern, 1990; Heikkinen, 1992–93) because they reject its negative connotations. Many "new" opportunities, e.g. for membership of organizations, engagement in leisure pursuits and further education, are open to the "senior citizens" of today, alongside the traditional roles of grandparent and family adviser. People have greater freedom to focus their energies where they please. Older people also seem to acquire defences for dealing with the negative attributions of others. Although the changes associated with age are perceived almost uniformly negatively, most older people maintain high levels of well-being, preventing their fears from being realized by coping successfully with the threats that come their way (Bearon, 1989; Keller, Leventhal & Larson, 1989; Dittmann-Kohli, 1990). As a result they have a positive view of their own coping with ageing.

The attribution of the term "old" to oneself appears to come with the acceptance of the closeness of death. It has become an "end state" category (Munnichs, 1992). Death itself seems to be less a concern for older people than the process of dying and the maintenance of the self in the face of death. Long, disruptive illness, for example, which is out of the expected order of things, is feared (Williams, 1990).

It is a common theme in social gerontology nowadays to emphasize the increased opportunities for a long, active life and to minimize the physical and mental decline which can occur. People are told that they can continue to lead healthy and independent lives long into late life. This is true, but it also has the effect of concealing, and thus also inhibiting adjustment to, the harsher facts of later life, which are decline, dependency and death. Such points have already been made forcefully by commentators from the humanities (e.g. Cole, 1992), whose increasing involvement in the study of ageing is very welcome. The profound topics that now present themselves for study in this area of social gerontology—self, biography, personal control, meaning and death—are best pursued by science and the humanities in partnership.

PRACTICE IMPLICATIONS

Research on dementia care is a new but fast-growing area of interest and closely links academic understanding of the self with implications for practice (Jones & Miesen, 1992; Kitwood & Bredin, 1992). The practical lessons that have emerged from more general research on the ageing self are more diffuse, and there have been few attempts yet to systematize them. Breytspraak (1984, 1991) and Tobin (1989, 1991) have been notable pioneers in this respect. Breytspraak provides three important guidelines for professional responses to older people: avoid letting them be drawn into negative images of ageing, for example by enabling them to see that the source of their problems is in the situation they face, not in themselves; give control wherever possible, so that elders may take charge of their own lives; and promote activities that encourage a sense of integration and wholeness, such as reminiscence activities and guided autobiographies that help individualize older people. Each of these points can be expanded on.

Older people's own ageist responses to their situations need to be gently challenged where possible. Very often there will be other explanations for their difficulties which arise from the unjust distribution of resources within an ageist society. Self-blame is inappropriate. Older people should be encouraged to join their voices to those who protest and campaign for improvements.

Control likewise is a key issue in health and social care. Kaufman's (1987) research on stroke rehabilitation illustrates a frequent divergence between practitioner and patient goals, expectations and responses. Continuity of self-image is particularly important. Where medical authority does not recognize this and pursues its own goal regardless, conflict and breakdown are the likely outcomes. It is probable that future years will see increased consideration given to attempts to extend individual control over future eventualities in the management of physical and mental disability. The concept of a "living will" is one move in this direction. Yet, as the San Francisco research on the oldest-old shows, internal control is not an unequivocal good. Older people's own need for a sense of subjective control should not be assumed. Imposing this on the unwilling can be as anxiety-provoking as taking it away.

Individualization is the key theme emphasized in current gerontological literature. Personal identity rests on one's whole life story. Yet service providers often do not sufficiently acknowledge a person's past strengths as being relevant to their current condition. Instead, they may subtly pressurize their clients to accept an image of helplessness precisely in order to get help. The need for including the assessment of the positives in a person's life by means of biographical interviewing has been recognized in a variety of ways in applied research, for example in assessment for community care services (Gearing & Coleman, 1996) and in long-term care (Kivnick, 1991). Assessment schedules should help place "deficiencies" in their proper context, starting from people's own view of themselves and their lives.

Encouragement of reminiscence can also promote a sense of a life that has been lived well, despite the setbacks and missed opportuities. But, as noted earlier, life review counselling needs to be carried out sensitively, and should not be confused with the more superficial activity engaged in within most types of reminiscence groups (Haight, Coleman & Lord, 1995).

Service providers, particularly in residential settings, should be trained to be tolerant of the diverse and sometimes bizarre forms in which the individual self expresses itself (Tobin, 1989). The need for security evident in repetitive and exaggerated telling of one's story may be more pronounced in a fast-changing society with weaker cultural roots. Celebration of traditional festivals and religious services can have an important part to play in preserving a sense of continuity for those for whom they have been significant parts of their lives.

People follow diverse paths in the long processes of ageing. Some need to be provided with opportunities to re-assert their sense of integrity. But for some the past will be genuinely over. The various paths of continued engagement, disengagement and transcendence will be followed, sometimes by the same people at different times, in the course of ageing. Future research needs to examine not only the psychological manoeuvres employed in situations of change and loss in late life, but also the social practices and attitudes that foster an accepting and appreciative awareness of old age as the rightful end of the life course.

REFERENCES

Atchley, R.C. (1989). A continuity theory of normal aging. *The Gerontologist*, **29**, 183–190.
Atchley, R.C. (1991). The influence of aging or frailty on perceptions and expressions of the self: theoretical and methodological issues. In J.E. Birren, J.E. Lubben, J.C. Rowe & D.E. Deutchman (eds), *The Concept and Measurement of Quality of Life in the Frail Elderly* (pp. 207–225). New York: Academic Press.

Baltes, P.B. & Baltes, M.M. (1990). Psychological perspectives on successful aging: the model of selective optimization with compensation. In P.B. Baltes & M.M. Baltes (Eds), *Successful Aging: Perspectives from the Behavioral Sciences* (pp. 1–34). New York: Cambridge University Press.

Bearon, L.B. (1989). No great expectations: the underpinnings of life satisfaction for older women. *The Gerontologist*, **29**, 772–778.

Bengtson, V.L., Reedy, M.N. & Gordon, C. (1985). Aging and self-conceptions: personality processes and social contexts. In J.E. Birren & K.W. Schaie (Eds), *Handbook of the Psychology of Aging*, 2nd edn (pp. 544–593). New York: Van Nostrand Reinhold.

Bornat, J. (Ed.) (1994). *Reminiscence Reviewed: Perspectives, Evaluations, Achievements*. Buckingham: Open University Press.

Brandstädter, J. & Greve, W. (1994). The aging self: stabilizing and protective processes. *Developmental Review*, **14**, 52–80.

Breytspraak, L.M. (1984). *The Development of Self in Later Life*. Boston, MA: Little, Brown.

Breytspraak, L.M. (1991). The development of self in later life. In C. Blais (Ed.), *Aging into the Twenty-First Century* (pp. 265–278). Milton, MA: Captus University Publications.

Busse, E. (1985). Normal aging: the Duke longitudinal studies. In M. Bergener, M. Ermini & H.B. Stahelin (Eds), *Thresholds in Aging* (pp. 215–230). New York: Academic Press.

Busse, E. & Reckless, J. (1961). Psychiatric management of the aged. *Journal of the American Medical Association*, **175**, 645–648.

Butler, R.N. (1963). The Life Review: an interpretation of reminiscence in the aged. *Psychiatry*, **26**, 65–76.

Byrd, K.R. (1994). The narrative reconstructions of incest survivors. *American Psychologist*, **49**, 439–440.

Cohler, B.J. (1982). Personal narrative and the life course. In P.B. Baltes & O.G. Brim Jr (Eds), *Life-Span Development and Behavior*, Vol. 4 (pp. 205–241). New York: Academic Press.

Cole, T. (1992). *The Journey of Life: a Cultural History of Aging in America*. Cambridge: Cambridge University Press.

Coleman, P.G. (1986). *Ageing and Reminiscence Processes: Social and Clinical Implications*. Chichester: Wiley.

Coleman, P.G. (1993). Psychological ageing. In J. Bond, P. Coleman and S. Peace (Eds), *Ageing in Society: An Introduction to Social Gerontology*, 2nd edn (pp 68–96). London: Sage.

Coleman, P.G. (1994). Reminiscence within the study of ageing: the social significance of story. In J. Bornat (Ed.), *Reminiscence Reviewed* (pp. 8–20). Milton Keynes: Open University Press.

Coleman, P.G., Aubin, A., Ivani-Chalian, C., Robinson, M. & Briggs, R. (1993). Predictors of depressive symptoms and low self-esteem in a follow-up study of elderly people over ten years. *International Journal of Geriatric Psychiatry*, **8**, 343–349.

Coleman, P.G., Ivani-Chalian, C. & Robinson, M. (1993). Self-esteem and its sources: stability and change in later life. *Ageing and Society*, **13**, 171–192.

Coleman, P.G. & McCulloch, A.W. (1990). Societal change, values and social support: exploratory studies into adjustment in late life. *Journal of Aging Studies*, **4**, 321–332.

Coupland, N., Coupland, J. & Giles, H. (1991). *Language, Society and the Elderly: Discourse, Identity and Ageing*. Oxford: Blackwell.

Cumming, E. & Henry, W. (1961). *Growing Old: The Process of Disengagement*. New York: Basic Books.

Dannefer, D. (1984). Adult development and social theory: a paradigmatic reappraisal. *American Sociological Review*, **49**, 100–116.

Dannefer, D. (1989). Human action and its place in theories of aging. *Journal of Aging Studies*, **3**, 1–20.

Dannefer, D. & Perlmutter, M. (1990). Development as a multidimensional process: individual and social constitutents. *Human Development*, **33**, 108–137.

Dittmann-Kohli, F. (1990). The construction of meaning in old age: possibilities and constraints. *Ageing and Society*, **10**, 279–294.

Dittmann-Kohli, F. (1994). Psychogerontology and the meaning of life. Inaugural lecture. The Netherlands: University of Nijmegen.

Erikson, E.H. (1950). *Childhood and Society*. New York: Norton.

Erikson, E.H., Erikson, J.M. & Kivnick, H.Q. (1986). *Vital Involvement in Old Age: The Experience of Old Age in Our Time*. New York: Norton.

Field, D. & Millsap, R.E. (1991). Personality in advanced old age; continuity or change. *Journal of Gerontology: Psychological Sciences*, **46**, 299–308.

Filipp, S.H. & Klauer, T. (1986). Conceptions of the self over the life span: reflections on the dialectics of change. In M.M. Baltes & P.B. Baltes (Eds), *The Psychology of Control and Aging* (pp. 167–205). Hillsdale, NJ: Erlbaum.

Frank, A.W. (1993). The rhetoric of self-change: illness experience as narrative. *The Sociological Quarterly*, **34**, 39–52.

Freden, L. (1982). *Psychosocial Aspects of Depression: No Way Out?* Chichester: Wiley.

Freeman, M. (1993). *Rewriting the Self: History, Memory, Narrative*. London: Routledge.

Freeman, M. & Robinson, R.E. (1990). The development within: an alternative approach to the study of lives. *New Ideas in Psychology*, **8**, 53–72.

Fromholt, P. & Larsen, S.F. (1991). Autobiographical memory in normal aging and primary degenerative dementia (dementia of Alzheimer type). *Journal of Gerontology: Psychological Sciences*, **46**, 85–91.

Fromm, E. (1976). *To Have or To Be*. New York: Harper and Row.

Gatz, M. & Karel, M.J. (1993). Individual change in perceived control over 20 years. *International Journal of Behavioral Development*, **16**, 305–322.

Gearing, B. & Coleman, P. (1996). Biographical assessment in community care. In J. Birren, G. Kenyon, J.E. Ruth, J.J.F. Schroots & T. Svensson (Eds), *Aging and Biography: Explorations in Adult Development* (pp. 265–282). New York: Springer.

Geertz, C. (1979). From the native's point of view: on the nature of anthropological understanding. In R. Rabinow & W.M. Sullivan (Eds), *Interpretive Social Science: A Reader*. Berkeley, CA: University of California Press.

Gerkin, C.V. (1989). Pastoral care and models of aging. *Journal of Religion and Aging*, **6**, 83–100.

Giles, H. (1991). "Gosh, you don't look it!": a sociolinguistic construction of ageing. *The Psychologist: Bulletin of the British Psychological Society*, **3**, 99–106.

Gubrium, J.F. (1986). *Oldtimers and Alzheimer's: The Descriptive Organization of Senility*. London: JAI Press.

Gutmann, D.L. (1994). *Reclaimed Powers: Towards a New Psychology of Men and Women in Later Life*, 2nd edn. Evanston IL: Northwestern University Press.

Hagberg, B. (1995). The individual's life history as a formative experience to aging. In B.K. Haight & J. Webster (eds), *The Art and Science of Reminiscing:*

Theory, Research, Methods and Applications (pp. 61–75). Washington DC: Taylor and Francis.

Haight, B.K., Coleman, P. & Lord, K. (1995). The linchpins of a successful life review: structure, evaluation and individuality. In B.K. Haight & J. Webster (Eds), *The Art and Science of Reminiscing: Theory, Research, Methods and Applications* (pp. 179–192). Washinton DC: Taylor and Francis.

Hazan, H. (1980). *The Limbo People: A Study of the Constitution of the Time Universe among the Aged*. London: Routledge and Kegan Paul.

Hazan, H. (1992). *Managing Change in Old Age*. Albany, NY: State University of New York.

Heidrich, S.M. & Ryff, C.D. (1993). The role of social comparisons processes in the psychological adaptation of elderly adults. *Journal of Gerontology: Psychological Sciences*, **48**, 127–136.

Heikkinen, R.L. (1992–93). Patterns of experienced aging with a Finnish cohort. *International Journal of Aging and Human Development*, **36**, 269–277.

James, W. (1890). *Principles of Psychology*. New York: Holt.

Jerrome, D. (1992). *Good Company: An Anthropological Study of Old People in Groups*. Edinburgh: Edinburgh University Press.

Johnson, C.L. & Barer, B.M. (1992). Patterns of engagement and disengagement among the oldest old. *Journal of Aging Studies*, **6**, 351–364.

Johnson, C.L. & Barer, B.M. (1996). *Life beyond 85 Years: the Aura of Survivorship*. New York: Springer.

Jones, G.M.M. & Miesen, B.M.L. (eds) (1992). *Care-giving in Dementia. Research and Applications*. London: Routledge.

Kaufman, S. (1986). *The Ageless Self: Sources of Meaning in Late Life*. Madison, WI: University of Wisconsin Press.

Kaufman, S. (1987). Stroke rehabilitation and the negotiation of identity. In S. Reinharz & G.D. Rowles (Eds), *Qualitative Gerontology* (pp. 82–103). New York: Springer.

Kaufman, S. (1988). Illness, biography and the interpretation of self following a stroke. *Journal of Aging Studies*, **3**, 217–227.

Keller, M.L., Leventhal, E.A. & Larson, B. (1989). Aging: the lived experience. *International Journal of Aging and Human Development*, **29**, 67–82.

Kitwood, T. (1997). *Dementia Reconsidered: the Person Comes First*. Buckingham: Open University Press.

Kitwood, T. & Bredin, K. (1992). Towards a theory of dementia care: personhood and well-being. *Ageing and Society*, **12**, 269–287.

Kivnick, H.Q. (1991). *Living with Care, Caring for Life: The Inventory of Life Strengths*. Minneapolis, MN: School of Social Work, University of Minnesota.

Koenig, H.G. (1993). *Aging and God: Spiritual Pathways to Mental Health in Midlife and Later Years*. New York: Haworth.

Kogan, N. (1990). Personality and aging. In J.E. Birren & K.W. Schaie (Eds), *Handbook of the Psychology of Aging*, 3rd edn (pp. 330–346). San Diego CA: Academic Press.

Krause, N. (1987). Life stress, social support and self-esteem in an elderly population. *Psychology and Aging*, **2**, 349–356.

Kuypers, J.A. & Bengtson, V.L. (1973). Social breakdown and competence: a model of normal aging. *Human Development*, **16**, 181–201.

Lachman, M.E. (1986). Locus of control in aging research: a case for multidimensional and domain-specific assessment. *Psychology and Aging*, **1**, 34–40.

Langer, E.J. (1989). Minding matters: the consequences of mindlessness-mindfulness. *Advances in Experimental Social Psychology*, **22**, 137–175.

Levin, J.S. (Ed.) (1994). *Religion in Aging and Health: Theoretical Foundations and Methodological Frontiers*. Thousand Oaks, CA: Sage.

Lieberman, M.A. & Tobin, S.S. (1983). *The Experience of Old Age: Stress, Coping and Survival*. New York: Basic Books.

Lund, D.A. (Ed.) (1989). *Older Bereaved Spouses: Research with Practical Applications*. New York: Hemisphere.

Markus, H.R. & Herzog, R.A. (1991). The role of the self-concept in aging. In K.W. Schaie & M.P. Lawton (Eds), *Annual Review of Gerontology and Geriatrics*, Vol. 11 (pp. 110–143). New York: Springer.

Markus, H. & Nurius, P. (1986). Possible selves. *American Psychologist*, **41**, 954–969.

Marshall, V.W. (1993). Social models of aging. Paper presented at the International Congress of Gerontology, Budapest.

McAdams, D.P. (1990). Unity and purpose in human lives: the emergence of identity as a life story. In A.I. Rabin, R.A. Zucker, R.A. Emmons & S. Frank (Eds), *Studying Persons and Lives* (pp. 148–200). New York: Springer.

McAdams, D.P. (1993). *The Stories We Live By: Personal Myths and the Making of the Self*. New York: William Morrow.

McAdams, D.P. & de St Aubin, E. (1992). A theory of generativity and its assessment through self-report, behavioral acts, and narrative themes in autobiography. *Journal of Personality and Social Psychology*, **62**, 1003–1015.

McAdams, D.P., de St Aubin, E. & Logan, R.L. (1993). Generativity among young, midlife, and older adults. *Psychology and Aging*, **8**, 221–230.

McCrae, R.R. & Costa, P.T. (1988). Age, personality and the spontaneous self-concept. *Journal of Gerontology: Social Sciences*, **43**, 177–185.

McCrae, R.R. & Costa, P.T. (1990). *Personality in Adulthood*. New York: Guilford Press.

Mertens, F. & Wimmers, M. (1987). Life-style of older people: improvement or threat to their health. *Ageing and Society*, **7**, 329–343.

Mills, M.A. & Coleman, P.G. (1994). Nostalgic memories in dementia—a case study. *International Journal of Aging and Human Development*, **38**, 203–219.

Munnichs, J.M.A. (1992). Ageing: a kind of autobiography. *European Journal of Gerontology*, **1**, 244–250.

Newton, E. (1980). *This Bed My Centre*. London: Virago Press.

Reker, G.T. & Wong, P.T.P. (1988). Aging as an individual process: toward a theory of personal meaning. In J.E. Birren & V.L. Bengtson (Eds), *Emergent Theories of Aging* (pp. 214–246). New York: Springer.

Robson, P.J. (1988). Self-esteem: a psychiatric view. *British Journal of Psychiatry*, **153**, 6–15.

Rodin, J. (1986). Aging and health: effects of the sense of control. *Science*, **233**, 1271–1276.

Rosenberg, M. (1979). *Conceiving the Self*. New York: Basic Books.

Rudinger, G. & Thomae, H. (1990). The Bonn longitudinal study of aging: coping, life adjustment and life satisfaction. In P.B. Baltes & M.M. Baltes (Eds), *Successful Aging: Perspectives from the Behavioral Sciences* (pp. 265–295). Cambridge: Cambridge University Press.

Ruth, J.E. & Oberg, P. (1992). Expressions of aggression in the life stories of aged women. In K. Bjorkqvist & P. Niemela (eds), *Of Mice and Women: Aspects of Female Aggression* (pp. 133–146). San Diego, CA: Academic Press.

Ryff, C.D. (1989). In the eye of the beholder: views of psychological well-being among middle-aged and older adults. *Psychology and Aging*, **4**, 195–210.

Ryff, C.D. (1991). Possible selves in adulthood and old age: a tale of shifting horizons. *Psychology and Aging*, **6**, 286–295.

Ryff, C.D. & Essex, M.J. (1992). The interpretation of life experience and well-being: the sample case of relocation. *Psychology and Aging*, **7**, 507–517.

Sabat, S.R. & Harré, R. (1992). The construction and deconstruction of self in Alzheimer's disease. *Ageing and Society*, **12**, 443–461.

Sarbin, T.R. (ed.) (1986). *Narrative Psychology: The Storied Nature of Human Conduct*. New York: Praeger.

Scott-Maxwell, F. (1968). *The Measure of My Days*. New York: Knopf.

Sherman, E. (1981). *Counseling the Aging: An Integrative Approach*. New York: Free Press.

Sherman, E. (1994). The structure of well-being in the life narratives of the elderly. *Journal of Aging Studies*, **8**, 149–158.

Sherman, E. & Webb, T.A. (1994). The self as process in late-life reminiscence: spiritual attributes. *Ageing and Society*, **14**, 255–267.

Sherrard, C.A. (1994). Elderly wellbeing and the psychology of social comparison. *Ageing and Society*, **14**, 341–356.

Smith, J. & Baltes, P.B. (1993). Differential psychological ageing: profiles of the old and very old. *Ageing and Society*, **13**, 551–587.

Thompson, P., Itzin, C. & Abendstern, M. (1990). *I Don't Feel Old: The Experience of Later Life*. Oxford: Oxford University Press.

Tobin, S.S. (1989). The effects of institutionalization. In K.S. Markides & C.L. Cooper (Eds), *Aging, Stress and Health* (pp. 139–163). Chichester: Wiley.

Tobin, S.S. (1991). *Personhood in Advanced Old Age: Implications for Practice*. New York: Springer.

Tornstam, L. (1994). Gerotranscendence: a theoretical and empirical exploration. In L.E. Thomas & S.A. Eisenhandler (Eds), *Aging and the Religious Dimension* (pp. 203–225). Westport: Greenwood Publishing Group.

Warnes, A.M. (1993). Being old, old people and the burdens of burden. *Ageing and Society*, **13**, 297–338.

Wenger, G.C. (1992). Morale in old age: a review of the evidence. *International Journal of Geriatric Psychiatry*, **7**, 699–708.

Whitbourne, S.K. (1985). The psychological construction of the life span. In J. Birren & K. Schaie (Eds), *Handbook of the Psychology of Aging*, 2nd edn (pp. 594–618). New York: Van Nostrand Reinhold.

Whitbourne, S.K. (1986). *The Me I Know: A Study of Adult Identity*. New York: Springer-Verlag.

Williams, R. (1990). *The Protestant Legacy: Attitudes to Death and Illness among Older Aberdonians*. Oxford: Clarendon Press.

Chapter 4

MENTAL HEALTH PROBLEMS IN LATE LIFE

Robert T. Woods*

INTRODUCTION

The dementias and depression are without doubt the major mental health problems encountered in older people. They have attracted most attention in relation to theories, assessment and treatment and are accordingly given prominence elsewhere in this volume. The current chapter aims to place these two groups of disorders within the broader spectrum of mental health problems, highlighting areas which would benefit from further investment of psychological resources. In discussing each area of difficulty in turn, a brief overview of its prevalence will be presented, to provide a perspective on the scale of mental health problems in late life. Fuller discussions of the epidemiological issues involved are to be found in Henderson (1989), Kay (1991) and Livingston & Hinchliffe (1993).

DEMENTIA

Epidemiology and diagnostic issues

The prevalence of the dementias has been the subject of numerous epidemiological studies internationally (e.g. Hofman et al., 1991). There are a number of differences between studies, but there is a broad consensus that the prevalence doubles for each increase of 5.1 years; 5% of the over-65s and 20% of the over-80s are widely accepted figures

* University of Wales, Bangor, UK

Psychological Problems of Ageing: Assessment, Treatment and Care. Edited by R.T. Woods.
© 1999 John Wiley & Sons Ltd.

(Livingston & Hinchliffe, 1993). The prognosis of the dementias should perhaps by definition be poor, and this is confirmed by most follow-up studies; however, where early cases are included, a proportion may show little deterioration for up to four years (Livingston & Hinchliffe, 1993). The prevalence rates for the different types of dementia are more difficult to ascertain, in view of the difficulty of making a definitive diagnosis during life; at present, neuropathological examination of the brain is essential in confirming which type of dementia was present. However, it is clear that, separately and in combination, Alzheimer's disease and multi-infarct dementia account for the majority of cases. In most countries, Alzheimer-type changes are more common, but in Japan, for example, the situation is reversed, presumably because of more general differences in vascular conditions. It is becoming clear that what has been thought of simply as Alzheimer's disease may include a number of different conditions. Lewy body dementia, for example, has only been considered in recent years as a potential diagnosis; such cases were probably in the past categorized as Alzheimer-type (Perry et al., 1990).

Neuropsychological aspects of the dementias are fully covered in Chapter 5 of this volume; issues of assessment, treatment and care are discussed extensively in a number of chapters. However, the boundaries of "dementia" are worth considering in more detail. Although the diagnosis of dementia is generally thought to be relatively clear-cut, this applies more to the moderate/severe cases; mild cognitive impairment poses much more difficulty, especially in the context of a single assessment. The presence of low mood adds further complications, which will be discussed later in relation to depression. Most epidemiological studies include a category reflecting the hinterland between "normality" and "dementia". Dawe, Procter & Philpot (1992) list a number of such diagnostic terms synonymous with mild memory impairment: benign senescent forgetfulness (BSF); mild dementia; very mild cognitive decline; questionable dementia; limited cognitive disturbance; minimal dementia; age-associated memory impairment (AAMI).

BSF was described initially by Kral (1962) as a static memory difficulty, in contrast to malignant memory problems which developed into a dementia. BSF was thought to reflect "normal" age-related changes in memory. This highlights neatly the central diagnostic problem, of identifying a decline in cognitive function against a backdrop of some decline being expected in any event. These non-dementia changes have become the focus of a new diagnostic category—age-associated memory impairment (AAMI)—which has aroused much controversy in recent years (see Deary, 1995). The definition has been very broad, taking as a comparative standard the memory performance of younger age groups, and it is likely that a large proportion of those over 50 could be included. The definition also includes the person complaining of poor memory, although subjective complaints have generally proved to have little relationship with objective performance, and may have a greater association with anxiety and depression (Dawe, Procter & Philpot, 1992). The debate on AAMI has raised issues as to what we mean by "normal"; if a condition is very common do we believe that it should not be treated? Should we search for a treatment for "normal ageing"? The perceived interest of the pharmaceutical industry in this area has led to calls for the costs and potential side-effects of treating a condition which is not disabling to be carefully considered (Deary, 1995). It is perhaps significant that psychological memory retraining techniques have been given little attention (Yesavage, Lapp & Sheikh, 1989; Scogin, 1992). Although the power of such approaches may be relatively weak, they are not associated with troublesome side-effects.

Clearly, if AAMI or whatever were a precursor of dementia, the balance of cost and benefit would be different. O'Brien & Levy (1993) argue that follow-up studies are required, using age-standardized norms, to identify those declining in relation to their peers. Generally, such follow-up studies show that only a small proportion of those with mild memory impairment progress to dementia (less than 10%) where the complaints are mainly subjective. For example, O'Brien et al. (1992) report that 8.8% of those attending a memory clinic and initially diagnosed as "normal" or having "memory loss associated with normal ageing" went on to develop a clear-cut dementia—slightly more than would have been expected from general population incidence figures. Where there is objective evidence of memory loss the proportion having dementia at follow-up is much greater (O'Brien & Levy, 1993).

Conventionally, dementia has been seen as qualitatively as well as quantitatively distinct from normal ageing; much has been achieved by emphasis on dementia as a disease, more common in older people but potentially striking at any age. However, it is possible to envisage normal ageing and dementia on a continuum, separated only by a necessarily arbitrary cut-off point (Huppert, 1994; Cohen, 1996). The essential distinction could perhaps be in the *rate*, rather than simply the absolute amount, of change. This model accounts for the appearance, in smaller numbers, of some of the neuropathological features of Alzheimer's, for example, in the brains of older people who died without dementia, as well as for the decline in cognitive function reported in normal ageing. The argument against such a model is usually based on the qualitative differences observed in cognitive changes between Alzheimer's and normal ageing. However, such differences are less where the Alzheimer's cases are mildly impaired (Dawe, Procter & Philpot, 1992), suggesting there may be a continuum of change. Such a model does suggest that distinguishing cases of early dementia may be a very difficult task, and may ultimately become a matter of definition, of setting a threshold of rate of change, as in effect is often the case in epidemiological studies.

Defining change presents particular psychometric problems. One concern has been that those who begin from a high level are less likely to cross any threshold of impairment. Those with a lifelong relatively low intellectual and educational level require only a small degree of change to enter the range of impairment. Those with high intellectual function and education have, it would appear, more resources in reserve to maintain their function. Certainly, those with low intellectual level are often given a diagnosis of dementia, which turns out not to be supported by monitoring the person over time. This may be attributable in part to the high educational loading of many of the screening tests available, such as the Mini-Mental State Examination (Orrell et al., 1992). It has been argued that education protects against dementia (Orrell & Sahakian, 1995), but the issue is a complex one (Gilleard, 1997). A highly intelligent person in a very demanding environment might in fact show signs of incipient dementia earlier than a person with a low intellectual level who is subject to few cognitive demands outside a well-established routine. Measures sensitive across the broad range of function, repeated over time to study rates as well as levels of change, are required to increase our understanding of a process so damaging in its final stages, yet so insidious in its onset.

Non-cognitive features

Although cognitive changes are universal in dementia, other features, whilst not present in every case, are common enough to merit attention in their own right. Indeed, it is likely that it is these features which contribute more than cognitive deficits to carer strain (Donaldson, Tarrier & Burns, 1998) and placement decisions. These "non-cognitive" features include depression, anxiety, hallucinations, delusions and challenging behaviours of various types (Burns, Jacoby & Levy, 1990, a,b,c). For example, delusions—often concerning theft—were reported by Burns et al. in about one-sixth of their sample of people with Alzheimer's disease, with another one-fifth having shown some ideas of persecution since their dementia began. Thirty percent had misidentification syndromes, for instance mistaking TV pictures or images in a picture or mirror for real people. Visual and auditory hallucinations were each noted in around one-tenth of the sample. Hallucinations and delusions are reported to be much more common in dementia of the Lewy body type, perhaps affecting as many as 80% of cases (McKeith et al., 1992).

Depression and anxiety become more difficult to assess accurately as cognitive impairment increases and self-report measures become less applicable. Measures of the observable features of depression have been developed to reduce the reliance on self-report, and informant ratings used (see Chapter 9). However, it is clear that features of anxiety and depression frequently coexist with dementia, potentially leading to additional disability, distress, restlessness and other disturbed behaviour. Ballard et al. (1996) report anxiety symptoms in 30% of their sample of people with dementia, and depressive features may occur in as many as a quarter of people with dementia (Reifler & Larson, 1990). Traditionally, assessment has sought to discriminate between those patients with a dementia and those with a depression; there needs to be greater awareness of the probability of a dual diagnosis.

"Challenging behaviour" in dementia encompasses a wide range of perceived difficulty. Aggression (verbal and/or physical), wandering, eating problems, shouting and screaming, sexual problems and toileting difficulties are amongst those most commonly described. The apparent prevalence of such problems varies widely, depending on the definitions used; imprecision abounds, with different types of behaviour mixed together, and the assumption made that the challenging behaviour is an inherent feature of the person rather than arising from an interaction between the person and his/her environment. Hope et al. (1997) suggest that there are three distinct behavioural syndromes in dementia: overactivity (including aimless walking); aggressive behaviour; and psychosis (hallucinations, persecutory ideas and extreme anxiety). The development of typologies of aggressive behaviour (Stokes, 1989; Ware et al., 1990) and wandering (Hope & Fairburn, 1990; Stokes, 1996) and the delineation of a variety of sexual problems (Haddad & Benbow, 1993) reflect the diversity of behaviours encompassed in these broad categories, reinforcing the notion that a multi-factorial and highly individualized understanding is required.

The extent to which behaviour change relates to specific areas or types of brain damage is unclear. Frontal lobe-type dementias are often thought to be associated with loss of control over behaviour. This leads in some cases to disinhibition, such as inappropriate sexual behaviour, or dangerous risk-taking. In other instances there is difficulty in initiating behaviour. This is seen most dramatically in the Diogenes syndrome, where the person shows gross self-neglect and apparent unawareness of the squalid conditions which result (Orrell, Sahakian & Bergmann, 1989). Other brain-behaviour relationships are less established. "Sundowning", an increase in restlessness and agitation in the evening, may be related to damage to the suprachiasmatic nucleus, which is involved in regulation of circadian rhythms; attempts have been made to link eating problems and aggression to particular brain lesions and neurochemical changes (Stokes, 1996). Challenging behaviour may arise less directly from brain damage, through the cognitive changes that occur or the psychiatric features mentioned above; misunderstandings, misinterpretations, misperceptions, acting on hallucinations and delusions may all lead to such behaviours. The effects of coexisting physical problems must also be considered; an acute confusional state, or delirium, arising from a urinary tract infection or a chest infection, say, on top of the dementia, may lead to added behavioural disturbance, including perhaps hallucinatory experiences; pain, which cannot be expressed readily, may emerge as disturbed behaviour; even constipation may increase restlessness and agitation. The effects of medication should also not be overlooked in terms of adverse reactions and unwanted side effects, and interactions between components of the "drug cocktail" on which some older people with dementia find themselves.

Psychologically, Stokes (1996) argues that challenging behaviour may best be understood as poorly communicated need. During development, a person learns to meet his/her basic needs in sophisticated and mature ways; this enrichment is stripped away by dementia, exposing a "dysfunctional and at times grotesque distortion of goal-directed communication and conduct" (Stokes, 1996, p. 676). Needs for emotional security and physical safety may be seen to lead to all manner of challenging behaviour; aggression to deal with the person who is seen as threatening; calling out continually to bring contact with a carer, who must be seen at all times, or appears not to exist; wandering to find someone or something familiar. Attempting to see the world from the perspective of the person with dementia is the key to understanding some of the difficulties in communication of need; as communication is a two-way process, the onus is then on those providing care to develop greater skills and expertise in hearing all that is being communicated, so that an appropriate response may be made (see Chapter 12, this volume).

DEPRESSION

Prevalence

The assumption is often made (mainly by younger people) that depression must be more common in older people. This is a complex issue; it is not acceptable simply to apply the same diagnostic instrument across all age groups and compare the rates obtained. Items on somatic symptoms or sleep patterns, for example, are much better indicators of depression in younger people; in older people they are likely to reflect changes occurring independent of mood state. Henderson (1994, 1990, 1989) reviews evidence indicating that rates of depression in elderly people are lower than in other age groups, when marital status and education are controlled for. This reflects the number who would be diagnosed as "cases" of depression. Henderson also suggests that if a dimensional, rather than a categorical, approach were adopted, older people might indeed have more depressive *symptoms*. Snowdon (1997) argues that among factors reducing the apparent prevalence of depression in later life are the emphasis on community samples, and the exclusion of people with dementia. Prevalence rates of depression in residential care are very high (around one-third of those without severe dementia; Ames, 1991) and as many as a quarter of people with dementia are said to have a coexisting depression (Reifler & Larson, 1990).

Reported rates of depression in older people do, then, vary greatly according to the sample, scales and diagnostic criteria used. A representative study is reported by Lindesay, Briggs & Murphy (1989). They surveyed nearly 1000 elderly people in an urban area, identifying 4.3% as having a severe depression and a further 13.5% having a mild to moderate degree of depression. A number of studies of the prognosis of depression in late life have been undertaken. These reflect the efficacy of the usual treatment regime, which in most cases has been antidepressant medication. As many as a third of patients with depression remain depressed three years later, with only around 20% sustaining a complete recovery (Livingston & Hinchliffe, 1993). Over the shorter timescale of a year, Burvill (1993) suggests that nearly half (47%) make a complete recovery and do not relapse within a year; 18% recover, but then relapse within 12 months; and 24% remain depressed or make only a partial recovery. The remaining 11% die within the year. Although there continues to be some debate regarding the interpretation of such figures (e.g. Baldwin, 1991), it is clear that a substantial number of older people with depression do not recover with the standard treatments and that relapse is a major issue.

Life events

The mechanisms underlying depression in older people are not well understood, especially regarding the factors leading to depression occurring for the first time in this phase of life. In older people, as with younger adults, the prevalence of adverse life events and difficult life circumstances is greater in the 12 months preceding the onset of the depression than in a control sample (e.g. Murphy, 1982; Lam et al., 1987). However, the direction of causality is by no means clear (Davies, 1996), as patients may have had previous depressive episodes. It is important to recognize that many older people experience adverse life events without becoming depressed, and that many episodes of depression are not preceded by adverse circumstances.

Although later life is often characterized as a time of great adversity and multiple losses, surveys appear to show that older people experience fewer adverse life events than younger respondents, who also report the occurrence of more desirable events. The most common events are health-related, affecting either the respondent or a close relative (Davies, 1996).

The meaning of an event or difficulty will vary from individual to individual. Lam et al. (1987) reported that among a group of older people who had all experienced adverse life circumstances, those who were depressed showed negative cognitions on standard scales. Typically, they would tend to over-generalize from a specific event, or blame themselves for events not within their control, and have a negative view of themselves, the world and the future. An event perceived as a threat is more likely to lead to anxiety, whereas events perceived as losses relate to depression. Events threatening the person's social roles and social identity may be particularly difficult, reducing the person's ability to exert control in important areas of life (Krause, 1994). From a developmental perspective, the extent to which the event is normative or "on-time" is important, as will be evident in relation to bereavement (see below). Where the event can be anticipated, expected and seen as part of a normal process, adjustment is likely to be better than where the event comes as an untimely shock.

Consideration of specific life events, such as retirement or relocation, indicates that in fact the "event" is part of a "process" and cannot be considered in isolation from what precedes and follows it. Thus, the impact of a change of home will be influenced by any factors necessitating the move (physical or mental health changes or a bereavement, for example). The amount of control and choice exercised by the individual and the amount of preparatory adjustment that is possible, together with the extent of change required, will be important factors also (Orrell & Davies, 1994). Depression in residents of old people's homes is often attributed to the impoverished environment typically provided. It may, however, more accurately be seen as the end-point of a process beginning with the contemplation of the move (Lindesay, 1995; Davies, 1996).

Similarly, retirement is both an event and a process (Bossé et al., 1996). About 30% of retirees find the transition stressful, although the event comes close to the bottom of a list of stressful events in order of perceived stressfulness. Around one-third of retirees report the state of being retired as stressful—however, this should be compared with two-thirds of workers who report work as stressful! The myth that retirement is a dreaded and dreadful event ignores the reality of many jobs, which are demanding, monotonous and oppressive and which, in certain cases, have a damaging effect on physical health, from which retirement provides a welcome relief. Factors shown to influence whether a person falls into the minority who do find retirement stressful include:

- The extent of control exerted by the individual; involuntary, enforced, unexpected retirement is most stressful.
- The presence of other stressful life events or difficulties; poor health or inadequate finances predict poor adjustment, for example.
- The importance of work to the individual's sense of worth and identity.

The notion that retirement inevitably places strain on a marital relationship also appears to be a myth (Bossé et al., 1996), with continuity in the relationship being evident. Overall, retirement appears to be a normative, anticipated life event, which for many is a desired event, but which is problematic for around one-third of individuals.

Social support

Cervilla & Prince (1997) report that elderly people having social support deficits of various kinds had an increased risk of depression. Murphy (1982) reported that the absence of a confiding relationship increases vulnerability to depression in older people. However, having a confidant made no difference to outcome of the depressive disorder at follow-up. Murphy argues that the vulnerability factor is in fact a long-standing difficulty in forming intimate relationships. However, the process by which the capacity to develop confiding relationships has a protective effect has yet to be satisfactorily elaborated (Davies, 1996). There are a number of aspects of social support which could usefully be explored in relation to depression—the effects of different types of social networks (Wenger, 1995, 1997), the relationship with loneliness (which might be defined as dissatisfaction with one's level of social support), the role of companionship and the contrasting impact of social support from family compared with that received from friends or from service-providers.

Day-centres are often seen as the "solution" to social isolation in the older person vulnerable to depression, but may not provide the type of relationship which would make a difference to the person's mood or feelings of loneliness. For some, it is only relationships with close family or valued friends which will meet the need for social support.

Physical health

Physical health and depression are intertwined in later life. The most common adverse life events and difficulties in later life relate to physical health problems. In samples of older adults with physical health problems, levels of depression are typically raised. Depression in older people is sometimes mistaken for a physical health problem and vice versa—generalized complaints of fatigue, lethargy and pain may prove difficult to evaluate (Pitt, 1995). Seeking to arrive at a single explanation for a person's presenting problems is likely to be unhelpful, as multiple pathologies are common.

In many instances, depression in the presence of physical health problems appears to reflect a difficulty in coping with and adjusting to the changed circumstances which accompany the physical health difficulty. A fit, vigorous 74 year-old woman trips over a paving stone on her way home from her regular Bingo game; she fractures her femur, and does not recover full mobility; she is depressed. She is missing her regular social contacts, as she can no longer go out alone; she now needs help to keep her home clean and for shopping; from being fiercely independent she now has to accept help from outsiders; she sees her grandchildren less often, as she is now unable to look after them to give their parents a break. She grieves for her lost roles and life; she cannot see any prospect for improvement. She is frequently in pain and discomfort, and the smallest daily task is now a major effort. She is angry with the doctors who did not succeed in restoring her mobiliy, and is suing the authorities responsible for the loose paving stone. Her relationship with the medical services is often difficult; her lack of recovery of mobility has at times been attributed to her "lack of motivation", which seems to reflect the lack of energy and drive, arising perhaps from her depression. Thus, her depression is potentially both a reaction to a major physical health problem and a factor delaying recovery.

Such a scenario might follow any number of physical health difficulties; however, there are some which are said to have a specific association with depressive disorders (see Chapter 10). These include Parkinson's disease and stroke. For example, one-fifth of patients are found to be depressed six months post-stroke; although there have been suggestions that depression is more common with strokes located in particular parts of the brain, the evidence on this is conflicting (see Skilbeck, 1996; and Chapter 10, this volume). It is important to remember that a condition such as Parkinson's disease will be experienced as a dynamic process; there are any problems that were encountered pre-diagnosis; the diagnostic assessment, the seeking to understand/accept the diagnosis and its impact on the family; periods of the condition responding to medication; periods when it appears to be out of control or deteriorating rapidly, etc. etc. The person's adjustment can only be understood in the context of what has led up to the present situation, not simply in relation to current symptoms. Coping mechanisms appropriate at one stage may not be useful at another; early on, for example, denial may have a protective function, later it may obstruct useful interventions.

Acute onset conditions (such as stroke) present particular problems for adjustment, with a sudden, rapid loss of function. With an amputation, the person may have to adjust to a radically altered body-image, and a grief-like process appears to be frequently encountered in such a context. Some conditions, such as stroke, myocardial infarction or cancer, are perceived as especially life-threatening, alerting the person to the possibility of death, which may impact on efforts to cope. Families may become over-protective, which in itself may add to depression, in taking away control from the individual.

Chronic arthritis is a painful, disabling condition. Barlow, Williams & Wright (1997) have reported that a programme of six weekly sessions teaching self-management principles is effective in increasing participants' self-efficacy, i.e. the person's confidence in his/her ability to control or manage the various aspects of the condition. Pain and depression were significantly reduced, and participants reported greater use of cognitive techniques such as distraction to reduce symptoms. They also exercised more frequently. Improved communication was reported with medical services, a key area of difficulty for many older people with chronic health problems, who often feel that their problems are not taken seriously enough by their doctors. Doctors, of course, often feel powerless to help with such chronic difficulties. The results of this and similar studies suggest that health psychology could make a major impact on the experience of chronic illness for many older people, and that cognitive techniques aimed at building up the person's sense of control and self-efficacy may have an important role in this. Pain management programmes and psychological treatment for depression in chronic illness (see Chapter 10) all have the potential for reducing disability, which often has components going beyond the functional impairment set by the physical problem.

Depression and cognitive impairment

Considerable attention has been given over the years to the diagnostic distinction between dementia and depression—the archetypal referral to the clinical psychologist practising in old age psychiatry. However, to make such a discrimination purely on the grounds of cognitive function ignores two key facts. First, people with dementia may well be depressed; the two diagnoses are not mutually exclusive. It is important to identify and treat depression in this context, as in any other. Secondly, some people with depression, while not having a dementia as such, may show cognitive impairments. This patient group has been variously described as having a "pseudodementia" or the "reversible dementia of depression". It is debatable whether either label is of much help, in that the impairments may not much resemble dementia (Poon, 1992), and the extent of their reversibility has been questioned (Abas, Sahakian & Levy, 1990).

It has proved difficult to identify clearly the nature of cognitive impairments in depression; Poon (1992) argues that they tend to be small and related to task and sampling factors. Some studies have suggested that cognitive deficits in depression may relate to the use of a more conservative response bias, being less prepared to "guess" the answer (Gainotti & Camillo, 1994). There are clear indications of heterogeneity amongst older people with depression; some show no cognitive impairment, whilst others do perform poorly (Speedie et al., 1990). The cognitively impaired also have more subjective cognitive complaints, particularly on recent memory and concentration (O'Boyle, Amadeo & Self, 1990).

Some efforts have been made to identify a neuropathological basis in those patients showing impairment (Nussbaum, 1994), and subcortical dysfunction has been proposed as a possible model (Massman et al., 1992). However, Sahakian (1991), while acknowledging some similarities, points out differences from both subcortical and cortical dementia patterns of dysfunction. Beats, Sahakian & Levy (1996) report significant impairments on tests sensitive to frontostriatal dysfunction in a group of elderly depressed patients. Some of these deficits, especially in response latencies, remained after the patient had made a clinical recovery from depression. Again, it is noted that the deficits seen in patients with frontal lobe lesions or in Parkinson's disease or other sub-cortical dementias do not provide an adequate model of these findings. Depressed patients show milder deficits, across a broader range of functions, including memory. An interesting finding on a problem-solving task was that depressed patients were particularly sensitive to an initial failure, showing a "catastrophic response"; where the initial attempt was successful, their problem-solving efficiency was relatively good. This suggests an interaction between cognitive style and impaired performance.

Several studies have shown depressed patients to occupy a position midway between normal controls and people with dementia on a variety of indices of brain function and structure; Pearlson et al. (1989) have extended this by demonstrating that on CT scanning, depressed patients with cognitive impairment fall between people with dementia and depressed patients without cognitive impairment. The possibility that some structural changes have occurred is supported by findings such as those of Abas, Sahakian & Levy (1990) indicating that cognitive function does not return completely to normal when the depression lifts. Beats, Sahakian & Levy (1996) conclude that there may be "structural disruption to fronto-subcortical neural circuitry that is made manifest during depressive illness by altered patterns of neurotransmitter activity".

BEREAVEMENT

Later life is often characterized as being a time of loss, and it is certainly the case that a number of older people experience multiple losses. As well as the death of friends and family, significant losses may occur in other domains also—pets, home, work, health, a sense of independence, for example. Many of the fears that younger people have regarding their own ageing relate to the anticipation of such losses, leading to the supposition that old age must necessarily be a time of grief and misery. The fact that generally this is not the case suggests perhaps that older people are coping with the losses that are experienced remarkably well, and raises the question as to whether age differences in grief might be occurring.

The evidence suggests that, in comparisons with younger adults, older adults tend to experience fewer severe grief reactions, showing lower levels of distress and mental health problems (e.g. Breckenridge et al., 1986; McKiernan, 1996). However, there are two factors to consider before concluding that grief is indeed less severe in older people. First, there is the possibility that the expression of grief may differ in older people. For example, there are suggestions of a different time-course, with a longer recovery time in older people; or physical symptoms may be more frequent in older people. Second, differences may relate to the degree to which the death was expected or seen as timely. The death of a younger person is more likely to be sudden and unexpected. The death of any older person is less likely to be perceived as untimely. Much of the apparent age difference in grief intensity relates to this factor. In fact, with increasing age the expectedness of a death has less influence on the grief reaction. Anticipation of the death, i.e. where the death results from a terminal illness rather than a sudden trauma, reduces the grief intensity for the younger bereaved person, but less so for the older person. Perhaps the strain on the older person of providing care through a protracted illness outweighs the knowledge that death is the likely outcome; or perhaps the death is not actually expected, the day-to-day routine of care-giving goes on, and seems not to have a predictable end. The importance of the perceived timeliness of the death is further reinforced by the severe intensity of grief in older people who lose an adult child.

Depression is by no means universal in bereavement, and most older people adjust emotionally and socially without major mental health problems. The identification of the significant minority who do experience difficulties is complicated by the overlap between the symptoms of depression and the features of grief, such as sadness, tearfulness, loss of appetite and sleep problems. This leads to elevated scores on most self-report measures of depression. Depression appears to be distinct in the person tending to have a negative self-image and feeling a failure. Most studies suggest that the increase in frequency of depression amongst bereaved older adults tends to be much less evident at a follow-up assessment a year or two later. However, there is agreement that features of grief continue for a significant number, beyond the period of two or three years where risk of mental health problems is increased. McKiernan (1996) suggests that for older people the "normal" grief response may involve living with the grief rather than "getting over it", the readjustment phase common to stage theories of grief work. As with other life events discussed above, there is the event of bereavement, but also the state of being bereaved, which for many who lose a spouse will involve living alone, perhaps for the first time. Loneliness is a significant issue for many bereaved people.

The effect of bereavement on the person's physical health is mainly in the immediate aftermath of the loss, and a longer-term impact is not reported. However, the bereaved are at increased risk of mortality (Stroebe & Stroebe, 1993), particularly older men. The causes of death include heart disease, which has led to the idea of the excess mortality arising from a "broken heart". However, other causes are also implicated, including an increased risk of suicide (McKiernan, 1996).

A number of risk factors for adjustment difficulties in bereavement have been considered. Low self-esteem, or a sense of the bereavement being out of control are among the characteristics of bereaved people that are implicated. Where the person had a relationship where tasks were rigidly divided, and now has difficulty in taking on or learning the skills required to take on the deceased person's roles, adjustment may be problematic. Social support that is received early in the bereavement and is perceived as helpful can be a protective factor.

Traditionally, "abnormal bereavement reactions" were identified either by time elapsed since the event, or by comparison with a notional template of the stages of grief a person would need to pass through in order to carry out their "grief-work" and reach the final stage of resolution. The former approach assumes that a "normal" grief reaction will lose its intensity in six months, a year, two years or whatever; in fact, the evidence suggests that those at risk can be identified fairly early, through their negative self-image and low self-esteem, and/or in relation to particularly difficult losses (e.g. that of an adult child, or after extended, exhausting care-giving), and/or where social support is particularly low, perhaps where the couple were completely enmeshed, living for each other, with few outside contacts or interests. The stage theories of grief have generally been found wanting, in relation to an orderly progression from one stage to the next, and Stroebe & Stroebe (1991) have emphasized the wide variation in "normal" ways of coping with grief; they challenge the idea of grief-work being a necessary path to adjustment, suggesting that, for some, continuing avoidance of talking about the loss may be adaptive, rather than a sign of psychopathology. The acid test is the person's adjustment, distress and mental health, rather than the path being taken through the bereavement.

In psychological interventions with bereaved people, there is a fine line to be drawn between pathologizing a normal adjustment process, and offering support to those at risk of physical and mental health problems. Bereavement counselling needs to be targeted at those at risk; grief therapy at those experiencing particular difficulties. Kavanagh (1990) outlines possible interventions in a cognitive-behavioural therapy framework, the strategies including guided mourning (controlled exposure to stimuli associated with the deceased person), where avoidance is an issue; gradual activation, taking up former roles, developing new ones, so that the person gains reinforcement from other areas of life; increasing social support; cognitive therapy, tackling negative cognitions, e.g. of self-blame and guilt. Knight (Chapter 11, this volume) discusses further aspects of grief therapy.

SUICIDE

Suicide rates

Suicide rates provide a dramatic, if unrefined, index of mental health dysfunction in a population. In the UK, a reduction in suicide rate is the major mental health target arising from the Health of the Nation initiative. This has led to a burgeoning interest in the topic, which it must be hoped will not focus too narrowly on completed suicide alone, but will recognize that such traumatic events represent the tip of the iceberg of suffering and malaise.

In general, older people are more likely than any other age group to die by committing suicide; on the other hand, they are much less likely to attempt suicide unsuccessfully. Rates vary greatly from area to area and internationally. Some of this variation is explicable in terms of differences in systems of recording the occurrence of a suicide. For example, in England, where coroners have the responsibility for determining the cause of death, practice differs markedly as to the level of evidence of intent that is required before a verdict of suicide is reached, rather than recording the cause of death as open. However, data from a large number of countries indicate that elderly males have the highest rate of suicide in virtually every country (Cattell, 1994). The international variation is such that the suicide rate among men aged 60 and over in 1985–86 varied from 16.1 per 100 000 population in Ireland; 19.9 in England and Wales; 43.4 in the USA; 64.7 in Japan; 93.7 in France; to 156.9 in Hungary. Rates among men over 80 were typically even higher (Lindesay, 1991b). Generally, suicide rates in older people, in the UK at least, appear to have levelled off during the 1980s.

Much has been written to seek to "explain" differences between and within countries over time. Lindesay (1991b) describes the complex interaction between risk factors arising from age effects, cohort membership and the period in history being considered. Period effects include the well-known reduction following the detoxification of domestic gas supplies in the UK and the impact of wars. Cohort effects have proved difficult to identify so far, but it would not be surprising if attitudes to suicide differed between generations. Age effects might include the loss of income and status following retirement, possibly an especially powerful risk factor for men. It is not poverty *per se* that is associated with suicide: rates are low in some of the most disadvantaged groups, who have lived with adversity throughout their lives. Rather, it is those who experience financial hardship for the first time in late life who are at increased risk. It should not be assumed that the age effect will be universal; Lindesay (1991b) points out that in India, suicides become less frequent with age, a pattern that may be repeated in those who have settled in the UK from India. Although this has been attributed to the respect and support given to older members of the community, it should be noted that rates have been high in older men in Japan, where there has also been a strong tradition of venerating older people.

Methods

Methods adopted vary greatly also. In a study in London (Cattell, 1988), drug overdose was the predominant method used by one-third of men and two-thirds of women. Men were twice as likely to use a violent means—drowning, hanging, jumping from a height, etc. Use of car exhaust fumes has increased in recent years in older men, and the main drugs implicated in self-poisonings have shifted from the barbiturates to analgesics and benzodiazepines (Lindesay, 1991b). Guns are rarely used in the UK, except in rural areas where shotguns are more accessible. In the USA, virtually 80% of suicides in men aged 65 and over are carried out with a firearm.

Precipitants

Precipitants of suicide in older people in Cattell's 1988 series included physical illness, especially pain (21% complained of pain prior to their death); poor adjustment to a stroke; bereavement, isolation and loneliness; hospital discharge and, conversely, the fear of hospitalization. This latter factor received strong support from Loebel et al. (1991). As many as 44% of elderly suicides leaving an indication of their reasons mentioned their anticipatory fear of being placed in a nursing home. Alcohol is often associated with the act, 29% having alcohol in their blood at post mortem (Cattell, 1988); its disinhibiting effects may facilitate the act, and its interaction with other drugs may potentiate their effects. Alcohol abuse is a risk factor for suicide at all ages, and 79% of Cattell's series showed depressive symptoms prior to death.

Attempted suicide

Attempted suicide is less common in older people: in one study the rate was estimated as a quarter of that in the 15–65 age group (Pierce, 1987). Merrill & Owens (1990) have been among those to conclude that the profile of suicide attempters is much closer to that of those who take their own lives in older people than in younger age groups. The implication is that the parasuicidal gesture, where the person harms him/herself as a cry for help, or to angrily manipulate others, without strong suicidal intent, is less common in older people. However, such a pattern certainly does occur (Lindesay, 1991b), and a range of suicidal intent was found in the sample studied by Pierce (1987). The issue must also be raised of whether such gestures are in fact more likely to lead to death in older patients, who may misjudge the lethality of the method, and their own increased sensitivity to drug effects.

The characteristics of older people taken to hospital with deliberate self-harm (DSH) have been documented by Pierce (1987). Men showed the same rate of attempted suicide as women, in contrast to completed suicide. In most cases the method adopted was a drugs overdose, involving hypnotics, analgesics, minor tranquillizers and antidepressants in various combinations. The more violent methods have, of course, a higher lethality, and so are less frequently seen in attempted suicide. Depression was diagnosed in 93% of cases, although in nearly one-third of these cases depression was judged to be secondary to housing or financial problems or poor physical health. In fact, 63% were suffering from significant physical illnesses, and in 18% pain or demoralization arising from the illness had clearly led to the attempt. Social isolation was indicated by high proportions widowed and/or living alone. A measure of suicidal intent indicated that men had higher levels of intent to kill themselves than the female patients; high-intent patients also tended to be slightly older, and the overall level of intent was much higher than for younger samples. The rate of repeat non-fatal and fatal attempts was also lower than in other age groups; the few who did later kill themselves had high intent scores at the time of the initial attempt. In Nowers's (1993) sample, 6% had killed themselves within a year of the attempt, which is considered in fact to be a high proportion compared with younger groups.

Younger samples typically show a greater preponderance of alcohol abuse and personality disorder, which were relatively rare in Pierce's sample. Draper (1994) identified alcohol/substance abuse in 32% of a smaller sample of over-65s evaluated after a suicide attempt, together with 26% having personality dysfunction. Depression was still the most common mental health disorder, present in 87% of cases. Organic brain disease was also more common in Draper's series (29%), often in men over 75. Pierce identified few such cases, but emphasized their clinical significance, a combination of confusion, depression and disinhibition leading to impulsive but very dangerous attempts at self-harm.

Hopelessness

While depression is clearly the predominant factor in suicide and attempted suicide in older people, it is widely recognized that hopelessness is involved in linking depression and suicidal intent (MacLeod, Williams & Linehan, 1992). It involves a strong expectation that positive outcomes will not occur or that negative outcomes are inevitable. Hill et al. (1988)

have shown that suicidal ideation in older people is predicted by scores on Beck's Hopelessness Scale, as well as by level of depression and by physical health ratings. There is considerable scope for greater application with older people of the cognitive models developed with younger attempted suicide patients. Deficits identified in younger groups include poor interpersonal problem solving and reduced ability to regulate affect, as well as hopelessness. Processes such as a difficulty in retrieving autobiographical memories at a specific, rather than a general, level and, similarly, a difficulty in anticipating specific positive experiences would be worth investigating further in the context of late life (MacLeod, Williams & Linehan, 1992; Morris & Morris, 1991). In younger people this work has led to new therapeutic approaches, emphasizing a problem-solving approach.

Attitudes to suicide

Attitudes to suicide are perhaps more ambivalent in relation to older people than with younger age groups. Seven of Cattell's (1988) series of 104 cases were judged to be "rational deaths", there being no evidence of mental illness. Do older people not have the right to take their own lives, to exercise control over the ultimately inevitable outcome? Carpenter (1993) argues that older people have a unique claim to an ethical, unobstructed suicide, recognizing their developmental autonomy, their wisdom and their experience. Others, such as Lindesay (1991b), counter that ageism and therapeutic nihilism underly attempts to explain away elderly suicides as rational choices. The debate will doubtless continue, especially at a time when public attitudes to voluntary euthanasia appear to be softening. Clearly, there is much depression to be treated, much pain that can be relieved, many precautions that can reduce the risk of an impulsive attempt. Suicide can never be eradicated; in some cultures, at some points in history, it has been an honourable death; in the UK, within living memory, it was a criminal act. The debate is an important one; psychologists particularly should bear in mind that depression, negative cognitions and hopelessness are not an inevitable response to adversity in older people (Lam, et al., 1987); however, they should also not underestimate the extent of suffering endured by some older people.

ANXIETY

Prevalence rates for various forms of anxiety disorder were reported from Lindesay, Briggs & Murphy's (1989) large urban community survey (see

Table 4.1). Around 13% have a generalized or phobic anxiety disorder. It is of interest that 60% of those with phobic anxiety do not have a coexisting depression, as the impression is sometimes given that anxiety in older people is secondary to depression. The zero prevalence of panic disorders is probably an artefact of the diagnostic criteria, which require three panic attacks in the preceding three weeks for the diagnosis to be made. It is likely that older people are able to prevent such attacks by avoidance strategies, at the cost of greater dependency and disability (Livingston & Hinchliffe, 1993).

Often, presentations of phobic anxiety appear to have a fairly clear precipitant—a fall, a heart attack or a mugging in the street, perhaps. It is worth considering, then, some of the specific fears most commonly associated with older people.

Table 4.1   Prevalence of anxiety disorders in an urban community sample

Disorder	Prevalence (%)
Generalized anxiety	3.7
Phobic disorder:	
Agoraphobia	7.8
Social phobia	1.3
Specific phobia	2.1
Total	10.0
Total without co-occurring depression	6.1
Panic disorder	0.0

Reproduced from Lindesay, Briggs & Murphy (1989), with permission

Fear of crime

The often quoted paradox is that, whilst older people particularly fear crime, they are in fact the least likely group to be victimized (Lindesay, 1995). Is their fear then irrational, or does it reflect a sensible degree of caution? Lindesay (1991a) discusses a number of factors that may contribute to the level of fear reported. These include, first, the impact of older people going out less than younger people; their relative risk may perhaps then be just as high on the occasions when they do go out. Secondly, there is much less of a reduction in crimes involving an attack on the victim, which are, of course, the most feared crimes, involving personal safety. Thirdly, older people may have a sense of greater vulnerability to attack. For them, the consequences may be more severe than for a younger person, since they have less physical resilience and reduced social support available to aid recovery. Lindesay (1997) reports, from a community sample, that fear of crime and phobic disorder in older people are associated. This may be mediated through the person with a phobic disorder having a greater perceived sense of personal vulnerability.

Fear of falling

Fear of falling (FOF) has a major impact on an older person's ability to go out, and may lead to the person becoming housebound. It is not based on experience of falling in every case. Howland et al. (1993) report that in a sample of older people living in the community, FOF was the most common fear. Downton & Andrews (1990) and Tinetti et al. (1994) both report FOF in just over 40% of their large samples of older people (aged over 75 and over 72 respectively). Correlates of FOF include self-rated health and previous falls (Howland et al., 1993), anxiety and depression, usual walking pace and subjective dizziness (Downton & Andrews, 1990; Tinetti, Richman & Powell, 1990). Tinetti, Richman & Powell (1990) suggest that avoidance of activity related to FOF leads to lower confidence and self-efficacy in avoiding falls. Just under half of those with a FOF acknowledged avoidance of everyday activity because of it (Tinetti et al., 1994). In such cases, FOF may then become a risk factor for further falls (Spano & Forstl, 1992).

Fear of dying

Younger people appear to be more fearful of *death*, whilst the concerns of older people focus around *dying*, about the circumstances and process of their death (McKiernan, 1996). Fears concerning the process—pain, suffocation, choking, and so on—are relatively common (Fry, 1990) and play a role in some anxiety problems. "Minor" heart attacks, transient ischaemic attacks and more chronic breathing problems may all produce sensations readily "misinterpreted" as being fatal (Pitt, 1995). The role of hyperventilation and catastrophic cognitions in exacerbating chronic, debilitating conditions such as emphysema is poorly understood. Many patients are relieved when asked to report their thoughts at such times to find that their thoughts of dying may be discussed openly and safely.

Methods of helping patients to reduce hyperventilation are discussed by Holden (1988). These include the provocation test, used routinely with younger patients. This involves the person being encouraged to hyperventilate under controlled conditions; the aim is to help them experience the link between their symptoms and their breathing. Holden warns that this procedure should be used cautiously with older patients. She recommends the use of controlled breathing procedures, where the patient is taught to breathe at a slower rate, in a relaxed rhythm.

A case of "choking phobia" has been reported by Ost (1992). A 68-year-old woman could not swallow fluids because she feared she would get water in her windpipe and accordingly (her catastrophic misconception) suffocate and die. An exposure and modelling approach was attempted initially, but little progress was achieved. Only when the catastrophic cognition was targeted, through educational input and behavioural experiments, was there a dramatic change in the patient's fluid intake. This was maintained at one-year follow-up.

Treatment approaches

Few reports of psychological therapy for older people experiencing phobias are available, despite the effectiveness of these approaches with younger people and the large number of older people with phobic anxiety (perhaps 10%—see Table 4.1). There are some single-case reports on fear of going out (Woods & Britton, 1985, p. 195) and fear of dogs (Thyer, 1981). The larger studies tend to involve elderly people in institutions having fears of aspects of institutional life such as using lifts (Hussian, 1981) and being raised on a hoist and lowered into a whirlpool bath (Downs, Rosenthal & Lichstein, 1988). Graded exposure can be a helpful procedure, especially when combined with the person learning skills to monitor and control his/her anxiety level, using relaxation and breathing procedures, distraction or positive coping self-talk. Graded exposure involves working up a hierarchy of gradually more feared situations, coping with and mastering each before moving to the next. A patient with a fear of going out would first simply stand at the door, then go a few feet, then a little further, each step being under the person's control; homework tasks to consolidate progress made in sessions would be an important treatment component. Flooding would rarely be appropriate with an elderly patient; this involves exposing the person directly to the feared stimulus, and remaining in the feared situation until the anxiety subsides. There is a concern that the high levels of arousal that might be generated could be counter-productive. There is little research-based evidence addressing such technical issues with older populations, however. It should be noted that the behavioural focus of these approaches does not detract from the importance of cognitive processes; a recent patient, treated for a fear of falling after recovery from a hip replacement operation, was maintaining her anxiety by thinking, "I'm going to fall, I'm going to fall" whenever a piece of furniture or other safe object was out of reach. During the process of graded exposure she learned to distract herself from this thought and, as her range of walking successfully increased, was able to dispense with it.

King & Barrowclough (1991) provide an excellent account of cognitive behaviour therapy (CBT) with elderly patients with generalized anxiety and panic. They report a series of 10 cases with a mean age of 73 (range 66–78). All had a diagnosis including panic (five) or generalized anxiety disorder (two) or both (three). Seven also were judged to have depression, two of these also showing hypochondriasis. Six showed evidence of agoraphobia. Three had significant medical conditions. Seven of the patients had previously been treated with benzodiazepines or antidepressants, with no effect. All lived in the community and were seen for an average of eight sessions.

The notion of a "catastrophic cognition" is central to the CBT view of panic. It occurs where the person believes that he/she is experiencing a life-threatening illness or disastrous event, such as a heart attack, inability to breathe, a collapse, a loss of control or death. As mentioned previously, this often occurs in the context of hyperventilation, which produces a number of physical sensations readily misinterpreted, such as dizziness, tremor, chest pain and nausea. Essentially, the treatment involves helping the patient reinterpret the symptoms being experienced as non-threatening, allowing the catastrophic cognition to be challenged and its power diminished. King & Barrowclough achieved this through means such as identifying thoughts and behaviour (including avoidance) leading to anxiety, both during sessions and through homework tasks; encouraging re-attributions using cognitive restructuring procedures, such as self-monitoring and behavioural experiments; and teaching techniques of controlled breathing to reduce the effects of hyperventilation.

All but one of the 10 patients showed a decrease in symptoms following intervention, and these improvements were generally maintained at follow-up three to six months post-treatment, with eight patients showing no symptoms at all at this stage. A number of patients showed improvement post-treatment on the Beck Anxiety and Depression Inventories; five of the seven patients who were initially depressed moved into the non-depressed range post-treatment, supporting the utility of this approach even where depression is also present.

This approach has much to commend it also where hypochondriasis is the major presenting problem; while such patients will, of course, resist any suggestion that "it's all in the mind", many are able to accept that anxiety-reduction procedures may be helpful in coping with any symptoms, pain or discomfort that is being experienced (as, indeed health psychology has demonstrated in a variety of health problems). Arena, Hightower & Chong (1988), for example, have demonstrated the effectiveness of relaxation therapy for long-standing tension headache in older people aged 62—80. Only seven sessions of progressive muscle relaxation training were required; over half the subjects using medication were able to reduce the amount used.

OBSESSIVE-COMPULSIVE DISORDER (OCD)

OCD is relatively rarely encountered in older people, with a prevalence of less than 1% (Flint, 1994; Eastwood & Lindesay, 1995). Effective treatment procedures have been developed with younger patients; response prevention, for example, would be worth attempting with an elderly person with compulsive behaviour (Rowan et al., 1984). Obsessional ruminations, such as thinking about killing babies or children, are difficult to treat, but some success has been achieved with repeatedly exposing the person to the rumination. The rationale here is that it is removing the thought that reduces anxiety and so maintains the rumination, which becomes linked with anxiety relief. Habituating to the rumination may break this paradoxically rewarding sequence of mental events.

POST-TRAUMATIC STRESS DISORDER (PTSD)

The effects of traumatic experiences, especially in combat, have long been recognized. The development of the diagnostic category of PTSD has enabled the whole range of traumatic experiences to be construed within a coherent framework, leading to an explosion of research and development of therapeutic approaches. Current definitions have as their starting point that the event is outside the range of normal human experience; that the event is re-experienced through flashbacks, dreams, etc; that there are symptoms of increased arousal and avoidance of stimuli associated with the trauma; and that the problems have gone on for at least a month.

Present-day cohorts of older people have been exposed to a number of potentially traumatizing events during their lifetimes. The Second World War particularly will have had an impact on the lives of many (Davies, 1997). Bonwick & Morris (1996) cite evidence of a 16% rate of PTSD among veterans of the Second Word War; it is suggested that as well as there being some people in whom the symptoms have persisted over the years, there are others for whom the traumatic stress has remained latent until reactivated by the process of ageing. With retirement or enforced inactivity through ill-health, nightmares reappear, as if the person had coped for so long by keeping busy and occupied, containing the distress (Hunt, 1997). For others, the anniversaries of various war-time events, shown at length in the media, reawaken "forgotten" memories (Hilton, 1997).

Prisoners of war appear to have even higher rates of PTSD, 40 years on. Speed et al. (1989) report that 29% of POWs fulfilled the PTSD criteria currently, compared with 50% rated retrospectively as at one year after repatriation. Having been tortured during captivity and the proportion of body weight lost were the best predictors of PTSD in this sample. Other studies (e.g. Sutker, Aliain & Winstead, 1993) have found even higher rates (up to 70%) of PTSD in POWs; much will depend on the sample studied, in relation to their specific experiences of imprisonment. A study from the UK of 30 former Far East POWs identified 30% as having PTSD, but as many as 90% had at least one intrusive or avoidant symptom (Neal et al., 1995).

It is, of course, not only those who were members of the armed forces who suffered traumatic events during the Second World War. Waugh (1997) examined the impact on older women who lived through the trauma of air-raids, and found a 16% prevalence of PTSD, associated with avoidant coping. Davies (1994) has drawn attention to the civilian evacuation in the UK, when schoolchildren, expectant mothers and mothers with young children were moved away from towns and cities at threat of being bombed, to the relative safety of the countryside. There is surprisingly little research on the long-term effects of the separation from their parents on the children involved, some of whom had very poor relationships with their foster parents.

The long-term effects of the Holocaust have been more extensively studied. Kuch & Cox (1992) report that 46% of Holocaust survivors continue to have PTSD. Exposure to atrocities, such as the death camps, is associated with PTSD. However, Robinson et al. (1990) emphasize that, despite their mental suffering, by and large survivors have been successful and raised warm families; there is a strong sense of survivors feeling a special responsibility to live their lives as a "testament to those who perished".

Clearly, the above examples indicate the potential long-term effects of exposure to trauma. Can PTSD also be acquired by exposure to trauma in late life? Reports from a few recent disasters are available. Elderly survivors of the Lockerbie disaster, where a village in Scotland was devastated by a plane suddenly crashing into its midst, have been interviewed by Livingston et al. (1992). Overall, most older survivors met the criteria for PTSD and showed similar responses to younger people, except that the older people also had a very high incidence of co-existing major depression. Loss of friends and exposure to human remains were related to the diagnosis of PTSD. Livingston, Livingston & Fell (1994) report a follow-up study carried out three years after the disaster. The results indicated that many patients had recovered and were less distressed. However, 16% still fulfilled the criteria for PTSD at this time. Nearly one-third of the sample remained on anxiolytics/hypnotics three years on. Goenjian et al. (1994) report a comparison of older and younger victims of the 1988 earthquake in Armenia. They found that the higher the exposure to the effects of the earthquake, the greater the rate of PTSD. Older people showed more arousal and less intrusive symptoms than younger people. Understandably, loss of family members in the disaster was related to the severity of the stress reaction.

Does exposure to trauma earlier in life protect if further trauma is encountered in late life? Solomon & Prager (1992) compared the reactions of Holocaust survivors with those of other older people living in Israel during the Gulf war, when Israelis were subject to missile attacks. Holocaust survivors showed increased vulnerability, reporting more distress and anxiety and perceiving higher levels of danger.

Most of the examples described so far have been trauma shared by a number of people. More personal trauma is also important, but less studied to date. Being involved in or witnessing a road accident or a mugging, etc., may precipitate a stress reaction. Rape would be another example of a trauma occasionally experienced by an older person. Recent publicity regarding child sexual abuse has contributed to a number of older women being able to talk about the abuse they experienced as children; often this has had a devastating effect on the person's life, and may be associated with intrusive thoughts and nightmares.

Treatment for PTSD typically involves debriefing—talking through the experience in great detail—and encouragement of emotional processing of the event in a safe environment (see Robbins, 1994, for a case example). Bonwick (1998) describes a group treatment programme for elderly war veterans with PTSD. Thomas & Gafner (1993) describe a case of a Second World War veteran treated with eye movement desensitization and reprocessing (EMDR). This therapy often appears to act very quickly (two sessions in this case). There is certainly no basis at present for therapeutic pessimism with PTSD in older people, even when the trauma was many years ago, and the symptoms appear ingrained.

PARANOID PSYCHOSIS

The prevalence of paranoid psychosis in older people (sometimes described as paraphrenia or as schizophrenia of late onset) is thought to be less than 2% (Livingston & Hinchliffe, 1993; Howard, 1993). However, the social isolation of many such patients probably makes their identification in community studies difficult. There have been suspicions of cognitive impairment associated with the disorder, and some abnormalities have been identified in imaging studies. Howard (1993) concludes that most such patients show a mild degree of cognitive impairment and a slow progressive deterioration, but that relatively few actually develop a dementia as such.

Treatment for paraphrenia has mainly involved major tranquillizers. With younger psychotic patients, considerable progress has been made in developing cognitive interventions for delusional beliefs (e.g. Birchwood & Tarrier, 1992; Birchwood & Shepherd, 1992; Fowler, Garety & Kuipers, 1995). There is scope for such psychological interventions to be piloted with older patients also. A rare example of a behavioural intervention which successfully reduced the frequency of paranoid speech in a 68-year-old patient is reported by Carstensen & Fremouw (1981).

SUBSTANCE ABUSE

Alcohol

It is generally thought that older people consume less alcohol, and that the proportion of people with a drinking problem declines with age (Ticehurst, 1995). However, alcohol abuse remains a significant mental health problem in late life. Saunders et al. (1989) surveyed just over 1000 people over the age of 65 living in the community, randomly selected from general practitioner lists in Liverpool, UK. The prevalence of current drinking problems was 0.94%. Three years later, most of the problem drinkers identified had reduced their drinking drastically because of health difficulties. The number of older people drinking regularly declined with age, with a trend towards less alcohol being consumed. Around one-fifth of both male and female regular drinkers consumed more than the recommended safe limits for alcohol intake.

Reductions in alcohol consumption in late life may be attributed in part to physiological changes, with the person being less able to tolerate alcohol, becoming intoxicated having consumed less. Physical health problems, reduced social opportunities and financial constraints may also play a part. Rates of problem drinking appear to be higher in more affluent areas (Livingston & Hinchliffe, 1993). It is thought that there is also a subgroup who drink more than previously, and indeed some who develop alcohol-related problems for the first time, perhaps as a way of coping with bereavement, loneliness, pain and discomfort (Ticehurst, 1995; Atkinson, 1994). For others, alcohol abuse reflects a continuing pattern.

Denial is often encountered amongst older people with a drinking problem (Saunders et al., 1989). Identification of difficulties in this area may be indirect: falls, confusion, cognitive impairment, depression and social difficulties may be among the manifestations that bring the person to the attention of health services. Home visits and discussion with relatives and friends are often helpful in indicating where problems may lie. Some screening tools are available, but their utility in community settings is not clear (Beresford, 1993).

Treatment may be made more complex by the effects of alcohol-related cognitive impairment, as well as by denial. Where the problem drinking arises in late life from loss or a difficulty in coping with hardship, interventions targeted at the central problem may be helpful. In general, as with younger patients, many reject or drop out of treatment programmes. There is no evidence that older people fare worse in treatment than younger patients (Janick & Dunham, 1983). A number of specific programmes for older people have been described. For example, Dupree, Broskowski & Schonfeld (1984) report on a behavioural treatment programme for elderly alcohol abusers. As well as examining the ABC (antecedents, behaviour and consequences) of drinking behaviour, problem-solving skills were taught. Those completing the programme tended to be late-onset drinkers, widowed, with higher motivation and a more internal locus of control. Improvements were related to increased social networks. Kashner et al. (1992) reported that an "elder-specific" programme, including the use of reminiscence, peer-group support and respect for age, was more effective in promoting abstinence than a "traditional" confrontational approach. However, better controlled intervention studies are required to highlight the effective components of treatment for this difficult problem.

Benzodiazepines

"After tobacco and alcohol, benzodiazepine consumption is associated with the greatest risk of abuse and dependence in the elderly" (Ticehurst, 1995, p. 187). Whilst benzodiazepine use is falling in younger people, rates are declining much more slowly in older people. They are used both as anxiolytics and as hypnotics, in response perhaps to the high rate of sleep problems reported by older people (see Morgan, 1996).

Sullivan et al. (1988) carried out a community survey of over 1000 older people in Liverpool. Just under 13% were taking benzodiazepine medication initially; at three-year follow-up, over 60% of these individuals continued to do so, despite current recommendations for their use to be short-term. Apart from a general concern about the long-term use of benzodiazepines, there are specific concerns about their use with older people, being linked with falls and confusion (Higgitt, 1992). At follow-up, over one-tenth of the total sample were taking benzodiazepines as a sleeping medication, reflecting the high prevalence of sleep disorders in older people, but in apparent disregard of the well-established loss of a hypnotic effect within a few weeks. Rebound effects and withdrawal reactions help to convince patients they are receiving some benefit from the drug, in that they feel worse when they stop it.

Effects of benzodiazepines on cognitive function have been demonstrated repeatedly in younger people. The potential to improve cognition by discontinuing benzodiazepines in older people has been demonstrated by Salzman et al. (1992). Nursing-home residents discontinuing—after several months or years on the drugs—showed improved working and episodic memory compared with those who remained on the medication.

Some older people are responding to the widespread publicity and requesting help to withdraw from benzodiazepine use. There is some evidence that psychological techniques such as anxiety management, support in gradual withdrawal, reappraisal of symptoms, etc., are helpful to older people in assisting this process. Jones (1990/1991) reports a randomized controlled trial in primary care settings. Over 200 patients completed the study. Twice as many (39%) treated cases succeeded in reducing or stopping their medication over the nine-month period of the trial compared with control-group patients (20%). Treatment was provided by a practice nurse offering counselling and relaxation therapy, under the supervision of a clinical psychologist.

With the widespread use of benzodiazepines as hypnotics for older people with sleeping difficulties, greater attention should be given to psychological treatments for insomnia as an alternative free of side-effects, and with potentially enduring effects on sleep patterns. These approaches have proven effectiveness, but often have not been extensively evaluated with older people (Morin & Azrin, 1988; Morgan, 1996). There are three main approaches: stimulus control procedures, which aim to reinforce the link between the bedroom and sleep, and weaken the association between being in bed and lying awake; relaxation-based methods, reducing arousal and anxiety levels; and cognitive approaches, aimed at reducing the thoughts which can delay sleep onset. These may be used in combination, and might also involve education about how sleep patterns may change with age, and that this need not be viewed as a problem. Routines and behaviours possibly contributing might also be identified, e.g. day-time naps, caffeine intake before bed, etc. Morgan & Gledhill (1991) and Espie (1991) provide details of these methods.

PERSONALITY DISORDER

Personality (or character) disorders are rarely discussed in detail in relation to older adults, perhaps because there has been concern regarding the at times pejorative use of this diagnostic label. There is a danger that the term simply becomes associated with those patients who are difficult to like and to help, where the professional's heart sinks as they arrive for their appointment or telephone once again. Yet if one were to ask the clinical psychologist member of a community mental health team what his/her distinctive contribution to the team's work might be, in many cases it would be to offer therapeutic help to exactly these individuals, who absorb the resources of service providers in a manner often disproportionate to the apparent severity of their difficulties. Their problems are chronic, "crises" occur frequently, the patient either does not comply with treatment, or appears to do so but shows no change; they have a long history of previous therapy attempts.

A definition of personality disorders is provided by Abrams (1995):

> enduring patterns of dysfunctional behaviour which pervade multiple facets of a person's life. Usually there is an interpersonal focus, and always there is impairment in functioning.

In the multi-axial DSM (*Diagnostic and Statistical Manual of Mental Disorders*, 4th edn, American Psychiatric Association, 1994), the primary mental health problems, depression, anxiety and so on, are situated on Axis 1, with the personality disorders grouped in clusters on Axis 2. This allows for a number of possible patterns of relationship between Axis 1 and Axis 2 disorders. For example, particular personality patterns might make the person more vulnerable to develop a particular Axis 1 syndrome; or the personality might influence the expression of the Axis 1 disorder, or its prognosis; or a severe, long-standing Axis 1 syndrome, such as depression or schizophrenia might damage the person's personality. Each of these patterns of interaction—and others—may be seen in older adults, e.g. a suspicious person developing a paranoid disorder; a person with anxiety problems, presenting in a histrionic fashion; a person who has had depressive episodes over many years, who has never returned to his/her original level of social function. However, it should also be noted that apparent personality disorders may be manifestations of the Axis 1 syndrome, so that with the remission of the depressive disorder, say, the disordered personality also returns to normal (Thompson, Gallagher & Czirr, 1987). It will be evident from these considerations that diagnostic problems abound with these disorders. This is exacerbated in the case of older people, as the diagnostic criteria "do not address issues relevant to the lives of ageing persons" (Abrams, 1995). Thus, there may appear to be fewer personality disorders in older people meeting DSM criteria. To an extent, this may also reflect a maturation process—some of the more dramatic/emotional disorders may be described as "immature". These include Cluster B disorders, such as narcissistic, borderline, histrionic and antisocial (see also Chapter 11). However, Cluster A disorders—paranoid and schizoid—and Cluster C—avoidant, dependent and obsessive-compulsive—may be more likely to endure into late life. The circumstances of late life for some may bring to the fore difficulties that had been coped with previously, e.g. living in close proximity to others in an institutional environment may be problematic for a person who coped by avoiding close contact with others.

A cognitive perspective places great emphasis on the person's schema, his/her basic rules of life, often acquired very early in life, which continue to have a powerful influence. A number of older people with personality disorders, from the author's clinical experience, have suffered sexual abuse or trauma as children. They may take forward schemata from these experiences with profound effects in later life. It is these schemata which need to be identified in the context of cognitive-behavioural therapy, and re-examined. Dick, Gallagher-Thompson & Thompson (Chapter 10, this volume) discuss schema change therapy, as a more advanced form of cognitive therapy for working with these powerful belief systems. Thompson, Gallagher & Czirr (1987) have indicated that personality disorder is associated with fewer good outcomes for psychological therapies, including standard cognitive behaviour therapies. Therapy needs to be active, structured and focused, with relatively limited, carefully selected goals. Working on the Axis 1 disorder may be helpful, in giving the person skills for tackling the Axis 2 problems.

CONCLUSION

This chapter has covered the broad range of mental health difficulty experienced by older people. Depression and the dementias have rightly been the major concern of psychologists working with older people, but this chapter illustrates the uncharted territory awaiting further psychological exploration, and the potential diversity of work with older people. Old age psychiatrists have carried out much of the groundwork of description and definition. Clinical psychologists now have a key role in aiding the understanding, assessment and treatment of the full spectrum of mental health problems affecting older people.

REFERENCES

Abas, M.A., Sahakian, B.J. & Levy, R. (1990). Neuropsychological deficits and CT scan changes in elderly depressives. *Psychological Medicine*, **20**, 507–520.

Abrams, R.C. (1995). Personality disorders. In J. Lindesay (Ed.), *Neurotic Disorders in the Elderly* (pp. 154–171). Oxford: Oxford University Press.

American Psychiatric Association (1994). *Diagnostic and Statistical Manual of Mental Disorders*, 4th edn. Washington, DC: American Psychiatric Association.

Ames, D. (1991). Epidemiological studies of depression among the elderly in residential and nursing homes. *International Journal of Geriatric Psychiatry*, **6**, 347–354.

Arena, J.G., Hightower, N.E. & Chong, G.C. (1988). Relaxation therapy for tension headache in the elderly: a prospective study. *Psychology and Aging*, **3**, 96–98.

Atkinson, R.M. (1994). Late onset problem drinking in older adults. *International Journal of Geriatric Psychiatry*, **9**, 321–326.

Baldwin, B. (1991). The outcome of depression in old age. *International Journal of Geriatric Psychiatry*, **6**, 395–400.

Ballard, C., Boyle, A., Bowler, C. & Lindesay, J. (1996). Anxiety disorders in dementia sufferers. *International Journal of Geriatric Psychiatry*, **11**, 987–990.

Barlow, J.H., Williams, B. & Wright, C.C. (1997). Improving arthritis self-management among older adults: "just what the doctor didn't order". *British Journal of Health Psychology*, **2**(2), 175–186.

Beats, B.C., Sahakian, B.J. & Levy, R. (1996). Cognitive performance in tests sensitive to frontal lobe dysfunction in the elderly depressed. *Psychological Medicine*, **26**, 591–603.

Beresford, T.P. (1993). Alcoholism in the elderly. *International Review of Psychiatry*, **5**, 477–483.

Birchwood, M. & Shepherd, G. (1992). Controversies and growing points in cognitive-behavioural interventions for people with schizophrenia. *Behavioural Psychotherapy*, **20**, 305–342.

Birchwood, M. & Tarrier, N. (Eds) (1992). *Innovations in the Psychological Management of Schizophrenia*. Chichester: Wiley.

Bonwick, R. (1998). Group treatment programmes for elderly war veterans with PTSD. *International Journal of Geriatric Psychiatry*, **13**(1), 64–67.

Bonwick, R. & Morris, P. (1996). Post-traumatic stress disorder in elderly war veterans. *International Journal of Geriatric Psychiatry*, **11**, 1071–1076.

Bossé, R., Spiro, A. III & Kressin, N.R. (1996). The psychology of retirement. In R.T. Woods (Ed.), *Handbook of the Clinical Psychology of Ageing* (pp. 141–157). Chichester: Wiley.

Breckenridge, J.N., Gallagher, D., Thompson, L.W., & Peterson, J. (1986). Characteristic depressive symptoms of bereaved elders. *Journal of Gerontology*, **41**, 163–168.

Burns, A., Jacoby, R. & Levy, R. (1990a). Psychiatric phenomena in Alzheimer's disease. I: Disorders of thought content. *British Journal of Psychiatry*, **157**, 72–76.

Burns, A., Jacoby, R. & Levy, R. (1990b). Psychiatric phenomena in Alzheimer's disease. II: Disorders of perception. *British Journal of Psychiatry*, **157**, 76–81.

Burns, A., Jacoby, R. & Levy, R. (1990c). Psychiatric phenomena in Alzheimer's disease. IV: Disorders of behaviour. *British Journal of Psychiatry*, **157**, 86–94.

Burvill, P.W. (1993). Prognosis of depression in the elderly. *International Review of Psychiatry*, **5**, 437–443.

Carpenter, B.D. (1993). A review and new look at ethical suicide in advanced age. *Gerontologist*, **33**, 359–365.

Carstensen, L.L. & Fremouw, W.J. (1981). The demonstration of a behavioural intervention for late-life paranoia. *Gerontologist*, **21**, 329–333.

Cattell, H. (1994). Suicidal behaviour. In J.R.M. Copeland, M.T. Abou-Saleh & D.G. Blazer (Eds), *Principles and Practice of Geriatric Psychiatry* (pp 607–614). Chichester: Wiley.

Cattell, H.R. (1988). Elderly suicide in London: an analysis of coroners' inquests. *International Journal of Geriatric Psychiatry*, **3**, 251–261.

Cervilla, J.A. & Prince, M.J. (1997). Cognitive impairment and social distress as different pathways to depression in the elderly: a cross-sectional study. *International Journal of Geriatric Psychiatry*, **12**, 995–1000.

Cohen, G. (1996). Memory and learning in normal ageing. In R.T. Woods (Ed.), *Handbook of the Clinical Psychology of Ageing* (pp. 43–58). Chichester: Wiley.

Davies, A.D.M. (1996). Life events, health, adaptation and social support in the clinical psychology of late life. In R.T. Woods (Ed.), *Handbook of the Clinical Psychology of Ageing* (pp. 115–140). Chichester: Wiley.

Davies, S. (1994). Long term psychological effects of the civilian evacuations in World War II Britain: a review and a case example. *PSIGE Newsletter*, **48**, 29–31.

Davies, S. (1997). The long-term psychological effects of World War Two. *Psychologist*, **10**(8), 364–367.

Dawe, B., Procter, A. & Philpot, M. (1992). Concepts of mild memory impairment in the elderly and their relationship to dementia—a review. *International Journal of Geriatric Psychiatry*, **7**, 473–479.

Deary, I.J. (1995). Age-associated memory impairment: a suitable case for treatment? *Ageing and Society*, **15**, 393–406.

Donaldson, C., Tarrier, N. & Burns, A. (1998). Determinants of carer stress in Alzheimer's disease. *International Journal of Geriatric Psychiatry*, **13**(4), 248–256.

Downs, A.F.D., Rosenthal, T.L. & Lichstein, K.L. (1988). Modelling therapies reduce avoidance of bath-time by the institutionalised elderly. *Behavior Therapy*, **19**, 359–368.

Downton, J.H. & Andrews, K. (1990). Postural disturbance and psychological symptoms amongst elderly people living at home. *International Journal of Geriatric Psychiatry*, **5**, 93–98.

Draper, B. (1994). Suicidal behaviour in the elderly. *International Journal of Geriatric Psychiatry*, **9**, 655–661.

Dupree, L.W., Broskowski, H. & Schonfeld, L. (1984). The Gerontology Alcohol Project: a behavioral treatment program for elderly alcohol abusers. *Gerontologist*, **24**, 510–516.

Eastwood, M.R. & Lindesay, J. (1995). Epidemiology. In J. Lindesay (Ed.), *Neurotic Disorders in the Elderly* (pp. 12–30). Oxford: Oxford University Press.

Espie, C. A. (1991). *The Psychological Treatment of Insomnia*. Chichester: Wiley.

Flint, A.J. (1994). Epidemiology and comorbidity of anxiety disorders in the elderly. *American Journal of Psychiatry*, **151**, 640–649.

Fowler, D., Garety, P. & Kuipers, L. (1995). *Cognitive Behaviour Therapy for Psychosis*. Chichester: Wiley.

Fry, P.S. (1990). A factor analytic investigation of home-bound elderly individuals' concerns about death and dying, and their coping responses. *Journal of Clinical Psychology*, **46**, 737–748.

Gainotti, G. & Camillo, M. (1994). Some aspects of memory disorders clearly distinguish dementia of the Alzheimer's type from depressive pseudodementia. *Journal of Clinical and Experimental Neuropsychology*, **16**, 65–78.

Gilleard, C.J. (1997). Education and Alzheimer's disease: a review of recent international epidemiological studies. *Aging & Mental Health*, **1**(1), 33–46.

Goenjian, A.K., Najarian, L.M., Pynoos, R.S. & Steinberg, A.M. (1994). Posttraumatic stress disorder in elderly and younger adults after the 1988 earthquake in Armenia. *American Journal of Psychiatry*, **151**, 895–901.

Haddad, P.M. & Benbow, S.M. (1993). Sexual problems associated with dementia. Part 1: Problems and their consequences. *International Journal of Geriatric Psychiatry*, **8**, 547–551.

Henderson, A.S. (1989). Psychiatric epidemiology and the elderly. *International Journal of Geriatric Psychiatry*, **4**, 249–253.

Henderson, A.S. (1990). The social psychiatry of late life. *British Journal of Psychiatry*, **156**, 645–653.

Henderson, A.S. (1994). Does ageing protect against depression? *Social Psychiatry and Psychiatric Epidemiology*, **29**, 107–109.

Higgitt, A. (1992). Dependency on prescribed drugs. *Reviews in Clinical Gerontology*, **2**, 151–155.

Hill, R.D., Gallagher, D., Thompson, L.W. & Ishida, T. (1988). Hopelessness as a measure of suicidal intent in the depressed elderly. *Psychology and Aging*, **3**, 230–232.

Hilton, C. (1997). Media triggers of post-traumatic stress disorder 50 years after the Second World War. *International Journal of Geriatric Psychiatry*, **12**(8), 862–867.

Hofman, A., Rocca, W.A., Brayne, C. et al. (1991). The prevalence of dementia in Europe: a collaborative study of the 1980–1990 findings. *International Journal of Epidemiology*, **20**, 736–748.

Holden, U.P. (1988). *Neuropsychology and Ageing: Definitions, Explanations and Practical Approaches*. London: Croom Helm.

Hope, R.A. & Fairburn, C.G. (1990). The nature of wandering in dementia: a community-based study. *International Journal of Geriatric Psychiatry*, **5**, 239–245.

Hope, T., Keene, J., Fairburn, C., McShane, R. & Jacoby, R. (1997). Behaviour changes in dementia 2: are there behavioural syndromes? *International Journal of Geriatric Psychiatry*, **12**(11), 1074–1078.

Howard, R. (1993). Late paraphrenia. *International Review of Psychiatry*, **5**, 455–460.

Howland, J., Peterson, E.W., Levin, W.C. & Fried, L. (1993). Fear of falling among the community dwelling elderly. *Journal of Aging and Health*, **5**, 229–243.

Hunt, N. (1997). Trauma of war. *Psychologist*, **10**(8), 357–360.

Huppert, F.A. (1994). Memory function in dementia and normal ageing—dimension or dichotomy? In F.A. Huppert, C. Brayne & D. O'Connor (Eds), *Dementia and Normal Ageing*. Cambridge: Cambridge University Press.

Hussian, R.A. (1981). *Geriatric Psychology: A Behavioral Perspective*. New York: Van Nostrand Reinhold.

Janik, S.W. & Dunham, R.G. (1983). A nationwide examination of the need for specific alcoholism treatment programs for the elderly. *Journal of Studies on Alcohol*, **22**, 193–198.

Jones, D. (1990/1991). Weaning elderly patients off psychotropic drugs in general practice: a randomised controlled trial. *Health Trends*, **22**, 164–166.

Kashner, T.M., Rodell, D.E., Ogden, S.R., Guggenheim, F.G. & Karson, C.N. (1992). Outcomes and costs of two VA inpatient treatment programs for older alcoholic patients. *Hospital and Community Psychiatry*, **43**, 985–989.

Kavanagh, D.J. (1990). Towards a cognitive-behavioural intervention for adult grief reactions. *British Journal of Psychiatry*, **157**, 373–383.

Kay, D.W.K. (1991). The epidemiology of dementia: a review of recent work. *Reviews in Clinical Gerontology*, **1**, 55–66.

King, P. & Barrowclough, C. (1991). Clinical pilot study of cognitive-behavioural therapy for anxiety disorders in the elderly. *Behavioural Psychotherapy*, **19**, 337–345.

Kral, V.A. (1962). Senescent forgetfulness, benign and malignant. *Journal of the Canadian Medical Association*, **86**, 257–260.

Krause, N. (1994). Stressors on salient social roles and well-being in later life. *Journal of Gerontology*, **49**, P137–P148.

Kuch, C. & Cox, B.J. (1992). Symptoms of PTSD in 124 survivors of the Holocaust. *American Journal of Psychiatry*, **149**, 337–340.

Lam, D.H., Brewin, C.R., Woods, R.T. & Bebbington, P.E. (1987). Cognition and social adversity in the depressed elderly. *Journal of Abnormal Psychology*, **96**, 23–26.

Lindesay, J. (1991a). Fear of crime in the elderly. *International Journal of Geriatric Psychiatry*, **6**, 55–56.

Lindesay, J. (1991b). Suicide in the elderly. *International Journal of Geriatric Psychiatry*, **6**, 355–361.

Lindesay, J. (1995). Psychosocial factors. In J. Lindesay (Ed.), *Neurotic Disorders in the Elderly* (pp. 56–71) Oxford: Oxford University Press.

Lindesay, J. (1997). Phobic disorders and fear of crime in the elderly. *Aging & Mental Health*, **1**, 81–85.

Lindesay, J., Briggs, K. & Murphy, E. (1989). The Guys/Age Concern survey: prevalence rates of cognitive impairment, depression and anxiety in an urban elderly community. *British Journal of Psychiatry*, **155**, 317–329.

Livingston, G. & Hinchliffe, A.C. (1993). The epidemiology of psychiatric disorders in the elderly. *International Review of Psychiatry*, **5**, 317–326.

Livingston, H.M., Livingston, M.G., Brooks, D.N. & McKinlay, W.W. (1992). Elderly survivors of the Lockerbie air disaster. *International Journal of Geriatric Psychiatry*, **7**, 725–729.

Livingston, H.M., Livingston, M.G. & Fell, S. (1994). The Lockerbie disaster: a three year follow-up of elderly victims. *International Journal of Geriatric Psychiatry*, **9**, 989–994.

Loebel, P.J., Loebel, J.S., Dager, S.R. & Centerwall, B.S. (1991). Anticipation of nursing home placement may be a precipitant of suicide among the elderly. *Journal of American Geriatrics Society*, **39**, 407–408.

McKeith, I., Fairbairn, A., Perry, R., Thompson, P. & Perry, E. (1992). Neuroleptic sensitivity in patients with senile dementia of Lewy body type. *British Medical Journal*, **305**, 673–678.

McKiernan, F.M. (1996). Bereavement and attitudes to death. In R.T. Woods (Ed.), *Handbook of the Clinical Psychology of Ageing* (pp. 159–182). Chichester: Wiley.

MacLeod, A.K., Williams, J.M.G. & Linehan, M.M. (1992). New developments in the understanding and treatment of suicidal behaviour. *Behavioural Psychotherapy*, **20**, 193–218.

Massman, P.J., Delis, D.C., Butters, N. & Dupont, R.M. (1992). The subcortical dysfunction hypothesis of memory deficits in depression: neuropsychological validation in a subgroup of patients. *Journal of Clinical and Experimental Neuropsychology*, **14**, 687–706.

Merrill, J. & Owens, J. (1990). Age and attempted suicide. *Acta Psychiatrica Scandinavica*, **82**, 385–388.

Morgan, K. (1996). Managing sleep and insomnia. In R. T. Woods (Ed.), *Handbook of the Clinical Psychology of Ageing* (pp. 303–316). Chichester: Wiley.

Morgan, K. & Gledhill, K. (1991). *Managing Sleep and Insomnia in the Older Person*. Bicester: Winslow Press.

Morin, C.M. & Azrin, N.H. (1988). Behavioral and cognitive treatments of geriatric insomnia. *Journal of Consulting & Clinical Psychology*, **56**, 748–753.

Morris, R.G. & Morris, L.W. (1991). Cognitive and behavioural approaches with the depressed elderly. *International Journal of Geriatric Psychiatry*, **6**, 407–413.

Murphy, E. (1982). Social origins of depression in old age. *British Journal of Psychiatry*, **141**, 135–142.

Neal, L.A., Hill, N., Hughes, J., Middleton, A. & Busuttil, W. (1995). Convergent validity of measures of PTSD in an elderly population of former prisoners of war. *International Journal of Geriatric Psychiatry*, **10**, 617–622.

Nowers, M. (1993). Deliberate self-harm in the elderly: a survey of one London borough. *International Journal of Geriatric Psychiatry*, **8**, 609–614.

Nussbaum, P.D. (1994). Pseudodementia: a slow death, *Neuropsychology Review*, **4**, 71–90.

O'Boyle, M., Amadeo, M. & Self, D. (1990). Cognitive complaints in elderly depressed and pseudodemented patients. *Psychology and Aging*, **5**, 467–468.

O'Brien, J.T., Beats, B., Hill, K., Howard, R., Sahakian, B. & Levy, R. (1992). Do subjective memory complaints precede dementia? A three-year follow-up of patients with supposed "benign senscent forgetfulness". *International Journal of Geriatric Psychiatry*, **7**, 481–486.

O'Brien, J.T. & Levy, R. (1993). Age-associated memory impairment. International *Journal of Geriatric Psychiatry*, **8**, 779–780.

Orrell, M.W., Sahakian, B.J. & Bergmann, K. (1989). Self neglect and frontal lobe dysfunction: case conference. *British Journal of Psychiatry*, **155**, 101–105.

Orrell, M., Howard, R., Payne, A., Bergmann, K., Woods, R., Everitt, B.S. & Levy, R. (1992). Differentiation between organic and functional psychiatric illness in the elderly: an evaluation of four cognitive tests. *International Journal of Geriatric Psychiatry*, **7**, 263–275.

Orrell, M. & Davies, A.D.M. (1994). Life events in the elderly. *International Review of Psychiatry*, **6**, 59–72.

Orrell, M.W. & Sahakian, B.J. (1995). Use it or lose it: does education protect against dementia? *British Medical Journal*, **310**, 951–952.

Ost, L. (1992). Cognitive therapy in a case of choking phobia. *Behavioural Psychotherapy*, **20**, 79–84.

Pearlson, G.D., Rabins, P.V., Kim, W.S. & Speedie, L.J. (1989). Structural brain CT changes and cognitive deficits in elderly depressives with and without reversible dementia ("pseudodementia"). *Psychological Medicine*, **19**, 573–584.

Perry, R.H., Irving, D., Blessed, G., Fairbairn, A.F. & Perry, E.K. (1990). Senile dementia of the Lewy body type: a clinically distinct form of Lewy body dementia in the elderly. *Journal of Neurological Science*, **95**, 119–139.

Pierce, D. (1987). Deliberate self-harm in the elderly. *International Journal of Geriatric Psychiatry*, **2**, 105–110.

Pitt, B. (1995). Neurotic disorders and physical illness. In J. Lindesay (ed.), *Neurotic Disorders in the Elderly* (pp. 46–55). Oxford: Oxford University Press.

Poon, L.W. (1992). Towards an understanding of cognitive functioning in geriatric depression. *International Psychogeriatrics*, **4**(Suppl. 2), 241–266.

Reifler, B.V. & Larson, E. (1990). Excess disability in dementia of the Alzheimer's type. In E. Light & B.D. Lebowitz (Eds), *Alzheimer's Disease Treatment and Family Stress* (pp. 363–382). New York: Hemisphere.

Robbins, I. (1994). The long term consequences of war trauma: a review and case example. *PSIGE Newsletter*, **48**, 26–28.

Robinson, S., Rapaport, J., Durst, R. & Rapaport, M. (1990). The late effects of Nazi persecution among elderly Holocaust survivors. *Acta Psychiatrica Scandinavica*, **82**, 311–315.

Rowan, V.C., Holborn, S.W., Walker, J.R. & Siddiqui, A.R. (1984). A rapid multi-component treatment for an obsessive-compulsive disorder. *Journal of Behaviour Therapy and Experimental Psychiatry*, **15**, 347–352.

Sahakian, B.J. (1991). Depressive pseudodementia in the elderly. *International Journal of Geriatric Psychiatry*, **6**, 453–458.

Salzman, C., Fisher, J., Nobel, K., Glassman, R., Wolfson, A. & Kelley, M. (1992). Cognitive improvement following benzodiazepine discontinuation in elderly nursing home residents. *International Journal of Geriatric Psychiatry*, **7**, 89–93.

Saunders, P.A., Copeland, J.R.M., Dewey, M.E., Davidson, I.A., McWilliam, C., Sharma, V.K., Sullivan, C. & Voruganti, L.N.P. (1989). Alcohol use and abuse in the elderly: findings from the Liverpool longitudinal study of continuing health in the community. *International Journal of Geriatric Psychiatry*, **4**, 103–108.

Scogin, F. (1992). Memory training for older adults. In G. Jones & B. Miesen (eds), *Care-giving in Dementia* (pp. 260–271). London: Routledge.

Skilbeck, C. E. (1996). Psychological aspects of stroke. In R. T. Woods (Ed.), *Handbook of the Clinical Psychology of Ageing* (pp. 283–301). Chichester: Wiley.

Snowdon, J. (1997). Depression in old age: questions concerning prevalence studies. *International Journal of Geriatric Psychiatry*, **12**, 1043–1045.

Solomon, Z. & Prager, E. (1992). Elderly Israeli Holocaust survivors during the Persian Gulf War: a study of psychological distress. *American Journal of Psychiatry*, **149**, 1707–1710.

Spano, A. & Forstl, H. (1992). Falling and the fear of it. *International Journal of Geriatric Psychiatry*, **7**, 149–151.

Speed, N., Engdahl, B., Schwartz, J. & Eberly, R. (1989). Post traumatic stress disorder as a consequence of the POW experience. *Journal of Nervous and Mental Disease*, **177**, 147–153.

Speedie, L., Rabins, P.V., Pearlson, G.D. & Moberg, P.J. (1990). Confrontation naming deficit in dementia of depression. *Journal of Neuropsychiatry and Clinical Neurosciences*, **2**, 59–63.

Stokes, G. (1989). Managing aggression in dementia: the do's and don'ts. *Geriatric Medicine*, April, 35–40.

Stokes, G. (1996). Challenging behaviour in dementia: a psychological approach. In R.T. Woods (Ed.), *Handbook of the Clinical Psychology of Ageing* (pp. 601–628). Chichester: Wiley.

Stroebe, M. & Stroebe, W. (1991). Does "grief-work" work? *Journal of Consulting & Clinical Psychology*, **59**, 479–482.

Stroebe, M.S. & Stroebe, W. (1993). The mortality of bereavement: a review. In M.S. Stroebe, W. Stroebe, & R.D. Hansson (Eds), *Handbook of Bereavement*. Cambridge: Cambridge University Press.

Sullivan, C.F., Copeland, J.R.M., Dewey, M.E., Davidson, I.A., McWilliam, C., Saunders, P., Sharma, V.K. & Voruganti, L.N.P. (1988). Benzodiazepine usage amongst the elderly: findings of the Liverpool community survey. *International Journal of Geriatric Psychiatry*, **3**, 289–292.

Sutker, P.B., Aliain, A.N. & Winstead, D.K. (1993). Psychopathology and psychiatric diagnoses of World War II Pacific Theatre prisoner of war survivors and combat veterans. *American Journal of Psychiatry*, **150**, 240–245.

Thomas, R. & Gafner, G. (1993). PTSD in an elderly male: treatment with eye movement desensitization and reprocessing (EMDR). *Clinical Gerontologist*, **14**, 57–59.

Thompson, L., Gallagher, D. & Czirr, R. (1987). Personality disorder and outcome in the treatment of late-life depression. *Journal of Geriatric Psychiatry*, **21**, 133–146.

Thyer, B.A. (1981). Prolonged in-vivo exposure therapy with a 70 year-old woman. *Journal of Behaviour Therapy and Experimental Psychiatry*, **12**, 69–71.

Ticehurst, S. (1995). Alcohol and drug use. In J. Lindesay (Ed.), *Neurotic Disorders in the Elderly* (pp. 172–192). Oxford: Oxford University Press.

Tinetti, M.E., Mendes-de-Leon, C.F., Doucette, J.T. & Baker, D.I. (1994). Fear of falling and fall-related efficacy in relationship to functioning among community living elders. *Journal of Gerontology*, **49**, M140–147.

Tinetti, M.E., Richman, D. & Powell, L. (1990). Falls efficacy as a measure of fear of falling. *Journal of Gerontology*, **45**, P239–243.

Ware, C.J.G., Fairburn, C.G. & Hope, R.A. (1990). A community based study of aggressive behaviour in dementia. *International Journal of Geriatric Psychiatry*, **5**, 337–342.

Waugh, M.J. (1997). Keeping the home fires burning. *Psychologist*, **10**(8), 361–363.

Wenger, G.C. (1995). *Practitioner Assessment of Network Type (PANT)*. Brighton: Pavilion Press.

Wenger, G.C. (1997). Social networks and the prediction of elderly people at risk. *Aging & Mental Health*, **1**, 311–320.

Woods, R.T. & Britton, P.G. (1985). *Clinical Psychology with the Elderly*. London: Croom Helm/Chapman Hall.

Yesavage, J.A., Lapp, D. & Sheikh, J.I. (1989). Mnemonics as modified for use by the elderly. In L.W. Poon, D.C. Rubin & B.A. Wilson (eds), *Everyday Cognition in Adulthood and Late Life* (pp. 598–611). Cambridge: Cambridge University Press.

Chapter 5

THE NEUROPSYCHOLOGY OF ALZHEIMER'S DISEASE AND RELATED DEMENTIAS

*Robin G. Morris**

INTRODUCTION

Dementia has been defined simply as a global deterioration in mental functioning in an otherwise alert patient (Lishman, 1987). This simple definition encompasses at least 20 common causes of dementia (see Table 5.1), although many more exist (McKeith, 1994). As well as being global, many definitions suggest that the mental impairment should progress over time, for example, in the much used criteria from the research-orientated NINCDS–ADRDA (National Institute of Neurological and Communicative Disorders and Stroke, and the Alzheimer's Disease Association) Joint Working Group (NINCDS–ADRDA Work Group, 1982; Tierney et al., 1988), but not, incidentally, the DSM–IIIR (Diagnostic and Statistical Manual III–Revised) criteria. Nevertheless, although the different causes have much in common, they all result in differing degrees of changes in cognition, behaviour and personality (Miller & Morris, 1993). Even within the main diagnostic category, Alzheimer's disease (AD), there is considerable variation in the profile of decline, with different subgroups emerging, such as the familial subtypes of the disease (Agnew, 1996; Kennedy et al., 1993). Detailed neuropsychological study has provided a wealth of information which sets varying degrees of cognitive impairment in context and can relate them to the underlying neurobiological impairment (Morris, 1996).

* Institute of Psychiatry, London, UK

Psychological Problems of Ageing: Assessment, Treatment and Care. Edited by R.T. Woods.
© 1999 John Wiley & Sons Ltd.

Table 5.1 Possible causes of dementia, listing those which are most likely to occur in routine practice (see text)

Degenerative	Alzheimer-type dementia
	Lewy body dementia
	Parkinson's disease
	Non-Alzheimer dementia of frontal lobe type
	Pick's disease
	Huntington's disease
Vascular	Multi-infarct dementia
	Lacunar state
	Binswanger's disease
Following neurological insult	Dementia pugilistica
	Following open or closed head injury
	Cerebral anoxia
Infective	AIDS–dementia complex
	Creutzfeldt–Jakob disease
	Neurosyphilis
Toxic	Alcohol-related dementia
Space-occupying lesions	Chronic subdural haematoma
	Primary or metastatic intracranial tumour
Metabolic	Hypothyroidism
Other	Normal pressure hydrocephalus

Reproduced from McKeith, 1994, with permission

To establish these findings, a cognitive neuropsychological approach has been taken, splitting mental functioning into different domains and indicating how these might be dissociated in dementia. This work is now very substantial, and dealt with in some depth by both Miller & Morris (1993) and Morris (1996). Nevertheless, some of the most salient areas are discussed here, such as executive functioning, memory and language, since these have the closest relevance to clinical practice, including assessment and rehabilitation.

Indeed, neuropsychological study has shown several aspects, including elucidating cognitive impairments perhaps undetected by conventional neuropsychological investigation, such as the executive and language impairments seen early on in the course of dementia (Morris, 1989, 1994a, b; and see below). These findings have important implications for the early diagnosis of dementia. Another finding is that not all cognitive functions are impaired in the various forms of dementia. These preserved functions can be harnessed in the development of strategies for the management and rehabilitation of patients. Finally, the patterns of deficits are not random, but linked to damage in different areas of the brain, so providing a more rational approach to treatment or therapy. This chapter reflects these developments, attempting to link the theoretical approaches to understanding dementia to clinical practice. Before doing this, some of the most important neurobiological changes that underpin neuropsychological changes are outlined in the section below.

NEUROBIOLOGY OF THE DEMENTIAS

The biological cause of dementia has not always been readily accepted and it is salutary to note that even until the late 1970s, attempts to produce purely psychological or environmental explanations were still taken seriously (see Miller, 1977, for a brief review). These included psychodynamic explanations of dementia and the concept that dementia resulted from negative interactions with an impoverished environment or societal expectations. In this sense, the dementias initially suffered the same fate as some other psychiatric disorders, with theorists eschewing a biological explanation or diagnostic approach until the neuropathological and neurochemical evidence for biological abnormalities became unassailable. In addition, it gradually became established that what was originally termed "senile dementia" was largely AD in old age, and that there was the same disease process as in the "pre-senile" form, to be distinguished from the cognitive changes associated with normal ageing (Morris, 1991b). AD became sufficiently well accepted that the Alzheimer's Disease Society is widely recognized as the main charitable body relating to dementia. Alternative approaches do still exist, and these largely serve to provide a reminder that a reductionist approach is in danger of failing to understand the syndrome from the viewpoint of the person with dementia (Kitwood, 1996).

AD, the "flagship" dementia, is associated with enlargement of the ventricles and sulci of the brain, reflecting brain shrinkage (Lantos & Cairns, 1994). These changes overlap considerably with the effects of normal ageing, as is the case with the neuropathological markers of AD, senile plaques, neurofibrillary tangles and granulovacuolar degeneration (Esiri, 1991). The location of changes gives a strong clue as to what neuropsychological changes to expect. For example, the neuropathological markers tend to be seen in association areas of the brain, which are concerned with the high-level multimodal integration of information, spanning language, visuospatial processing and executive functions. Less affected are primary association areas, preserving the sensory processing of information (Bondareff et al., 1988). This is reflected in the deficits associated with AD, where low-level auditory and visual processing are relatively preserved, contrasting with higher-order cognitive processes (Nissen et al., 1985). The pattern of impairment is correlated with changes in blood flow to the brain, where the principal areas of hypometabolism are mainly the cortical frontal and parietal association areas (Frackowiak et al., 1981; Friedland et al., 1985; Haxby et al., 1988, 1990).

A feature of degeneration in AD is the tendency to produce a disconnection between different regions of the brain, an important feature in understanding neuropsychological impairment. First, very severe degenerative changes are found in the pathways linking the neural substrate of memory to the rest of cortical processing. These pathways are to be found bilaterally within the mesial temporal lobes, where the flow of information to and from the hippocampal circuitry is funnelled through the entorhinal cortex, providing an interaction with frontal, parietal and temporal cortices (see Figure 5.1; Squire, 1992). In AD, neurofibrillary tangles are found in very large quantities in the entorhinal cortex and some of the connecting hippocampal structures, such as the CA1 field (Arriagada et al., 1992; Esiri, 1991). This may explain the profound memory impairment associated with AD and the susceptibility of the memory system in the early stages of the disease.

Another form of dissociation is between the cortical association areas themselves, particularly the link between the parietal lobes and the prefrontal cortex. Again, neurodegeneration is seen to be most severe in cortical tissue, from which emanate the long corticocortical association fibres between the cortices (Pearson et al., 1985; Rogers & Morrison, 1985; Lewis et al., 1987). This deterioration results in a desynchronization

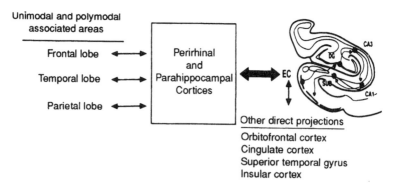

Figure 5.1   Schematic representation of the connectivity of mesiotemporal lobe memory circuitry. The width of the arrows corresponds to the relative proportions of inputs arising from the areas indicated. EC = entorhinal cortex; DG = dentate gyrus; SUB = subicular complex; CA3 and CA1 are fields of the hippocampus proper. Reproduced from Squire (1992), with permission

between brain regions measurable using electroencephalography (EEG) or positron emission tomography (PET) (Leuchter et al., 1992; Horwitz et al., 1987; Azari et al., 1992). It is only recently that the significance of these changes for neuropsychological functioning has been realized (Morris, 1994a, b, c). Essentially, they predict asynchronous cognitive activity, with difficulties in co-ordinating different mental processes efficiently (Morris, 1994a). This is precisely what has been observed through cognitive neuropsychological investigation, in that AD patients show specific patterns of impairment in executive processes (see below) (Morris & Baddeley, 1988; Morris, 1994b).

Another factor is the neurochemical changes seen in dementia. In AD there is a reduction in neurotransmitter activity, some of which originates within subcortical structures. This includes the impaired noradrenergic projection arising from the locus coerulus and the seratonergic projection from the raphe nucleus. The significance of these pathways is not known fully, but it is suggested they modulate attention abilities (Bondareff et al., 1987). The cholinergic projections from the basal forebrain have attracted more interest. This structure appears to send discrete, topographically arranged projections to the entire cortical mantle (Semba & Fibinger, 1989) and is again thought to modulate cortical activity. The cortical projection is focused on key structures such as the amygdala and the hippocampus, so depletion of cholinergic activity in these neuronal systems has been associated with memory and attentional impairment (Perry, 1994). Cholinergic treatments of AD (see e.g. Eagger, Levy & Sahakian, 1991) have produced one of the few forms of biological therapies that have been shown to be successful in relation to improving cognition, albeit modest in their effects (Ashford & Zec, 1993).

In other forms of dementia, the association between cognitive and neurobiological changes is either less well established or predictable. Nevertheless, general features can be established in relation to particular aetiologies. The cognitive decline found in Parkinson's disease (PD), which can extend into a dementing illness, may result from both cortical and subcortical changes. There is evidence for an overlap with AD, with neuropathological markers such as neuritic plaques and neurofibrillary tangles (de la Monte et al., 1989), and cortical hypoperfusion in similar cortical areas, including the parietal and temporal cortices (Spampinato et al., 1991). Bradyphrenia, or slowing of thought, is likely to relate to subcortical changes, but may affect cognitive processes also impaired in AD, for example executive processes (Morris & Baddeley, 1988). The more generalized features seen in neurodegenerative processes, such as PD and Huntington's disease, contrast with the less predictable changes in vascular dementias, which depend on the location of vascular events

(Metter & Wilson, 1993). With these dementias, including multi-infarct dementia, there are often accompanying neurological signs relating to motor control or primary sensory processing. These are quantified using the Hachinski Ischaemic Score (IS) (Hachinski et al., 1975; Rosen et al., 1980). It should be noted that differentiating the different forms of dementia on the basis of the neuropsychological profiles is not particularly accurate, suggesting that all forms can produce a similar effect on cognition. Despite this, detailed investigation has tended to identify different patterns of impairment which provide insights into the dementias overall.

ATTENTIONAL DYSFUNCTION

Impairments in attention are frequently seen in relation to brain damage (Mattis, 1976), and the ability to attend to, and therefore process, incoming information forms the basis of higher-order cognition. Gross impairments in attention are associated with confusional states resulting, for example, from bodily metabolic disturbances or illnesses such as urinary tract infection. They should be differentiated from the milder attentional impairments in people with dementia, who are basically "alert" and able to focus on what is happening around them. This is borne out by experimental work described below, which essentially shows that attentional impairment lies in the sequencing and manipulation of cognitive activity in response to more than one stimulus or mental activity, rather than loss of "alertness".

Vigilance

The clinical notion of "alertness" appropriately translates in part into the cognitive concept of vigilance, being able to detect reliably the existence of a stimulus and respond readily (Allport, 1989). AD patients seem to be surprisingly intact on vigilance tasks. For example, Lines et al. (1991) required subjects to listen to a train of short tones and indicate the number by pointing to a choice array of numbers (1–15). They also had to push a button when a target digit (7) appeared on a computer screen. In neither case did the AD patients show impairment in comparison with elderly matched controls.

"Phasic" attention also appears to be unimpaired. This refers to the ability to maintain a state of readiness for very short periods, for example milliseconds. This ability is under voluntary control and essentially mobilizes cognitive resources in the "direction" of the expected stimulus.

Phasic alertness was explored by Nebes & Brady (1993), using a task in which the subject had to press one of two keys according to the position of a "square" presented on a computer screen (top or bottom). To induce phasic attention, a warning tone was presented. This usually produces a more rapid response, with the benefit optimal with an approximate 300 ms interval between tone and the presentation of the squares. AD patients were found to be significantly slower to respond overall, but the key result was that the degree of benefit induced by the tone was the same as in the elderly controls. Changes in response speed as the delay deviated from the optimal period were also matched.

Shifting attention

Being able to switch attention from one stimulus to another at will is vital for a person to interact flexibly with his/her environment. Normally, a person can shift attention between different external inputs to scan and fixate individual faces in a crowd (Humphreys & Bruce, 1989) or to "tune into" a particular conversation at a party. The cognitive components that underpin this ability have been identified by Posner et al. (1984a) and include engaging or focusing attention, disengagement, and shifting (or moving). In the visual domain, there is some evidence for the impairment in dementia being at the disengagement stage, as will be seen below.

A preliminary study by Freed et al. (1989) found visual attentional shift deficits only in a sub-sample of AD patients who were thought to have locus coerulus degeneration. However, a more substantial and modified study by Parasuraman et al. (1992) has shown a very significant impairment. In their task the patient had to respond to one of two response keys according to whether a vowel or a consonant was presented. In addition, preceding the letter by 200, 500 or 2000 ms, was an arrow which pointed either towards the letter or away. Normally, if the arrow points towards it, it increases the speed of the response, but if away, inhibits it. Because "towards" arrows are used 80% of the time, the person usually shifts attention to the position indicated by the arrow. For the "away" arrows, the person engages attention in an incorrect position and then has to redirect attention to the correct place. AD patients were found to have the normal facilitation effect, but showed a much larger inhibitory effect with the "away" arrows. This indicates that they were less able to disengage their attention from the inappropriate visual field.

Impairments in shifting attention are consistent with what is known about the neurobiology of AD. There is substantial evidence that shifting attention is controlled at least in part by the posterior parietal regions of the brain, particularly the right side (La Berge, 1990; Posner, Walker, Friedrich & Rafal, 1984b), precisely one of the regions that show substantial neurophysiological change (Haxby et al., 1986; Horwitz et al., 1987; Grady et al., 1988; Peterson et al., 1988). Indeed, Parasuraman et al. (1992) found that right hypometabolism measured using positron emission tomography was found more frequently in patients who tended to show the attentional shift deficit.

In the auditory domain, there are parallels with the attentional shift deficit. Here the technique used is the dichotic listening task, in which strings of digits or words are presented simultaneously to each ear for remembering. There is clear evidence that patients with dementia have difficulty on this task (Grady et al., 1989). If left to his/her own devices, a right-handed person will report the list presented to the right ear first, showing greater accuracy with the list presented in that ear. However, this effect is modifiable by instructing the person to recall either the left- or right-ear list first. In AD, the effect has been found to be unmodifiable, for example showing no reduction in the right-ear superiority when instructed to recall the left-ear list first (Mohr et al., 1990; Bouma & Van Silfhout, 1989). This suggests that AD patients may be less able to switch attention at will, directing it towards the left ear.

DEMENTIA AS A DYSEXECUTIVE SYNDROME

A third type of attention is the ability to sequence and co-ordinate more than one activity at a time. This also involves selective attentional processes, since the person has to move between mental activities in the process of sequencing and may even cope with several types by switching backwards and forwards between them in a process referred to as "time sharing". In ordinary life there are many instances in which it is necessary to carry out several activities simultanously, such as driving a car and holding a conversation, or doing an everyday task whilst listening to the radio. There is substantial evidence that these abilities are impaired early in the course of Alzheimer's disease (Becker, 1988; Becker, Bajulaiye & Smith, 1992; Morris, 1992; 1994a). Baddeley (1986) has coined the term "dysexecutive syndrome" to characterize patients who have difficulties in this sphere, following the development of the Working Memory Model (Baddeley & Hitch, 1974; Baddeley, 1992).

The model describes the cognitive mechanisms that underpin executive functioning (see Figure 5.2). A prime component is the central executive system (CES), which co-ordinates and schedules mental processes. The CES is part of a cluster of modular components that are used to keep material within working memory. The components of the CES can be thought to be in themselves a cluster of cognitive processes which interact with each other (Barnard, 1985). Separated off from the CES is the articulatory loop system (ALS), responsible for recycling verbal information within immediate memory, for example when a person is attempting to remember a telephone number temporarily (Baddeley, 1986). The equivalent temporary store of visuospatial material is termed the "visuospatial scratchpad" (Baddeley, Thomson & Buchanan, 1975; Logie & Marchetti, 1991).

The CES has been explored by a series of tests that combine more than one task simultaneously. These dual tasks effectively "stress" the resources of the CES, revealing a putative deficit. First, AD patients show very substantial impairment on tests which require a person to remember a small amount of information while their attention is divided by another task, the Peterson & Peterson (1959) procedure. There are several variations of this test, including presenting three words or consonants and distracting the person by counting backwards for periods of up to 30 seconds, in all of which AD patients show a significant impairment (Corkin, 1982; Kopelman, 1985; Morris, 1986). Morris (1986) even found robust impairment with very simple distracter tasks, such as saying the word "the" repeatedly in the retention interval or tapping the experimenter's table in a rhythmic fashion.

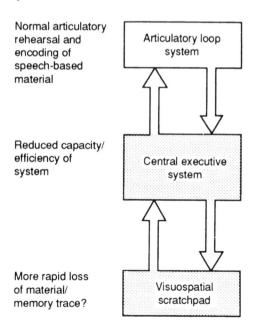

Figure 5.2 The working memory model, showing areas of impairment in Alzheimer's disease, as indicated by shading

A series of more controlled studies of divided attention had been conducted by Baddeley et al. (1986, 1991). The primary task is to track a moving stimulus on a computer screen using a light pen. The speed of the stimulus is adjusted to suit the speed and accuracy of the subject. "Tracking" is then combined with other tasks, including counting from one to five continuously, detecting tones and recalling strings of digits. In the last task, the number used was adjusted to match the memory span of each subject. AD patients were severely impaired with tone detection and tracking (Baddeley, 1986) and began to show an impairment with the counting task on follow-up (Baddeley et al., 1991).

Articulatory loop system

These impairments have been interpreted as a breakdown of the time-sharing capacity of the CES. Other studies have investigated the storage components of the model, in particular the articulatory loop system (ALS). This system recycles verbal material in a more automatic fashion, for example contributing to verbal memory span performance. One way of investigating the ALS is to measure the size of what is called the word length effect, the propensity for longer words (e.g. "association" and "university") to be less well recalled than shorter words (e.g. "sun" and "hate") in immediate memory. The effect relates to the longer time taken to cycle such words through the ALS, producing greater opportunity for forgetting. Morris (1984), however, has shown that the effect is undiminished in AD, despite a decline in memory span overall. This has also been repeated with series recall of objects shown on cards, where objects with longer names are less well recalled (Morris, 1992). Another method of exploring the ALS is to measure the rate of articulatory rehearsal. The rate determines how much material can be recycled, and hence how much can be retained. Morris (1984, 1987a, b) estimated the rate by requiring subjects to read strings of digits as rapidly as possible, finding no impairment in AD patients. These and other experiments which have explored the degree to which phonological (the sound form of words) encoding is intact (Morris, 1984) all point towards an unimpaired ALS system, at least at the early stage of AD.

Visuospatial scratchpad

The visuospatial counterpart of the ALS, the visuospatial scratchpad (VSSP), is involved in remembering visual material in a temporary "snapshot" fashion. For example, when a person is distracted from viewing a scene, a temporary visual record can be maintained, helping retain a sense of visual continuity. Performance on many visual tasks may be reliant on the integrity of the VSSP.

Studies of the VSSP tend to suggest a deficit in AD. For example, patients are impaired on the Corsi Block Span task, in which they have to tap out a sequence on an array of nine blocks from memory (Spinnler et al., 1988). In addition, AD patients are consistently impaired on the delayed matching to sample task, in which an item is shown which then has to be picked out from other items after a short delay. Part of the Cambridge Automated Neuropsychological Test Battery includes a delayed matching to sample task which shows a pattern on a computer screen, which has to be identified from four others later on, with the subject responding using a touch-sensitive screen facility (Morris et al., 1987). AD patients were not only impaired, but showed greater rates of forgetting overall (Morris et al., 1987; Sahakian et al., 1988). A more recent study by Money, Kirk & McNaughton (1992) found a similar impairment, using filled circles of different sizes. One difficulty, however, in interpreting these deficits as VSSP impairments is the high CES demands of the task, which may also contribute to the deficits. Nevertheless, it seems likely that the VSSP is impaired, contrasting with an intact ALS.

An explanation for the dysexecutive syndrome

As indicated above, recent theorizing about AD has related the CES impairment to a breakdown in synchronous activity between the association areas of the cortex (Morris, 1994a, b, c), relating to the damage to the corticocortical pathways and the increased dysynchrony measured between tertiary association areas using both electroencephalography (EEG) and positron emission tomography (Leuchter et al., 1992; Horwitz et al., 1987; Morrison et al., 1986). To illustrated this further, Figure 5.3 shows the method used to investigate synchrony in the EEG study by Leuchter et al. (1992). The similarity of EEG activity in different brain regions is measured and a metric coherence computed. Figure 5.3 shows the brain regions, with coherence between regions across the Rolandic (central) fissure compared to that within frontal, or parietal and temporal regions. Maximal dysynchrony was found across the Rolandic fissure in AD, but between parietal and temporal regions in patients with multi-infarct dementia.

The CES system has been associated with the frontal lobes (Baddeley, 1992), but in order to co-ordinate mental activity in other cortical areas there must be continuous transfer of information between different brain

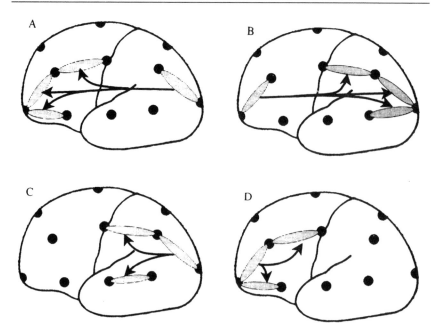

Figure 5.3   Electrode sites used for measures of brain coherence in AD by Leuchter et al. (1992). Coherence variables were grouped in four combinations. A is posterior–anterior coherence transmitted via the superior longitudinal fasciculus. B represents transmission in the anteroposterior direction. C and D show connectivity within either the anterior or the posterior brain. The AD patients had systematic decreases in coherence with the anterior and posterior linkage. Reproduced from Leuchter et al. (1992), with permission

regions. Thus a breakdown of transfer would impair the ability to direct and control mental processes. Difficulties with coherence might particularly impair performance on tests of divided attention, but leave performance on tasks more reliant on the ALS, such as immediate memory span, more intact.

The clinical implications for this deficit have been discussed by Morris (1994b). These include the difficulties, observed by Alberoni et al. (1992), that AD patients have in keeping track of conversations involving several people. In addition, rehabilitation approaches should take into account the need to avoid splitting the attention of a patient.

EPISODIC MEMORY

A major feature of the dementias (although not necessarily discriminative) is the substantial impairment in memory for events, be it over a period of minutes, days or weeks. This has been termed "episodic" memory to distinguish it from semantic memory, which encompasses knowledge about the world, including facts, rules and concepts (Tulving, 1983). The impairment underlies the temporal and spatial disorientation experienced by many patients with dementia. Episodic memory testing forms part of almost all neuropsychological tests for dementia, and formal testing has shown deficits across a range of tasks, including recall of prose passages, lists of words and sentences (Morris & McKiernan, 1994). The difficulties posed by memory impairment in AD change as the disease progresses, as illustrated in Table 5.2. Early memory impairment can be indistinguishable from the memory lapses commonly experienced by anyone, but they are of greater frequency. The increasing severity is eventually accompanied by the behavioural disturbances seen in the latter stages of dementia.

One way of viewing the cause of the deficit is as a primary impairment of neurological structures supporting episodic memory overlaid by secondary deficits in areas (for example, attention, semantic processing) that

Table 5.2   Stages in the development of memory impairment in dementia

---

Stage 1   Mild memory impairment
- Mild memory lapses occur, but cause only a few problems for the person and are often falsely attributed to other factors, such as the effects of normal ageing, stress or depression.
- These lapses include forgetting errands, failing to pass on messages and becoming disoriented in unfamiliar surroundings. Memory for episodes in the near distant past, including conversations with people, is poor.
- These types of memory problems do not necessarily indicate a progressive neuropsychological impairment.

Stage 2   Mild to moderate memory impairment
- Memory impairment is more pronounced and starts to have a significant effect on daily living activities. At this point, the person may seek medical help (usually prompted by a relative or friend) and is likely to become reliant on a carer.
- Memory errors include forgetting familiar people or friends, becoming disoriented even in familiar surroundings, confusing the time of day or day of the week, and becoming increasingly unable to keep track of daily events.

Stage 3   Severe memory impairment
- Memory errors include forgetting close relatives. Marked signs, such as confabulation and paramnesia, become apparent.
- Memory errors become more severe and can present safety problems for the person, such as wandering, or forgetting to turn off the gas stove. Loss of information about person may occur, for example details of personal information such as relatives' names.

From Miller & Morris (1993), with permission

contribute to memory functioning (Morris, 1991a; Morris & Kopelman, 1986). The primary deficit can be related to damage to mesiotemporal lobe structures known to be involved in memory, as indicated above (see Figure 5.1). Damage to the entorhinal cortex effectively lesions the cortical inputs and outputs between the rest of the cortex and is compounded by damage within the hippocampus proper, including the CA1 fields. Arriagada et al.'s (1992) neuropathological study shows how the system has a hierarchical vulnerability in relation to the formation of neurofibrillary tangles, with impairment of the entorhinal cortex tending to occur first, followed by the CA1 field, the amygdala, and the association and sensory cortices (see Figure 5.4). At one year's duration the CA1 field of the hippocampus proper is maximally affected, with the disease process spreading with more severity to the entorhinal cortex, the amygdala and the inferotemporal cortex by the fifth year. Notably, recent studies indicate that neurofibrillary tangles, rather than senile plaques, tend to correlate more highly on ratings of dementia (Arriagada et al., 1992; Morris, 1991a; Wilcock & Esiri, 1982).

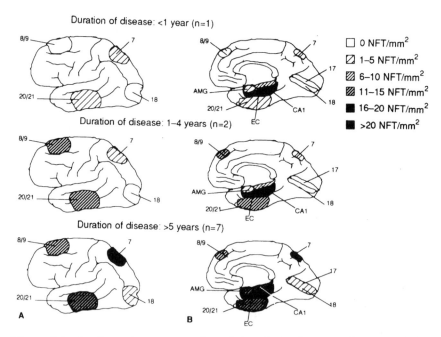

Figure 5.4 A schematic representation of the relation between density and distribution of neurofibrillary tangles (NFT) and duration of AD (A = lateral view, B = medial view), taken from Arriagada et al. (1992). On the right is the legend which gives the density in number of NFTs mm² by the different shading. EC = entorhinal cortex; AMG = amygdala; numbers refer to Brodmann map areas of the neocortex. Reproduced from Arriagada et al. (1992), with permission

Overlaying this primary deficit are additional processing impairments. These include not being able to "cluster" words into a semantic framework to improve recall. An example is Weingartner et al.'s (1983) finding of an inability to be cued by specific category words to aid retrieval. In addition, there is substantial evidence that AD patients fail to make use of semantic orientating instructions, for example presenting a word then using the question, "Is the word a type of bird?". These instructions normally provide much stronger memory for the word than others which cue phonological or orthographic processing, but not so in AD (Corkin, 1982; Martin et al., 1985). Since semantic cuing is used as the basis of many memory rehabilitation techniques, this is an important finding, because AD patients may not benefit in the normal fashion.

Cuing the patient at retrieval has ameliorated the memory impairment in certain cases (e.g. Morris, Wheatley & Britton, 1983). There is evidence that memory can be improved only if the right type of cuing is employed. For example, Martin et al. (1985) used semantic/praxic cues in which patients had to pantomime a movement or series of movements associated with an object. The movements were used as a cue at recall and successfully improved performance in AD patients. This result has been replicated with a variety of related procedures (Bird & Luszcz, 1991; Granholm & Butters, 1988; Tuokko & Crockett, 1989). In the most recent study, Bird & Luszcz (1991) used a semantic cue when presenting pictures of objects (e.g. find the animal) and used the same cue at retrieval. Again, memory was boosted in AD patients, but crucially only when the same cue was used at presentation and recall. At a cognitive level, this effect is consistent with Tulving's (1983) "encoding specificity" principle, where memory retrieval involves re-activating the same processes that take place at encoding (Tulving & Thomson, 1973). In AD, the encoding and retrieval processes may be so damaged that supporting both processes by cuing may be needed to ameliorate memory impairment. The implication for rehabilitation of patients with AD is that cuing the patient at retrieval may not be sufficient to improve memory, but the same cues should be used when the material is first encountered.

To summarize, the memory deficit in AD should not be seen in isolation and may reflect semantic or language impairments. Added to this are the deficits in executive functioning that may impair the ability to attend to material correctly and hence remember it later on. For example, in a conversation, even in the early stages of dementia, a person may have his/her attention disrupted from the main content of what is being said.

AUTOBIOGRAPHICAL MEMORY

A common experience is that people with dementia are relatively good at remembering what has happened to them in the distant past, for example stories from their young adult period or childhood. These personally experienced events are called autobiographical or "remote" memories, to indicate their longevity. Objective testing confirms this impression, but with some qualification.

Remote memories are difficult to assess objectively, but various procedures have been used. These include the Famous Faces Test (Albert, Butters & Levin, 1979), which consists of presenting the faces of people famous across different decades, between 1920 and 1975. AD patients have been found to be impaired on this test by Sagar et al. (1988), but show a uniform reduction. An alternative is the "cue word" technique in which high-frequency nouns are presented (e.g. the words "bird" or "tree") (Crovitz & Shiffman, 1974). The person then uses the word to remind them of an experience. The consistency of reporting can be checked by using the same procedure after 24 hours. Sagar et al. (1988) found that AD patients produced stories with significantly less rich detail, indicating impoverished memories overall.

Closest to ordinary reminiscence is to ask the person simply to talk about events that have been important in his/her life, a technique used originally by Cohen & Faulkner (1988) to investigate age differences in remote memory. The memories can then be dated approximately in relation to the age of the person. Normally, the proportion of early memories is much greater, with a "dip" in middle age, rising again for recent memories. Fromholt & Larsen (1991) have conducted a study with AD patients showing the same proportions, but an overall decline (see Figure 5.5). This has the effect of abolishing "middle-aged' memories almost completely, with the person being left with distant memories in reminiscence. One implication of this finding is that a person with AD may be left with few or no memories about his/her middle age. Morris (1994a) has recently speculated that this accounts for why some patients with dementia start thinking they are living in an earlier age; they have no "middle" memories to orientate them to the approximate present.

Neurologically, what accounts for the relative preservation of distant memories, in contrast to the eventual profound loss of episodic memories? One possibility stems from the proposed gradual shift of memory traces from the primary memory structures, such as the hippocampus and the entorhinal cortex, as suggested by Squire (1992) and others. Longer-term memories reside in association areas (unimodal or

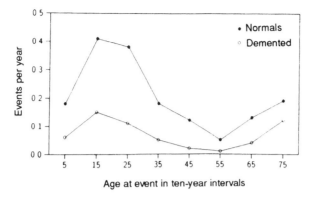

Figure 5.5   Distribution of autobiographical memories (mean number of events per year) across decades of life span in normal participants and patients with dementia. Reproduced from Fromholt & Larsen (1991), with permission

multimodal) and are less affected by the disease process. The distant memories recalled may have been recounted many times over a long period and so be "overlearned" and thus more resistant to the effects of a deteriorating memory system. Despite this, the neural structures that support these structures are still damaged to a certain extent, hence the reduction in even the most distant memories.

LANGUAGE AND SEMANTICS

More dramatic changes in language functioning in the context of dementia may indicate an arteriosclerotic form, although subtle changes do exist even in the early stages of AD (see Table 5.3). One of the most obvious is word-finding difficulties, accompanied by naming deficits. To some extent these are compensated for by the person "talking round the word", leading to circumlocutory and somewhat vague expressive language (Morris, 1992). Later on, comprehension becomes overtly impaired, particularly with complex material, the syntax of spoken language is simplified and the content becomes more devoid of meaning.

The characteristics of language breakdown and assessment are dealt with more thoroughly by Miller & Morris (1993) and by Morris & McKiernan (1994). However, one way of conceptualizing it is to compare the changes to more specific forms of aphasia. In 1985, Cummings, Benson & Hill suggested that the language profile most closely resembled transcortical sensory aphasia, which is characterized by poor comprehension, but preserved articulation and repetition of words. As the dementia progresses,

Table 5.3 Progression of language impairment associated with dementia

Early dementia
  Word-finding difficulties
  Naming impairment
  Circumlocutory discourse

Moderate dementia
  Impaired comprehension, particularly with complex material
  Simplified syntax
  Content vague and sometimes meaningless
  Paraphasias
  Verbal perseveration

Severe dementia
  Meaningless repetition of words
  Repetition of nonsense words
  Mutism

Reproduced from Morris & McKiernan (1994), with permission

this pattern was found to change to become more like Wernicke's or global aphasia. Perhaps this is the reason why Wernicke's aphasia can easily be initially confused with moderate dementia. More recently, Whitworth & Larson (1989) used the Boston Diagnostic Aphasia Examination (BDAE) (Goodglass & Kaplan, 1983) and found the general pattern in AD to be fluent, grammatical and articulate, but with loss of content and comprehension. Generally, this can be seen as a reduction of less complex linguistic forms, with a reduction of semantics, hence the term coined by Emery (1988), "regressive dysphasia", to describe the language breakdown in AD.

A removal of content reflects a more fundamental change in cognition in relation to language functioning, namely a deterioration in "semantic memory". As indicated above, this is the more permanent representation of concepts, rules about the world and knowledge, including, for example, the meaning of words (Tulving, 1983). Breakdown in semantic memory can be seen across a range of tasks. For example, Morris (1987a) has shown a gross impairment in the ability to learn abstract simple concepts, such as "matching to sample" in a learning paradigm. A breakdown in existing semantic memories is seen on tests of verbal fluency, for example the ability to produce a series of words which fit into particular categories, e.g. words beginning with a specific letter, or animals or fruits. Patients with dementia are consistently impaired on such tasks, producing less exemplars of the categories (Goldstein et al. 1992; Rosen, 1980). A second feature is the loss of the ability to name objects successfully. Some of this deficit can be attributed to visuoperceptual difficulties, but not all (Huff, Corkin & Growdon, 1986), and semantic impairment is reflected in the production of inappropriate names with associated meaning (Hodges, Salmon & Butters, 1990a; Smith, Murdoch & Chenery, 1989).

The fact that these represent semantic memory impairment rather than mere retrieval difficulties is supported by testing item knowledge across a range of tasks, which would presumably vary in terms of retrieval load. For example, Huff, Corkin & Growdon (1986) report that AD patients are more likely not to comprehend the meaning of a word relating to a particular object if they have difficulty naming it. Chertkow & Bub (1990) found that matching the name of an object to a picture of it was more impaired if the patient could not name the object (tested on a different occasion). Confirming these findings, Hodges, Salmon & Butters (1990b) have reported correlations between errors relating to the same item across a range of tests, including additionally sorting into categories and providing definitions of words.

The breakdown in semantic memory is seen in the loss not only of the knowledge of meaning of words, but of the rules that govern social interaction, or at least their description of them. These have been characterized as "scripts" or knowledge about the typical sequence of events in everyday situations, for example "going to a doctor" or "eating at a restaurant" (Abott, Black & Smith, 1985; Galambos, 1983). Typically, AD patients tend to be able to describe only the most frequent and central aspects of a script, but not the more peripheral detail, and are poorer at deciding whether two events come from the same script (Grafman et al., 1991; Weingartner et al., 1983). More research is needed to determine whether this translates into changes in appropriate social behaviour.

DISCUSSION AND CONCLUSIONS

In summary, neuropsychological impairment in dementia is widespread and heterogeneous, but the complex picture of decline can be understood more fully by detailed neuropsychological investigation. These endeavours should lead to an increased understanding of dementia, and provide the basis of clinical assessment and remediation. A primarily cognitive approach aims at providing an explanation or description of different deficits within dementia, rather than treating it as a simple disease or collection of diseases. This means that therapeutic strategies can be tailored to individual disabilities or cognitive deficits, with different approaches appropriate for each. For example, some of the cuing approaches used in remediating word-retrieval deficits might be appropriately used, but these are different in kind from the strategies used to ameliorate the dysexecutive syndrome associated with AD. Mnemonic aids can be employed to help reduce the disabling effect of the episodic memory disturbance, whilst therapies such as reminiscence (Baines, Saxby & Ehlert, 1987) can utilize preserved remote memories, as indicated by Fromholt & Larsen (1991). In other words, focusing on understanding the different deficits should in turn provide substantial insights into assessment and intervention processes.

REFERENCES

Abott, V., Black, J.B. & Smith, E.E. (1985). The representations of scripts in memory. *Journal of Memory and Language*, **24**, 179–199.

Agnew, S. (1996). Familial subtypes of Alzheimer's disease. In R.G. Morris (Ed.), *The Cognitive Neuropsychology of Alzheimer's Disease*. Oxford: Oxford University Press.

Alberoni, M., Baddeley, A.D., Della Sala, S. & Logie, R. (1992). Keeping track of a conversation: impairments in Alzheimer's disease. *International Journal of Geriatric Psychiatry*, **7**, 639–646.

Albert, M.S., Butters, N. & Levin, J. (1979). Memory of remote events in chronic alcoholics and Korsakoff patients. In H. Begleiter & B. Kissen (eds), *Alcoholic Intoxication and Withdrawal*. New York: Plenum.

Allport, A. (1989). Visual attention. In M.I. Posner (Ed.), *Foundations of Cognitive Science* (pp. 631–682). Cambridge, MA: MIT Press.

Arriagada, P.V., Growdon, J.H., Hedley-Whyte, T. & Hyman, B.T. (1992). Neurofibrillary tangles but not senile plaques parallel duration and severity of Alzheimer's disease. *Neurology*, **42**, 631–639.

Ashford, J.W. & Zec, R.F. (1993). Pharmacological treatment in Alzheimer's disease. In R.W. Parks, R.F. Zec & R.S. Wilson (Eds), *Neuropsychology of Alzheimer's Disease and Other Dementias* (pp. 589–614). Oxford: Oxford University Press.

Azari, N.P., Rapoport, S.I., Grady, C.L., Shapiro, J.A., Salerno, A., Gonzalez-Aviles & Horwitz, B. (1992). Patterns of interregional correlation of cerebral glucose metabolic rates in patients with dementia of the Alzheimer's type. *Neurodegeneration*, **1**, 101–111.

Baddeley, A.D. (1986). *Working Memory*. Oxford: Oxford University Press.

Baddeley, A.D. (1992). Working memory. *Science*, **255**, 556–559.

Baddeley, A.D., Bressi, S., Della Sala, S., Logie, R. & Spinnler, H. (1991). The decline of working memory in Alzheimer's disease. *Brain*, **114**, 2521–2542.

Baddeley, A.D. & Hitch, G. (1974). Working memory. In G.A. Bower (Ed.), *Recent Advances in Learning and Motivation*, Vol. 8. New York: Academic Press.

Baddeley, A.D., Logie, R., Bressi, S., Della Sala, S. & Spinnler, H. (1986). Dementia and working memory. *Quarterly Journal of Experimental Psychology*, **38A**, 603–618.

Baddeley, A.D., Thomson, N. & Buchanan, M. (1975). Word length and the structure of short-term memory. *Journal of Verbal Learning and Verbal Behavior*, **14**, 575–589.

Baines, S., Saxby, P. & Ehlert, K. (1987). Reality orientation and reminiscence therapy: a controlled crossover study of elderly confused people. *British Journal of Psychiatry*, **151**, 222–231.

Barnard, P. (1985). Interacting cognitive subsystems: a psycholinguistic approach to short-term memory. In A. Ellis (Ed.), *Progress in the Psychology of Language*, Vol. 2. Hillsdale, NJ: Erlbaum.

Becker, J.T. (1988). Working memory and secondary memory deficits in Alzheimer's disease. *Journal of Clinical and Experimental Neuropsychology*, **6**, 739–753.

Becker, J.T., Bajulaiye, O. & Smith, C. (1992). Longitudinal analysis of a two-component model of the memory deficit in Alzheimer's disease. *Psychological Medicine*, **22**, 437–445.

Bird, M. & Luszcz, M. (1991). Encoding specificity, depth of processing, and cued recall in Alzheimer's disease. *Journal of Clinical and Experimental Neuropsychology*, **13**(4), 508–520.

Bondareff, W., Mountjoy, C.Q., Roth, M. et al. (1987). Age and histopathologic heterogeneity in Alzheimer's disease. Evidence for subtypes. *Archives of General Psychiatry*, **44**, 412–417.

Bondareff, W., Raval, J., Colletti, P.M. & Hauser, D.L. (1988). Quantitative magnetic resonance imaging and the severity of dementia in Alzheimer's disease. *American Journal of Psychiatry*, **145**, 853–856.

Bouma, A. & Van Silfhout, B. (1989). Dichotic listening in patients with Alzheimer's disease. *Journal of Clinical and Experimental Neuropsychology*, **11**, 369.

Chertkow, H. & Bub, D. (1990). Semantic memory loss in dementia of the Alzheimer's type. *Brain*, **113**, 397–417.

Cohen, G. & Faulkner, D. (1988). Life span changes in autobiographical memory. In M.M. Gruneberg, P.E. Morris & R.N. Sykes (eds), *Practical Aspects of Memory: Current Research and Issues*, Vol. 1 (pp. 277–282). Chichester: Wiley.

Corkin, S. (1982). Some relationships between global amnesias and the memory impairment in Alzheimer's disease. In S. Corkin, K.L. Davis, J.H. Growden, E. Usdin & R.J. Wurtman (Eds), *Alzheimer's Disease: A Report of Research in Progress*. New York: Raven.

Crovitz, H.F. & Schiffman, H. (1974). Frequency of episodic memories as a function of their age. *Bulletin of the Psychonomic Society*, **4**, 517–518.

Cummings, J.L., Benson, D.F. & Hill, M.A. (1985). Aphasia in dementia of the Alzheimer type. *Neurology*, **35**, 394–396.

de la Monte, S.M., Wells, S.E., Hedley-Whyte, T. & Growdon, J.H. (1989). Neuropathological distinction between Parkinson's plus Alzheimer's disease. *Annals of Neurology*, **26**, 309–320.

Eagger, S.A., Levy, R. & Sahakian, B.J. (1991). Tacrine in Alzheimer's disease. *Lancet*, **337**, 989–992.

Emery, O. (1988). Language and memory processing in senile dementia Alzheimer's type. In L. Light & D.M. Burke (Eds), *Language, Memory and Aging* (pp. 113–147). Cambridge: Cambridge University Press.

Esiri, M. (1991). Neuropathology. In R. Jacoby & C. Oppenheimer (Eds), *Psychiatry in the Elderly* (pp. 113–147). Oxford: Oxford University Press.

Frackowiak, R.S.J., Pozzili, C., Legg, N.J., Du Boulay, G.H., Marshall, J., Lenzi, G.L. & Jones, T. (1981). Regional cerebral oxygen supply and utilization in dementia. A clinical and physiological study with oxygen-15 and positron tomography. *Brain*, **104**, 753–788.

Freed, D.M., Corkin, S., Growdon, J.H. & Nissen, M.J. (1989). Selective attention in Alzheimer's disease: characterising cognitive subgroups of Alzheimer's disease. *Neuropsychologia*, **27**, 325–339.

Friedland, R.P., Budinger, T.F., Koss, B. & Ober, A.B. (1985). Alzheimer's disease: anterior–posterior and lateral hemisphere alterations in cortical glucose utilization. *Neuroscience Letters*, **53**, 235–240.

Fromholt, P. & Larsen, S.F. (1991). Autobiographical memory in normal aging and primary degenerative dementia (dementia of Alzheimer type). *Journal of Gerontology: Psychological Sciences*, **46**(3), 85–91.

Galambos, J.A. (1983). Normative studies of six characteristics of our knowledge of common activities. *Behavior Research Methods and Instrumentation*, **15**, 327–340.

Goldstein, F.C., Green, J., Presley, R. & Green, R.C. (1992). Dysnomia in Alzheimer's disease: an evaluation of neurobehavioral subtypes. *Brain and Language*, **43**, 308–322.

Goodglass, H. & Kaplan, E. (1983). *The Assessment of Aphasia and Related Disorders*, 2nd edn. Philadelphia, PA: Lea & Febiger.

Grady, C.L., Grimes, A.M., Partronas, N., Sunderland, T., Foster, N.L. & Rapoport, S.I. (1989). Divided attention, as measured by dichotic speech performance in dementia of the Alzheimer's type. *Archives of Neurology*, **46**, 317–320.

Grady, C.L., Haxby, J.V., Horwitz, B., Sundram, M., Berg, G., Schapiro, M. et al. (1988). A longitudinal study of early neuropsychological and cerebral metabolic changes in dementia of the Alzheimer type. *Journal of Clinical and Experimental Neuropsychology*, **10**, 576–596.

Grafman, J., Thompson, K., Weingartner, H., Martinez, R., Lawlor, B.A. & Sunderland, T. (1991). Script generation as an indicator of knowledge representation in patients with Alzheimer's disease. *Brain and Language*, **40**, 344–358.

Granholm, E. & Butters, N. (1988). Associative encoding and retrieval in Alzheimer's and Huntington's disease. *Brain and Cognition*, **7**, 335–347.

Hachinski, V.C., Iliff, L.D., Zihka, E., Duboulay, G.H., McAllister, V.L., Marshall, J., Russell, R.W.R. & Symon, L. (1975). Cerebral blood flow in dementia. *Archives of Neurology*, **32**, 632–637.

Haxby, J., Grady, C., Duara, R. et al. (1986). Neocortical metabolic abnormalities precede non memory cognitive defects in early Alzheimer-type dementia. *Archives of Neurology*, **43**, 882–885.

Haxby, J.V., Grady, C.L., Koss, E., Horwitz, B., Heston, L., Shapiro, M., Friedland, R.P. & Rapoport, S.I. (1990). Longitudinal study of cerebral metabolic asymmetries and associated neuropsychological patterns in early dementia of the Alzheimer type. *Archives of Neurology*, **47**, 753–760.

Haxby, J.V., Grady, C.L., Koss, E., Horwitz, B., Shapiro, M., Friedland, R.P. & Rapoport, S.I. (1988). Heterogenous anterior–posterior metabolic patterns in dementia of the Alzheimer's type. *Neurology*, **38**, 1853–1863.

Hodges, J.R., Salmon, D.P. & Butters, N. (1990a). Differential impairment of semantic and episodic memory in Alzheimer's and Huntington's disease: a controlled prospective study. Journal of Neurology, *Neurosurgery and Psychiatry*, **53**, 1089–1095.

Hodges, J.R. Salmon, D.P. & Butters, N. (1990b). Semantic memory impairment in Alzheimer's disease: failure of access or degraded knowledge. *Neuropsychologia*, **30**(4), 301–314.

Horwitz, B., Grady, C.L., Schlageter, N.L., Durara, R. & Rapoport, S.I. (1987). Intercorrelations of regional cerebral glucose metabolic rates in Alzheimer's disease. *Brain Research, Amsterdam*, **407**, 295–306.

Huff, F.J., Corkin, S. & Growdon, J.H. (1986). Semantic impairment and anomia in Alzheimer's disease. *Brain and Language*, **28**, 235–244.

Humphreys, G.W. & Bruce, V. (1989). *Visual Cognition: Computational, Experimental and Neuropsychological Perspectives*. Hillsdale, NJ: Erlbaum.

Kennedy, A.M., Newman, S., McCaddon, A., Ball, J., Roques, P., Mullan, M., Hardy, J., Chartier-Harlin, M.C., Frackowiak, R.S.J., Warrington, E.K. & Rossor, M.N. (1993). Familial Alzheimer's disease. *Brain*, **116**, 309–324.

Kitwood, T. (1996). A dialectical framework for dementia. In R.T. Woods (ed.), *Handbook of the Clinical Psychology of Ageing*. Chichester: Wiley.

Kopelman, M.D. (1985). Rates of forgetting in Alzheimer-type dementia and Korsakoff's syndrome. *Neuropsychologia*, **23**, 623–628.

La Berge, D. (1990). Thalamic and cortical mechanisms of attention suggested by recent positron emission tomographic experiments. *Journal of Neuroscience*, **2**, 358–372.

Lantos, P.L. & Cairns, N.J. (1994). The neuropathology of Alzheimer's disease. In A. Burns & R. Levy (Eds), *Dementia* (pp. 185–207). London: Chapman and Hall.

Leuchter, A.F., Newton, T.F., Cook, I.A., Walter, D.O. & Lachenbruch, P.A. (1992). Changes in brain functional connectivity in Alzheimer-type and multi-infarct dementia. *Brain*, **115**, 1543–1561.

Lewis, D.A., Campbell, M.J., Terry, R.D. & Morrison, J.H. (1987). Laminar and regional distribution of neurofibrillary tangles and neuritic plaques in Alzheimer's disease: a quantitative study of visual and auditory cortices. *Journal of Neuroscience*, **7**, 1799–1808.

Lines, C.R., Dawson, C., Preston, G.C., Reich, S., Foster, C. & Traub, M. (1991). Memory and attention in patients with senile dementia of the Alzheimer type and normal elderly subjects. *Journal of Clinical and Experimental Neuropsychology*, **13**(5), 691–702.

Lishman, W.A. (1987). *Organic Psychiatry*, 2nd edn. Oxford: Blackwell.

Logie, R.H. & Marchetti, C. (1991). Visuospatial working memory: visual, spatial or central executive? In R.H. Logie & M. Denis (Eds), *Mental Images in Human Cognition* (pp. 105–115). Amsterdam: Elsevier Science Publishers.

Martin, A., Browers, P., Cox, C. & Fedio, P. (1985). On the nature of the verbal memory deficits in Alzheimer's disease. *Brain and Language*, **25**, 232–341.

Mattis, S. (1976). Mental status examination for organic mental syndrome in the elderly patient. In L. Bellak & T.B. Karasu (eds), *Geriatric Psychiatry*. New York: Grune and Stratton.

McKeith, I. (1994). The differential diagnosis of dementia. In A. Burns & R. Levy (Eds), *Dementia* (pp. 39–57). London: Chapman and Hall.

Metter, E.J. & Wilson, R.S. (1993). Vascular dementias. In R.W. Parks, R.F. Zec & R.S. Wilson (Eds), *Neuropsychology of Alzheimer's Disease and Other Dementias* (pp. 416–437). Oxford: Oxford University Press.

Miller, E. (1977). *Abnormal Ageing*. Wiley, Chichester.

Miller, E. & Morris, R.G. (1993). *The Psychology of Dementia*. Chichester: Wiley.

Mohr, E., Cox, C., Williams, J., Chase, T.N. & Fedio, P. (1990). Impairment of central auditory function in Alzheimer's disease. *Journal of Clinical and Experimental Neuropsychology*, **12**, 235–246.

Money, E.A., Kirk, R.C. & McNaughton, N. (1992). Alzheimer's dementia produces a loss of discrimination but no increase in rate of memory decay in delayed matching to sample. *Neuropsychologia*, **30**(2), 133–143.

Morris, R.G. (1984). Dementia and the functioning of the articulatory loop system. *Cognitive Neuropsychology*, **1**, 143–157.

Morris, R.G. (1986). Short-term forgetting in senile dementia of the Alzheimer's type. *Cognitive Neuropsychology*, **3**, 77–97.

Morris, R.G. (1987a). Articulatory rehearsal in Alzheimer-type dementia. *Brain and Language*, **30**, 351–362.

Morris, R.G. (1987b). The effect of concurrent articulation on memory span in Alzheimer-type dementia. *British Journal of Clinical Psychology*, **26**, 233–234.

Morris, R.G. (1987c). Matching and oddity learning in moderate to severe dementia. *Quarterly Journal of Experimental Psychology*, **39**, 215–227.

Morris, R.G. (1989). Neuropsychological aspects of dementia. *Current Opinions in Psychiatry*, **2**, 66–71.

Morris, R.G. (1991a). Neuropsychological studies of memory functioning in Alzheimer-type dementia. In J. Weinmann & J. Hunter (Eds), *Memory: Neurochemical and Abnormal Perspectives* (pp. 163–187). London: Harwood Academic.

Morris, R.G. (1991b). Cognition and ageing. In R. Jacoby & C. Oppenheimer (Eds), *Psychiatry in the Elderly* (pp. 58–88). Oxford: Oxford University Press.

Morris, R.G. (1992). Patterns of short-term memory impairment in Alzheimer's disease. In L. Backman (Ed.), *Memory Functioning in Dementia* (pp. 3–25). Amsterdam: Elsevier.

Morris, R.G. (1994a). Recent developments in the neuropsychology of dementia. *International Journal of Psychiatry*, **4**, 85–107.

Morris, R.G. (1994b). Working memory in Alzheimer's disease. *Neuropsychology*, **8**, 544–554.

Morris, R.G. (1994c). Working memory in Alzheimer's disease: a dysconnection syndrome? International Conference on Working Memory. Cambridge: Magdalene College.

Morris, R.G. (Ed.) (1996). *The Cognitive Neuropsychology of Alzheimer's Disease*. Oxford: Oxford University Press.

Morris, R.G. & Baddeley, A.D. (1988). Primary and working memory functioning in Alzheimer-type dementia. *Journal of Experimental and Clinical Psychology*, **51**, 757–766.

Morris, R.G., Evenden, J.L., Sahakian, B.J. & Robbins, T.W. (1987). Computer-aided assessment of dementia: comparative studies of Alzheimer-type dementia and Parkinson's disease. In S.M. Stahl, S.D. Iversen & E.C. Goodman (Eds), *Cognitive Neurochemistry* (pp. 21–36). Oxford: Oxford University Press.

Morris, R.G. & Kopelman, M.D. (1986). The memory deficits in Alzheimer-type dementia: a review. *Quarterly Journal of Experimental Psychology*, **38**, 575–602.

Morris, R.G. & McKiernan, F. (1994). Neuropsychological investigation of dementia. In A. Burns & R. Levy (Eds), *Dementia* (pp. 327–354). London: Chapman and Hall.

Morris, R.G., Wheatley, J. & Britton, P.G. (1983). Retrieval from long-term memory in senile dementia: cued recall revisited. *British Journal of Clinical Psychology*, **22**, 141–142.

Morrison, J., Scherr, S., Lewis, D., Campbell, M., Bloom F., Rogers, J. et al. (1986). The laminar and regional distribution of neocortical somatostatin and neuritic plaques: implications for Alzheimer's disease as a global neocortical disconnection syndrome. In A. Scheibel, A. Wechsler & M. Brazier (Eds), *The Biological Substrates of Alzheimer's Disease* (pp. 115–131). Orlando, FL: Academic Press.

Nebes, R.D. & Brady, C.B. (1993). Phasic and tonic alertness in Alzheimer's disease. *Cortex*, **29**, 77–90.

NINCDS–ADRDA Work Group (1982). Criteria for the clinical diagnosis of Alzheimer's disease. Journal of Neurology, *Neurosurgery and Psychiatry*, **53**, 23–32.

Nissen, M.J., Corkin, S., Buonanno, F.S., Growden J.H., Wray, S.H. & Bauer, J. (1985). Spatial vision in Alzheimer's disease: general findings and a case report. *Archives of Neurology*, **42**, 667–671.

Parasuraman, R., Greenwood, P.M., Haxby, J.V. & Grady, C.L. (1992). Visuospatial attention in dementia of the Alzheimer's type. *Brain*, **115**, 711–733.

Pearson, R.C.A., Esiri, M.M., Hiorns, R.W., Wilcock, G.K. & Powell, T.P.S. (1985). Anatomical correlates of the distribution of the pathological changes in the neocortex in Alzheimer's disease. *Proceedings of the National Academy of Sciences USA*, **82**, 4531–4534.

Perry, E.K. (1994). Cholinergic component of cognitive impairment in dementia. In A. Burns & R. Levy (Eds), *Dementia* (pp. 143–157). London: Chapman and Hall.

Peterson, L.R. & Peterson, M.J. (1959). Short-term retention of individual verbal items. *Journal of Experimental Psychology*, **58**, 193–198.

Peterson, S.E., Fox, P.T., Miezin, F.M. & Raichle, M.E. (1988). Modulation of cortical visual responses by direction of spatial attention measured by PET. *Investigative Ophthalmology and Visual Science*, **29** (Abstract Issue), 22.

Posner, M.I., Cohen, Y., Choate, L.S., Hockey, R. & Maylor, E. (1984a). Sustained concentration: passive filtering or active orienting? In S. Kornblum & J. Requin (Eds), *Preparatory States and Processes* (pp. 49–65). Erlbaum, Hillsdale, NJ, pp. 49–65.

Posner, M.M., Walker, J.A., Friedrich, F.J. & Rafal, R.D. (1984b). Effects of parietal injury on covert orienting of attention. *Journal of Neuroscience*, **4**, 1863–1874.

Rogers, J. & Morrison, J.H. (1985). Quantitative morphology and regional and laminar distributions of senile plaques in Alzheimer's disease. *Journal of Neuroscience*, **5**, 2801–2808.

Rosen, W.G. (1980). Verbal fluency in aging and dementia. *Journal of Clinical Neuropsychology*, **2**, 135–146.

Rosen, W.G., Terry, R.D., Fuld, P.A., Katzman, R. & Peck, A. (1980). Pathological verification of ischemic score differentiation of dementia. *Annals of Neurology*, **7**, 486–488.

Sagar, H.J., Corkin, S., Cohen, N.J. & Growden, J.H. (1988). Remote-memory function in Alzheimer's disease and Parkinson's disease. *Brain*, **111**, 698–718.

Sahakian, B.J., Morris, R.G., Evenden, J.L., Heald, A., Levy, R., Philpot, M., & Robbins, T.W.R. (1988). A comparative study of visuo-spatial memory and learning in Alzheimer-type dementia and Parkinson's disease. *Brain*, **111**, 695–718.

Semba, K. & Fibinger, H.C. (1989). Organisation of central cholinergic systems. *Progress in Brain Research*, **79**, 37–63.

Smith, S.R., Murdoch, B.E. & Chenery, H.J. (1989). Semantic abilities in dementia of the Alzheimer's type: 1. Lexical semantics. *Brain and Language*, **36**, 314–324.

Spampinato, U., Habert, M.O., Mas, J.L., Bourdel, M.C., Ziegler, M., de Recondo, J., Askienazy, S. & Rondot, P. (1991). (99m Tc)-HMPAO SPECT and cognitive impairment in Parkinson's disease: a comparison with dementia of the Alzheimer's type. *Journal of Neurology, Neurosurgery and Psychiatry*, **54**, 787–792.

Spinnler, H., Della Sala, S., Bandera, R. & Baddeley, A.D. (1988). Dementia, ageing and the structure of human memory. *Cognitive Neuropsychology*, **5**, 193–211.

Squire, L.R. (1992). Memory and the hippocampus: a synthesis from findings with rats, monkeys, and humans. *Psychological Review*, **99**(2), 195–231.

Tierney, M.C., Fisher, R.H., Lewis, A.J., Zorzitto, M.J., Snow, W.G., Reid, D.W. et al. (1988). The NINCDS-ADRDA work group criteria for the clinical diagnosis of probable Alzheimer's disease: a clinicopathologic study of 57 cases. *Neurology*, **38**, 359–364.

Tulving, E. (1983). *Elements of Episodic Memory*. New York: Oxford University Press.

Tulving, E, & Thomson, D.M. (1973). Encoding specificity and retrieval processes in episodic memory. *Psychological Review*, **80**, 352–373.

Tuokko, H. & Crockett, D. (1989). Cued recall and memory disorders in dementia. *Journal of Clinical and Experimental Neuropsychology*, **11**, 278–294.

Weingartner, H., Grafmann, J., Boutelle, W., Kaye, W. & Martin, P. (1983). Forms of memory failure. *Science*, **221**, 380–382.

Whitworth, R.H. & Larson, C.M. (1989). Differential diagnosis and staging of Alzheimer's disease with an aphasia battery. *Neuropsychiatry, Neuropsychology and Behavioural Neurology*, **4**, 255–265.

Wilcock, G.K. & Esiri, M.M. (1982). Plaques, tangles and dementia. A quantitative study. *Journal of Neurological Science*, **56**, 343–356.

Chapter 6

COMMUNITY CARE: PSYCHOLOGICAL PERSPECTIVES

*Chris Gilleard**

INTRODUCTION

Community care has become the mainstay policy for the provision of health and welfare services for older people in most Western societies. The fundamental tenet of community care is that the management of illness and disability should involve the least possible disruption to the life circumstances and choices of the individual. In practical terms this means restricting the use of hospital, nursing-home and residential-home beds to those whose illness and associated disability cannot be managed effectively from or within their own home environment. As far as older people are concerned, this policy has been promulgated through the use of enhanced health and social domiciliary services and the contraction of the number of hospital longstay beds, now restrictively targeted or channelled to people most "in need". This policy has been incorporated into English law through the NHS and Community Care Act 1990 (HMSO, 1990). The terms of this Act as it affects the development of community care in Britain can be summarized as follows:

1. The separation of the role of purchasing from that of providing health and social care, health authorities becoming purchasers of health care, and local authorities purchasers of social care.
2. The requirement that local authorities, as the key purchasers of care, and in conjunction with local health authorities, prepare plans

* Springfield Hospital, London, UK

Psychological Problems of Ageing: Assessment, Treatment and Care. Edited by R.T. Woods.
© 1999 John Wiley & Sons Ltd.

outlining how they intend to ensure the provision of appropriate services for people in their community.

3. The requirement that such services are provided only after an adequate assessment of an individual's needs and expressed wishes, taking account of both the potential client and his/her informal carer(s).

4. The transfer of responsibility to the local authority for purchasing nursing and residential home places for those whose needs are such that they cannot be met in any other way.

5. The dissemination of information about services that are available, including the criteria for providing such services.

Three features of the Act have created a significant shift in the social context of managing the illnesses and disabilities of later life. The first element is that care has to be planned; the second that it has to be targeted; and the third that it has to be costed. Community care plans are meant to demonstrate the responsibility of local authority social service departments, in conjunction with the appropriate health authorities, to outline how their purchasing intentions will ensure that the local community's needs for health and social care provision are met adequately and effectively. At the individual user/client level, individual care management requires a plan outlining the most adequate and effective package or programme of care that will meet the individual's needs. As for targeting, it is evident that by planning services around population and personal needs, some system of client/user priority has to be established to ensure that those with the greatest need for care are given due priority, and that their most pressing and serious needs are met first, so that health and social care resources are not used inefficiently. Finally, it is clear that, given finite resources, making the best use of health and social care budgets demands an effective method of determining the costs of services in order that the most efficient purchasing decisions are made for each programme of care required for a particular user/client. These three features of the Act create a particular tension between the empowerment associated with the "user/client" status, with its apparent entitlement to make choices of services that will best meet the individual's needs, and the very real constraints demanded by an explicitly finite purchasing plan, which delimits the resources available to purchase care for a given population/community. Central to this tension is the ambiguous role of assessment as the principal means of accessing services.

The psychological consequences of these policies appear to be many and varied. First, there is the well-acknowledged problem that community care of chronically ill and disabled people can increase the burden on family and friends, leading to loss of earnings and poorer mental and physical health for the carers, despite saving the state considerable sums of money (see Henwood & Wicks, 1984, who estimate that informal care "costs" as much as the British Government's total health and personal social services bill for the over-75s; or the Family Policy Studies Centre report, which estimated the replacement costs of informal care at between £15 and £25 billion per annum: Family Policy Studies Centre, 1989). Balancing the costs and benefits of a particular combination of services for an older person from the point of view of a health authority or local authority social services department will lead to an emphasis on the immediately accountable costs of domiciliary care, day care or institutional care. The personal and social costs to carers, their families and even to the clients themselves may be ignored as largely unquantifiable and relevant only in so far as they presage a breakdown of informal care.

Second, there is the very real problem of determining the most accurate means of assessing the needs for community, hospital and/or residential services to maximize the benefits for a particular client. This is really a question of predictive validity. How well do care assessments provide information that determines the best pattern of care and the most favourable outcome for the client? This in turn raises the question of the construct validity of the outcomes one is seeking to achieve or predict for a client. Which particular psychological, social and physical factors should form the criteria for judging whether or not the health and welfare services have met a client's needs successfully? This is an especially important issue in relation to progressive conditions such as dementia. The role of assessment is meant to be central in determining appropriate care management and effective care outcomes. However, issues need to be raised concerning the reliability and validity of care assessment methodologies: at present most community care assessment schemes are simply taken as having face validity without any consideration being given to what might be termed their "psychometric" properties.

Within the community of older people, there is growing concern about lost or limited access to services which previously had been assumed to belong to them as a group "of right". Such concerns vary from one local authority to another, and from one health authority to another. They may be about local authority day centres, lunch clubs or home-help services, or hospital longstay wards, day hospitals or numbers of acute admission beds. With a finite budget for social care, local authority cutbacks on services are becoming more common as welfare spending is focused on a numerically smaller, more tightly targeted group of people presenting with the most severe disabilities. While there may well be justification for local and health authorities to consider how best to use their financial resources to achieve the most beneficial outcomes for their communities, the immediate fallout from these complex decisions can be extremely distressing to those who had become reliant upon the existing patterns of social care.

Finally, the continuing process of health and social care reform has begun a cultural reconceptualization of the older person, not as patient or pensioner, but as a "customer" or "client" of the service. The personal and behavioural implications of this shift from citizen to consumer have hardly begun to be addressed. But if the impact of these policy changes is to be managed to the benefit of older people, the shift in perspective needed must be achieved in a way that enables older people to be more self-confident clients or customers in their future dealings with service providers.

This chapter will focus upon the above themes—addressing the "burden of care" associated with community care policies; the nature of care assessment and its associated outcomes; and the shifting perspective of older people—considering both the challenge of becoming users and consumers and the threats this poses to people's rights to welfare as "old age citizens".

THE BURDEN OF COMMUNITY CARE

Illness and disability become increasingly common the longer one lives. The rise in the over-75 year-old population in Britain over the last 25 years is mirrored in most other developed societies. Most older people's needs are met through their own efforts and those of their family, friends and neighbours. For a minority this involves some degree of dependence, and that usually means that one particular person within their social network acquires special status as a carer. For most such carers, this responsibility is not especially onerous, and offers a mixture of satisfaction and frustration common to most adult relationships. However, for a small, but still significant, minority of carers, the responsibilities can be particularly heavy, and their dependant may require regular assistance and/or supervision to prevent serious harm arising. Within this group of carers and older dependants, mental health problems play a particularly significant role.

Research into the impact of caring for an older person with serious mental health problems, particularly dementia, is extensive. A number of reviews (e.g. Baumgarten, 1989; Morris, Morns & Britton, 1988) have indicated that carers looking after people with dementia experience considerable distress. However, most studies have focused on carers who are already in touch with services of one kind or another. Community-based studies relying upon case ascertainment methods to identify people with dementia indicate less dramatic levels of carer morbidity.

Nevertheless, they too suggest that, compared with matched controls, relatives looking after people with mild to moderate dementia are more stressed, more socially restricted and more likely to use medication (Graftstrom et al., 1992); and those looking after someone with moderate to severe dementia experience even greater strain, although not necessarily more psychiatric symptomatology (Eagles et al., 1987; O'Connor et al., 1988; 1990). Compared with most of the elderly population, people with dementia are more likely to present greater social and health morbidity problems (Johnston et al., 1987); to receive more extensive domiciliary health and social care services (Foster, Kay & Bergmann, 1976; O'Connor et al., 1989); to spend time in hospital (Kay et al., 1970); and to become institutionalized (Adolfsson et al., 1981; Opit & Pahl, 1993). From this one may conclude that dementia presents a major problem for health and social care services and that, faced with this problem, many families end up unable to provide the level of care required to keep their relative in the community.

Of course, it is true that other chronic, disabling conditions occasion considerable stress to carers, including depression, Parkinson's disease and cancer (Liptzin, Grob & Eisen, 1988; Dura et al., 1990; Rabins et al., 1990). However, unlike most people with dementia, people with other chronic, degenerative diseases usually have an understanding of their disability and present less need for supervision to prevent harm coming to themselves or to others. The limited awareness that people with dementia have of their disability makes this group of elderly people the most formidable challenge to the policies of community care.

Impact of community support services

Is enhanced domiciliary support enough to make an impact on the personal well-being of the carer and prevent the collapse of community care or at least delay institutional admission? While a number of studies have examined the impact of existing community services on people with dementia and their carers, few give unequivocal evidence that any one service is universally beneficial. Home helps have been reported to reduce the strain of caring for elderly confused people (Levin, Sinclair & Gorbach, 1986). Likewise, positive reports of in-home support and sitter services have been made (Turvey & Toner, 1990). Studies of day care (Panella, Littiston & Brush, 1984; Gilleard, 1987; Wells et al., 1990) also suggest that it offers real benefits to some carers, but few, if any, observable benefits to the users of the service. Institutional respite care seems to offer even fewer benefits to carers (Lawton, Brody & Saperstein, 1989) and none to users (Seltzer et al., 1988), who may be adversely affected

(Hirsch et al., 1993). While respite services are valued by carers (Levin, Moriarty & Gorbach, 1994), their benefits to users of the services seem minimal at best. Most studies examining the significance of "service use" have tended to indicate that higher rates of community-based service use are more, rather than less, likely to lead to subsequent institutionalization (see Colerick & George, 1986; Cohen et al., 1993).

Intensive care management services

The research evidence indicates that home care, day care and respite care do not significantly reduce the likelihood of admission into long-term care. This has led some to suggest that only by innovative and intensive home support services can community care be successfully implemented with this client group. However, the results of specialist intensive home-care support teams suggest that they too may offer little, if any, real positive outcomes judged by successful community placement (Askham & Thompson, 1990; O'Connor et al., 1991). The strongest evidence of achieving successful community care for older people with dementia must come from the series of studies conducted by Davies, Challis and their colleagues in the Personal Social Services Research Unit at the University of Kent in Canterbury. This work provides a unique focus on research into case management systems for older people. Beginning with the initial project in Kent, these researchers have meticulously documented the impact of care management systems on rates of institutionalization and mortality, and indicators of personal well-being, among those exposed or not exposed to this system of social care (Challis & Davies, 1980, 1988; Challis et al., 1992). Clearly, a number of older people with dementia were included in and, to varying degrees, benefited from the various demonstration projects. However, mainstream intensive care management programmes targeting most older people with dementia may not have quite the same outcomes (see Davies, 1992).

The care programme approach (Department of Health, 1990) and care assessment and management (Department of Health, 1992) rely heavily on the belief that by offering flexible, comprehensive, carefully planned packages of services to older people, specifically designed for the individual and taking account of the existing resources and level of support available to the person, most older people can continue to live successfully in the community. However, service research conducted to date does not offer strong empirical support for this belief (Callahan 1989; Meyers & Master, 1989; Jack, 1993). The impact of the policy changes enacted in the health and welfare services in Britain remains to be seen.

Families looking after older relatives with dementias and other serious mental health problems are still facing the same difficulties outlined earlier. The status of older people living alone in the community and suffering from dementia and other serious mental illness remains problematic. At present there is little evidence of any major shifts in the overall patterns of care (see Lewis, Dunn & Vetter, 1994). The changes that the new community care policies have introduced, changes in approaches to managing the care of older people with mental health problems, are, however, very real, and of great significance to psychologists working in the field. These practices will be considered in more detail in the next section.

ASSESSMENT AND CARE MANAGEMENT

Services have become much more targeted. Issues of eligibility and entitlement to services have become matters less of interpretation than of formalization, relying upon clinical and resource criteria that are part explicit and part implicit. In this shift away from universal provision, the importance of correctly assessing individual need takes on extra significance. There has been a marked evolution of ideas about assessment of older people and the relative contributions that professionals and patients can make to successfully completing an audit of the needs with which the older person presents in a particular service setting. Many of the concerns are centred on the contrast between traditional specialist referral and assessment processes and multi-agency, open-access, cross-disciplinary assessment procedures.

Assessment: multi-agency, multidisciplinary—or specialist?

The current emphasis of assessment is based upon a single, holistic and comprehensive examination considering functional capacity, emotional, cognitive and behavioural stability, and personal social and material resources. Standard assessment forms are being produced by local authority social services departments asking a series of questions which the assessor is supposed to answer during or after his/her meeting with client and carer. The possible requirement for a more detailed assessment is contained in the general guidelines about community care assessment methods (Social Services Inspectorate, 1992). However, assessment forms are rarely developed with immediate reference to the psychometric principles of reliability and validity. There is very little research on the inter-rater reliability, test–retest reliability and predictive validity of the assessments currently employed in order to determine eligibility for services. Meanwhile, healthcare providers increasingly are using standardized assessment methodologies, in part to support multidisciplinary involvement in the assessment process (see Collighan et al., 1993) and in part to formalize resource utilization decisions (Carpenter, Main & Turner, 1995; Fries et al., 1994). Whilst considerable care has been expended in the development of assessment instruments in the healthcare field, the same cannot be said of developments in the assessment of needs for social care. No doubt this reflects a historical difference in the underlying traditions of social casework compared with clinical medicine, but the implications of employing measures of unknown reliability, let alone uncertain validity, are serious. Research shows clearly that, in the field of mental health at least, large and significant discrepancies exist between elderly, mentally frail patients' accounts of their problems and those given by their families (Reifler, Cox & Hanley, 1981). At the same time, perceptions of "risk" may be subject to professional bias and preconceptions, while interprofessional differences in rating the severity of problems have frequently been reported. How much balance should and can be achieved between specialist assessments and generic assessments remains an open question. How much professional judgements (observing signs) should outweigh personal reports (recording symptoms) depends importantly upon the outcome criteria one is seeking to achieve. One professional may assess an older person for his/her "need" for social contact and consider that met if the person agrees to go to a day centre, while another may interpret his/her reports of loneliness as the expression of a long-standing personality disorder, unlikely to respond to any psychosocial or psychopharmacological intervention, and do nothing. In terms of the relative validity of these two assessments, it is a moot point which more adequately reflects appropriate planning and targeting of services.

The criteria for involving a clinical psychologist in conducting neuropsychological examination of a patient or client are, of course, equally unclear. While direct requests for such assessments typically come from psychiatrists, GPs or geriatricians, i.e. after some presumed medical assessment has been conducted, it is perfectly possible for social care managers and staff to include as an option in their assessments a referral for neuropsychological assessment. Developing "criteria" for such assessments should ideally take place within the context of a multiprofessional team, where the potential customers and the potential providers seek agreement about who to refer, when to refer, and what outcomes are expected after referral. Part of the goal of effectively targeting services does depend upon accurate professional assessment. If an older person's sadness and lack of socialization are the result of a depressive illness, then prescribing antidepressants might be the more effective and appropriate response to help the person maintain his/her usual lifestyle, while attendance at a day centre, or provision of a volunteer "sitter", may not. The formalization of assessment that accompanies the targeting of resources tends to institutionalize the assessment process as a "once and for all" decision. As many clinicians would point out, however, additional information may alter the picture and change the nature of the "need". Likewise, changing health and social circumstances may invalidate earlier assessments. The stability and the predictive value of assessments are crucial concerns if the assessment process is to be the central key to unlocking costly services. It is clear that, at a population level, gross indicators of cognitive and functional capacity do have powerful predictive value in determining outcomes of care (Donaldson & Jagger, 1983), suggesting that, in non-acute settings, assessments of mental and functional competence and social care networks possess an adequate degree of stability and predictive validity to warrant their employment in allocating resources. However, it could be argued that, as the costs consequent upon an assessment decision rise, so too should the level of specialization of the assessment and its associated costs. Thus, for example, a decision about the need for long-term care of a not-so-old person with probable Alzheimer's dementia involves a potentially large and continuous cost consequent upon the outcome of the assessment. In such circumstances it can be argued that a detailed medical and neuropsychiatric/ neuropsychological assessment is warranted to see whether some other alternative "formulation" of the person's problems might not emerge.

In short, there are complex issues arising concerning the nature of generic and specialist assessment methods applied to determine the need for health and/or social care. This complexity hinges to a great extent upon concerns which have long occupied psychometricians: issues of reliability and validity. As experience with such generic multidisciplinary assessment forms grows, it may turn out that they represent extremely cost-effective ways of ensuring that the most appropriate care is given to those in need. The work cited above, of Collighan et al (1993), suggests that too much specious professionalism has developed around the topic of specialist assessments.

Management: co-ordinating care, delivering care and supporting carers

Current policy supports a more flexible response to the assessed needs of an older person. Care planning and care management are meant to facilitate a broader, more imaginative response to health and social care needs. In reality it is unclear through what processes such imaginative flexibility is likely to arise. Research asking users and carers suggests some ways forward, but most service providers continue to respond according to the resources they currently have or once controlled. Effective continuing care management of elderly disabled people within the community requires an expansion of training and an equivalent expansion of care options. The role of psychologists working in multidisciplinary mental health teams can be to support the development of flexible care strategies that consider, first and foremost, ways of enabling older people with mental infirmity to benefit from services that are acceptable to them, and which are presented in ways that address their needs and not the needs of others who insist that "something must be done". Traditionally, psychologists have been called in when people present problems—rejecting services, rejecting help or acting in such a way that help is put off. This has tended to foster a trouble-shooting, "behaviour modification" strategy that can too easily target and objectify the person presenting the problem. Operating according to the client's perspective may be difficult, especially if he/she is severely demented, but seeking to involve significant others in drawing up care management strategies is one way of giving voice to the patient or client. The work of people like Feil (1989, 1992) and Kitwood (1993) has done much to re-orientate psychologists to the reality of the person behind the disabilities of his/her dementia. Of course, there is still scope for working actively in partnership with carers, but acknowledging the difficulties of care does not necessitate fostering the notion of the social or psychological death of the person with dementia. Clinical psychologists—and other healthcare professionals—will need to develop skills to become effective and sensitive keyworkers, co-ordinating care across services as well as between disciplines within the same service. This expanding role for psychologists working with older people will have significant repercussions for pre- and post-qualification training within this speciality.

CHALLENGING THE CULTURE OF WELFARE: CONSUMERS, CLIENTS AND CARERS

The diminished status and passivity associated with being assessed and judged "in need"—whether of financial, social or health resources—are central features in many of the arguments put forward by the proponents of "structured dependency" theory (Walker, 1981; Townsend, 1981). The provision of health and social care as a civic responsibility may ensure universal availability, but it has also been seen as fostering a sense of induced helplessness, leaving many people ill-served and ill-treated, and yet uncomplaining. The interest in consumerism and the user perspective in health and social care has been stimulated by the NHS and Community Care Act, and developments such as the Patient's Charter and the Community Care Charter have focused thinking about the relationship between purchaser, provider and recipient of health and social care. It seems a laudable aim for older people and their families to be involved in framing the services they receive and helping tailor care to best meet the needs of users and carers. However, the fact that the purchaser of that care is an organization unaccountable to the users/clients means that the users' power to influence care is considerably less, mediated almost entirely by purchasing authorities. Radical proposals for direct consumer funding of care services made by William Laing (1991) remain unexplored options and there are few signs of care managers acting as the agents of their clients/customers.

Equally, the requirement to involve carers in the assessment process has meant less in practice than it might in theory. What tends to be the focus of such assessments is the likelihood that the informal carer can cope, and when doubts about coping arise, the critical level of service provision that the carer may find tolerable in order to prevent this. The likelihood of admission to an institutional "bed" has consistently been found to be more strongly related to carer characteristics (e.g. level of distress, attitudes towards care, physical health, practical assistance offered, closeness of kin relationship, etc.) than to the clinical characteristics of the older person's illness (Morycz, 1985; Opit & Pahl, 1993; Levin, Moriarty & Gorbach, 1994, especially pp. 125–139).

While it is easy to argue that the aim of involving clients/carers in planning and providing good-quality care has not been achieved, nevertheless there are signs that for some older people, opportunities for a more active role in their care have been made available and have been seized (see Thornton & Tozer, 1994). These are a minority, it seems. In a recent overview of assessment issues and community care, Caldock & Nolan (1994) point out from their own studies that "users, particularly older individuals, have few ideas of their rights and only a very limited understanding of the assessment process" (Caldock & Nolan, 1994, p. 4). Their findings about carers largely reiterate the same point: a lack of information about services and a consequent lack of clear expectations of them. It is not uncommon to find that families looking after ill old people are unable to articulate what sorts of additional help or services might best meet their needs. The cultural shift required to educate and empower a whole new social group about their rights and responsibilities may have been going on for some time, but affecting younger generations more than the present generation of elderly people. The baby boom generation of the middle and late 1940s will be reaching old age towards the turn of the century. Unlike contemporary elderly people, they have grown up accustomed to challenging societal assumptions from their early youth through to middle age, and, having spent their working life in settings more fluid and less structured by class, are less likely to be intimidated by professional power.

This more informed, and less accepting, generation of third-agers eventually may realize the aims of current social policy, i.e. greater user involvement and more family consultation. In the meantime, there are ways that psychologists can contribute to these goals. The first is bringing a more user-orientated perspective into health and social care services. This may involve developing regular user and carer forums which the services can consult, regularly including carers and users in devising and revising clients' care programmes, and accessing advocacy systems that can serve as the consumerist voice for those with neither the social nor the psychological means to speak for themselves. In some senses the onus is upon the providers to demonstrate the fact that they are making an effort to see things not solely from the point of view of the service, but also from the point of view of the community for whom the service is being purchased. The psychological process of attitude change would seem of particular relevance here.

The second way that psychologists can be actively involved is in promoting a programme of cultural awareness amongst users and carers, increasing their understanding of the care programme approach, the Patient's Charter, the Community Care Charter and issues surrounding care assessment and care management. At the level of individual practice, this might involve explaining to the user/carer what the psychologist is going to do, why they are going to do that, how it might help and when the proposed intervention will stop or be reviewed. Many older people cannot be seen in an outpatient setting and invariably will be seen at home, or in a day-care setting. Visits from different professionals can be confusing, and it may not be easy to know who each professional is and why they are there. Simply leaving a copy of the care programme may not be enough. It is important for each professional to be clear about his/her role in relation to the patient, and equally to explain clearly his/her role with the patient and the implications for the particular care plan. Working on the process of accounting to clients and carers more fully and more informatively about the services they can and will receive is an important step towards empowering the user to share responsibility for his/her own care and treatment. Emerging from a gradual shifting of the balance of power in client/professional contacts, this change can be the opportunity for psychologists to demonstrate their own commitment to providing a service that is accessible and understandable to those that use it.

The third means of developing a psychological framework for user and carer involvement is to make practical sense of terms like "needs assessment", "empowerment", "advocacy", "holistic assessment" and "personal dignity" as applied to some of the most seriously ill and disabled users of the service. Thinking around some of the issues involved in consulting people with dementia, considering what a holistic assessment is and how it differs from a request to test for "? dementia", looking at how to minimize the indignities of dementia instead of resolving problems by minimizing the humanity of the person, seeking to discuss family concerns with the client present rather than holding hurried conversations in out-of-the-way kitchens and corridors—these are just some examples of how psychologists can make a reality of what otherwise can seem like the rhetoric of policy makers who have never had to deliver a service to ill and disabled people.

REFERENCES

Adolfsson, R., Gottfries, C., Nystrom, L. & Winblad, B. (1981). Prevalence of dementia disorders in institutionalised Swedish old people. *Acta Psychiatrica Scandinavica*, **63**, 225–244.

Askham, J. & Thompson, C. (1990). *Dementia and Home Care: A Research Report on a Home Support Scheme for Dementia Sufferers*. Age Concern Institute of Gerontology Research Paper No. 4. London: Age Concern.

Baumgarten, M. (1989). The health of persons giving care to the demented elderly: a critical review of the literature. *Journal of Clinical Epidemiology*, **42**, 1137–1148.

Caldock, K. & Nolan, M. (1994). Assessment and community care: are the reforms working? *Generations Review*, **4**, 2–7.

Callahan, J.J. (1989). Play it again, Sam—there is no impact. Gerontologist, 29, 5–6.

Carpenter, G.I., Main, A., Turner, G.F. (1995). Case mix for the elderly inpatient: resource utilisation groups (RUGs) validation project. *Age and Ageing*, **24**, 5–13.

Challis, D., Chessum, R., Chesterman, J., Luckett, R. & Traske, K. (1992). Case management. In F. Laczko & C.R. Victor (Eds), *Social Policy and Elderly People* (pp. 137–162). Aldershot: Avebury.

Challis, D. & Davies, B. (1980). A new approach to community care for the elderly. *British Journal of Social Work*, **10**, 1–18.

Challis, D. & Davies, B. (1988). The community care approach: an innovation in home care by social services departments. In N. Wells & C. Freer (Eds), *The Ageing Population: Burden or Challenge?* (pp. 191–202). London: Macmillan.

Cohen, C.A., Gold, D.P., Shulman, K.I., Wortley, J.T., McDonald, G. & Wargon, M. (1993). Factors determining the decision to institutionalise dementing individuals: a prospective study. *Gerontologist*, **33**, 714–720.

Colerick, E.J. & George, L.K. (1986). Predictors of institutionalization among caregivers of patients with Alzheimer's disease. *Journal of the American Geriatrics Society*, **34**, 493–498.

Collighan, G., Macdonald, A., Herzberg, J., Philpot, M. & Lindesay, J. (1993). An evaluation of the multidisciplinary approach to psychiatric diagnosis in elderly people. *British Medical Journal*, **306**, 821–824.

Davies, B. (1992). Resources, needs and outcomes in community services: why academic caution is useful. In K. Morgan (Ed.), *Gerontology: Responding to an Ageing Society* (pp. 215–248). London: Jessica Kingsley.

Department of Health (1990). *The Care Programme Approach for People with a Mental Illness Referred to the Specialist Psychiatric Services*. HC(90)23/LASS. London: Department of Health.

Department of Health (1992). *Implementing Community Care: Model for Purchasing Care for Elderly People*. London: HMSO.

Donaldson, L.J. & Jagger, C. (1983). Survival and functional capacity: three year follow up of an elderly population in hospitals and homes. *Journal of Epidemiology and Community Health*, **37**, 176–179.

Dura, J.R., Haywood-Niler, E. & Kiecolt-Glaser, J.K. (1990). Spousal caregivers of persons with Alzheimer's and Parkinson's disease dementia: a preliminary comparison. *Gerontologist*, **30**, 332–339.

Eagles, J.M., Craig, A., Rawlinson, F., Restall, D.B., Beattie, J.A.G. & Besson, J.A.O. (1987). The psychological wellbeing of supporters of the demented elderly. *British Journal of Psychiatry*, **150**, 293–298.

Family Policy Studies Centre (1989). *Family Policy Bulletin No. 6*. London: Family Policy Studies Centre.

Feil, N. (1989). Validation: an empathic approach to the care of dementia. *Clinical Gerontologist*, **8**, 89–94.

Feil, N. (1992). Validation therapy with late-onset dementia populations. In G. Jones & B.M.L. Miesen (Eds), *Caregiving in Dementia* (pp. 199–218). London: Routledge.

Foster, E.M., Kay, D.W.K. & Bergmann, K. (1976). The characteristics of old people receiving and needing domiciliary services: the relevance of psychiatric diagnosis. *Age and Ageing*, **5**, 245–251.

Fries, B.E. & Cooney, L.M. (1985). Resource utilisation groups: a patient classification for long term care. *Medical Care*, **23**, 100–122.

Fries, B.E., Schneider, D.P., Foley, W.J. et al. (1994). Refining a case mix measure for nursing homes: resource utilisation groups (RUG-III). *Medical Care*, **32**, 668–685.

Gilleard, C.J. (1987). Influence of emotional distress among supporters on the outcome of psychogeriatric daycare. *British Journal of Psychiatry*, **150**, 219–223.

Graftstrom, M., Fratiglioni, L., Sandman, P.O. & Winblad, B. (1992). Health and social consequences for relatives of demented and non-demented elderly: a population based study. *Journal of Clinical Epidemiology*, **45**, 861–870.

Henwood, M. & Wicks, M. (1984). *The Forgotten Army: Family Care and Elderly People*. London: Family Policy Studies Centre.

Hirsch, C.H., Davies, H.D., Boatwright, F. & Ochango, G. (1993). Effects of a nursing home respite admission on veterans with advanced dementia. *Gerontologist*, **23**, 523–528.

HMSO (1990). *NHS and Community Care Act 1990*. London: HMSO.

Jack, R. (1993). Care management and social services: welfare or trade fair? *Generations Review*, **2**, 4–6.

Johnston, M., Wakeling, A., Graham, N. & Stokes, F. (1987). Cognitive impairment, emotional disorder and length of stay of elderly patients in a district hospital. *British Journal of Medical Psychology*, **60**, 133–139.

Kay, D.W.K., Bergmann, K., Foster, E., McKechnie, A. & Roth, M. (1970). Mental illness and hospital usage in the elderly. *Comprehensive Psychiatry*, **11**, 26–35.

Kitwood, T. (1993). Toward a theory of dementia care: the interpersonal process. *Ageing and Society*, **13**, 51–67.

Laing, W. (1991). *Empowering the Elderly: Direct Consumer Funding of Care Services*. London: Institute of Economic Affairs, Health and Welfare Unit.

Lawton, M.P., Brody, E.M. & Saperstein, A.R. (1989). A controlled study of respite service for caregivers of Alzheimer's patients. *Gerontologist*, **29**, 8–16.

Levin, E., Sinclair, I. & Gorbach, P. (1986). The effectiveness of home help services with confused people and their families. *Research Policy and Planning*, **3**, 1–7.

Levin, E., Moriarty, J. & Gorbach, P. (1994). *Better for the Break*. London: HMSO.

Lewis, P.A., Dunn, R.B., Vetter, N.J. (1994). NHS and Community Care Act 1990 and discharges from hospital to private residential and nursing homes. *British Medical Journal*, **309**, 28–29.

Liptzin, B., Grob, M.C., Eisen, S.V. (1988). Family burden of demented and depressed elderly psychiatric inpatients. *Gerontologist*, **28**, 397–401.

Meyers, A.R. & Master, R.J. (1989). Managed care for high risk populations. *Journal of Ageing and Social Policy*, **1**, 197–215.

Morris, R., Morris, L.W. & Britton, P.G. (1988). Factors affecting the wellbeing of the caregivers of dementia sufferers. *British Journal of Psychiatry*, **153**, 147–156.

Morycz, R.K. (1985). Caregiver strain and the desire to institutionalize family members with Alzheimer's disease. *Research on Aging*, **7**, 329–362.

O'Connor, D.W., Pollitt, P.A., Hyde, J.B., Brook, C.P.B. & Roth, M. (1988). Do general practitioners miss dementia in elderly patients? *British Medical Journal*, **297**, 1107–1110.

O'Connor, D.W., Pollitt, P.A., Brook, C.P.B. & Reiss, B.B. (1989). The distribution of services to demented elderly people living in the community. *International Journal of Geriatric Psychiatry*, **4**, 339–344.

O'Connor, D.W., Pollitt, P.A., Roth, M., Brook, C.P.B. & Reiss, B.B. (1990). Problems reported by relatives in a community study of clinical dementia and morbidity. *British Journal of Psychiatry*, **156**, 835–841.

O'Connor, D.W., Pollitt, P.A., Brook, C.P.B., Reiss, B.B. & Roth, M. (1991). Does early intervention reduce the number of elderly people with dementia admitted to institutions for long term care? *British Medical Journal*, **302**, 871–875.

Opit, L. & Pahl, J. (1993). Institutional care for elderly people: can we predict admissions? *Research Policy and Planning*, **10**, 2–5.

Panella, J., Littiston, B.A. & Brush, H.A. (1984). Day care for dementia patients: an analysis of a four-year program. *Journal of the American Geriatrics Society*, **32**, 883–886.

Rabins, P.V., Fitting, M.D., Eastham, J. & Zabora, J. (1990). Emotional adaptation over time in caregivers for chronically ill elderly people. *Age and Ageing*, **19**, 185–190.

Reifler, B.V., Cox, G.B. & Hanley, R.S. (1981). Problems of the mentally ill elderly as perceived by patients, family and clinicians. *Gerontologist*, **21**, 165–170.

Seltzer, B., Rheaume, Y., Volicer, L. et al. (1988). The short term effects of in-hospital respite on the patient with Alzheimer's disease. *Gerontologist*, **28**, 121–124.

Social Services Inspectorate (1992). *Care Management and Assessment: The Practitioners' Guide*. London: HMSO.

Thornton, P. & Tozer, R. (1994). *Involving Older People in Planning and Evaluating Community Care: A Review of Initiatives*. York: Social Policy Research Unit, University of York.

Townsend, P. (1981). The structured dependency of the elderly: a creation of social policy in the twentieth century. *Ageing and Society*, **1**, 5–28.

Turvey, T. & Toner, H. (1990). *An Evaluation of a Home Based Dementia Support Service*. Report No. 1. Fife: Alzheimer's Scotland Fife Dementia Service.

Walker, A. (1981). Towards a political economy of old age. *Ageing and Society*, **1**, 73–94.

Wells, Y.D., Jorm, A.F., Jordan, F. & Lefroy, R. (1990). Effects on caregivers of special day care programmes for dementia sufferers. *Australian and New Zealand Journal of Psychiatry*, **24**, 1–9.

Chapter 7

FAMILY CAREGIVING: RESEARCH AND CLINICAL INTERVENTION

Steven H. Zarit and Anne B. Edwards*

INTRODUCTION

Among the most dramatic demographic changes of the twentieth century is the increasing survival of people to old age. Old age was once a rare event, achieved by a very small proportion of each generation; now, reaching age 65, 75 and even 85 is commonplace and increasingly expected. This growth in the proportion of older people in the population includes many who are healthy and independent, but also an unprecedented number who need assistance. Help for disabled elderly persons is provided first and for the longest period of time by family members. They do this despite major changes in structure and roles of contemporary families that potentially limit the amount of assistance they can provide, such as increased participation of women in the workforce and smaller family size. While families have always assisted their elders, they are doing so now more often and for longer periods of time. Even in the Scandinavian countries, where public policies encouraged the development of formal service systems to free younger generations to participate fully in the workforce, family care continues to have a predominant and, as the population ages, an ever more important role in assisting elders (Thorslund, 1991).

As family caregiving has grown increasingly more frequent, it has emerged as a singularly challenging and often stressful event in the life span. Much of the research conducted on family caregiving has been concerned with identifying stresses of family care, as well as with factors which are associated with individual differences in the experience of stress. These

* Pennsylvania State University, Pennsylvania, USA

Psychological Problems of Ageing: Assessment, Treatment and Care. Edited by R.T. Woods.
© 1999 John Wiley & Sons Ltd.

studies form a strong foundation for clinical intervention, as they identify potentially modifiable aspects of the situation. A smaller, but important, clinical research literature has identified promising approaches which can help families manage care of their elderly relatives more effectively and with less strain on themselves.

In the following sections, we shall review the demographic changes that have brought about the prominence of family caregiving, and which identify potential resources and limitations for families in meeting the challenge of caring for elderly relatives. We shall then examine research which documents the stresses associated with family caregiving and with individual differences in the experience of stress. Finally, we shall explore promising clinical interventions to assist caregiving families.

BASIC DEFINITIONS

Before proceeding to the literature, we want to offer a definition and suggest some boundaries to family caregiving. Caregiving can be defined by asking people to identify themselves as caregivers for an older relative, or by using an operational definition of caregiving, for example, that the family member provides help on a regular basis with at least one activity of daily living. These approaches can lead to different definitions of who is a caregiver (Blum, Kelly & Gatz, 1989). Some people providing daily help to an older person may not identify themselves as caregivers, while others who give little or no assistance may consider themselves to be caregivers.

For the purposes of this chapter, we define caregiving as interactions in which one family member is helping another on a regular (i.e. daily, or nearly so) basis with tasks that are necessary for independent living. Included are "instrumental" tasks, such as managing finances, transportation, shopping, cooking and housework, as well as "personal" tasks, such as bathing, dressing and toileting. In the case of disabilities involving dementia, the "care recipient" may also require some ongoing supervision. A relationship develops into caregiving when an older person becomes dependent on another's help to complete tasks and another family member (e.g. spouse or child) provides or arranges for this assistance. In other words, caregiving constitutes a change in ongoing patterns of exchange in response to a new disability, which results in one or more people providing regular help to the elder.

We distinguish this situation from family relationships where one person may feel emotionally or physically "burdened", and may even label the situation as "caregiving", but where interactions do not include providing regular assistance with daily living tasks. Caring for an elderly person emerges, as we describe later, from a context of ongoing family exchanges. Children provide tangible and emotional support to parents on an ongoing basis, and parents reciprocate in complementary ways. Likewise, an older married couple provide mutual, and often complementary, assistance to one another, for instance when sharing household tasks. These ordinary and routine exchanges may involve conflict and distress and, as the family ages, may come to be labelled by one or more of the involved parties as "caregiving". We have encountered instances where conflict between mother and daughter, which had been lifelong, is called "caregiving" by the daughter, now that her mother is older. The daughter may present herself as overburdened and emotionally drained by her mother's demands, although the character of their interactions has probably not changed much over the years.

These situations are important clinically, because they represent the ageing of ingrained family conflicts, but they should be carefully differentiated, both in research and in clinical settings, from those circumstances in which new dependencies have developed. Of course, new dependencies may re-awaken or intensify longstanding family problems. Nonetheless, we feel this distinction between longstanding and changing patterns of exchange is important and basic. In research, it allows us to identify how changes in the family result in new problems and stresses. Clinicians, in turn, will make more effective interventions if they differentiate between acute disruptions that may be amenable to practical interventions, and longstanding relationship problems that may be highly resistant to change. Incorrectly calling an interaction "caregiving" can precipitously shift the power in the family, needlessly worsening the "care recipient's" well-being and access to resources.

This distinction between usual family exchanges and caregiving can, of course, sometimes be difficult to make. Some patterns of help may develop gradually over a period of many years, such as when a parent becomes dependent on a child for assistance with managing finances. A spouse may gradually take over a few household tasks in response to increasing disability. By later life, most couples probably have some specialization of functioning that developed in response to minor disabilities, such as when a husband opens jars for a wife who has arthritis in her shoulder and fingers. When there is no dramatic change or event, these situations may go on for many years, with the "caregiver" making gradual accommodations to the other person's disability, and perhaps never labelling him/herself as "caregiver".

As this discussion implies, people will identify themselves as "caregivers" in different ways, and in response to different situations. In fact, identification of oneself as a "caregiver" and socialization into the role may be a major transition for families, with implications for how they subsequently adapt to the demands placed on them (Aneshensel et al., 1995). For this chapter, we shall limit our discussion to caring for people who need regular assistance with daily living tasks, recognizing that some of the carers may not identify themselves as such, and that some people nominating themselves as caregivers may not meet this definition.

Within the definition of caregiver lies a distinction between "primary" and "secondary" caregivers. In most caregiving situations, one family member assumes the major responsibility for assisting a disabled elder. When the elder lives with a relative, either a spouse, child or other relative, that person almost always takes on most caregiving activities. When an elder lives alone, proximity and kin relationship usually determine who takes on the main caregiving role, with daughters being most likely to assume this responsibility (Stone, Cafferata & Sangl, 1987). Other family members may assist the primary caregiver by providing occasional relief or by taking the responsibility for specific tasks, such as when a son handles his mother's finances, while her daughter manages daily care needs. Most of what is known about caregiving to date concerns primary caregivers. How patterns of care develop, change and become differentiated over time, as well as the potential for conflict between primary and secondary caregivers, are important but relatively overlooked issues.

THE DEMOGRAPHICS OF CAREGIVING

Caring for a dependent elderly person has become a focus of research as well as a salient issue for individuals primarily as a result of the major demographic changes that have taken place in the industrialized world. The first of these changes concerns life expectancy. In the USA, for example, life expectancy at birth was 47 years in 1900. This figure increased rapidly throughout the twentieth century, and in 1989 life expectancy at birth had reached an all-time high of 75.3 years (US Bureau of the Census, 1992b). From 1950 to 1980, the rate of increase of the elderly population was greater than that of the entire US population. During this period, the population of those people 75 years or older increased at a more rapid pace than that of those aged 65–74 (Doty, Liu & Wiener, 1985). This makes the very old the fastest-growing segment of the US population.

The European Community has experienced similar ageing of its population. In 1960, the average life expectancy for someone in the European Community at birth was 67.6 years for men and 73.4 years for women. By 1990, men could expect to live 73.9 years, and women 76.4 years

(Eurostat, 1993b). If these trends increase, there will be twice as many people over the age of 60 living in the European Community in 2020 as there were in 1960 (Eurostat, 1993a).

Fertility rates have also had considerable influence on the overall age structure of the population. There has been an overall decline in birth rates in the industrialized countries, thereby leading to an even greater relative increase in the elderly. Fluctuations within this overall trend, baby booms and busts, create transitional periods with unusual balances between cohorts. In the USA, for example, the 1920s saw a decline in the birth rate, and birth rates remained low throughout the Depression and the Second World War. The cohorts born during this time are entering old age now. So, although we are seeing a steady increase in the elderly population now, the most dramatic increase will not occur until after 2011, when the baby boom generation begins to reach age 65 (US Bureau of the Census, 1992b). The population of people 65–84 years of age is expected to grow 73% between 2010 and 2030, and after 2030 the population over age 85 is expected to double (US Bureau of the Census, 1992a). The dramatic ageing of the population will have far-reaching effects, not only for the elderly themselves but for the population as a whole.

While many older people are healthier than those of earlier cohorts, significant numbers have chronic illnesses, and need assistance with everyday activities. This need for assistance is strongly associated with age. Among persons 65–69 years of age, only 9.3% needed help with at least one activity of daily living, while this figure rose to 45.4% for those over the age of 85 (US Bureau of the Census, 1990). Because more elderly people are living with disabilities due to chronic illness, more people are needed to care for their elderly relatives.

Using a probability sample drawn from Medicare records in the USA, Stone and her colleagues (Stone, Cafferata & Sangl, 1987) projected that approximately 2.2 million caregivers were providing unpaid care to 1.6 million non-institutionalized disabled elderly people with one or more activities of daily living (ADL) limitations. However, by combining the findings of a number of large surveys, Brody (1985) estimated that 5 million people were caring for their parents at any one point in time. This does not take into account the number of people caring for a spouse, which is the most frequent form of caregiving. In 1986, spouses constituted 44% of those providing assistance with at least one ADL to someone 65 years of age or older because of a health problem (US Bureau of the Census, 1990). Studies have shown that spouses are more likely than adult children to provide care at home (Soldo & Myllyuoma, 1983; Enright, 1991).

The increase in the number of people needed to care for an elderly relative has an especially high impact on women. Sixty-seven percent of those who provided assistance to someone in another household and 56% of those who provided assistance to someone in their household were women (US Bureau of the Census, 1990). Daughters are more likely to be the primary caregivers for impaired parents than are sons. When a daughter is the primary caregiver, male siblings provide much less additional care than female siblings, when proximity to the primary caregiver is constant (Brody et al., 1989). Even in networks where there is only one adult child to provide care, the participation of only males is about half that of only females (Coward & Dwyer, 1990). Within the spousal relationship, even though husbands and wives tend to spend similar amounts of time caring for their spouse, husbands receive more help from informal sources than do wives (Enright, 1991).

When taking into account the proportion of total caregiving time that is provided by informal caregivers, the importance of studying informal caregivers is fully illustrated. Less than 15% of all caregiving days in the community were provided by formal services (Doty, Liu & Wiener, 1985). Family members are still the primary source of care for the elderly.

CAREGIVING AT A DISTANCE

In addition to changes in the proportion of elderly in the population, some modern social changes are adding to the challenges and complexities of family caregiving. The migration of children away from their elderly parents is seen as a problem facing the elderly in the USA (Siegel, 1980; Soldo, 1980) as well as in the European Community (Hermanova, 1995). With increasing geographic mobility and smaller family size, this situation is occurring with growing frequency. In 1962, 28% of the elderly with a surviving child lived with a child. By 1979, that percentage had dropped to 18% (Crimmins & Ingegneri, 1990).

Children caring from a distance face special challenges. They may have difficulty obtaining accurate information about daily problems their parent faces, and deciding when an intervention is ncessary. While local resources may be available to help older people remain in their own homes, children living at some distance may find it hard to identify and monitor home help or other services. Sometimes, parents and children will disagree over the need for help. As an example, children may hire a helper, such as a homemaker, to provide some assistance in the home, only to have the parent dismiss this person.

When questions about parents' ability to remain in their own home are raised, children living at a distance may consider moving them to their own community, or into their own home. This decision is exceedingly difficult, because all of the available alternatives are likely to have drawbacks. Failure to relocate someone who needs help may result in serious injury or even death. Arranging for and monitoring help at a distance can be time-consuming and frustrating for children. On the other hand, moving parents from their long-term residence may take them away from friends and other supports. While they may be able to perform common daily activities, such as shopping, housework or even driving in a familiar setting, they may not be able to adjust to the move to a new community, and may lose some functional competencies. Children may unreasonably expect that disabled parents will be able to re-establish an independent lifestyle after a move, making new friends and initiating new activities, only to find that the parent has become increasingly dependent on them for social needs and other activities. Parents may even insist that they could go back to their homes again, increasing the feelings of tension and guilt in their children.

Another change in the family structure that could affect the lives of the elderly and their adult children alike is the increase in the proportion of one-child families. The proportion of one-child families has increased steadily and reached a high of 40% in the USA in the 1980s (Falbo, 1984). This means that many children are the sole family member available to provide help when their elderly parent needs assistance. Only children tend to feel more responsibility for their parents (Barnes, Given & Given, 1992), because they know that arrangements for the care of their parents rests on their shoulders. This knowledge can be beneficial. Adult children with siblings feel abandoned by other members of the family and have a negative reaction to caregiving to a greater extent than children with no siblings (Barnes, Given & Given, 1992). Caregivers' expectation of assistance by other family members shapes how well they adjust to the caregiving role. In the case of only children, the expectation of help from others is not there, which explains the lack of negative adjustment.

RESEARCH ON FAMILY CAREGIVING PROCESSES AND OUTCOMES

Models of caregiving stress

Caregiving for a disabled elder has been identified as one of the most stressful and disruptive events in the family life cycle. Many adverse and unwanted consequences have been identified. Caregiving can interfere with other aspects of one's life, such as when a daughter's providing care to an ailing mother interferes with her employment or takes time away from her husband or children. Many caregivers may experience strong negative emotions, such as anger and depression. Furthermore, these stresses are usually not short-term. Caregiving may persist for several years, presenting new and increasingly complex challenges for a family. Even events such as placement of the elder into an institution, or the elder's death, which are typically viewed as releasing caregivers from their burdens, present new, potentially disruptive stressors (Rosenthal & Dawson, 1991; Mullan, 1992; Zarit & Whitlatch, 1992).

We want to highlight from the outset that caregiving is a complex, multi-faceted process. There is no one pattern of caregiving or adaptation, neither are there distinct stages. Rather, caregiving is characterized by a great deal of individual variation at every point in the process. Families differ in their willingness and ability to take on this role, in their feelings of affection and obligation to the elder, and in the resources available to them for carrying out the role. Likewise, elders requiring help vary considerably in the type of their disability, their personality and past history of relationships with potential caregivers, and their willingness to accept help. Simple reductionist concepts, such as stages of caregiving, do not do justice to the wide variability of situations, neither can the processes and consequences of caregiving be captured by a single dimension of burden or other construct.

Perhaps the most critical point to emerge from research on family caregiving is that people adapt quite differently to similar situations. Feelings of distress or burden are influenced, but not dictated, by characteristics of the elder's disease or disability; neither are they dictated by the type or amount of care required. Some family caregivers assisting an elder with severe disabilities report little or no problems or distress, while others who are caring for someone with modest degrees of disability indicate they are overwhelmed or burned out by the care they are giving (e.g. Zarit, Reever & Bach-Peterson, 1980). These individual patterns become further differentiated over time, as some caregivers adapt successfully to chronic, deteriorating conditions, while others become progressively more burdened (Townsend et al., 1989; Zarit, Todd & Zarit, 1986; Aneshensel et al., 1995).

To explore these individual differences, researchers have been guided by theories of stress and adaptation (e.g. Lazarus & Folkman, 1984; Pearlin & Schooler, 1978). A particularly useful approach, the Stress Process Model, has been developed by Pearlin and his associates (Pearlin et al., 1990;

Aneshensel et al., 1995), to guide their longitudinal investigation of family care of people with dementing illnesses. This model, which is shown in Figure 7.1, will be used to organize findings from the research literature. By identifying potentially important dimensions of the stress process, the model can also guide clinicians in conducting assessments of caregiving families.

While the particular components of the model are explored below, three concepts are critical for understanding the process of adaptation over time. First, Pearlin and colleagues propose that a pivotal feature of chronically stressful situations such as caregiving is the potential for stress proliferation, that is, for the effects of the stressors associated with caregiving to spill over into or interfere in other areas of a person's life. As an example, a caregiving daughter may find she is arguing more with her husband, who feels neglected because of the time she now spends with her parent. The second concept is stress containment. Containment refers to the processes by which caregivers can limit or decrease the effects of caregiving stressors by using resources available to them. Resources can be psychological (e.g. having high self-esteem or good coping strategies), social (e.g. receiving instrumental or emotional support), or economic (e.g. high income, financial assistance). Because of these resources, caregivers experience less distress or burden in their situation over time than do others who have inadequate resources. Third, Pearlin (1993; Aneshensel et al., 1995) has posited that caregiving can be undertood as a career which goes through a developmental process of learning or socialization, and key transitional events, such as initial diagnosis of the

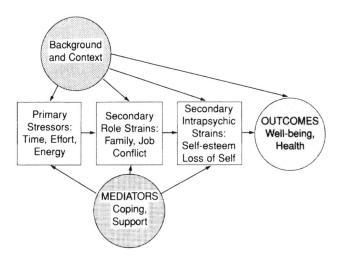

Figure 7.1 A model of caregiver stress. Adapted from Pearlin et al. (1990)

relative's illness and placement into an institution. A caregiver's adaptation, then, depends on stressors, resources and the particular point in his/her caregiving career.

Context of caregiving

Who is the caregiver?

As we have already seen, many different people may take on the role of caregiver. The kin relationship between caregiver and care recipient makes a difference in terms of feelings of commitment and obligation, and how difficult or distressing caregiving will be for them. In turn, feelings of commitment and obligation influence how long someone is willing to provide assistance. The closest relatives, spouses and perhaps also daughters, provide the most assistance for the longest period of time. A spouse caregiver almost always shares the same household with the care recipient, at least at the outset of caregiving, while daughters and other relatives are more likely to reside in separate households. When elders have a long-term, degenerative disorder, such as dementia, daughters often move them into their own household.

The available research describes committed caregivers who initially made the decision to become involved, and who remain deeply involved over time. Among this group, the amount of emotional distress experienced in comparable care circumstances differs according to their kin relationship to the care recipient. Typically, husbands caring for their wives report less emotional distress than wives caring for their husbands, even after controlling for severity of the elder's disease (Anthony-Bergstone, Zarit & Gatz, 1988; Schulz et al., 1993; Williamson & Schulz, 1990; Zarit & Whitlatch, 1992). Surprisingly, few differences are found between wives and daughters who are caregivers, once place of residence is controlled. That is, if wives are compared to daughters who share a household with the care recipient, they have similar commitments and feelings of emotional distress (Townsend et al., 1989; Goodman, Zarit & Steiner, 1994). In fact, daughters and wives appear strikingly similar in their commitment and feelings of obligation to the care recipient (Goodman, Zarit & Steiner, 1994). Surprisingly, kin relationship does not affect the likelihood of institutional placement or how long a caregiver keeps someone at home (Aneshensel, Pearlin & Shuler, 1993; Aneshensel et al., 1995). This is contrary to the expectation that spouses would be more likely to persist in the caregiving role than children. This lack of difference may be due to the fact that daughters who have become caregivers are a select group who made a deliberate decision, while spouses are more clearly expected to do so. Because of the small number of sons providing primary caregiving, little systematic information is available on them. In addition, not much is known about various other family members who provide care, such as siblings and grandchildren.

Kin relationship, of course, encompasses dyads which vary considerably in their past history and quality of their relationship. Someone who had a good relationship with the care recipient (Williamson & Schulz, 1990), or who believes providing assistance reciprocates for help the care recipient gave earlier in life (Goodman, Zarit & Steiner, 1994), may experience less emotional distress in the caregiving role.

The idea of reciprocity is important when determining why someone would become the primary caregiver for an elderly relative. Reciprocity can be an important reason for the choice children make to care for their dependent parents. Children can feel indebted to their parents for the care they received and even for giving them life (Berman, 1987). Blau (1981) describes this indebtedness as an irredeemable obligation toward parents. This perceived obligation can promote feelings of guilt and frustration among adult child caregivers.

Intergenerational exchange

When examining patterns of exchange between adult children and their elderly parents, a number of factors can influence the support elderly parents receive. Children and parents who have consistent contact are more likely to give or receive support (Hogan, Eggebeen & Clogg, 1993). In addition, the more children an elderly person has, the more likely they are to receive support (Eggebeen, 1992). When elderly parents are asked who they would receive support from, children are chosen more often than any other family member (Hogan, Eggebeen & Clogg, 1993).

Even though the elderly choose to receive support from their children, there are factors that affect the likelihood of their receiving support. Using data from the National Survey of Families and Households, Eggebeen (1992) explored the differences in patterns of exchange between elderly Americans and their non-coresidential children by marital status and family structure. He found that the likelihood of elderly people receiving support from their children varies by marital status of the elder. Divorced parents are less likely than widowed parents to be receiving support from their children. In fact, divorced parents and those who are married have about the same chance of receiving support from their children (Eggebeen, 1992). This is distressing, because married older adults can receive informal support from their spouses, while the sole main source of support for divorced elders is their children. As the divorce rate increases, there will be more and more adult children with divorced elderly parents. This can have a large impact in the amount of help given to parents. In addition, divorced elderly people tend to be more disadvantaged than those who are married or widowed (Uhlenberg, 1990), so they are most likely to have the greatest need for support.

Culture and socioeconomic status

Culture and socioeconomic status affect how caregiving is carried out in many different ways. Ethnic groups differ in values and beliefs about the importance of caring for their elderly, and, indeed, in how they view ageing and disability (e.g. Lawton et al., 1992; Mintzer et al., 1992). For some groups, care of the person at home takes a priority over everything else, while other groups are more likely to view professional help in a positive light.

Socioeconomic status (SES), or social class, probably has a complex relationship to the caregiving process. It would be generally expected that lower SES people would have fewer economic resources and therefore have more of the burden of care on themselves. In the USA, however, low-income caregivers often have greater access to publicly supported programmes than middle-class families, thus partly offsetting disadvantages due to their low income. They may also be more likely to be able to obtain help from an extended family and friendship network.

Primary stressors

Pearlin et al. (1990) have distinguished between primary stressors and secondary strains of caregiving. Primary stressors are those events and actions directly related to the elder's disability and to providing assistance. They include the need for assistance with activities of daily living and emotional or behavioural problems of the care recipient. By contrast, secondary strains involve changes in caregivers' lives that result from their efforts to respond to or manage primary care tasks. This distinction is useful, because it separates the events and activities specifically related to an elder's illness or disability from the ramifications those events may have for caregivers' lives. By making this distinction, clinicians can more effectively pinpoint the main sources of stress, and target their interventions appropriately.

The stress process model further differentiates between objective and subjective dimensions of primary stressors. Objective dimensions are the actual activities the caregiver engages in (e.g. assisting with dressing, responding to agitated or depressed behaviour). Subjective dimensions refer to the immediate impact these stressors have on the caregiver. This distinction reflects that the meaning or value that someone places on a specific event is a better predictor of its impact than an objective measure of the stressor (Lazarus & Folkman, 1984; Pearlin & Schooler, 1978).

Two distinct approaches have been used to evaluate the subjective impact of stressors. The first, drawn from the work of Lazarus & Folkman (1984), assesses how caregivers subjectively evaluate the stressfulness of specific caregiving events (e.g. Kinney & Stephens, 1989; Teri et al., 1992; Zarit, Todd & Zarit, 1986). Taking a somewhat different, though complementary approach, Pearlin and colleagues (Pearlin et al., 1990; Aneshensel et al., 1995) have developed three indicators which reflect the main subjective effects of caregiving. These primary subjective stressors are: role overload, that is, becoming physically or emotionally depleted by one's caregiving activities; role captivity, feeling trapped by one's responsibilities; and loss of the relationship with the other person. This last dimension is particularly pertinent for progressive disorders such as dementia. It reflects the sense of loss the caregiver feels for the person and what was valued in their relationship.

Primary objective stressors have positive but surprisingly small associations with outcome measures, such as depression or emotional distress. Assisting an elder with activities of daily living, including bathing, dressing and feeding, has generally not been found to be related to poor outcomes. Rather, care recipients who have frequent behavioural or emotional problems place more stress on caregivers (Aneshensel et al., 1995; Pruchno & Resch, 1989). When diagnosis is considered, caring for someone with a dementia or with another chronic mental disorder is generally much more difficult than assisting someone with physical care needs but few or no emotional or behaviour problems (Birkel, 1987; Pearson, Verma & Nellett, 1988).

Caregivers also rate behavioural and emotional problems as subjectively more distressing or stressful for them (Teri et al., 1992; Haley, Brown & Levine, 1987). Agitated and repetitive behaviours in dementia are generally rated as the most stressful. Teri and colleagues note that depressive behaviours, such as when the care recipient may cry or talk about dying, are also very problematic for families. Although clinical lore suggests that caregivers are often overwhelmed by dealing with care recipient's incontinence, this is not always the case. On average, incontinence is less stressful for caregivers than behavioural or emotional disturbances.

A much stronger relationship, with outcomes such as health and wellbeing, emerges when subjective primary stressors are added to the objective measures (Aneshensel, Pearlin & Schuler, 1993; Aneshensel et al., 1995). In particular, role overload and role captivity are important predictors, both in cross-sectional and longitudinal analyses, of how much distress caregivers experience. In other words, increases in role overload and role captivity result in greater emotional distress among caregivers, after controlling for level of objective stressors.

These findings indicate that knowing a specific event has occurred is not sufficient for determining if it is problematic or troublesome for a particular caregiver. The meaning the event has, as well as its subjective impact, has to be considered. A goal for clinical interventions is to assess what is specifically stressful about a situation, event or behaviour, and whether caregivers experience physical or emotional overload in response to the care demands placed on them. Clinicians who look only at caregiving activities and not their subjective impact will design interventions that miss the mark, and which do not relieve caregivers in the areas where they are most stressed.

Secondary role strains

Much of the media attention given to family caregiving has focused on its potential to disrupt other areas of the person's life, particularly to interfere with work, or with the caregiver's marital relationship. There is evidence of stress proliferation into these areas but, as with primary stressors, considerable individual differences are found. We shall discuss three specific role strains: family conflict, disruption of work and disruption of leisure and social activities.

Family conflict

Conflict with other family members over caregiving is quite common (Brody et al., 1989). Studies have begun documenting the types and frequency of family conflict. Using a sample of caregivers of dementia patients, Semple (1992) identified three dimensions of family conflict: over definitions of the elder's illness and how to provide care; over how and how much the family assists the care recipient; and over how they treat and assist the caregiver. All three types of family conflict are more commonly reported by adult children than spouse caregivers. Family conflict generally is associated with poorer outcomes, specifically feelings of depression and anger (Semple, 1992; Aneshensel et al., 1995; MaloneBeach & Zarit, 1995).

Investigating the specific daily interactions between the primary caregiver and other family members, MaloneBeach & Zarit (1995) found that giving advice and information was generally experienced as stressful. Providing information is usually viewed as a type of social support. These findings, however, suggest that relatives may be giving advice but not listening to the primary caregiver or finding out what is really needed in the situation.

When daughters are the primary caregivers, they may experience conflict with their sisters (Brody et al., 1989; Suitor & Pillemer, 1993). In turn, the sisters of caregiving daughters may feel guilty about not doing more (Brody et al., 1989). A caregiving daughter is more likely to feel support from her husband or from friends than from a sibling (Suitor & Pillemer, 1993; Brody et al., 1992).

Family tension and conflict can certainly antedate caregiving. Caregiving can also awaken or intensify longstanding family conflicts between parent and child or among siblings. Using longitudinal data that controls for prior levels of family conflict, Aneshensel et al. (1995) have also found that increases in primary stressors (particularly subjective stressors, such as role overload and role captivity) lead to increased levels of family conflict. In other words, there is a proliferation of stress whereby a worsening in basic elements of the care situation are associated with exacerbations of family tensions.

These findings have been drawn from long-term caregiving situations. There are many acute crises during which families make critical decisions, such as making decisions about a medical treatment, arranging for care following a hospitalization, or around death and dying. We know less about conflict that can emerge in short-term situations, such as when the older person must go to the hospital. Anecdotally, however, family members may frequently disagree with decisions, or may second-guess or undercut the primary caregiver. Transfer of assets, whether during the old person's life or afterwards, is, of course, another common source of family conflict.

A further source of family tensions is when caregiving affects the marital relationship. In a comparison of couples with and without an elderly parent with Alzheimer's disease, Creasey et al. (1990) found that wives with a parent with Alzheimer's disease tended to have a more negative relationship with their husbands than wives with a healthy parent. Husbands who had a parent with Alzheimer's disease did not experience comparable tensions. When Adamson et al. (1992) tested a model to find what aspects of the caregiving situation were associated with the marital relationship, they found that depression of the elder and caregiver burden were directly associated with marital happiness. Other variables, such as spouse burden and relationship closeness, affected marital happiness through their impact on caregiver burden. The primary caregiver is at greater risk than his/her spouse for marital conflict.

Disruption of work

A form of secondary role strain that is becoming a common concern is that of employment. Research on working caregivers has drawn from theories that address how people acclimate to the roles they acquire. Goode (1960) introduced the concept of role strain, or the difficulty in meeting the demands of multiple roles. In this view, role strain is seen as normal and even inevitable; therefore the task for everyone is to discover ways to reduce this strain.

Other theorists, however, have proposed that occupying more than one role simultaneously can be beneficial (Sieber, 1974). Marks (1977) took this idea one step further by trying to explain why some people have more than enough energy to meet the demands of all their roles. He proposed that an additional role may actually generate energy which can be used to complete the demands of other roles.

Role theories have been most commonly used to explain interactions between the roles of parent to a dependent child and that of worker. Recently, these theories have been applied to situations where someone is caring for a dependent adult and working. Within the caregiving literature, the competing commitment perspective conceptualizes that the other roles of caregivers are further demands on the caregivers' time. This perspective focuses on the time dimension of the conflicts among multiple roles and corresponds to the concept of "role overload" found in the role theory literature (Stoller & Pugliesi, 1989).

Workers caring for an elderly relative do face a challenge. In a study of caregiving women in different age groups, middle-aged women, the group that has the highest proportion of workers, had the strongest sense of responsibility concerning caregiving (Brody et al., 1983). In fact, when studying mothers and their daughter caregivers, Brody & Schoonover (1986) found that the mothers received the same amount of help whether their daughters worked or not.

Reports of strain are common among working caregivers (Scharlach & Boyd, 1989; Mutschler, 1994). With this finding comes the question of what contributes to that strain. The four main predictors of conflict between work and caregiving are: the elderly family member's emotional health; the number of caregiving tasks performed by the caregiver; the presence of children in the caregiver's residence; and having caregiving responsibilities when beginning the current job (Gibeau & Anastas, 1989).

In addition, sociodemographic variables such as the employee's gender, marital status, household income, job status, occupation, and flexibility of work schedule are related to employees' levels of absenteeism and stress (Neal et al., 1990). Other studies have found that the severity of disability of the elderly relative and the intensity of the caregiving responsibilities are related to work and caregiving conflict (Gibeau & Anastas, 1989).

Other factors need to be considered in addition to whether or not a caregiver is working. The type of occupation has an effect on the strain that caregivers experience as well. From information in the Survey of Informal Caregivers which was part of the 1982 US National Long Term Care Survey, Mutschler (1994) reports that production workers have less opportunity to adjust their work and care demands than do workers in executive, sales or clerical positions.

The effects of caring for an elderly relative have significant consequences in the workplace. A sizable number of caregivers leave their jobs within three months after becoming a caregiver (Franklin, Ames & King, 1994). Many workers generally try to rearrange their schedules or reduce their hours, rather than giving up their job (Mutschler, 1994). There are many different factors that contribute to the decision or need to leave a job because of caregiving responsibilities. Caregivers who leave their jobs or reduce their work hours tend to have relatives who have more severe disabilities (Brody et al., 1987; Stone & Short, 1990) and have faced work constraints for a longer period of time (Mutschler, 1994).

Workers express interest in work benefits that are designed to make work and caregiving easier. Benefits that generate the most interest are respite care, flexible work time, reduced hours without reduced benefits, adult day care, and job sharing. Caregivers using formal services understand that the availability of those services is critical if they are to maintain their employment and meet their family member's need for care (Gibeau & Anastas, 1989).

Disruption of leisure and social activities

Caregivers, and people in general, occupy many roles whether they work or not. Even the roles that caregivers take on when they participate in leisure or social activities can play an important part in the stress process of a caregiver. One of the most frequent consequences of caring for a frail elder is having to give up or restrict social activities (Horowitz, 1985; George & Gwyther, 1986). Social and leisure activities are closely linked to social support and, as a result, there are not many research studies which look at social activities exclusively.

In the first study devoted to limitations of social activities, Miller & Montgomery (1990) examined data from the 1982 National Long Term Care Survey. They found that caregivers who report social activity limitations also report greater objective and subjective time and task demands than those who report no limitations in social activities. When the severity of the elders' impairment was controlled for, the subjective appraisal of the nature of providing care was more important than objective care demands in predicting limitations in social activities. These results indicate that those people who perceive their caregiving situation as demanding may limit their social activities and lose a vital source of social support.

Secondary intrapsychic strain

One of the unique dimensions of the stress process model is the concept of "secondary intrapsychic strain". This concept captures an important feature of caregiving that has been hinted at in anecdotal accounts, namely, the tendency for caregivers to become so immersed in their role that they lose their sense of self. As caregiving becomes an all-consuming process, erosion of self-concept can occur, exacerbating the caregiver's overall well-being and hastening the breakdown of care arrangements (Skaff & Pearlin, 1992; Aneshensel et al., 1995).

Caregiving may also contribute in positive ways to self-concept. Caregivers may feel they are successfully and competently discharging an important obligation and they may feel they have gained some valuable experiences from doing so (Lawton et al., 1989). These positive attributions appear to be very important for many caregivers, but do not result in significant containment of stress over time (Aneshensel et al., 1995).

Modifiers of stress

We have emphasized from the outset that there is considerable variability in the outcomes of the chronic stressors of caregiving. A major source of these individual differences is the resources people have and use. Social support and coping are the most widely recognized and studied modifiers of caregiving stress. A related concept, one's sense of mastery or control, also contributes to adaptation in important ways.

Implicit in the concept of modifying variables is that people are not passive or helpless in the face of stress. Rather, they make active attempts to control, modify and understand the events with which they are confronted. There is a dynamic relation between stressors and resources, by which the use of effective approaches may lessen the impact of stressors and even how often they occur. Ineffective strategies, by contrast, can further aggravate the situation. We also believe that these resources are not fixed or immutable like traits. Instead, resources may become depleted over the course of a long period of chronic stress, or may become augmented, as caregivers learn new strategies for coping or seek out new sources of support (Pearlin & Skaff, 1995).

Social support

Social support is perhaps the most important modifying variable for family caregivers. In the face of problems that frustrate individual efforts at coping, as is often the case in chronic disease, social support can be an important source of help to caregivers. Supportive relationships can lessen their frustration and provide some relief from the ongoing pressures of caregiving (Hansson & Carpenter, 1994).

Social support has multiple dimensions, and has been studied in many different ways. For the sake of simplicity, we will emphasize two major categories of social support: instrumental support, or actual assistance in performing certain tasks, and emotional support, the extent to which other people reflect positive feelings to the caregiver. We shall consider support provided by informal sources, namely, family, friends or volunteers, and from formal or paid sources.

The idea that social support from family and friends decreases the effects of stress is widely held. Benefits have been found for both mental and physical health. Harper & Lund (1990) report that perceived social support was related to lower subjective burden among wives, husbands and daughters of dementia patients. Clipp & George (1990) report that caregivers who have high, stable support are less likely to experience a decline in their own health over time. Similarly, Kiecolt-Glaser and her colleagues (Kiecolt-Glaser et al., 1991) found that social support buffered the effects of chronic stress on the immune systems of spousal caregivers of Alzheimer's patients. Despite these generally positive findings, other studies have reported that social support has no benefits (e.g. Cosette & Lévesque, 1993; Stommel, Given & Given, 1990).

One reason for these discrepancies may be that studies have assessed different types of social support. Another source of differences may be that involvement with family and friends, but particularly family, can be a source of both support and conflict (e.g. Suitor & Pillemer, 1993; MaloneBeach & Zarit, 1995).

The effects of formal support are less clear-cut. Many caregivers in large-scale studies report using little or no formal help (e.g. Mullan, 1993; Stone, Cafferata & Sangl, 1987). Caregivers most in need of formal assistance may, paradoxically, be least likely to obtain help. Mullan (1993), for example, found that caregivers who were depressed were less likely to use formal services over time than non-depressed caregivers. Another complicating factor is that many family caregivers delay use of formal services until the situation has become critical. Noelker & Bass (1989) found that high levels of impairment among care recipients and declining health among caregivers predicted use of formal services. Similarly, many caregivers of dementia patients delay use of adult day care until late in the disease, when the benefits of day programmes are limited (Zarit et al., 1994). If formal services are introduced only when caregiving is breaking down, families may not gain the kind of relief intended by the programme.

Another complicating factor is how well formal and informal sources of assistance interface. Noelker & Bass (1989) suggest a framework for viewing the type of coordination of formal and informal help. They propose five patterns: kin independence, where the family provides all assistance; formal service specialization, in which agencies perform one or more tasks exclusively, while families assist with other tasks by themselves or in conjunction with agencies; dual specialization, where families and agencies assist with different tasks; supplementation, where agencies assist with tasks that are also provided by the family; and substitution, where agencies take over all tasks previously provided by the family. The pattern of interface may be related to how effectively formal services help caregivers. Some patterns of interface may be more adaptive at different points in a caregiver's career or for carrying out certain caregiving tasks, or some caregivers may do better with one type of interface than another. Formal help with bathing, for example, may be particularly helpful for many caregivers who do not have the strength or flexibility to assist a disabled elder in that task.

How informal and formal helpers interact with one another may be a critical factor in how much relief caregivers experience. Although caregivers generally view formal service providers as helpful, they often complain that services are not flexible or suited to their needs (MaloneBeach, Zarit & Spore, 1992). Agencies may take away caregivers' sense of control, for example, by not explaining what services the family is eligible for, or by not allowing families to make choices about the type and timing of services.

Coping

Coping represents the responses people make to stressors to avoid their harmful consequences (Pearlin & Schooler, 1978). Most research on coping has identified three broad categories of responses (e.g. Lazarus & Folkman, 1984; Pearlin & Skaff, 1995). Problem-focused coping includes strategies which are focused on management of the stressors or the situation which gave rise to them. Cognitive coping, in turn, represents efforts to manage the meaning of the stressful situation, for instance, relabelling a difficult problem as a learning experience. Finally, emotion-focused coping involves management of the symptoms of stress.

It has generally been reported that cognitive coping and problem solving are related to lower distress and emotion-focused coping to higher distress (e.g. Haley et al., 1987; Quayhagen & Quayhagen, 1988; Vitaliano et al., 1991). Clinical reports also emphasize that learning to manage stressors more effectively is helpful (e.g. Zarit, Orr & Zarit, 1985). The efficacy of a coping strategy, however, may depend to an extent on the nature of the stressor. When stressors are not easily modifiable, as is the case for some aspects of caregiving, then strategies which manage the meaning or consequences of these events may be more productive (Pearlin & Skaff, 1995). It is also important to consider that stressors and coping have a reciprocal relation. Stressors evoke coping responses, but effective efforts at management may lower the rate at which stressors occur. Ineffective coping, in turn, can lead to exacerbations of behavioural and emotional problems. As an example, confronting a dementia patient who asks to see her long-deceased mother is likely to make her more agitated and to increase the frequency of her request. By contrast, comforting her and reminiscing about her mother can be calming, and can lead to a reduction in the frequency of this behaviour.

Bledin and associates (Bledin et al., 1990) have proposed an intriguing link between expressed emotion (EE) and poor coping. EE refers to communication of negative emotions in speech and verbal behaviour, such as critical comments, hostility and the absence of warmth. EE has been found to be an important predictor of outcomes in schizophrenia. Bledin and associates found that higher rates of negative emotions were related to poor coping strategies among daughters who were caring for a parent with dementia. In turn, EE and poorer coping were associated with greater emotional strain. High levels of EE have also been reported to be associated with less frequent use of strategies to manage the meaning of stressors by caregivers (Vitaliano et al., 1989).

Mastery or control

A third resource, which is more abstract than social support or coping, is the sense that people have control over the events in their lives. Feelings of control have been found to be effective buffers for a variety of stressors

(Cohen & Edwards, 1989) and an important contributor to well-being and health of elderly in many different situations (Rodin, 1986). Using a family systems perspective, Boss and colleagues (Boss et al., 1990) report that greater ambiguity about family boundaries and mastery predicted depression among caregivers of dementia patients. Mastery reduces stress proliferation over time and may result in better adaptation following key transitions, such as placement in a nursing home (Aneshensel et al., 1995). As noted earlier, feelings of mastery or control may be important determinants of whether or not caregivers use and get relief from formal services (MaloneBeach, Zarit & Spore, 1992).

Outcomes of caregiving

Outcomes represent the effects caregiving has on well-being. There is considerable evidence that caregiving is associated with negative mental health consequences, particularly elevated rates of depression (e.g. Gallagher et al., 1989; Schulz, Visintainer & Williamson, 1990; Wright, Clipp & George, 1993). Rates of depression symptoms are high when caregivers are compared with non-caregiving samples who are similar in age and gender (e.g. Anthony-Bergstone, Zarit & Gatz, 1988; Jutras & Lavoie, 1995). Depression and other problems are generally lower among caregivers of physically impaired compared to cognitively impaired older people (Birkel, 1987; Tennstedt, Cafferata & Sullivan, 1992). Caregivers sharing a household with the care recipient are more likely than others to experience depressive and other mental health symptoms. Though most research has focused on depression, feelings of anger may be a particularly important dimension (Anthony-Bergstone, Zarit & Gatz, 1988).

Evidence is less clear concerning changes in health. While some studies have identified differences in health between caregivers and non-caregivers, other research has found no difference (e.g. Jutras & Lavoie, 1995; Schulz, Visintainer & Williamson, 1990; Wright, Clipp & George, 1993). The most intriguing evidence of the effects of caregiving on health is provided by a longitudinal investigation of immune system changes among spouse caregivers of Alzheimer's patients. Relative to age- and gender-matched controls, caregivers had more evidence of decrements in immune system functioning over time and also higher rates of infectious illness. Rates of depression were also higher among caregivers (Kiecolt-Glaser et al., 1991).

The question has also been raised about whether there might be positive outcomes or benefits of being a family caregiver (e.g. Lawton et al., 1989; Pearlin et al., 1990). Caregivers may, for example, gain a sense of having fulfilled an obligation or believe they have helped their relative in important ways. These positive benefits deserve more attention, because they may be at the heart of why some caregivers are willing to continue in this role, despite considerable personal sacrifice.

The timeframe in which outcomes are measured has often been compressed. In some cases, outcomes are measured simultaneously with predictors, or there is a short-term longitudinal design of six months or one year (but see Aneshensel et al. 1995, as an example of a long-term study of outcomes). Because caregiving often continues over several years, information on longer time spans is needed to examine more fully these various outcomes.

Longitudinal studies have found that caregivers vary a great deal over time in their functioning. Some caregivers decline in well-being, others improve, and some remain the same over time (e.g. Schulz et al., 1993; Townsend et al., 1989; Zarit, Todd & Zarit, 1986). As summarized earlier, some predictors of longitudinal outcomes have been identified. Decreases in well-being over time are related to higher rates of behavioral disturbances and proliferation of stress into other roles, while improved well-being is associated with better resources (Aneshensel et al., 1995).

The term "outcome" also has a larger meaning than "symptoms" or "burden". One way to conceptualize the outcome of caregiving is the extent to which families feel they have achieved their objectives, or feel that the sacrifices they made were balanced by the worth of what they were doing. Another type of outcome is the discontinuation of caregiving, such as when caregivers turn their relative over to another family member or to a nursing home. How caregivers make that decision and whether it represents a positive or negative outcome may very well be the most important issue in a caregiver's career. We shall turn to that issue in the following section.

Transitions in caregiving

Caregiving is a dynamic, evolving process which changes over time in relation to fluctuations in the elder's condition, depletion and/or augmentation of the caregiver's resources, and variability in secondary stressors which may impinge on the situation. The course of caregiving varies, depending on the nature of an elder's disability, if the condition is stable, improving or deteriorating. While there can be considerable heterogeneity, three important transitions affect caregivers in critical ways: entry into the role; placement of the elder into an institution; and bereavement (Aneshensel et al., 1995). We do not imply that these transitions form a series of ordered stages. In fact, many caregivers may never have to place their relative into an institution. There will also be other transitions during the caregiving career, around which families reorganize and rethink their involvement. These three transitions, however, are particularly pivotal points for many caregivers.

Entry into the caregiving role

Of these three transitions, we know the least about entry into the role. Who becomes a caregiver is, as we noted earlier, determined to an extent by social norms. Recognition of one's entry into the role may be sudden, such as when an elder has a stroke or fractures a hip. More typically, however, families respond to gradually growing needs as an elder's condition deteriorates slowly over time. Under those circumstances, some key event, such as if the older person wanders away from home and gets lost or is diagnosed with Alzheimer's disease, crystallizes the change in status and responsibilities of the caregiver.

Although we have little prospective or concurrent information on caregivers going through role acquisition, they are often quite explicit in retrospective reflections on what they would have liked during this process. In general, caregivers report that when they received a formal medical diagnosis of the elder's condition they were given little explanation of the meaning or consequences of the disorder (Aneshensel et al., 1995). They also received virtually no information about caregiving, potential formal resources they might utilize, or legal and financial implications. The one bit of advice likely to have been given is that they should consider nursing-home placement, an event which is usually many years away.

Institutionalization as a pivotal transition

In any chronic, debilitating condition, nursing-home placement is a compelling alternative to family care. Most families consider placement at least at some point during their caregiving career. Timing of placement is highly variable. For disorders with a predictable deteriorating course, such as dementia, placement can occur at any point, or not at all (Zarit, Orr & Zarit, 1985; Zarit, Todd & Zarit, 1986). Retrospective accounts identify the elder's behaviour as the main factor which led to placement. Prospective studies, however, have found that subjective indicators of stress, such as feeling trapped or burdened, are as important in leading to placement as the elder's behaviours or functional impairments (Zarit, Todd & Zarit, 1986; Aneshensel, Pearlin & Schuler, 1993).

Placement does not end the caregiving role, but represents a restructuring of it. While nursing-home placement reduces some stressors, there are also new problems and challenges. Studies following placement have found that most caregivers remain involved in the nursing home. They visit frequently, and typically assist with at least some activities of daily living (Aneshensel et al., 1995; Duncan & Morgan, 1994). While caregivers no longer have major responsibility for daily care, they now often interact with staff to ensure that their relative receives appropriate care. Learning how to interact with staff in an effective way and to accept differences in how staff provide care can be a major challenge. Because staff may change or rotate to different units, families feel there is no continuity in care or in their relationships with staff (Duncan & Morgan, 1994). Feeling they have lost control over the situation and concern that staff are not providing adequate care can be very distressing to families.

Another new stressor following placement, particularly in the USA, is the cost of care. Because nursing-home care is rarely covered by insurance, families can experience considerable economic strain. In particular, spouses of a nursing-home resident can expect to spend one half or more of their assets before government assistance programmes take over.

Nursing-home placement also places family caregivers, particularly spouses, in an ambiguous and undefined role. They are not widowed, but they also do not have the companionship and other benefits of being married. This ambiguous status has been described by Rosenthal & Dawson (1991) as "quasi-widowhood". Friends and even family do not know how to treat the person, or even how to talk about the placement. They may avoid the caregiver or avoid talking about what is meaningful to the caregiver. Caregivers may be excluded from social situations involving couples, because of the uncertainty surrounding their marital status. Caregivers may, in fact, receive more support and attention following the patient's death than after placement, because there are clear norms and expectations for behaviour toward people in mourning. Finally, many people experience guilt following placement, which contributes to their feelings of emotional distress.

Given the continuities in caregiving after placement and the new problems associated with it, it should not be surprising that caregivers continue to experience considerable emotional distress. Zarit & Whitlatch (1992; 1993) used a longitudinal panel of caregivers of dementia patients to compare people who placed their relative during a one-year time period with those who provided continuing care. Placement was associated with a decrease in primary subjective stressors, that is, feelings of burden directly associated with daily care routines, but there was little improvement in emotional well-being in the year following placement, compared to the group continuing care at home. In other words, caregivers who were depressed prior to placement often remained depressed following placement. Over a longer period of time, mood improves, but even up to four years following placement, about one quarter of caregivers experience significant emotional distress (Aneshensel et al., 1995).

Caregivers are often advised to place their relative out of the belief that that will lower the stress on them. As these results suggest, the benefits are far more limited, and placement typically leads to new stresses. These findings suggest that advice about placement should never be made casually. Furthermore, it is evident that caregivers need support following placement to help with the challenges of this transition.

Cessation of caregiving: bereavement and its aftermath

The final transition in caregiving is bereavement. Like placement, however, one's identity as a caregiver and the cumulative effects of caregiving do not end with the elder's death. Many caregivers continue feeling considerable emotional distress following their loss (Aneshensel et al., 1995; Bodnar & Kiecolt-Glaser, 1994). Over time, some recovery is evident, but even after an average of 20 months following the patient's death, former caregivers have more depressive symptoms than people from a non-caregiving control group (Bodnar & Kiecolt-Glaser, 1994).

CLINICAL INTERVENTIONS

As we have seen, caregiving places people at considerable risk with regard to their own health and emotional well-being. Although the elder's illness may be chronic and largely untreatable, many dimensions of the stress process are potentially modifiable. Clinical interventions which target these modifiable features of the caregiving situation can effectively lower stress on the family, while addressing the elder's care needs in optimal ways. These interventions can help caregivers manage their situation more effectively and make informed choices about providing care that reflect their values and those of their relative.

Our examination of clinical interventions will begin with assessment issues. Next, we shall consider clinical approaches for caregivers assisting a relative in the community. We shall conclude with a consideration of interventions around the key transition of nursing-home placement. Knight, Lutzky & Macofsky-Urban (1993) provide a meta-analysis of the effectiveness of interventions to reduce caregiver distress.

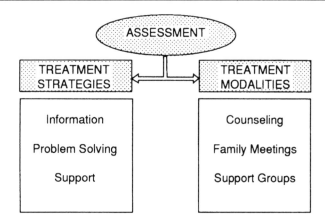

Figure 7.2 Treatment model for family caregivers

Assessment for interventions with caregivers

As with any clinical intervention, the foundation of a successful treatment is careful assessment. Assessment of caregivers is especially important because of the heterogeneity in stressors, resources, values and other factors that affect treatment. Interventions, of course, need to be tailored to a family's specific problems and concerns, rather than being based on theoretical notions of what caregivers ought to need.

A beginning point for assessment is often to clarify the medical diagnosis. The family may not have complete information about a diagnosis. In cases where the older person has not seen a geriatric specialist, there may be questions about whether or not the diagnostic process has been adequate. Because many potentially treatable disorders can cause symptoms that mimic dementia, it is imperative that these problems are ruled out before developing a caregiving intervention. Treatable components of other problems may also be overlooked, for instance, the use of vision and hearing aids in cases of sensory loss.

Assessment next proceeds to identify the unique stressors and resources in the caregiving situation. The stress process model, which was introduced earlier, can be used to guide the assessment process.

In identifying primary and secondary stressors, clinicians should keep in mind two important points. First, medical diagnosis is only the starting point. The problems facing a particular family can vary considerably. Even for disorders like dementia that follow a predictable course, there is a considerable variation in what types of problems families will encounter.

As an example, agitation is a common problem in the middle phases of dementing illnesses, but some patients exhibit little or no agitation. Rather than assuming that all dementia patients become agitated, the clinician needs to determine whether that problem is actually present.

A second consideration is that caregivers find problems stressful to varying degrees. As an example, one of us worked over a period of 10 years with a husband who was caring for his wife, who had dementia. During that time, the most stressful problem he faced was having to take over paying the household bills. Late in the disease, his wife became incontinent. While incontinence is a problem that many people regard as overwhelming, this caregiver did not find it stressful at all. Caregivers respond to any disability or problem in varied ways. Even potentially troubling and disturbing behaviour, such as thinking a deceased relative is alive, or becoming upset and agitated, may not bother or overwhelm some caregivers. The clinician, then, must assess which problems are stressful for this family, rather than assuming that everyone finds a particular problem difficult.

This principle applies to secondary stressors as well. As we discussed earlier, holding a job while giving care can add to one's stress, but it can also be an outlet which allows some caregivers to get away from the problems of their relative's illness. Similarly, reductions in social activities and even conflict with other family members may or may not be important to a particular caregiver. An important goal in assessment is to target those problems which are most distressing to a given caregiver, rather than to intervene for problems which someone else might find troubling.

In the process of identifying stressors, clinicians can also obtain information about resources and deficits in the situation, for example, coping strategies that are working well or poorly, or the absence of any coherent, effective way of managing the elder. Two particular problems are encountered in a small number of cases: abuse and suicidal ideation. Some caregivers are physically or psychologically abusive. In some instances abuse may occur out of mistaken ideas about care, for example, when a demented patient is restrained in bed as a way of controlling wandering. Suicidal thoughts are not uncommon, especially among husband caregivers. They may be considering ending their wife's life and their own. A standard clinical inquiry about suicidal and homicidal thoughts is warranted as part of one's assessment.

Treatment strategies

We have stressed throughout that family caregivers differ considerably from one another. Accordingly, clinical interventions require a flexible approach that addresses these individual differences. There are some general issues, however, that are likely to emerge in most caregiving situations. These issues include the need for information, improving management of stressors, and increasing emotional and instrumental support. Although there are many ways of addressing these issues, we shall present three clinical approaches that are especially promising: individual counseling, family counseling and support groups.

Education

A very important part of interventions with caregivers is identifying what information they have about their relative's illness, the implications of that illness, and their long-term options for care. At the point caregivers seek assistance, they often have very little information. Although their relative's condition is chronic and intractable, they may still be wondering about treatments that might reverse the disabilities. Some families may need help in deciding when it is appropriate to stop searching for a cure, so they can focus their energies on managing the illness.

When caring for someone with dementia or other mental health problems, caregivers often misinterpret behaviours in ways that lead to greater stress on themselves and on their relative. As an example, caregivers may believe that a dementia patient who asks the same question over and over again may be doing so to annoy or aggravate them. In turn, they will respond with anger or exasperation, which only increases the patient's agitation. In situations like that, it is important to teach families about the effects of their relative's illness and to help them interpret troubling behaviours as part of the illness.

In some instances, caregivers need to learn that their relative can no longer manage independently, or may not even be able to behave in rational or appropriate ways. Caregivers often have to develop an understanding that they must take charge of the situation. Helping them reach this point should be done carefully and with a great deal of support. It is not the role of clinicians to beat down a caregiver's denial, but rather to establish a non-judgemental relationship in which caregivers are able to explore their alternatives and develop a better understanding of their situation.

Another important issue for caregivers is to become familiar with legal and financial arrangements that affect the care of their relative. Legal issues, of course, vary considerably from one country to another. Among these issues are matters such as: getting legal authority to make decisions for a cognitively impaired or mentally disabled elder; deciding what to do about resuscitation and terminal-care decisions; and making financial arrangements for the elder's care. The latter is particularly important in the USA, where there is no government assistance for nursing homes until an elder has used up most personal resources.

Managing stressors

Caregivers often use inadequate or inappropriate methods for managing stressors, or they may not know how to respond at all. Disturbed behaviour or mood are especially problematic. Caregivers typically respond with confrontation or avoidance, neither of which is a particularly effective strategy. Training them in the use of simple behavioural management techniques can help bring a variety of everyday problems under control. These approaches have been useful for problems such as agitation, incontinence, wandering, not sleeping at night, and depressed mood. Solutions include changing the environmental cues that may trigger problem events, increasing activities as a way of heading off problems, and increasing reinforcement of appropriate behaviours (Zarit, Orr & Zarit, 1985).

The problems caused by secondary stressors often require extensive discussion and planning to come up with potential solutions. Solutions for conflict between the caregiver's work and the elder's needs, or for family disagreements, may emerge only after careful examination of options and alternatives.

These approaches to managing stressors requires a transition from educational efforts. Education helps caregivers understand what the patient cannot do, and why help is needed. This step aids the caregiver to accept the chronic illness and its consequences. Paradoxically, acceptance needs to lead to an active management approach. Many of the daily hassles of caregiving can be relieved through systematic examination of their antecedents and consequences, and alternative approaches for managing the situation. While giving up hope for their relative's recovery, caregivers learn to become more effective in their daily interactions.

Providing support

As discussed earlier, support includes both emotional and instrumental support. The clinician working with a caregiver is a very important source of emotional support. Although we have emphasized a didactic approach when working with caregivers, these interventions must always be made in the context of a supportive, non-judgemental relationship. Within the safety of this relationship, caregivers will be willing to take risks and try new behaviours that may improve their situation. The idea that caregivers can be assessed and then matched to services in one or two sessions is typically not realistic, because caregivers need more time to sort out their options and preferences, and to overcome feelings of hopelessness and helplessness that may have developed.

The clinician can also identify sources of emotional and instrumental support that may be available from family and friends. Caregivers sometimes isolate themselves unnecessarily. They may be afraid to ask for help, or may believe that other people should know what kind of help they need, volunteering it without their asking. Caregivers can sometimes be encouraged to reach out to these potential sources of support.

A major barrier for many families is use of formal services. While help from agencies can relieve caregivers of some of their burden, they are often reluctant to use services for a variety of realistic and unrealistic reasons. Examples of realistic reasons are: services may not be appropriate; service providers may be unreliable, such as when home health aids do not show up as scheduled; or services may be too expensive. Unrealistic reasons may include beliefs that it is wrong to use help, that the family should do everything by themselves, that no-one else can provide appropriate help, or that the elder will be harmed in some way by the formal service. Clinicians need to sort through the reasons why caregivers are reluctant to use help. In the case of realistic barriers, clinicians need to work with caregivers to identify alternatives. For unrealistic barriers, clinicians should encourage a process of testing out these beliefs and generating new ways of looking at the situation. This approach, which is drawn from cognitive-behavioural therapy (e.g. Beck et al., 1979), engages caregivers in an active, supportive process to identify and examine their beliefs.

Most caregivers are likely to think about nursing-home placement at least at some point in the course of their involvement. All too often, clinicians recommend placement precipitously, when other alternatives might be possible. It is important to proceed cautiously because, as we showed earlier, placement shifts, but does not relieve, caregiver distress. Placement can also be associated with negative effects for the older person. There is an increased risk of mortality following placement, even after controlling for health (Aneshensel, Pearlin & Schuler, 1993). Nursing homes also increase the rate of "excess disabilities" among older residents by restricting activity and taking away control over personal routines and activities (Zarit, 1980). In effect, placement represents a difficult choice which often must be made, but should never be suggested lightly, casually or without careful thought.

The role of clinicians is to give permission to caregivers to consider placement as one of the options available to them. In a collaborative way, clinician and family can explore the pros and cons of placement. Families need, however, to make this decision in their own way, consistent with their values and the resources available to them. There is no right time, neither should clinicians try to beat down the caregiver's resistance to placement. Some families may never place an elder, despite severe problems, while others will provide little or no informal care.

Clinical treatment approaches with caregivers

Counselling

A counselling relationship with the primary caregiver can be very useful. It can allow the caregiver to learn and try out new strategies and approaches for managing stressors and to consider alternatives and options for care. As noted above, the counselling relationship provides emotional support which may be pivotal in helping caregivers take a more active role in coping with their situation. Identifying possible formal services and overcoming barriers to their use is often a major focus. Counselling, of course, can address the caregiver's emotional distress. The focus often fluctuates between consideration of the caregiver's needs and trying new strategies for managing the situation.

Counselling can be brief or longer-term, depending on the complexity of the situation and the extent to which the elder's disability might bring up long-standing problems or concerns of the caregiver. Many caregivers benefit from a small number (five to ten) of sessions, which emphasize providing new information, trying out new approaches and obtaining additional support. Long-term counselling typically addresses pre-existing personal or interpersonal issues that the elder's disability has brought to the fore. As an example, disability in one member of a couple who were highly dependent on one another may result in very strong emotional reactions in the caregiver and considerable ambivalence about taking over activities previously performed by the spouse.

Family counselling

Family counselling is an especially powerful approach for working with caregivers. The family is potentially a major source of assistance. They can provide more flexible help than formal agencies. On the other hand, family conflict over caregiving can be a major source of distress to the primary caregiver. Family interventions which were designed to decrease conflict and increase instrumental and emotional support have proved to be a very effective way of lowering stress on the caregiver (Whitlatch, Zarit & von Eye, 1991; Mittelman et al., 1993).

Clinicians should plan for a family meeting carefully. It is important to learn in advance something about the family system (e.g. how the family solves problems, who is influential, what conflicts there are over caregiving, what long-standing conflicts there may be). Working collaboratively with the primary caregiver, the clinician plans who to invite. The timing of the meeting should occur at the point when caregivers have a good understanding of their situation, and when their efforts to manage stress more effectively would benefit from increased support from the family. Where to hold the meeting is another concern. We have found that family counselling often proceeds better in the caregiver's home, or in the home of another relative. Families are less defensive when they are on familiar ground, and may even be impressed by the clinician's commitment.

The family session recapitulates the process that primary caregivers have gone through. Typically, the session begins by examining what is known about the patient's condition and dispelling any misunderstandings about diagnosis or treatment. In cases of dementia, families may also benefit by asking questions about causes of the disease and learning more about why patients behave the way they do. Rather than lecturing, the clinician should be a resource who responds to questions from the family. When there is a consensus about the patient's situation, the focus can be turned to the caregiver. Caregivers can be asked what would help them. Some will be able to indicate what they would want, but others may need encouragement. (Preparation for asking for help would have taken place in individual sessions.) The family should be encouraged to problem-solve to meet the caregiver's needs. Only if they cannot do so should the clinician offer suggestions. Typically, the family's own solutions will be better, because they are more likely to work within that family system.

There are a number of steps clinicians can take to make the family session more successful. First and foremost is to avoid being drawn into a discussion of long-standing disagreements. This meeting should not be an opening for family therapy, which was not requested, neither is it likely to proceed quickly enough to help caregiver or patient. Rather, the focus needs to remain on how to help the caregiver. Second, the clinician should guide families to realistic plans. If someone is making unrealistic commitments, that will be more frustrating for everyone in the long run. Third, caregivers should encourage everyone to help, but also to avoid trying to equate the amounts of help being offered. It is important to point out that there are many different ways of helping, and that everyone should do what they can. One person may only be willing or able to call the primary caregiver, while another person volunteers to provide respite. While very different in the amount of effort, each type of help can be useful in its own way. Turning helping into a competition or an argument over whether or not someone is doing their share is likely to reflect long-standing family conflicts that will drain everyone's energy without helping the situation. Finally, as with any behaviourally-orientated task, the types of help to be provided should be specific, including who will do what and when it will take place.

We have found that one family session is adequate (Zarit, Orr & Zarit, 1985), although Mittelman and associates (1993) recommend at least one follow-up meeting. Even if a second meeting is not held, there should be follow-up with the primary caregiver to see if everyone has done what was agreed upon. The clinician can also be a resource that the family can turn to if there is a significant change in the situation.

Support groups

Support groups are a very popular intervention for family caregivers, especially for people assisting someone with a dementing illness. Part of a genuine grassroots movement, support groups arose in response to caregivers' feelings that they were not getting the information or help they needed from physicians, and that family and friends did not understand or support them. Research on support groups suggests they are not as effective as counselling or a combination of individual and family treatment in relieving the caregiver's emotional distress (Toseland et al., 1990; Whitlatch, Zarit & von Eye, 1991). On the other hand, there are many positive things that groups can do. Groups can be a very effective way of disseminating information about a disease, and particularly about different ways of coping with the consequences of it. Caregivers readily share information about which physicians or other providers are helpful, which home services are worth trying, and so on. They can also be very creative in groups in coming up with ideas for managing problem behaviours. There is also the understanding that results from talking with people who have shared a similar experience.

Groups can be organized in many different ways. They can have a professional or a peer leader. The group can be open to anyone who wants to attend a session, or it can be closed to a small number of participants. It is often useful to interview people before they attend a group to divert anyone who may be too upset at that time to benefit or who would in some way be inappropriate. On the other hand, it may not be possible to do that in every group. The format for the group can also vary. Some groups mainly discuss caregivers' problems and feelings, while other groups may bring in speakers. These different ways of structuring groups can achieve distinct goals. There is probably no one right way to run a support group. Rather, clinicians (or peer leaders) should consider what their goals are, and then structure the group optimally for achieving those ends.

As with any group, the leader must sometimes take an active role to mobilize the therapeutic potential of group interaction. Leaders must also restore a balance when, for example, one person dominates the conversation, or when there is a lot of conflict. As a group develops, leaders often find that they can step back a bit and let the members take the lead. The whole point of a support group, after all, is to learn from people in similar situations, so the more the members interact directly with one another, the better.

CONCLUSIONS

Caring for a disabled elder can be very stressful and demanding. As the population has aged, more people need help than ever before, often for long periods of time. Because of trends in modern society, this explosion of dependent elderly has occurred at the same time that the family's resources to care for them have declined. Women's working, high rates of divorce and remarriage, and generally stagnant economic conditions have reduced the resources families have for caring for the older generation. Caregiving is often very stressful for families, especially in cases of dementia and when the disability persists over long periods of time. While it may not be possible to improve the elder's condition significantly, there are often modifiable aspects of the care situation. As examples, building social support and improving how caregivers manage stress can alleviate some of their emotional distress. Clinical interventions can target these modifiable dimensions to reduce stress on caregivers. Interventions can include individual counselling with the caregiver, family counselling, and support groups. In the end, caregiving poses a considerable challenge to families and to society, but some straightforward clinical approaches can often be very helpful so that caregivers can assist their relative in the best possible ways, without excessive burden on themselves.

REFERENCES

Adamson, D., Feinauer, L., Lund, D. & Caserta, M. (1992). Factors affecting marital happiness of caregivers of the elderly in multigenerational families. *American Journal of Family Therapy*, **20**, 62–70.
Aneshensel, C., Pearlin, L.I., Mullan, J.T., Zarit, S.H. & Whitlach, C.J. (1995). *Profiles of Caregiving: The Unexpected Career*. New York: Academic Press, New York.

Aneshensel, C.S., Pearlin, L.I. & Schuler, R.H. (1993). Stress, role captivity, and the cessation of caregiving. *Journal of Health and Social Behavior*, **34**, 54–70.

Anthony-Bergstone, C.R., Zarit, S.H. & Gatz, M. (1988). Symptoms of psychological distress among caregivers of dementia patients. *Psychology and Aging*, **3**, 245–248.

Barnes, C.L., Given, B. & Given, C.W. (1992). Caregivers of elderly relatives: spouses and adult children. *Health and Social Work*, **17**, 282–289.

Beck, A.T., Rush, A.J., Shaw, B. F. & Emery, G. (1979). *Cognitive Therapy of Depression*. New York: Guilford.

Berman, H.J. (1987). Adult children and their parents: irredeemable obligation and irreplaceable loss. *Journal of Gerontological Social Work*, **10**, 21–33.

Birkel, R.C. (1987). Toward a social ecology of the home-care household. *Psychology and Aging*, **2**, 294–301.

Blau, Z.S. (1981). *Aging in a Changing Society*, 2nd edn. New York: Franklin Watts.

Bledin, K.D., MacCarthy, B., Kuipers, L. & Woods, R.T. (1990). Daughters of people with dementia: expressed emotion, strain and coping. *British Journal of Psychiatry*, **157**, 221–227.

Blum, M.J., Kelly, M. & Gatz, M. (1989). Empirically-defined caregivers vs. self-defined caregivers for aging parents. Paper presented at the meetings of the Gerontological Society of America, Minneapolis, MN.

Bodnar, J.C. & Kiecolt-Glaser, J.K. (1994). Caregiver depression after bereavement: chronic stress isn't over when it's over. *Psychology and Aging*, **9**, 372–380.

Boss, P., Caron, W., Horbal, W. & Mortimer, J. (1990). Predictors of depression in caregivers of dementia patients: boundary ambiguity and mastery. *Family Process*, **29**, 245–254.

Brody, E.M. (1985). Parent care as a normative family stress. *Gerontologist*, **25**, 19–29.

Brody, E.M., Hoffman, C., Kleban, M.H. & Schoonover, C.B. (1989). Caregiving daughters and their local siblings: perceptions, strains, and interactions. *Gerontologist*, **29**, 529–538.

Brody, E.M., Johnsen, P.T., Fulcomer, M.C. & Lang, A.M. (1983). Women's changing roles and help to the elderly: attitudes of three generations of women. *Journal of Gerontology*, **38**, 597–607.

Brody, E.M., Kleban, M.H., Johnsen, P.T., Hoffman, C. & Schoonover, C.B. (1987). Work status and parent care: a comparison of four groups of women. *Gerontologist*, **27**, 201–208.

Brody, E.M., Litvin, S.J., Hoffman, C. & Kleban, M.H. (1992). Differential effects of daughters' marital status on their parent care experiences. *Gerontologist*, **32**, 58–67.

Brody, E.M. & Schoonover, C.B. (1986). Patterns of parent-care when adult daughters work and when they do not. *Gerontologist*, **26**, 372–381.

Clipp, E.C. & George, L.K. (1990). Caregiver needs and patterns of social support. *Journal of Gerontology*, **45**, S102–111.

Cohen, S. & Edwards, J.R. (1989). Personality characterstics as moderators of the relationship between stress and disorder. In R.W.J. Neufeld (Ed.), *Advances in the Investigation of Psychological Stress* (pp. 235–283). New York: Wiley.

Cosette, S. & Lévesque, L. (1993). Caregiving tasks as predictors of mental health of wife caregivers of men with chronic obstructive pulmonary disease. *Research in Nursing and Health*, **16**, 251–263.

Coward, R.T. & Dwyer, J.W. (1990). The association of gender, sibling network composition and patterns of parent care by adult children. *Research on Aging*, **12**, 158–181.

Creasey, G.L., Myers, B.J., Epperson, M.J. & Taylor, J. (1990). Couples with an elderly parent with Alzheimer's disease: perceptions of familial relationships. *Psychiatry*, **53**, 44–51.

Crimmins, E.M. & Ingegneri, D.G. (1990). Interaction and living arrangements of older parents and their children. *Research on Aging*, **12**, 3–35.

Doty, P., Liu, K. & Wiener, J. (1985). An overview of long-term care. *Health Care Financing Review*, **6**, 69–78.

Duncan, M.T. & Morgan, D.L. (1994). Sharing the caring: family caregivers' views of their relationships with nursing home staff. *Gerontologist*, **34**, 235–244.

Eggebeen, D.J. (1992). Family structure and intergenerational exchanges. *Research on Aging*, **14**, 427–447.

Enright, R.B. (1991). Time spent caregiving and help received by spouses and adult children of brain-impaired adults. *Gerontologist*, **31**, 375–383.

Eurostat (1993a). Older people in the European Community: population and employment. *Rapid Reports, Population and Social Conditions (No. 1)*. Luxembourg: Eurostat.

Eurostat (1993b). Old people in the European Community: life expectancy. *Rapid Reports, Population and Social Conditions (No. 11)*. Luxembourg: Eurostat.

Falbo, T. (1984). *The Single-child Family*. New York: Guilford.

Franklin, S.T., Ames, B.D. & King, S. (1994). Acquiring the family eldercare role: influence on female employment adaptation. *Research on Aging*, **16**, 27–42.

Gallagher, D., Rose, J., Rivera, P., Lovett, S. & Thompson, L.W. (1989). Prevalence of depression in family caregivers. *Gerontologist*, **29**, 449–456.

George, I. & Gwyther, L. (1986). Caregiver well-being: a multidimensional examination of family caregivers of demented adults. *Gerontologist*, **26**, 253–259.

Gibeau, J.L. & Anastas, J.W. (1989). Breadwinners and caregivers: interviews with working women. *Journal of Gerontological Social Work*, **14**, 19–40.

Goode, W.J. (1960). A theory of strain. *American Sociological Review*, **25**, 483–496.

Goodman, C.R., Zarit, S.H. & Steiner, V. (1994). Self-appraisals as predictors of strain in caregiving. Paper presented at the meetings of the Gerontological Society of America, Atlanta, Georgia.

Haley, W.E., Brown, S.L. & Levine, E.G. (1987). Family caregiver appraisals of patient behavioral disturbance in senile dementia. *Clinical Gerontologist*, **6**, 25–34.

Haley, W.E., Levine, E.G., Brown, S.L. & Bartolucci, A.A. (1987). Stress, appraisal, coping, and social support as predictors of adaptational outcome among dementia caregivers. *Psychology and Aging*, **2**, 323–330.

Hansson, R.O. & Carpenter, B.N. (1994). *Relationships in Old Age: Coping with the Challenge of Transition*. New York: Guilford.

Harper, S. & Lund, D.A. (1990). Wives, husbands, and daughters caring for institutionalized and noninstitutionalized dementia patients: toward a model of caregiver burden. *International Journal of Aging and Human Development*, **30**, 241–262.

Hermanova, H. (1995). Healthy aging in Europe in the 1990s and implications for education and training in the care of the elderly. *Educational Gerontology*, **21**, 1–14.

Hogan, D.P., Eggebeen, D.J. & Clogg, C.C. (1993). The structure of intergenerational exchanges in American families. *American Journal of Sociology*, **98**, 1428–1458.

Horowitz, A. (1985). Family caregiving to the frail elderly. *Annual Review of Gerontology and Geriatrics*, **25**, 194–246.

Jutras, S. & Lavoie, J. (1995). Living with an impaired elderly person: the informal caregiver's physical and mental health. *Journal of Aging and Health*, **7**, 4.

Kahn, R.L., Wolfe, D.M., Quinn, R., Snoek, J.D. & Rosenthal, R.A. (1964). *Organizational Stress*. New York: Wiley.

Kiecolt-Glaser, J.K., Dura, J.R., Speicher, C.E., Trask, J. & Glaser, R. (1991). Spousal caregivers of dementia victims: longitudinal changes in immunity and health. *Psychosomatic Medicine*, **53**, 345–362.

Kinney, J.M. & Stephens, M.A.P. (1989). Caregiving hassles scale: assessing the daily hassles of caring for a family member with dementia. *Gerontologist*, **29**, 328–332.

Knight, B.G., Lutzky, S.M. & Macofsky-Urban, F. (1993). A meta-analytic review of interventions for caregiver distress: recommendations for future research. *Gerontologist*, **33**, 240–248.

Lawton, M.P., Kleban, M.H., Moss, M., Rovine, M.N. & Glicksman, A. (1989). Measuring caregiving appraisal. *Journal of Gerontology: Psychological Sciences*, **44**, P61–71.

Lawton, M.P., Rajagopal, D., Brody, E. & Kleban, M.H. (1992). The dynamics of caregiving for a demented elder among black and white families. *Journal of Gerontology: Social Sciences*, **47**, S156–164.

Lazarus, R.S. & Folkman, S. (1984). *Stress, Appraisal, and Coping*. New York: Springer.

MaloneBeach, E.E. & Zarit, S.H. (1995). Dimensions of social support and social conflict as predictors of caregiver depression. *International Psychogeriatrics*, **7**, 25–38.

MaloneBeach, E.E., Zarit, S.H. & Spore, D.L. (1992). Caregivers' perceptions of case management and community-based services: barriers to service use. *Journal of Applied Gerontology*, **11**, 146–159.

Marks, S.R. (1977). Multiple roles and role strain: some notes on human energy, time, and commitment. *American Sociological Review*, **41**, 921–936.

Miller, B. & Montgomery, A. (1990). Family caregiving and limitations in social activities. *Research on Aging*, **12**, 72–93.

Mintzer, J.E., Rubert, M.P., Loewenstein, D., Gamez, E. et al. (1992). Daughters caregiving for Hispanic and non-Hispanic Alzheimer patients: does ethnicity make a difference? *Community Mental Health Journal*, **28**, 293–303.

Mittelman, M.S., Ferris, S.H., Steinberg, G., Schulman, E., Mackell, J.A., Ambinder, A. & Cohen, J. (1993). An intervention that delays institutionalization of Alzheimer's disease patients: treatment of spouse caregivers. *Gerontologist*, **33**, 730–740.

Mullan, J.T. (1992). The bereaved caregiver: a prospective study of changes in well-being. *Gerontologist*, **32**, 673–683.

Mullan, J.T. (1993). Barriers in the use of formal services among Alzheimer's caregivers. In S.H. Zarit, L.I. Pearlin & K.W. Schaie (Eds), *Caregiving Systems: Formal and Informal Helpers* (pp. 241–260). Hillsdale, NJ: Erlbaum.

Mutschler, P.H. (1994). From executive suite to production line: how employees in different occupations manage elder care responsibilities. *Research on Aging*, **16**, 7–26.

Neal, M.B., Chapman, N.J., Ingersoll-Dayton, B., Emlen, A.C. & Boise, L. (1990). Absenteeism and stress among employed caregivers of the elderly, disabled adults, and children. In D.E. Biegel & A. Blum (Eds), *Aging and Caregiving: Theory, Research, and Practice* (pp. 160–183). Newbury Park, CA: Sage.

Noelker, L.S. & Bass, D.M. (1989). Home care for elderly persons: linkages between formal and informal caregivers. *Journal of Gerontology: Social Sciences*, **44**, S63-70.

Pearlin, L.I. (1993). The social contexts of stress. In L. Goldberger & S. Breznitz (Eds), *Handbook of Stress: Theoretical and Clinical Aspects*, 2nd edn. (pp. 303–315). New York: Free Press.

Pearlin, L.I., Mullan, J.T., Semple, S.J. & Skaff, M.M. (1990). Caregiving and the stress process: an overview of concepts and their measures. *Gerontologist*, **30**, 583–594.

Pearlin, L.I. & Schooler, C. (1978). The structure of coping. *Journal of Health and Social Behavior*, **19**, 2–21.

Pearlin, L.I. & Skaff, M.M. (1995). Stressors and adaptation in late life. Paper presented at the Mini White House Conference on Mental Health and Aging, Washington, DC.

Pearson, J., Verma, S. & Nellett, C. (1988). Elderly psychiatric patient status and caregiver perceptions as predictors of caregiver burden. *Gerontologist*, **28**, 79–83.

Pruchno, R.A. & Resch, N.L. (1989). Aberrant behaviors and Alzheimer's disease: mental health effects on spouse caregivers. *Journal of Gerontology: Social Sciences*, **44**, S177–182.

Quayhagen, M.P. & Quayhagen, M. (1988). Alzheimer's stress: coping with the caregiving role. *Gerontologist*, **28**, 391–396.

Rodin, J. (1986). Aging and health: effects of the sense of control. *Science*, **233**, 1271–1276.

Rosenthal, C.J. & Dawson, P. (1991). Wives of institutionalized elderly men. *Journal of Aging and Health*, **3**, 315–334.

Rosenthal, C.J., Sulman, J. & Marshall, V.W. (1993). Depressive symptoms in family caregivers of long-stay patients. *Gerontologist*, **33**, 249–257.

Scharlach, A.E. & Boyd, S.L. (1989). Caregiving and employment: results of an employee survey. *Gerontologist*, **29**, 382–387.

Schulz, R., Visintainer, P. & Williamson, G.M. (1990). Psychiatric and physical morbidity effects of caregiving. *Journal of Gerontology: Psychological Sciences*, **45**, P181–191.

Schulz, R., Williamson, G.M., Morycz, R. & Biegel, D.E. (1993). Changes in depression among men and women caring for an Alzheimer's patient. In S.H. Zarit, L.I. Pearlin & K.W. Schaie (eds), *Caregiving Systems: Informal and Formal Helpers* (pp. 119–140). Hillsdale, NJ: Erlbaum.

Semple, S.J. (1992). Conflict in Alzheimer's caregiving families: its dimensions and consequences. *Gerontologist*, **32**, 648–655.

Sieber, S.D. (1974). Toward a theory of role accumulation. *American Sociological Review*, **39**, 567–578.

Siegel, J.S. (1980). On the demography of aging. *Demography*, **17**, 345–361.

Skaff, M.M. & Pearlin, L.I. (1992). Caregiving: role engulfment and the loss of self. *Gerontologist*, **32**, 656–664.

Soldo, B.J. (1980). America's elderly in the 1980s. *Population Bulletin*, 35, 148.

Soldo, B.J. & Myllyuoma, J. (1983). Caregivers who live with dependent elderly. *Gerontologist*, **23**, 605–611.

Stoller, E.P. & Pugliesi, K.L. (1989). Other roles of caregivers: competing responsibilities or supportive resources. *Journal of Gerontology*, **44**, S231-S238.

Stommel, M., Given, C.W. & Given, B. (1990). Depression as an overriding variable explaining caregiver burden. *Journal of Aging and Health*, **2**, 81–102.

Stone, R.I., Cafferata, G.L. & Sangl, J. (1987). Caregivers of the frail elderly: a national profile. *Gerontologist*, **27**, 616–626.

Stone, R.I. & Short, P.F. (1990). The competing demands of employment and informal caregiving to disabled elders. *Medical Care*, **28**, 513–526.

Suitor, J.J. & Pillemer, K. (1993). Support and interpersonal stress in the social networks of married daughters caring for parents with dementia. *Journal of Gerontology: Social Sciences*, **48**, S1–8.

Tennstedt, S., Cafferata, G.L. & Sullivan, L. (1992). Depression among caregivers of impaired elders. *Journal of Aging and Health*, **4**, 58–76.

Teri, L., Truax, P., Logsdon, R., Zarit, S., Uomoto, J. & Vitaliano, P.P. (1992). Assessment of behavioral problems in dementia: the revised memory and behavior problems checklist. *Psychology and Aging*, **7**, 622–631.

Thorslund, M. (1991). The increasing number of very old people will change the Swedish model of the welfare state. *Social Science and Medicine*, **32**, 455–464.

Toseland, R.W., Rossiter, C.M., Peak, T. & Smith, G.C. (1990). Comparative effectiveness of individual and group interventions to support family caregivers. *Social Work*, **35**, 209–217.

Townsend, A., Noelker, L., Deimling, G. & Bass, D. (1989). Longitudinal impact of interhousehold caregiving on adult children's mental health. *Psychology and Aging*, **4**, 393–401.

Uhlenberg, P.R. (1990). Implications of increasing divorce for the elderly. Paper presented at the United Nations International Conference on Aging Population in the Context of the family, Kitakyushn, Japan, October.

US Bureau of the Census (1990). The need for personal assistance with everyday activities: recipients and caregivers. *Current Population Reports, Series P70–19*. Washington, DC: US Government Printing Office.

US Bureau of the Census (1992a). Growth of America's oldest-old population. *Profiles of America's Elderly, No. 2*. Washinton, DC: US Government Printing Office.

US Bureau of the Census (1992b). Sixty-five plus in America. *Current Population Reports, Special Studies, P23–178*. Washington, DC: US Government Printing Office.

Vitaliano, P.P., Becker, J., Russo, J., Magana-Amato, A. & Maiuro, R.D. (1989). Expressed emotion in spouse caregivers of patients with Alzheimer's disease. *Journal of Applied Social Sciences*, **13**, 216–250.

Vitaliano, P.P., Russo, J., Young, H.M., Teri, L. & Maiuro, R.D. (1991). Predictors of burden in spouse caregivers of individuals with Alzheimer's disease. *Psychology and Aging*, **6**, 392–402.

Whitlatch, C.J., Zarit, S.H. & von Eye, A. (1991). Efficacy of interventions with caregivers: a reanalysis. *Gerontologist*, **31**, 9–14.

Williamson, G. M. & Schulz, R. (1990). Relationship orientation, quality of prior relationship, and distress among caregivers of Alzheimer's patients. *Psychology and Aging*, **5**, 502–509.

Wright, L.K., Clipp, E.C. & George, L.K. (1993). Health consequences of caregiver stress. *Medicine, Exercise, Nutrition, and Health*, **2**, 181–195.

Zarit, S.H. (1980). *Aging and Mental Disorders*. New York: Free Press.

Zarit, S.H., Orr, N.K. & Zarit, J.M. (1985). *The Hidden Victims of Alzheimer's Disease: Families under Stress*. New York: New York University Press.

Zarit, S.H., Reever, K.E. & Bach-Peterson, J. (1980). Relatives of the impaired elderly: correlates of feelings of burden. *Gerontologist*, **20**, 649–655.

Zarit, S.H., Steiner, V., Goodman, C.R., Greene, R., Ferraro, E., Stephens, M.A.P. & Townsend, A. (1994). Predictors of short-term and sustained use of adult day care. Paper presented at the meetings of the Gerontological Society of America, Atlanta, Georgia.

Zarit, S.H., Todd, P.A. & Zarit, J.M. (1986). Subjective burden of husbands and wives as caregivers: a longitudinal study. *Gerontologist*, **26**, 260–270.

Zarit, S.H. & Whitlatch, C.J. (1992). Institutional placement: phases of the transition. *Gerontologist*, **32**, 665–672.

Zarit, S.H. & Whitlatch, C.J. (1993). Short and long term consequences of placement for caregivers. *Irish Journal of Psychology*, **14**, 25–37.

Chapter 8

INSTITUTIONAL CARE

*Robert T. Woods**

INTRODUCTION

The concept of an institution for older people is not a popular one; internationally, policies emphasize care in the community; families agonize and feel great guilt over decisions to place the older person in such a place; older people themselves almost universally express horror at the thought of ending their days in an old people's home or a longstay hospital ward; staff often perceive their jobs as of low value, morale may be low, recruitment difficult. The adjective "institutional" has come to imply regimented or unimaginative, and the verb "institutionalize" to make dependent and apathetic. The Oxford Dictionary definition of an "institution" as "a society or organization founded especially for charitable, religious, educational or social purposes" (or the building used by such an organization) has been overwhelmed by all the negative connotations associated with decades of care systems that have fulfilled the stereotypes only too well (see, for example, Townsend, 1962).

Those who have over many years sought to provide care in a personalized, imaginative way, which actively engages residents and encourages independence, have faced many obstacles in the quest for a new culture of care (Woods, 1995), but significant progress can be identified. Efforts have been made to replace the word "institution" with more acceptable generic euphemisms, such as "alternative homes", "residential facilities" and "continuing care", and there is increasing recognition that care in the community may be just as regimented, impersonal and disempowering as the facilities it was intended to replace. Indeed, it has

* University of Wales, Bangor, UK

Psychological Problems of Ageing: Assessment, Treatment and Care. Edited by R.T. Woods.
© 1999 John Wiley & Sons Ltd.

been known for many years that the apathy, inactivity and dependence that are often attributed to the impact of the institutional environment on the older person in fact commence before admission, whilst the person is still in the community (Tobin & Lieberman, 1976; Clough, 1981). These reflect the problems leading to the decision to enter a residential environment, as well as a process of change in the person's self-perception to one where few, if any, valid social roles remain. The institution may not do enough to combat this process, but it probably does not set it in train.

It is possible to debate whether or not, ideally, there should be any institutional care at all; Townsend (1962) argued that many of the drawbacks he identified in residential care arose from the context of communal living with a group of virtual strangers from diverse backgrounds, and could not be readily remedied even by more liberal policies. In like manner, advocates of social role valorization (see Stirling, 1996) have at times argued that, because living in an institution is not a valued option, then it should not form part of the care spectrum offered. However, pragmatically, the care system is so dependent on the residential sector that it is not going to be dispensed with in the near future; it is possible, at least intuitively, to identify better and worse care environments, and there is an important task to be undertaken in identifying the conditions for higher-quality care and the means of achieving these. More positively, it can be argued that, for some older people, a form of alternative home may be the best way of providing the care required (Clough, 1981). Older people with dementia living alone and requiring 24-hour monitoring and supervision in view of the danger they present to themselves and/or others are a case in point. Clough's definition of the primary function of residential care is worth repeating: "to provide a living base in which basic physical needs are met in a way which allows the individual the maximum potential for achieving mastery".

In the UK (and in the USA—see Knight et al., 1998) in the last few years there have been extensive changes in the provision of institutional care. There is much greater diversity of provision than ever before, with less reliance on hospital care. This has been welcome in many respects. For example, in the UK the hospital provision was typically a Victorian asylum, miles from the person's home, or an equally grim, but usually less rural, workhouse from the same era. However, such inadequate facilities have not been, by and large, replaced by alternative community provision, but by residential and nursing homes provided usually by the private and voluntary sectors. Many of these aspire to high standards of care, but the financial constraints imposed by the statutory funding agencies create considerable pressures, and there is a discernible trend towards larger homes and less favourable conditions of service for staff in an effort to reduce unit costs. It is regrettable that inspection and monitoring procedures have not developed at the same rate as the growth in decentralization of provision.

There is a concern that the existence of a readily available pool of residential provision is likely to hinder the development of complex care-packages to help those older people who require a great deal of input, such as 24-hour monitoring, to remain at home. The institutional alternative seems to provide a convenient way of meeting all the person's needs in one fell swoop, quite possibly at a lower cost than providing the same level of care in the person's own home. There is concern that arrangements are made for older people that would be unacceptable in other client groups; thus, in learning disabilities, an eight-bed unit for people with profound disabilities would be considered too large, whereas for older people it might be dismissed as too small to be economically viable. The alternative is not simply augmenting family care: many of those entering residential care live alone, and have outlived close family members.

During the 1980s in the UK, public funding of residential and nursing-home placements was not on the basis of assessed need, and so a perverse incentive to place older people in homes was operating. The NHS and Community Care Act 1990 has ended funded placements without assessment, but incentives for the development of innovative care packages to provide viable alternatives to institutional care are not in force. Entry to institutional care must not be seen as an easy option, or indeed as a solution. Improvements are needed in assessments for care needs to take into account all the ramifications for the older person of the various options. Remaining at home and entering an institution will both have their risks and benefits for the older person, and both must be carefully considered in each individual case. Developing measures that allow comparisons of quality of life for older people across community and residential provision is necessary if there is to be a rational basis for the development of care provision. As Zarit & Edwards (Chapter 7, this volume) point out, institutional care should not even be regarded as a certain means of reducing distress experienced by family caregivers.

QUALITY IN INSTITUTIONAL CARE

What characterizes a residential setting of high quality? Anyone who has visited even a few such places will have some ideas as to what differentiates those with a poor quality of care from those where higher standards are achieved (although agreement, even between experienced raters, might be surprisingly low—Gibbs & Sinclair, 1992). A fairly immediate indication will be the level of activity and interaction within the home; Woods & Britton (1985) provide a detailed review, documenting the often very low levels of engagement to be found. Doing nothing or sleeping typically appear as the predominant activities, and interactions with staff (and other residents) are typically minimal and, with staff, are usually task-related, in relation to dressing, washing, feeding and so on. Bowie & Mountain (1993) used detailed direct observation in seven longstay hospital wards for people with dementia to answer the question, "What happens in a day in the life of a longstay demented patient?" and arrived at the succinct answer "Not a lot": 86.7% of time observed was spent in (apparently) purposeless motor activity, antisocial or inappropriate behaviour or simply doing nothing.

These are fairly crude indices; increasing activity may not reflect an improvement if the activities are seen by the residents as meaningless and irrelevant, or if participation is virtually enforced. The quality of interaction is, of course, as relevant as the quantity (Carstensen & Erickson, 1986); this consideration has led to the development of measures such as Dementia Care Mapping (Kitwood & Bredin, 1992) and the Quality of Interactions Schedule (Dean, Proudfoot & Lindesay, 1993b), designed to address the quality dimension as well as the quantitative aspect (see Brooker, 1995, for a review).

Another immediate impression may be the "homeliness" of the facility. The size and scale of the unit, the provision of single rooms for residents, the type and style of furnishing, the presence of personal touches and possessions, and the absence of a "clinical" feel or of unpleasant odours may all contribute to this aspect. For example, in a relatively impoverished hospital context, Mountain & Bowie (1992) found that "a large number of patients only possessed a core of toiletries . . . and did not have items such as ornaments, pictures or jewellery".

However, probably the most important indication of the quality of the institution comes from observing the attitudes of staff to the recipients of care. Are residents treated as individuals, unique people with their own needs and preferences, or en bloc, as if all have the same needs? Are residents treated with respect, and efforts made to preserve dignity? Are residents addressed as adults, or are they talked down to in a patronizing, infantilizing, devaluing fashion? Are explanations given regarding care procedures, choices offered, or is the person treated as a passive, inanimate object to be cleaned and changed in a dehumanizing manner?

Kitwood (1996; 1997) describes a person-centred care approach, emphasizing respect for the individuality, value and worth of the person with dementia. This resonates with the values arising from the application of "normalization" or "social-role valorization" principles to this context (Stirling, 1996; Holden & Woods, 1995 pp. 122) The important point here is that indicators of quality based on these considerations can be constructed. Institutions will differ markedly in their quality, reflected in these attributes, and, at least in principle, improvements in quality of care should be attainable. This is not a universally accepted view. Booth's (1985) major comparative survey of residential homes found:

> The differences between regimes are little more than a veneer on the massive uniformity of institutional life. The common features of residential institutions are so dominant in their effects as to mask or suppress any influence that small differences in the social environments of homes exert (p. 234).

In the next section will be reviewed some of the promising developments internationally that suggest this may be an over-pessimistic conclusion, in relation to dementia care at least. It will become clear that achieving high quality in institutional care is an intricate task, requiring inputs at many levels; it is a goal that must not be abandoned simply because of its complexity. Lawton (1994) argues that the dynamic character of the structure of institutions shows that most institutional elements may be "shaped toward higher-quality care".

The emphasis here on institutional environments specifically for people with dementia is justified in view of Lawton's "environmental docility" model (Parmelee & Lawton, 1990), which suggests that the person with lowered competence and function is more likely to be shaped by and vulnerable to environmental contingencies. Older people with intact cognitive function are thought to be more able to themselves shape the environment to suit their individual needs; people with dementia are much more at the mercy of their physical, social and interpersonal surroundings.

DEVELOPMENTS IN INSTITUTIONAL CARE FOR PEOPLE WITH DEMENTIA

Special care units

Special care units for people with dementia are identified by Carr & Marshall (1993) as a widespread development. Often these are planned to be small and local to the area from which the residents come, and to be more domestic in scale and style than the longstay hospital units they often replace. Single rooms are much more likely to be available in such units; they represent a major improvement in the care environment, offering greatly increased scope for privacy, for the person to have more of their own possessions with them and to have a meaningful personal space to which it is worth being orientated.

This is very much an international trend, although there are variations in implementation in different countries. In the USA, for example, units still tend to be large, often as many as 80–120 beds "to optimize service production costs and regulatory requirements" (Regnier & Pynoos, 1992), although these may be arranged in clusters of, say, eight or 12. Sloane et al. (1995) quote an average bed size of 35.9, with only a quarter of units containing 19 or fewer residents.

In the context of these special care units, as Carr & Marshall (1993) reflect, the trend in the UK and Australia is very definitely towards "homely" care. What is achieved is always a compromise; there will be as many different conceptions of "home" as there are residents on a unit; this emphasizes the importance of the person having his/her own room, some personal living space. In the UK, regulations for the registration of residential and nursing homes are such that further compromises are necessary, to meet stringent fire and hygiene standards, for example. The same issues have arisen in the USA, where Lawton (1994) describes "homelike" furnishings as having become obsolete because of such stipulations.

In France, a small homely unit for dementia care would be described as a "cantou", a word meaning "hearth", reflecting that home is around the fireside (Ritchie et al., 1992). These often have one large communal room, with the residents' bedrooms and bathrooms etc. opening off the main room, dispensing with confusing corridors and reducing the load on spatial memory. The kitchen area might typically be in a corner of the communal room, with food preparation a central interest and activity. In the UK, having the kitchen accessible to residents, having the same staff involved in cooking and resident care and involving residents in food preparation might well all be seen as impossible in view of hygiene and safety standards. Could such standards be balanced against a higher quality of life?

Among the special care units developed in the UK, the "domus" units have been particularly influential. Lindesay et al. (1991) describe "the domus philosophy", which is aimed at tackling staff attitudes and fears which lead to poor quality of life in institutional settings for people with dementia. Emphasis is given to seeking to maintain the independence and preserved abilities of the person with dementia, through having an active role in the life of the domus, where the intention is to apply domestic rather than hospital standards of safety and hygiene.

The principles of the domus philosophy (Lindesay et al., 1991) are:

1. The domus is the person's home for life.
2. The needs of the staff should be considered equally with those of the residents.
3. The domus aims to correct the avoidable consequences of dementia, and accommodate those that are unavoidable.
4. Residents' individual psychological and emotional needs may take precedence over the physical aspects of care.

In Sweden, "group living homes" have been developed. These typically consist of a group of four flats in an ordinary housing block, in which eight people with dementia live, each having his/her own room and possessions, with 24-hour staff cover for the unit as a whole. Wimo et al. (1991) indicate that such a project can be a cost-effective alternative to institutional care, with anecdotal reports of enhanced function. Such units are unable to manage severe physical disabilities, which may be a problem as a resident's condition deteriorates, with a number of residents eventually moving on to nursing-home or hospital-type placements in view of decline in physical health and mobility (Malmberg & Zarit, 1993). This is in contrast to the domus units, which aim to provide a home for life, but is similar to the situation in other countries, where special care units are seen as not able to manage the more severe manifestations of behavioural problems or of physical frailty (Sloane et al., 1995). This difference may reflect the fact that the movement towards special care units in the UK has largely been driven by the need to replace longstay psychogeriatric hospitals, whereas elsewhere it has been the problems of managing relatively physically fit, ambulant, active people with dementia in a nursing-home setting that have fuelled the development of new models of care.

The physical environment

Most of these developments involve a change to the caregiving regime, as well as a change to the physical environment; arguably it is the former that is more important, in that negative staff attitudes and practices would negate the effects of the best physical environment. However, the design of the building can have some influence on both the regime and the residents more directly, if only by providing certain constraints on what may be attempted. Keen (1989), in reviewing architectural influences, argues there has been little consideration given to the contribution the buildings themselves might make to the problems. Similarly, Regnier & Pynoos (1992) state that: "facilities that are managed well are often kept from pursuing their most effective work because negative aspects of the environment are antagonistic to therapeutic goals" (p. 782). They discuss 12 environmental and behavioural principles of design which have an impact on the quality of life and function of older people with cognitive impairment:

1. Privacy, e.g. own room.
2. Provide opportunities for social exchange and interaction.
3. Control, choice and autonomy: promote opportunities for residents to make choices and control events that influence outcomes.
4. Orientation and wayfinding: an environment that is easy to comprehend.
5. Safety and security: ensure user will sustain no harm, injury or undue risk.
6. Accessibility and functioning: can the person manipulate features of the environment?
7. Provide a stimulating environment that is safe but challenging.
8. Sensory aspects: allow for changes in visual, auditory and olfactory senses.
9. Familiarity: use historical reference and solutions influenced by tradition to give a sense of continuity and familiarity.
10. Aesthetics and appearance: attractive, provocative and non-institutional designs.
11. Personalization: mark it as the property of a single, unique individual.
12. Adaptability: flexible enough to fit changing personal characteristics.

These authors exemplify these principles in practice in the USA in relation to design features in residential facilities. In the UK, some architects are now taking an imaginative approach to designing environments for people with dementia (e.g. Manser, 1991). Norman (1987) draws attention to a number of design features that appeared helpful in her study of innovative units for people with severe dementia:

1. Single-storey buildings.
2. Ample, safe space for walking indoors and outdoors.
3. Individual private rooms.
4. Easy orientation and identification of key facilities.
5. Minimal distances between sitting, dining, bedroom and lavatory provision.

6. Kitchenette facilities.
7. Minimal boundaries between staff and resident "territory".
8. Easy access to shops.
9. Good transport facilities.
10. Dignified non-institutional furnishing and decoration with opportunity to furnish/decorate own room.

There is clearly considerable convergence between the various accounts, particularly in relation to privacy, through single rooms, safety and orientation aids. However, despite this growth of interest in design, and the significant changes that have been achieved, there is, as Parmelee & Lawton (1990) indicate, little empirical research specifically evaluating design features. This may be in part because of the difficulties inherent in examining such complex, interrelated issues. It is not even established, for example, that reducing the size of the unit has beneficial effects; smaller units almost inevitably necessitate a higher staff:resident ratio, and this may be the crucial factor. Providing "wandering paths" which safely return the person to their starting point, and using colour, architectural and other features to distinguish areas within the unit, have also not been adequately evaluated. Netten (1989, 1993) has examined the relationship between architectural complexity of residential homes and the person with dementia's ability to find his/her way around; different factors were shown to operate in large, communal homes compared with those homes where residents lived together in small groups. Small group homes tended to assist orientation, with the presence of meaningful decision points acting as helpful landmarks.

For many years attempts have been made to arrange the environment so as to encourage social interaction, for example through grouping of furniture around coffee tables, rather than around the walls of a large dayroom (see Woods & Britton, 1985; Wattis & Church, 1986). The emphasis was on breaking up a large waiting-room type of space into smaller, more social areas; now "homely" units are being designed so that the living areas are more immediately conducive to a social atmosphere. More homely dining rooms also encourage social interaction, with residents helping each other more (Davies & Snaith, 1980).

The care environment

Much more empirical research on the effects of changing the pattern of care is available, although, as Sloane et al. (1995) demonstrate, this is a very difficult area in which to carry out well controlled research, in view of the many interacting factors and sources of potential bias operating.

In a Swedish hospital, Melin & Gotestam (1981) report an evaluation of a change of regime, emphasizing choice and encouraging self-reponsibility, for 21 patients with dementia. Three specific areas were targeted: first, residents were allowed more autonomy in helping themselves to coffee and cakes, with the aim of creating more choice and a more natural social situation; secondly, meal times were altered so that free choice and un-limited time were offered to avoid patients being fed if they were too slow; thirdly, activity materials—games, books, jigsaws, etc.—were provided and patients were encouraged to use them. The changes were introduced se-quentially, allowing a multiple baseline design for the experimental group. In comparison to a control group, social interaction during afternoon coffee increased greatly in the experimental group and eating skills improved following the meal-time changes; their level of activity increased when encouraged to use the recreational materials. The results provide strong support for the use of such an approach, encouraging independence and choice, particularly where the existing milieu may have led to under-functioning and patients not using all their skills and abilities to the full.

Brane et al. (1989), also from Sweden, evaluated "integrity-promoting care". This involved staff in a nursing home being trained and supported in implementing individualized care, with patients encouraged to participate more in decisions and activities. Staff were trained to allow more time to residents so that they could go at their own pace and not be rushed. Changes to the physical environment aimed at achieving a more home-like atmophere with domestic-style furnishing, and personalized clothing and possessions were also encouraged. Changes over the three-month interven-tion period and at a follow-up six months later were compared with those of a control group in a second nursing home. Patients in the integrity-promoting care group were reported to have become less confused, anx-ious and distractible; there were also improvements in mood and motor performance. Many of the benefits remained at the follow-up evaluation.

Ritchie et al. (1992) report an evaluation of the impact of the cantou units, described above, on people with dementia, in comparison with long-term hospital care. Residents in the cantou units were more mobile and less dependent in daily activities, had better language skills and interacted more with other residents. However, there were indications that these differences arose from differences in the patients admitted to the two types of care; although there was considerable overlap in degree of dementia, it appeared that the benefits of the cantou became less evident as the condi-tion progressed. Ritchie et al. conclude that both types of care are required, and the issue becomes who is more appropriately cared for in each setting; they suggest that the hospitals could benefit from incorporating some of the features of the cantou, such as the involvement of families.

A detailed evaluation of the Swedish group-living units by Annerstedt, Gustafson & Nilsson (1993) compared a group of people with dementia moved from institutional care to such units with a control group who remained. Cognitive and mood changes favoured the group-living group over a six-month period; although both groups declined over a full year, there were indications of this being less marked in the group-living residents.

In the UK, the first evaluation of the domus principles in practice (Lindesay et al., 1991) compared a new (but not purpose-built) and relatively large (27 beds) unit with this philosophy with two typical psychogeriatric longstay wards on a cross-sectional basis. Although the populations of each unit would be expected to be broadly comparable, and indeed were in terms of cognitive impairment, age and length of time in long-term care, residents of the domus were rated as less impaired in self-care and in communication and orientation. Higher levels of activity and staff–resident interaction were observed in the domus setting.

Dean, Briggs & Lindesay (1993a) report a prospective evaluation of two further domus units; only one of these catered for people with dementia, and so the results in relation to that unit alone will be presented here. Patients were assessed in a longstay hospital ward prior to moving to the purpose-built domus (12 beds), and were then monitored at intervals during their first year of residence. Improvements were identified in cognitive function, self-care and communication skills; again, increased levels of activities and interactions were observed. Some dramatic changes were observed: one patient spoke for the first time in five years within a week of moving to the domus. The increases in staff–resident interaction have been demonstrated to have been of good quality (Dean, Proudfoot & Lindesay, 1993b), with a marked reduction in negative interactions by the end of the first year of operation of the domus, in comparison with the hospital ward. Skea and Lindesay (1996) report a third evaluation, involving a domus-type home and a community hospital ward offering enhanced care. Again there are positive results favouring the domus unit, with an increase in both quantity and quality of interactions, and increases in residents' rated communication skills. Some, less marked, improvements were also noted on the enhanced care hospital ward, compared with a traditional hospital unit. The improvements in quality of life in domus units do have a cost: staff–resident ratios are higher than in the hospital wards, and the costs are accordingly higher (Beecham et al., 1993). This is in contrast to the cantou units in France, which were established in part to lower the costs of care.

However, a caution that additional resources are not a simple guarantee of positive care is provided by the research group evaluating three experimental NHS nursing homes for people with dementia (Sixsmith et al., 1993a). Like the domus units, the new homes aimed to provide a homely living environment and individualized care. Comparing these homes with two other homes and a hospital ward, using techniques to estimate the amount of staff time spent on various activities, it was found that the additional resources were used in routine care, rather than in what the authors describe as life-enhancing care, such as social interaction and group activities. In a further article, Sixsmith, Stilwell & Copeland (1993b) show that in one of the three homes "rementia" could be observed. After admission to the home, residents' functional level tended to improve for some time, before beginning gradually to decline, as would be the expectation in dementia. It is difficult to draw conclusions from this data, as it is not clear what were the factors leading to this pattern of change in one home and not the other two. We would also want to emphasize that positive care has not been seen as additional to other "routine" care by other researchers, but as an approach that transforms every type of interaction; it is not just reflected in numbers of activity sessions with people at this level of impairment, but equally in the way the person is helped to dress, bathe and have a meal. Thus, the way staff resources are deployed is vital, but it is the use to which each interaction is put that is of prime importance.

THE INSTITUTIONAL SYSTEM

In practice, lasting changes have often proved difficult to implement in institutional care (see Woods & Britton, 1985). Special care units might seem from the above discussion to be a welcome development, but in the USA, Gold et al. (1991) indicated that their quality is extremely variable, ranging from the excellent to the execrable. This section discusses some of the complex interacting factors at work; failure to address the complexity of the factors involved has often tended to reduce the long-term impact of interventions in institutional care.

An institution is a complex system, or rather a set of overlapping and interlocking systems. Moos & Schaefer (1987) describe the influences on an individual member of staff as arising from two major systems:

1. Environmental system:
   (a) Organizational
       Physical/architectural aspects of the home
       Structure and policies of the home
       Work social climate
   (b) Non-work stressors and resources

2. Personal system:
    (a) Work-related
         Type of job and work role
    (b) Non-work
         Personal resources—self-esteem, values, intellectual abilities
         Sociodemographic characteristics

The cognitive appraisal of these two systems and their interaction by the staff member influences the person's coping responses and accordingly his/her work performance and morale, and so ultimately the quality of care and resident outcomes. At any and every stage of this process, reciprocal feedback can occur, and all processes are seen as transactional.

Moos & Schaefer emphasize the importance of the work social climate, the "atmosphere" of the workplace, in relation to staff morale. This is evident, for example, when a member of staff reports that the residents are no problem, for all the complexity and diversity of their care needs— rather, it's the other staff who make life difficult! A number of influences on the work climate are described: the staff group and their characteristics, values, commitment to the work and client group, personality and communication skills are clearly important in relation to the extent to which staff are friendly to and support each other; however, also important are the organizational structure and policies, the clarity with which these are communicated, the style of management—controlling or supportive, high-pressured or encouraging autonomy, with staff making their own decisions—and the contribution made by the physical surroundings to a pleasant workplace.

Several aspects of this model are worthy of comment:

1. The impact of non-work stressors and resources, and their two-way relationship, are acknowledged. The work performance of a member of staff who is under stress outside work may well be affected; stress at work may well affect the staff member's personal life and relationships. The institution does not have impervious boundaries.
2. The role of cognitive appraisal is highlighted; it is the person's perception of the policies or the management style or whatever which are important. For example, in an unpublished study (Wills & Woods, 1994) of staff in a new, purpose-built, homely dementia-care unit, staff rated the physical comfort aspect lower than staff working in a crumbling Victorian asylum, shortly to close. Exploration of this odd finding suggested that staff in the special-care unit had very high expectations of what "homely" care should provide (and of themselves), which could not be met even by a specially designed unit; the

hospital staff, on the other hand, were much more accepting of the environment as it was, knew nothing different and so did not down-rate it. Benjamin & Spector (1990) asked staff in three different care facilities to rate a number of potential stressors; staff in a unit where the philosophy encouraged staff to express their emotional needs rated items relating to communication difficulties with residents, or residents being unresponsive, as particularly stressful, compared with staff in units where physical care was given emphasis. Staff's appraisal of what is expected of them is likely to influence areas of tension and stress.

3. The individual's values and personal characteristics are seen as inter-acting with organizational factors. Different people may benefit from different management styles, say; some may prefer more autonomy, others a more hierarchical structure. Job satisfaction and morale must be seen as an interaction between an individual's needs from the work setting and the environment, not a fixed feature of the work-place. Wright (1988) argues that negative attitudes among staff in nursing homes are determined by the sociocultural environment of the nursing home; it is not that staff simply bring with them negative attitudes towards old people, rather that the culture and ethos of the home, characteristics of the staff group as a whole and the nature of the residents' difficulties interact dynamically to shape the repertoire of available skills, coping strategies and management techniques of staff members which "translate attitudes into actions".

4. The type of work, the interaction with residents, and the problems to be dealt with have an influence on the environmental and personal systems, but again are subject to cognitive appraisal. Thus, the staff members' perception of a resident's challenging behaviour, say ver-bal abuse, will affect its impact on their morale; it will make a big difference, for example, if it is seen as directed at them personally, rather than as arising from the resident's condition.

A large-scale study of nurses' job satisfaction and quality of care received by patients in hospital psychogeriatric wards, reported by Robertson et al. (1995), adds support to this type of model. They identified a strong rela-tionship between nurses' job satisfaction and quality of care (evaluated through direct observation). However, they concluded that this associa-tion was best understood as arising from ward and hospital management practices, contributing to both quality of care and staff morale, with the latter two variables then reinforcing each other through a mutual feed-back system. Thus, high quality of care may lead to high job satisfaction, which may lead to higher quality of care and so higher job satisfaction, and so on.

One gap in the model that should be highlighted is the role of relatives. Again, staff at times identify their relationship with relatives as more problematic than that with residents. Relatives may be seen as constantly critical, interfering or as having abandoned the resident. For their part, relatives may be experiencing considerable stress (Zarit & Whitlatch, 1993; Zarit & Edwards, Chapter 7, this volume) and guilt feelings may be strong (Woods & Macmillan, 1994; Woods, 1997). There is some evidence that relatives' distress is related to negative perceptions of staff functioning, and there have been attempts to establish a more collaborative relationship between staff and relatives (Hansen, Patterson & Wilson, 1988). Duncan & Morgan (1994) report that relatives (of cognitively impaired residents) do desire an ongoing relationship with staff members, and that they appraise high quality care as much on the social and emotional aspects as on the technical competence.

CHANGING STAFF ATTITUDES

In considering the evaluation of a service, it is helpful to consider three components: structure, process and outcomes. In this analysis, the physical environment and philosophy of care form part of the given structure and among the outcomes discussed above are aspects thought to contribute to residents' quality of life, such as residents' functional level, activity and interaction. Outcomes relating to relatives have also been evaluated (e.g. Woods & Macmillan, 1994), but might be seen as secondary (but to some extent related) to residents' quality of life. Outcomes for staff, on the other hand, are essentially process measures, important means to the desired outcomes for residents. The central issue in improving the quality of institutional care is how to make a difference to staff behaviour, as the key aspect of service delivery. Moos & Schaefer's model suggests that a wide range of interventions could make a difference, but that a multi-level approach will be required for the best chance of success. Unless structural changes succeed in making a difference to staff outcomes, their impact on residents with dementia is likely to be limited.

The emphasis in the literature so far has been more on staff outcomes such as morale, attitudes, job satisfaction and burnout, rather than on changing behaviour *per se*. It is presumed that the desired behavioural change, and associated quality of care improvements, will flow from changes in these areas. This notion receives some support from studies such as that by Robertson et al. (1995), discussed above, which demonstrated the relationship of the job satisfaction level of a group of staff to quality of care provided. Generally, there is a pressing need for staff outcomes in empirical studies to move beyond stated self-reported attitudes to encompass observed behaviour. Wright (1988) has pointed out some of the difficulties with the "attitudes to old people" scales that have typically been used, and most attitude scales are subject to the bias of the respondent giving the answers they feel to be socially desirable.

There has been particular concern that staff burnout might lead to poor-quality care. Burnout involves physical and emotional exhaustion, demoralization, negative job attitudes and loss of concern for clients; it may affect the staff member outside the work setting as well as within it. It is sometimes thought of as arising from intense involvement over a long period of time, perhaps with difficult clients, where improvements are limited or non-existent, and where there is little support from colleagues and superiors.

Astrom et al. (1990) report that just over a quarter of a sample of 557 nursing staff working in dementia care in Sweden were assessed as being at risk of burnout. Qualified nursing staff had lower levels of burnout than nurses' aides. In the UK, Macpherson et al. (1994) administered the General Health Questionnaire (GHQ), a general screening measure for distress, to 188 staff working in a varied sample of 16 institutional care settings for older people, and concluded that they were no more subject to emotional upset than the general population, contrary to the usual picture of such carework being a highly stressful occupation. Again, just over a quarter of the predominantly female sample were over the threshold for "caseness", but this should be compared with the norm of a third of the general female population scoring at this level or above. GHQ scores were positively related to staff reports of assaults by residents over the previous week, and distressed staff were more likely to report shouting back at aggressive residents, and to feel less supported at work. The authors caution that, although their response rate was fairly good (67%), it may be that more stressed individuals chose not to respond, or were already on long-term sick leave (as were half the care staff in one old people's home). The association of higher levels of distress with both higher reported levels of assaults by residents and greater likelihood of shouting back reflects the likely vicious-circle interaction of the staff member's mood and behaviour with his/her perceptions of the resident's behaviour.

Similar levels of "casesness" using the GHQ with residential care staff have been reported by staff of two out of three homes evaluated by Baillon et al. (1996). In the third home, which had been under threat of closure, 63% scored above the relevant GHQ cut-off point. Moniz-Cook, Millington & Silver (1997) also report different levels of distress among staff in different homes, and indicate that moderate levels of burnout may be reported even where GHQ scores are low.

It can be argued that one way of protecting against distress arising from burnout is to distance oneself from the care recipients, not to become involved in their lives or to empathize with them. Someone adopting such a distancing coping strategy might appear to have some aspects of burnout (negative job attitudes, low involvement with residents), but without any emotional distress. On the other hand, someone initially with high empathy, an ability to identify with the residents' experience, might develop burnout, which would reduce his/her ability to empathize, but would be accompanied by emotional and somatic upset. Astrom et al. (1990) identified a weak negative correlation between burnout and empathy. Higher empathy scores were related to more positive attitudes (Astrom et al., 1991).

In Canada, Chappell & Novak (1992) interviewed 245 nursing assistants in long-term care homes for elderly people. Burden and burnout levels were thought to be high, and were more likely in those reporting that they lacked a sense of reward in their job. Training in work with residents with cognitive impairment appeared to be related to lower feelings of burnout and perceived job pressure, although neither the proportion of patients with cognitive impairment being cared for nor the behavioural problems of patients related to burden. Support from family and friends was another ameliorating factor. Perceived workload was a major source of stress, and Chappell & Novak (1992) join with Astrom et al. (1990) in calling for reduced workloads to reduce the burden on staff. Benjamin & Spector (1990) similarly reported that "there have been insufficient staff on duty" was the item most frequently rated as stressful in their study of three different care environments. However, as noted above, having more staff is no guarantee of improved quality of care. Baillon et al. (1996) indicate that organizational factors may be as stressful for staff as caring for residents, and the need for a careful consideration of the whole system is reinforced by Moniz-Cook et al. (1997), who suggest that each home may need an individualized staff development programme.

Hallberg & Norberg (1993) report introducing regular systematic clinical supervision together with implementation of individualized care planning on an experimental dementia-care ward, and comparing the impact on staff over a 12-month period with a control group of staff on another similar ward. The results indicated that nurses' burden in caring for severely demented patients reduced; positive changes were mainly in aspects of the nurse–patient relationship. Berg, Hansson & Hallberg (1994) elaborate on these findings. Creativity and a climate of innovation improved significantly among nurses on the experimental ward; there was no change on the control ward. Importantly, nurses' sense of tedium and burnout decreased significantly. Hallberg and Norberg (1995) suggest that the intervention helped nurses to see patients' lives as meaningful and opened the way to achieving cooperative relationships with individual patients.

These findings are important in indicating ways in which positive staff outcomes may be achieved. However, these may be viewed as secondary to positive outcomes for residents. Some of the studies on new developments in dementia care reporting benefits to residents have also included staff measures. For example, in Sweden, Alfredson & Annerstedt (1994) report the outcome for staff of the change to group living discussed above, which had positive effects on the residents involved. They report that training and ongoing support/supervision for staff in the group-living schemes resulted in increased knowledge and new emotional and social attitudes, increased motivation, job satisfaction and quality of work compared with staff in traditional institutions.

Staff job satisfaction and morale have also been evaluated in relation to the domus evaluations described previously (Lindesay et al., 1991; Dean, Briggs & Lindesay, 1993a; Skea & Lindesay, 1996). The acknowledgement of staff needs in the domus is perhaps reflected in their reporting higher levels of job satisfaction than staff in the hospital wards from where the patients moved. Dean et al. comment that this higher morale may be related to the higher staff:resident ratio in the domus, staff's appreciation of the competence of their supervisor and managers, staff's freedom to make decisions and do their job in their own way, knowing that what they said was important and valued, and gaining a strong sense of accomplishment from being kept busy using all their skills to help others. In the most recent study (Skea & Lindesay, 1996) the improvement was apparent only after 12 months; there may be a need for a "settling down" period with any innovation.

In such complex multifaceted interventions, teasing out the process of change is virtually impossible; however, the general assumption is that resident outcomes arise from changes in staff behaviour, and that staff attitude change will be a necessary prerequisite for this. Ingstad & Gotestam (1987), in looking at the staff involved in Melin & Gotestam's (1981) intervention, suggest that, with their relatively simple environmental interventions, staff attitudes changed positively as a result of seeing the behaviour change in their residents. This is a useful reminder of the interactive nature of these variables, and the power of a positive feedback system.

Seeing is not always believing, however. In the USA an effective method to reduce levels of incontinence in nursing homes has been developed: "prompted voiding" (Schnelle et al., 1993). Its efficacy has been shown in a number of studies. It involves a little extra input from staff, but demonstrably reduces the number of times a patient has to be changed out of wet clothing—a benefit for all concerned. Time after time the research team report that as soon as the demonstration programme is over, staff stop carrying out the required procedures, despite extensive training and clear feedback on the approach's success. The team have now developed a "quality control" procedure, involving regular checks on practice, which maintains the programme much better than general exhortations and demonstrations. Training programmes alone often prove insufficient to change staff behaviour and practices, and methods of monitoring and reinforcing appropriate practice on an on-going basis are recommended to maintain staff performance (Burgio & Burgio, 1990). To an extent, dementia care mapping (DCM), the detailed observational method developed by Kitwood & Bredin (1992), can be used in this way (Brooker et al, 1998). Using DCM, staff may be able to gain a sense of ownership over the monitoring process, rather than it being perceived simply as a management tool. This is aided by training staff in the mapping methods and perhaps involving them in mapping other units. By giving feedback on the performance of a staff group, rather than on an individual staff member's behaviour, there is scope for staff to work together on action plans for change.

An important function of management in institutional settings is to set clear expectations, and, just as importantly, to indicate their importance by monitoring regularly and systematically that these standards are being met. It is tempting to blame staff attitudes for all the problems encountered in institutional care, but it is the framework provided by the structure, policies and management of the home that allows negative attitudes to take hold, or conversely nurtures positive attitudes, encourages creativity, supports staff and recognizes each resident and staff member as an individual person. Person-centred care (Kitwood, 1997) will be more demanding on staff, requiring a greater degree of empathy and identification with the person with dementia, a closer human relationship to elicit and nurture well-being in the person with dementia; if it is to be achieved, there is an even greater requirement for sensitive management structures within organizations to provide the clarity of communication, supervision and support that staff will undoubtedly require.

REFERENCES

Alfredson, B.B. & Annerstedt, L. (1994). Staff attitudes and job satisfaction in the care of demented elderly people: group living compared with long-term care institutions. *Journal of Advanced Nursing*, **20**, 964–974.

Annerstedt, L., Gustafson, L. & Nilsson, K. (1993). Medical outcome of psychosocial intervention in demented patients: one-year clinical follow-up after relocation into group living units. *International Journal of Geriatric Psychiatry*, **8**, 833–841.

Astrom, S., Nilsson, M., Norberg, A. & Winblad, B. (1990). Empathy, experience of burnout and attitudes towards demented patients among nursing staff in geriatric care. *Journal of Advanced Nursing*, **15**, 1236–1244.

Astrom, S., Nilsson, M., Norberg, A., Sandman, P.O. & Winblad, B. (1991). Staff burnout in dementia care—relations to empathy and attitudes. *International Journal of Nursing Studies*, **28**, 65–75.

Baillon, S., Scothern, G., Neville, P. G. & Boyle, A. (1996). Factors that contribute to stress in care staff in residential homes for the elderly. *International Journal of Geriatric Psychiatry*, **11**, 219–226.

Beecham, J., Cambridge, P., Hallam, A. & Knapp, M. (1993). The costs of domus care. *International Journal of Geriatric Psychiatry*, **8**, 827–831.

Benjamin, L.C. & Spector, J. (1990). The relationship of staff, resident and environmental characteristics to stress experienced by staff caring for the dementing. *International Journal of Geriatric Psychiatry*, **5**, 25–31.

Berg, A., Hansson, U.W. & Hallberg, I.R. (1994). Nurses' creativity, tedium and burnout during 1 year of clinical supervision and implementation of individually planned nursing care: comparisons between a ward for severely demented patients and a similar control ward. *Journal of Advanced Nursing*, **20**, 742–749.

Booth, T. (1985). *Home Truths*. Aldershot: Gower.

Bowie, P. & Mountain, G. (1993). Using direct observation to record the behaviour of long-stay patients with dementia. *International Journal of Geriatric Psychiatry*, **8**, 857–864.

Brane, G., Karlsson, I., Kihlgren, M. & Norberg, A. (1989). Integrity-promoting care of demented nursing home patients: psychological and biochemical changes. *International Journal of Geriatric Psychiatry*, **4**, 165–172.

Brooker, D.J.R. (1995). Looking at them, looking at me; a review of observational studies into the quality of institutional care for elderly people with dementia. *Journal of Mental Health*, **4**, 145–156.

Brooker, D., Foster, N., Banner, A., Payne, M. & Jackson, L. (1998). The efficacy of Dementia Care Mapping as an audit tool: report of a 3-year British NHS evaluation. *Aging & Mental Health*, **2**(1), 60–70.

Burgio, L. D. & Burgio, K. L. (1990). Institutional staff training and management: a review of the literature and a model for geriatric, long-term care facilities. *International Journal of Aging & Human Development*, **30**(4), 287–302.

Carr, J.S. & Marshall, M. (1993). Innovations in long-stay care for people with dementia. *Reviews in Clinical Gerontology*, **3**, 157–167.

Carstensen, L.L. & Erickson, R. (1986). Enhancing the social environments of elderly nursing home residents: are high rates of interaction enough? *Journal of Applied Behavior Analysis*, **19**, 349–355.

Chappell, N.L. & Novak, M. (1992). The role of support in alleviating stress among nursing assistants. *Gerontologist*, **32**, 351–359.

Clough, R. (1981). *Old Age Homes*. London: Allen & Unwin.

Davies, A.D.M. & Snaith, P. (1980). The social behaviour of geriatric patients at meal-times: an observational and an intervention study. *Age and Ageing*, **9**, 93–99.

Dean, R., Briggs, K. & Lindesay, J. (1993a). The domus philosophy: a prospective evaluation of two residential units for the elderly mentally ill. *International Journal of Geriatric Psychiatry*, **8**, 807–817.

Dean, R., Proudfoot, R. & Lindesay, J. (1993b). The Quality of Interactions Schedule (QUIS): development, reliability, and use in the evaluation of two domus units. *International Journal of Geriatric Psychiatry*, **8**, 819–826.

Duncan, M.T. & Morgan, D.L. (1994). Sharing the caring: family caregivers' views of their relationships with nursing home staff. *Gerontologist*, **34**, 235–244.

Gibbs, I. & Sinclair, I. (1992). Residential care for elderly people: the correlates of quality. *Ageing and Society*, **12**, 463–482.

Gold, D.T., Sloane, P.D., Mathew, L.J., Bledsoe, M.M. & Konanc, D.A. (1991). Special care units: a typology of care settings for memory-impaired older adults. *Gerontologist*, **31**, 467–475.

Hallberg, I.R. & Norberg, A. (1993). Strain among nurses and their emotional reactions during 1 year of systematic clinical supervision combined with the implementation of individualized care in dementia nursing. *Journal of Advanced Nursing*, **18**, 1860–1875.

Hallberg, I. R. & Norberg, A. (1995). Nurses' experiences of strain and their reactions in the care of severely demented patients. *International Journal of Geriatric Psychiatry*, **10**, 757–766.

Hansen, S.S., Patterson, M.A. & Wilson, R.W. (1988). Family involvement on a dementia unit: the resident enrichment and activity program. *Gerontologist*, **28**, 508–510.

Holden, U.P. & Woods, R.T. (1995). *Positive Approaches to Dementia Care*, 3rd edn. Edinburgh: Churchill Livingstone.

Ingstad, P.J. & Gotestam, K.G. (1987). Staff attitude changes after environmental changes on a ward for psychogeriatric patients. *International Journal of Social Psychiatry*, **33**, 237–244.

Keen, J. (1989). Interiors: architecture in the lives of people with dementia. *International Journal of Geriatric Psychiatry*, **4**, 255–272.

Kitwood, T. (1996). A dialectical framework for dementia. In R. T. Woods (Ed.), *Handbook of the Clinical Psychology of Ageing* (pp. 267–282). Chichester: Wiley.

Kitwood, T. (1997). *Dementia Reconsidered: the Person Comes First*. Buckingham: Open University Press.

Kitwood, T. & Bredin, K. (1992). A new approach to the evaluation of dementia care. *Journal of Advances in Health and Nursing Care*, **1**, 41–60.

Knight, B. G., Woods, B., Kaskie, B. & Phibbs, E. (1998, in press). Community mental health services in the United States and in the United Kingdom: a comparative systems approach. In B. Edelstein (Ed.), *Clinical Geropsychology* (Comprehensive Clinical Psychology, Vol. 7). New York: Elsevier.

Lawton, M.P. (1994). Quality of care in residential accommodation in the USA. In J.R.M. Copeland, M.T. Abou-Saleh & D.G. Blazer (Eds), *Principles and Practice of Geriatric Psychiatry* (pp. 975–979). Chichester: Wiley.

Lindesay, J., Briggs, K., Lawes, M., Macdonald, A. & Herzberg, J. (1991). The domus philosophy: a comparative evaluation of a new approach to residential care for the demented elderly. *International Journal of Geriatric Psychiatry*, **6**, 727–736.

Macpherson, R., Eastley, R.J., Richards, H. & Mian, I.H. (1994). Psychological distress among workers caring for the elderly. *International Journal of Geriatric Psychiatry*, **9**, 381–386.

Malmberg, B. & Zarit, S.H. (1993). Group homes for people with dementia: a Swedish example. *Gerontologist*, **33**, 682–686.

Manser, M. (1991). Design of environments. In R. Jacoby & C. Oppenheimer (Eds), *Psychiatry in the Elderly* (pp. 550–570). Oxford: Oxford University Press.

Melin, L. & Gotestam, K. (1981). The effects of rearranging ward routines on communication and eating behaviours of psychogeriatric patients. *Journal of Applied Behavior Analysis*, **14**, 47–51.

Moniz-Cook, E., Millington, D. & Silver, M. (1997). Residential care for older people: job satisfaction and psychological health in care staff. *Health & Social Care in the Community*, **5**, 124–133.

Moos, R.H. & Schaefer, J.A. (1987). Evaluating health care work settings: a holistic conceptual framework. *Psychology and Health*, **1**, 97–122.

Mountain, G. & Bowie, P. (1992). The possessions owned by long-stay psychogeriatric patients. *International Journal of Geriatric Psychiatry*, **7**, 285–290.

Netten, A. (1989). Environment, orientation and behaviour; the effect of the design of residential homes in creating dependency among confused elderly residents. *International Journal of Geriatric Psychiatry*, **4**, 143–152.

Netten, A. (1993). *A Positive Environment? Physical and Social Influences on People with Senile Dementia in Residential Care*. Aldershot: Ashgate.

Norman, A. (1987). *Severe Dementia: The Provision of Long-stay Care*. London: Centre for Policy on Ageing.

Parmelee, P.A. & Lawton, M.P. (1990). The design of special environments for the aged. In J.E. Birren & K.W. Schaie (Eds), *Handbook of the Psychology of Aging* (pp. 464–488). San Diego: Academic Press.

Regnier, V. & Pynoos, J. (1992). Environmental intervention for cognitively impaired older persons. In J.E. Birren, R.B. Sloane & G.D. Cohen (eds), *Handbook of Mental Health and Aging* (pp. 763–792). San Diego: Academic Press.

Ritchie, K., Colvez, A., Ankri, J., Ledesert, B., Gardent, H. & Fontaine, A. (1992). The evaluation of long-term care for the dementing elderly: a comparative study of hospital and collective non-medical care in France. *International Journal of Geriatric Psychiatry*, **7**, 549–557.

Robertson, A., Gilloran, A., McGlew, T., McKee, K., McKinley, A. & Wight, D. (1995). Nurses' job satisfaction and the quality of care received by patients in psychogeriatric wards. *International Journal of Geriatric Psychiatry*, **10**, 575–584.

Schnelle, J.F., Newman, D., White, M., Abbey, J., Wallston, K.A., Fogarty, T. & Ory, M.G. (1993). Maintaining continence in nursing home residents through the application of industrial quality control. *Gerontologist*, **33**, 114–121.

Sixsmith, A., Hawley, C., Stilwell, J. & Copeland, J. (1993a). Delivering "positive care" in nursing homes. *International Journal of Geriatric Psychiatry*, **8**, 407–412.

Sixsmith, A., Stilwell, J. & Copeland, J. (1993b). Rementia: challenging the limits of dementia care. *International Journal of Geriatric Psychiatry*, **8**, 993–1000.

Skea, D. & Lindesay, J. (1996). An evaluation of two models of long-term residential care for elderly people with dementia. *International Journal of Geriatric Psychiatry*, **11**, 233–241.

Sloane, P.D., Lindeman, D.A., Phillips, C., Moritz, D.J. & Koch, G. (1995). Evaluating Alzheimer's special care units: reviewing the evidence and identifying potential sources of bias. *Gerontologist*, **35**, 103–111.

Stirling, E. (1996). Social role valorization: making a difference to the lives of older people? In R. T. Woods (Ed.), *Handbook of the Clinical Psychology of Ageing* (pp. 389–422). Chichester: Wiley.

Tobin, S.S. & Lieberman, M.A. (1976). *Last Home for the Aged*. San Francisco, CA: Jossey-Bass.

Townsend, P. (1962). *The Last Refuge*. London: Routledge & Kegan Paul.

Wattis, J. & Church, M. (1986). *Practical Psychiatry of Old Age*. London: Croom Helm.

Wimo, A., Wallin, J.O., Lundgren, K., Ronnback, E., Asplund, K., Mattsson, B. & Krakau, I. (1991). Group living, an alternative for dementia patients: a cost analysis. *International Journal of Geriatric Psychiatry*, **6**, 21–29.

Woods, R.T. (1995). The beginnings of a new culture in care. In T. Kitwood & S. Benson (Eds), The *New Culture of Dementia Care* (pp. 19–23). London: Hawker Publications.

Woods, R. T. (1997). Why should family caregivers feel guilty? In M. Marshall (Ed.), *State of the Art in Dementia Care* (pp. 39–44). London: Centre for Policy on Ageing.

Woods, R.T. & Britton, P.G. (1985). *Clinical Psychology with the Elderly*. London: Croom Helm/Chapman and Hall.

Woods, R.T. & Macmillan, M. (1994). Home at last? Impact of local "homely" care on relatives of people with dementia. In D. Challis, B. Davies & K. Traske (Eds), *Community Care: New Agendas and Challenges from the UK and Overseas* (pp. 75–85). Aldershot: Ashgate.

Wright, L.K. (1988). A reconceptualization of the "negative staff attitudes and poor care in nursing homes" assumption. *Gerontologist*, **28**, 813–820.

Zarit, S.H. & Whitlatch, C.J. (1993). The effects of placement in nursing homes on family caregivers: short and long term consequences. *Irish Journal of Psychology*, **14**, 25–37.

Chapter 9

PSYCHOLOGICAL ASSESSMENT OF OLDER PEOPLE

Robert T. Woods*

INTRODUCTION

Psychometric assessment was traditionally the major task of clinical psychologists with "the elderly". Now treatment and management of the problems of older people and those who care for them predominate. Assessment remains none the less important: any worthwhile treatment programme must be founded on a careful assessment and formulation. However, it is now psychological assessment in its widest sense that must be considered. The questions and concerns to be addressed by the assessment and its content must also be re-evaluated. This chapter will accordingly cover the full range of psychological assessment with older adults in the context of the purposes for which assessment may be used. Assessment of a range of areas, not only cognitive functions, will be discussed. Examples will be given of the tests, scales and procedures that may be used, but the ever-growing number of these means that a comprehensive account of each is not feasible. Clinical psychologists tend to have their own personal repertoire of measures which they use and with which they are familiar; the selection here includes many of the most widely-used, but inevitably is incomplete. The book *Assessment of the Elderly*, edited by Beech & Harding (1990) provides useful reviews of a number of the specific assessment measures commonly used with older people, as well as discussions of general themes. Miller & Morris (1993), Morris & McKiernan (1994), Morris & Kopelman (1992), Storandt & VandenBos (1994) and

* University of Wales, Bangor, UK

Psychological Problems of Ageing: Assessment, Treatment and Care. Edited by R.T. Woods.
© 1999 John Wiley & Sons Ltd.

Davies (1996) provide detailed accounts of neuropsychological assessment, whilst Little & Doherty (1996) discuss other types of assessment fully.

WHY ASSESS THE OLDER PERSON?

A preoccupation of psychological assessment with older people has been differential diagnosis, particularly between depression and dementia. However, formal psychological assessments have been used for a number of other purposes:

- The measurement of the occurrence, and extent, of decline in cognitive functioning.
- The early detection of Alzheimer's disease and other dementias.
- The characterization and differentiation of the cognitive deficits in the various dementias.
- Monitoring change over time, e.g. describing the natural history of dementia.
- Evaluating the response of the older person to a range of interventions (e.g. exercise, drugs, psychological interventions) and examining side-effects (e.g. of anti-depressants on memory).
- Identification of patients suitable for particular treatments.
- Identification of the person's needs so that appropriate placements and services for the older person may be selected.
- Assessment of competence, e.g. to drive, or to handle financial affairs.
- Provision of feedback to older people and/or their carers, regarding the person's strengths and weaknesses (including neuropsychological deficits) and possible compensatory strategies.
- Evaluating the effects of service provision of various types on the older person and his/her supporters.

A basic distinction should be drawn between diagnostic assessment and descriptive assessment. The former has the primary aim of discriminating, and eventually assigning the patient to some category or other. The latter aims to delineate the patient's profile of psychological functioning, the pattern of abilities and deficits, thus providing information potentially useful for a number of the above purposes. The purpose of an assessment must always be carefully clarified, as different strategies and procedures will be indicated for different objectives.

Diagnostic assessment

Considerable energy has been expended over the years in developing tests which discriminate between groups of older people diagnosed as having depression or dementia, and—most importantly for the assessment of the individual case—have low rates of error in category allocation. Examples of these tests include various WAIS indices, learning and speed tests (such as the Kendrick Cognitive Tests for the Elderly), discussed in more detail below.

A major difficulty is that the tests are generally developed and standardized on clear-cut cases of depression and dementia. The very cases (i.e. the less clear-cut) where psychological assessment might be requested to aid diagnosis may actually be excluded from the standardization groups! Typically where the diagnosis is doubtful the psychological test results are equivocal. This is illustrated by the Kendrick Tests, which identified nearly perfectly clear-cut acute cases but misclassified almost half of a sample of long-stay psychiatric patients (Kendrick, Gibson & Moyes, 1979; Gibson, Moyes & Kendrick, 1980).

Base-rates must also be considered. A diagnostic test's usefulness depends on the relative proportions of the diagnostic groups amongst those actually to be tested. A large preponderance of one group means an extremely high level of discrimination will be required of the test if it is to be more efficient than simply allocating all the patients to the extremely frequent diagnostic group. Strictly speaking, cut-off points for different diagnoses need to be determined locally according to these base-rates.

Using clinical diagnosis to validate the tests inevitably introduces error, as diagnosis can never be a totally reliable procedure. On average, across 18 studies, ten per cent of cases initially diagnosed as organic dementia were later rediagnosed as depression (Desrosiers, 1992). Diagnostic tests validated only against a clinical diagnosis made at one point in time will be inadequate. In order to validate tests purporting to discriminate between the various forms of dementia it will probably be necessary to rely on post-mortem data rather than clinical diagnoses for some time to come.

The emphasis on making the dementia vs. depression distinction using cognitive tests seems to ignore two salient facts (see Chapter 4). First, depression in older people is itself associated with a degree of cognitive impairment; secondly, for as many as a quarter of people with a dementia, a dual diagnosis of depression is also appropriate. A good rule of thumb here is that depressed mood should routinely be assessed, and that where it is present, appropriate treatment should be offered; judgement about enduring cognitive impairment may have to be suspended until either the person's depression lifts or the progression of the cognitive impairment makes itself evident over time.

Refraining from using psychological tests simply as diagnostic tests is a good reminder that diagnosis consists of bringing together a variety of types of information about a person, of which cognitive test results are only one. In this differential diagnosis other features, such as mood, behaviour, history of the disorder and so on, are usually as relevant as cognitive status.

Descriptive assessment

Here the emphasis is on describing aspects of the patient's psychological function and changes in them. This may still aid diagnosis. The difference here is that a poor score on, say, a learning test leads immediately to an evaluation of possible reasons for failure, not to a diagnostic statement that probably reflects only one of several explanations of poor test performance.

Descriptive assessment has its own problems. Perhaps as a result of the traditional emphasis on diagnostic testing, the range of psychological functions that can be readily assessed is fairly limited, the effects of repeated assessment have not been ascertained for many tests and the relationship between test results and real-life behaviour is often uncertain.

If this type of assessment is pursued, however, it becomes possible to offer a distinctly psychological contribution to the care of the older person. Assessment of change in function enables the effects of interventions (psychological or otherwise) to be evaluated, or the rate of change, say in a person with dementia, to be estimated. A detailed description of current levels and patterns of ability and dysfunction and of changes in these over time can be of assistance in counselling patients and/or their carers. This may assist in developing strategies for adapting to or coping with the deficits (Moniz-Cook & Woods, 1997).

Descriptive assessment may be validated by its predictive power in certain instances, for example, where it is used to aid placement, or allocation of treatments or support services, or to measure rate of decline.

ASSESSING COGNITIVE ABILITIES

Intellectual function

Two major measures of global intellectual function have been extensively used. Raven's Progressive Matrices (Standard and Coloured) and the Mill

Hill Vocabulary Scale (Raven, 1982) provide indications of performance and verbal intellectual levels respectively; they are fairly simple and quick to administer. Limited old-age norms are available. The Coloured version is particularly useful with older patients, being briefer and less susceptible to floor effects in those with lower levels of function. The Matrices may be particularly useful with patients with limited verbal ability, e.g. following a dominant hemisphere CVA, and have been shown to predict outcome in this context (David & Skilbeck, 1984). Care should be taken, however, that results are not invalidated on this test through visual neglect or visual field deficits.

The Wechsler Adult Intelligence Scales (WAIS) are more time-consuming, requiring a highly trained tester, but tap a richer variety of skills and modalities. As they can only be used individually, the assessor is able to observe the patient's approach to the tasks and to consider alternative hypotheses for apparent deficits. The most widely used version of the WAIS, the WAIS-R (Wechsler, 1981) was standardized in the USA on a representative sample of adults up to age 75. When assessing someone above this age, norms are available for groups of 75–79 year-olds and for those 80 and over (Ryan, Paolo & Brungardt, 1990; Ivnik et al, 1992a). It is to be hoped that the future revisions of the WAIS will include well-standardized age-norms for those over 80 years old. When examining and comparing the scores of individual subtests, it is essential to use the age-scaled subtest scores (*not* the scores used for calculating IQ), as these allow for comparison with the person's age-peers, rather than with young adults. Tables provided by Crawford (1997) allow the reliability of subtest differences to be assessed using age-scaled scores.

The WAIS-R is a lengthy test for older people. A number of short forms have been evaluated by Crawford, Allan & Jack (1992a) on a normal sample, which reflected the age distribution of over 16s in the UK, so that around a quarter were over 60. They provide regression equations and tables for calculating Full Scale, Verbal and Performance IQs from combinations of two, four, six and seven subtests. Generally, the more subtests administered, the better the prediction. For older people specifically, a four subtest short form (Comprehension and Vocabulary, Block Design and Object Assembly) was developed by Britton & Savage (1966) for the WAIS; by consulting Crawford et al.'s equations it can confidently be used with the WAIS-R. Crawford et al. suggest substituting Similarities for Vocabulary, as the latter is now less likely to be used as an indicator of pre-morbid function (see below). The verbal and performance sub-tests included in both these short forms should give good estimates of the Verbal and Perceptual Organisation factors which emerge reliably in factor analytic studies of the WAIS-R (Crawford et al., 1989a).

Much effort has been expended on developing methods of assessing whether or not the person's current level of intellectual function represents a decline from previous levels. In view of what is known of the differing trajectories of distinct domains of cognitive function over the life span, this is perhaps a rather simplistic approach, but one which does have clinical relevance in relation to disorders associated with global cognitive decline. A number of the available strategies have been reviewed by van den Broek & Bradshaw (1990).

Ideally, a comparison would be made with a measure of intellectual function administered during the person's middle years. Such an assessment is rarely, if ever, available. Alternatively, the current assessment is treated as a baseline, and then repeated after an appropriate time interval, to indicate whether any decline is on-going. This latter approach will not detect a non-progressive change occurring before the first testing. In both instances some caution is required. Where possible, the same measure should be used on each occasion, as each test of intellectual function may produce slightly different IQ estimates. Practice effects and normal variability in cognitive function must be taken into account. These considerations can mean that quite a large change—of 15 IQ points, say—may have to be present for it to be considered clinically significant.

Some guide to pre-morbid function may be provided by demographic variables, such as occupation, level of education and so on. Attempts have been made to draw up regression equations to make quantitative predictions using these variables, with limited success (Crawford et al., 1989b). Particularly with the current generation of older people, where educational opportunities were even less equitably available than today, these indices are likely to be unreliable in the individual case. They may be used in a positive sense, in that, for example, an older person who achieved well in higher education and/or in one of the professions might be safely assumed to be of above average intellectual level; however, no assumptions could be made regarding someone who left school at 14, and worked as, say, a labourer.

Another approach makes use of the apparent differential decline in various aspects of cognitive function. A number of formulae have been devised to compare WAIS sub-tests which are thought to "hold" and "don't hold", producing various Deterioration Quotients. Or the Verbal and Performance IQs have been compared to produce a Verbal–Performance Discrepancy Score. Essentially these indices have proved to be of little value in discriminating older people with a dementia from those who are unimpaired (Savage et al., 1973; van den Broek & Bradshaw, 1990). Partly this relates to the wide variability in patterns of cognitive function in the normal population; a person may have a fairly large difference between Verbal and Performance IQs, greater than could be attributed to errors of measurement, without this being particularly unusual. Another factor is the variability in patterns of change, between individuals and within the same person at different stages of the disorder. Thus at first performance abilities may well show more decline, but verbal abilities may later decline more, reducing the discrepancy, with performance levels showing a "floor" effect.

Vocabulary test scores have been evaluated as a possible indicator of pre-morbid intellectual levels and the comparison between the Mill Hill Vocabulary Scale and Raven's Progressive Matrices as an indication of decline was on this basis. Whilst vocabulary is still used in studies of normal ageing (e.g. Holland & Rabbitt, 1991) as a stable index of life-long levels, it has been shown to decline in dementia (O'Carroll, Baikie & Whittick, 1987) and tests of word-reading ability are now thought to give a more accurate index of pre-morbid intellectual level (Nelson & McKenna, 1975). The National Adult Reading Test (NART; Nelson, 1982) consists of words unlikely to be read correctly unless the person is familiar with them. The Revised form (Nelson & Willison, 1991) has been standardized against the WAIS-R. Other data is available on the Schonell Reading Test in conjunction with both the WAIS and Raven's Matrices (Ruddle & Bradshaw, 1982). In each case a predicted intellectual level is derived from the reading test score and compared with the current assessed level. The Schonell is particularly useful for those patients who are able to read very few of the NART words, as it is more sensitive in the low-average range. Conversely, it has a low "ceiling", so that the NART must be used with those of above average ability. The NART has been criticized for being over-long, and Beardsall & Brayne (1990) have shown the first 25 of the 50 items to give a good estimate of overall performance. Beardsall & Huppert (1994) have further modified the NART, by placing each word in the context of a sentence, so that the words are not seen in isolation. It is suggested that this version, the Cambridge Contextual Reading Test (CCRT), may produce more accurate estimates of pre-morbid function (Beardsall, 1998). Other possible problems with the NART have been described by Baddeley, Emsley & Nimmo-Smith (1993) who are developing the "Spot the Word" test as an alternative. This lexical decision test requires the subject to choose which of two letter strings presented is actually a word. Unfortunately, norms for older people have yet to be published (Baddeley, Emsley & Nimmo-Smith, 1992). Beardsall & Huppert (1997) have shown that performance levels on this test are affected by fairly mild degrees of cognitive impairment, and suggest that its main use will be where the person being assessed has an articulatory problem.

Despite the usefulness of these tests in descriptive assessment of the older person, the use of the discrepancy between pre-morbid and current intellectual level as a diagnostic index should be treated with as much caution as any other attempt to arrive at a diagnostic formulation from only one type of evidence.

Memory and learning

Primary memory is typically assessed using the digit-span test from the WAIS-R and the visual span from the Wechsler Memory Scale—Revised (Wechsler, 1987). A number of measures of secondary memory are available, reflecting different memory modalities, and, to an extent, different aspects of the memory process; unfortunately, the relationship of test paradigms to models of memory is not always clear. Among memory tests currently available are:

Kendrick Object Learning Test (OLT; Kendrick, 1985). This test, involving free recall of a number of common objects presented pictorially, is acceptable to patients, but would benefit from a recognition or cued-recall format. It does have two parallel forms and data on six-week re-test aids its longitudinal use. The OLT Quotient should be calculated, giving a descriptive measure of the patient's performance in relation to his/her peer group; the diagnostic index is not recommended.

Recognition Memory Tests (Warrington, 1984). This test uses a forced-choice recognition format, where the patient is required to indicate which of two stimuli he/she was shown previously. The test is in two parts, using single words and faces, respectively, with 50 items in each. The test enables an interesting comparison to be made between verbal and non-verbal aspects of memory. Norms are available up to age 70; the recognition format tends to be more acceptable than free recall, but leads to a high chance level, with moderately impaired patients with dementia performing at chance levels. A briefer version is now available, complete with normative data on older people (Clegg & Warrington, 1994).

The Rivermead Behavioural Memory Test (Wilson, Cockburn & Baddeley, 1985). Designed to quickly and simply assess everyday memory, and to reflect real-life performance more than conventional tests, this battery contains a useful variety of memory tests, including—unusually—tests of prospective memory i.e. remembering to do something in the future, rather than some past event. The four parallel forms are especially useful for re-assessment purposes, and there is a useful supplement to the test manual, giving norms for 119 older adults, aged 70–94 (Cockburn &

Smith, 1989). Ironically some of the most useful sub-tests are very similar to conventional tests, e.g. prose recall, face recognition and orientation; the behavioural aspects play a relatively minor role. The scoring system does not allow detailed interpretation of performance on particular sub-tests in comparison with the standardization sample.

Wechsler Memory Scale—Revised (Wechsler, 1987). The original scale was much criticized, but widely used as a brief test rapidly covering a variety of areas of memory function. The revised version takes many of the criticisms on board, but in so doing has become much more unwieldy and daunting for use with older people. Five indices may be derived from the full battery: general memory; attention/concentration; verbal memory; visual memory; and delayed recall. In contrast to the Rivermead Behavioural Memory Test, many of the items appear meaningless, and motivation may be an issue for some patients, e.g. in attempting to learn pairings of words that have no apparent association, in the paired-associates sub-test. However, many of the subtests stand as tests in their own right (e.g. logical memory, digit span, paired associates) and subtests may be used selectively. Norms in the manual are up to age 74 only at present. Normative data on over 400 people aged 56–94 are provided by Ivnik et al. (1992b).

Fuld Object Memory Evaluation (Fuld, 1977). This ambitious test begins with the patient identifying by touch (and sight, if necessary) 10 objects hidden in a bag. The objects are removed and memory for them tested over five trials using a selective reminding paradigm (the subject is told on each occasion only those items he/she is unable to recall); delays are filled with verbal fluency tasks and a measure of recognition memory is also included. Even mood is assessed by contrasting the number of "happy" and "sad" words produced in a given time interval in two of the verbal fluency tasks. Norms are available for various populations, including some up to age 90, and there are two parallel forms. However, the test often feels over-demanding for older patients; perhaps a simpler version should be developed?

The Benton Visual Retention Test (Benton, 1974) is a commonly used test of immediate visual memory (Crookes & McDonald, 1972). A series of 10 line drawings of shapes of increasing complexity are shown to the patient for 10 seconds each; most cards have two large central figures and one small peripheral figure. The patient draws them immediately after each is removed. The copying version of the test (where the stimuli are not removed) provides a control for the effects of visuo-spatial, rather than memory difficulties. A detailed scoring system allows for analysis of the type of errors made. Norms for older people are available (Benton, Eslinger & Damasio, 1981).

The Doors and People Test (Baddeley, Emslie & Nimmo-Smith, 1994) allows a direct comparison of verbal and non-verbal memory. For the non-verbal material, photographs of a huge variety of doors are preferred to faces, as it is thought the latter may be processed differently from other non-verbal stimuli. The test also incorporates both free recall and recognition components, with the person choosing from four options, so that chance scores are relatively low. There is a multiple-trial, learning component for both verbal and non-verbal material, and a test of delayed recall in each modality. All in all, it provides a fairly comprehensive analysis of the person's memory, and has reasonable norms for older people. As yet it has no parallel forms, so repeated testing may be a problem. For an older person with reasonable vision and hearing, without severe impairment, it is an acceptable test, which often captures the person's interest and attention.

Speed

The Digit Copying Test, one of the Kendrick Cognitive Tests for the Elderly measures psycho-motor speed simply and acceptably. It is preferable to the WAIS Digit Symbol Test as it is less complex and relies less on memory and comprehension of instructions. The Digit Copying Quotient should be calculated to facilitate comparison with other aspects of the patient's abilities. Speed of performance may be impaired both in dementia and, to a lesser extent, in depression. In a number of research studies, reaction time tests have been used, and these would be an obvious method of assessing speed of information processing. However, these have usually been associated with the various computerized test batteries that have been developed (see below).

Language

Many aphasia batteries exist, but none specifically for older people. The *Schuell Minnesota Aphasia Test* is wide-ranging, has a useful short form (Powell, Bailey & Clark, 1980) and has been standardized on normal elderly people (Walker, 1980). The *Token Test* (DeRenzi & Vignolo, 1962; DeRenzi & Faglioni, 1978) tests comprehension of instructions of increasing linguistic complexity, and is useful in delineating the extent of a receptive deficit. The *Frenchay Aphasia Screening Test* (FAST) (Enderby et al., 1986), designed for use with stroke patients, may be useful as a a brief, easily administered screening test for language problems.

Many batteries include a naming test; a specific test of nominal dysphasia—the *Graded Naming Test*—has been produced by McKenna & Warrington (1983), which comprises 30 line drawings of increasing difficulty. Norms are available up to age 70. Williams et al. (1989) present data on a similar test—the *Boston Naming Test*—for patients with dementia and normal controls, and suggest a 30-item version of the original 60-item test. In dementia the difficulty in naming is thought to also reflect difficulty in recognizing the object, whereas the dysphasic may clearly recognize the object but still be unable to name it (Kirshner, Webb & Kelly, 1984).

Verbal fluency may be assessed by asking the patient to name as many words as possible beginning with a certain letter in a particular time (Whitehead, 1973) or name members of a particular set (for example country names; Isaacs & Akhtar, 1972). Hart, Smith & Swash (1988) provide data on a small number of patients with Alzheimer-type dementia and normal elderly controls on both types of fluency tests. There is some evidence that verbal fluency scores are highly correlated with verbal intellectual level (Miller, 1984), and so the approach of Crawford, Moore & Cameron (1992b) in using NART scores to derive a predicted verbal fluency score for comparative purposes has much to commend it.

Stevens et al. (1992) report the use of verbal fluency tests and the Boston Naming Test in a memory clinic context, and provide some useful data on their usefulness in assessing early dementia.

The *Anomalous Sentences Repetition Test* (Weeks, 1988) involves the patient in repeating a number of "sentences", which while syntactically correct, do not make sense. This is an area of function thought to be particularly sensitive to the effects of dementia, and the test has been designed very much with diagnosis in mind, rather than as an index of an aspect of language function. There are four parallel forms, the test is brief and reported to be acceptable to patients, with norms up to and beyond age 80. Data on its use in clinical settings would be of interest.

Executive functioning

Problems in this area of assessment are usually thought of as reflecting dysfunction of the frontal lobe type. The higher level skills of planning, problem-solving and flexible thinking may be involved in many different tasks, and clues to such difficulties may be gathered from careful observation of the person's performance on a variety of tasks. Perseveration of response may be seen, or the person's attempt at a constructional task may be disorganized. The *WAIS-R Similarities subtest* may point to difficulties in abstract thinking.

Verbal fluency is a frequently used indicator of frontal lobe dysfunction, and may also be seen as a measure of semantic memory; some of the tests available for initial letter and category fluency were described above, in the section on Language.

The *Wisconsin Card Sorting Test* is probably the best known test of executive function, requiring the patient to sort cards according to an undisclosed rule, which may reflect either the number or colour or the shape of symbols on the cards. The patient's task is to discern the correct rule from feedback given card by card; the rule is then changed, and the patient must discover the new rule. A short form is available (Nelson, 1976), as the full test would be extremely demanding for most older patients. Norms for older people are available (e.g. Axelrod & Henry, 1992).

The *Weigl Colour Form Sorting Test* provides a much simpler test of the person's ability to switch response-set. The patient is given a number of different shapes of different colours, and asked to sort them; having sorted them into piles of similar shape or colour, the patient is asked to sort them a different way. A patient with a severe dysexecutive difficulty will perseverate and sort them as previously, apparently being unable to perceive the second dimension on which they might be sorted. Colour tends to be the preferred sorting dimension for patients with dementia (Grewal, Haward & Davies, 1985, 1986).

The *Trail Making Test*, Part A, requires the patient to draw lines connecting in sequence numbers displayed on a page, and is a measure of psychomotor speed and perceptual organization. Part B requires letters and numbers to be connected alternately, maintaining the sequence of each, e.g. A–1–B–2–C–3, etc. This additionally requires cognitive flexibility, and may give a guide to executive function. Norms for older adults are provided in Spreen & Strauss (1991). This source also provides older adult norms for the *Stroop Test*, where the person has to name the colour in which a word is printed, ignoring the word itself, which will be the name of a different colour. The person has to inhibit reading the colour word, and this slows performance in colour identification, a phenomenon particularly marked in patients with frontal lobe difficulties.

Perceptual abilities

Perceptual difficulties may become apparent in a variety of tests; a difficulty in naming pictures of objects in a memory task, or an inability to carry out a simple psychomotor task such as the *Digit Copying Test*, for example. A test such as the *Benton Visual Retention Test*, described above, is useful in giving an indication of copying a design, as well as having a separate memory component. Other clinical tests of drawing ability, such as drawing a clock (Shulman, Shedletsky & Silver, 1986; Sunderland et al., 1989; Bourke et al., 1995) or drawing a house (Moore & Wyke, 1984) can also be informative. Contrasting the person's ability to draw an object, such as a house, spontaneously with their ability to copy a given design, may give indications whether spatial relationships have become completely disorganised, or whether an external cue can assist in their expression. Sub-tests of the WAIS-R, especially Block Design and Object Assembly, provide further evidence of the person's visuo-spatial abilities.

Most of the above tests involve a constructional element; the *Visual Object and Space Perception Battery* (VOSP) (Warrington & James, 1991) includes a number of sub-tests which may be useful in addressing the perceptual element of perceptuo-motor skills more directly. However, older adult norms are limited. Particularly following a right hemisphere stroke, unilateral visual neglect is a common, but often unrecognized, feature. The person behaves as if no sensory input is being received from the contralateral side of visual space. Clock and other drawing tasks may reveal the problem, with the left hand side of the drawing incomplete, but more systematic tests, such as cancellation or line bisection tasks, are more useful (Skilbeck, 1996). In the former, the patient with neglect will miss target letters, digits or symbols on the left hand side of the array; in the latter, the patient when asked to draw a cross in the middle of a line will typically respond with a cross in the right hand half of the line. Several of these tasks are included in the *Behavioural Inattention Test* (BIT) (Wilson, Cockburn & Halligan, 1987), as well as in other batteries (see Skilbeck, 1996).

Neuropsychological tests

Neuropsychological batteries developed for use with younger patients should be used cautiously unless old-age norms are available. For example, normal old people show poor performance on some parts of the *Halstead–Reitan Battery* (Klisz, 1978) and on other neuropsychological tests (Benton, Eslinger & Damasio, 1981). Generally, length and difficulty-level make such batteries unsuitable for older people, although Blackburn and Tyrer (1985) report positively on the value of a shortened version of *Luria's Neuropsychological Investigation* in older patients. More straightforward clinical testing will be informative with many older patients.

Examples of such a clinical approach are provided by Holden & Woods (1995), Holden (1995) and Church & Wattis (1988).

It was hoped that automated testing would allow cognitive assessment of patients untestable conventionally (Miller, 1980). A number of reports of the development of such methods have appeared (e.g. Carr, Woods & Moore, 1986b; Sahakian, 1990; Simpson et al., 1991). The capabilities of microcomputers provide an excellent opportunity to devise a new generation of tests, emphasizing success rather than failure, suitable for repeated use, and taking into account information-processing models currently used in experimental psychology, including consideration of the strategies the patient adopts. Using response speed measures allows differentiation between patients even in error-free performance. Computer graphics can be used to increase the attractiveness and interest of the materials and the various studies have reported that such batteries are well received by older people, including those with dementia. There is some evidence that performance is enhanced through the use of a touch sensitive screen, rather than through response buttons (Carr, Woods & Moore, 1986a). The *CANTAB* battery of tests (Sahakian, 1990) is now the best developed commercially available system. Considerable development work has taken place on normal samples and clinical groups, and a wide range of tests cover many cognitive functions, including memory and learning, attention, executive functions and visuo-spatial skills.

Brief cognitive assessment

By using brief cognitive tests clinicians can quantify clinical data in a structured and standardized form. Such tests should always have been given before patients are referred for detailed cognitive assessment, as simple tests of information and orientation have often proved at least as valid as more detailed cognitive tests (e.g. Pattie & Gilleard, 1979). Many such tests exist; the 12-item Information/Orientation subtest of the *Clifton Assessment Procedures for the Elderly* (CAPE) is widely available, and has been extensively researched (Pattie, 1988). The CAPE also includes a concentration test and screening items for reading and writing as well as a behaviour rating scale (see below). Other frequently used tests include Hodkinson's (1972) 10-item *Abbreviated Mental Test* (AMTS) and the rather longer *Mini-Mental State Examination* (MMSE; Folstein, Folstein & McHugh, 1975).

Which of the various tests is used in practice will depend on the setting, how brief the test has to be and personal preference. The various measures have high inter-correlations (e.g. Orrell et al., 1992), and all are liable to be influenced by the patient's level of education; those with a below average education may score poorly on such tests, despite being unimpaired; those with a high level of education may maintain high scores despite actual cognitive decline. The MMSE has been shown to be particularly susceptible to this effect (e.g. Christensen & Jorm, 1992). The MMSE also may be criticized for combining a number of items tapping quite distinct areas of function (memory, concentration, praxis, etc.) into a single total score. Different patients may have identical scores but quite different patterns of performance on this test. Orrell et al. (1992) indicate that it is the memory and orientation items that discriminate best between groups of depressed and dementing patients.

Assessing other areas of function is important in describing the pattern of impairment, e.g. dementia with dysphasia, or dementia of frontal type. To achieve this, a profile is required rather than a single score. The *Middlesex Elderly Assessment of Mental State* (MEAMS; Golding, 1989) achieves just this, including 12 brief neuropsychological screening tests, including orientation, naming, drawing, arithmetic and perceptual tasks. It is brief, easy to administer and available in two parallel forms. Some clinical data are already available—as these grow, the usefulness of the test will be enhanced. The Cambridge examination for mental disorders of the elderly (*CAMDEX*; Roth et al., 1988) is a psychiatric diagnosis scale for older people that includes *CAMCOG*, a screening test again covering a range of neuropsychological functions and incorporating the MMSE and AMTS. Each area of function has relatively few items, but it is reported to show sufficient differentiation at higher levels of function to be of value in the detection of mild dementia (Huppert, 1991; Huppert et al., 1996).

As one of the key issues in cognitive assessment relates to whether or not the person has shown an abnormal amount of cognitive decline, informant questionnaires have been developed to supplement cognitive tests. The best known of these is the *Informant Questionnaire of Cognitive Decline in the Elderly* (IQCODE) (Jorm, Scott & Kacomb, 1989). This is now available as a 12-item scale, and appears to perform at least as well as the MMSE as a screening instrument (Stephens & Jorm, 1994).

Example of descriptive cognitive assessment

Referral

Mrs G, a 74 year-old retired primary school headteacher, was referred in view of occasional memory lapses; on several occasions she had become completely lost whilst driving, not knowing what town she was in, despite it being a place well-known to her. The referring physician commented that she had a history of hypertension.

Assessment

Mrs G was seen at home on two occasions, where she lives alone with a sister living close by. As well as the problems with driving, she recounted how she would walk into a room and forget why she had gone there, and that she would occasionally forget appointments. She had begun to use memory aids, always making a shopping list and marking days off on the calendar. There was a hint of vagueness as she talked about her past life, with some of the details not being at all clear.

Results

National Adult Reading Test. Mrs G made four errors in reading the 50 irregular words on this test, giving an estimated life-long IQ of 126, consistent with her educational and occupational history.

Rivermead Behavioural Memory Test. Mrs G's overall profile score on this test was 11 (maximum possible 24). The test manual supplement for older people suggests this score is below the 2.5th percentile for someone of Mrs G's age and estimated IQ level.

The profile of performance on the various subtests is of interest. She scored maximum points on orientation, including being able to give the correct date. She performed well on the two recognition tasks, and was able to learn and remember a route around the room relatively well. However, her prospective memory was extremely poor, as was her free recall, especially after a delay. In recalling a brief memory passage, she was able immediately to give back the initial phrases of the passage, but then elaborated details not present in the original. After 20 minutes, although the story bore some tenuous relation to the original, there was no evidence of recall of the specific incident described.

WAIS-R sub-tests. Mrs G did poorly on the Block Design and Similarities Subtests of the WAIS-R. Using the age-scaled scores for her age group, her scores were 5 and 6, respectively, both well below average, and representing a clear deficit in performance. On the Block Design items, she placed the blocks in a line, and seemed to be unable to plan a strategy for tackling the task. On Similarities, she had some difficulty in abstract thinking. Both these deficits may be considered as reflecting frontal lobe dysfunction. Her Digit Span age-scaled score was 10, which, although average for her age, might represent a change for someone of Mrs G's general intellectual level.

Digit Copying Test.   On this test of psychomotor speed, her performance appeared unimpaired, with a Test Quotient of 112.

Verbal Fluency.   On being given 60 seconds each to produce words beginning with "F", "A" and "S" respectively, Mrs G produced an average of 11 words per letter. She was able to name 9 items that might be bought in a supermarket in a minute. All these scores are below average for someone of Mrs G's intellectual level, and are supportive of the hypothesis of frontal lobe dysfunction.

Geriatric Depression Scale.   Mrs G scored 2 on the 15-item short form of this scale. She said that she feels helpless when she is not able to find something she needs, but did not feel that she had more problems with memory than most people. There was no evidence for depressed mood.

Feedback

The results were discussed in detail with Mrs G together with her sister (with Mrs G's permission). Mrs G remembered clearly items from one testing session to the next (despite having had a holiday in the meantime), and had a good grasp of day-to-day events. Strengths as well as problem areas were discussed, in relation to the different tests used. Both had wondered about "dementia", but were not entirely sure what this meant. Mrs G had had an aunt who, at 90, had become very confused and been admitted to hospital. It was explained that the definition of dementia involved simply a loss from a previous level in some areas of function, but that there are many causes and types, which may have different implications. For Mrs G, the likelihood was of the changes relating to vascular damage in specific areas of the brain—possibly mini-strokes— and that medication, such as aspirin, aimed at preventing further strokes could be helpful to her. Mrs G found useful a diagram of the brain, indicating the relatively specific areas of possible dysfunction, e.g. frontal areas for verbal fluency, Block Design and Similarities; fronto-temporal in relation to recall difficulties. She found it reassuring that many aspects were still working normally, and that her success in using memory aids showed that she could find ways of coping with her problems. Mrs G's sister commented that earlier in life, Mrs G would readily become anxious over the smallest problem; now she felt she was more relaxed and accepting than ever before in her life, almost to the extent of a character change. This change may also relate to frontal lobe changes, and hopefully will make it easier for Mrs G to face the inevitability of giving up her car.

Conclusion

This assessment contributed to the diagnostic issues, but went well beyond them in providing feedback which Mrs G and her sister found useful. Understanding the person's own thoughts and fears about diagnosis is essential before giving feedback; his/her image of ageing and memory, dementia or Alzheimer's disease will have been conditioned by personal experiences or media images. The good performance on orientation tests is quite common in frontal-type dementias, which may be missed if too much reliance is placed on screening measures having only items of this type.

Practical considerations

Several practical points are important:

1. Sensory deficits are more common in older people. Care must be taken that the patient can see and hear adequately, with glasses or hearing aid if necessary. Large print versions of some tests (e.g. the NART) are available; other tests have items that could be presented in enlarged versions if required. Ensure that the testing room is quiet and free from distracting noises. If the sensory impairment is severe and uncorrectable, tests using only the unimpaired modalities will be needed. With deaf patients, written instructions can be useful for some tests. With practical tasks, check that painful joints or tremors are not making the test too difficult for the person, and note any effects on performance. Where the person's first language is not English, check whether interpretation is required; it is usually preferable to use a professional interpreter, with some prior knowledge of the tests, rather than a family member. Be cautious in interpreting the results of verbal tests, even where the person appears to understand and speak some English.
2. Older patients may take longer to adjust to the testing situation and often more time needs to be spent putting the patient at ease, establishing an atmosphere of cooperation and trust, and establishing with the person the purpose of the assessment and its benefits.
3. The patient is likely to be helped by supportive encouragement during testing. This usually has to be of a general nature; often it is useful to explain that everybody fails on some items because of the test-

design. Patients often underestimate their performance level and realistic positive evaluations are often possible. Unrealistic praise where the patients's failure is blatantly evident is unhelpful.

4. The session should be paced gently—a rushed, pressured session will increase the apparent impairment level. Several short sessions are preferable to a lengthy one, to minimize the effects of fatigue. Ending each session on a note of success helps to maintain future cooperation.

5. The difficulty level of the tests used should be carefully reviewed so that the patient experiences as little overt failure as possible, particularly early in the session. Tests exposing the older patient to repeated overt failure are stressful, reduce cooperation and should be used with caution. It is sometimes suggested that tests should resemble "real-life" situations as closely as possible, and this may have advantages in predicting the patient's function outside the test session. Paradoxically, tests that appear too similar to real-life tasks may increase the stress on the patient, whereas tests that are more in the form of a game may be more acceptable.

6. It is wise to commence the assessment with some brief, wide-ranging tests, to give an indication of possible areas of strength and weakness. If for any reason the assessment is cut short, there may still be some conclusions that can be drawn from a relatively brief contact.

7. In selecting tests, there are clearly a wealth of possible measures available. As well as difficulty level, consider whether the test in question has appropriate norms relevant to the person being assessed, and whether it has parallel forms, as reassessment is fairly common in work with older people.

ASSESSING MOOD AND WELL-BEING

Several self-report "life-satisfaction" and "morale" scales have been developed specifically for older people. Among those widely used have been the *Philadelphia Geriatric Center (PGC) Morale Scale* (Lawton, 1975) and the *Life Satisfaction Index* (LSI), which is available in a number of forms (Twining, 1990) including the brief version described by Bigot (1974). This has eight items on two sub-scales, "acceptance–contentment" and "achievement–fulfilment". Gilleard, Willmott & Vaddadik (1981) provide useful normative clinical data and suggest that the latter subscale reflects a more stable attitudinal component of morale, based on past life achievements and experiences.

The PGC Morale Scale and the LSI show considerable overlap with depression scales, although demoralization and depression in the elderly are not necessarily identical constructs (Gurland, 1980). Gilleard, Willmott & Vaddadik (1981) used the LSI and *Schwab Depression Scale* to monitor depression in the elderly. Gallagher, Nies & Thompson (1982) report normative and reliability data on the *Beck Depression Inventory* with normal and depressed elderly people and conclude that it is an adequate clinical screening instrument. The *Geriatric Depression Scale* (Yesavage, Brinic & Rose, 1983) has a simpler response format (Yes/No) than the Beck, and is now extensively used as a self-report measure for depression in older people. The original scale had 30 items, but a 15-item short form is available (Sheikh & Yesavage, 1986). O'Neill et al. (1992) suggest that this scale is more effectively administered by a rater, rather than being given to the older person to complete. An alternative is the *SELFCARE (D) Scale*, which has been developed as a 12-item self-report measure for use in primary care settings (Bird et al., 1987). The *Hospital Anxiety & Depression Scale* (HADS) (Kenn et al., 1987) allows a structured assessment of anxiety as well as depression, an aspect not addressed specifically by most of the available scales.

A number of observer-rated scales are available (see Montgomery, 1988), which may assist in overcoming some of the problems inherent in self-report measures with older people (such as visual acuity problems, inappropriateness of items etc.). In assessing patients with cognitive impairment for mood disturbance—where self-report may be particularly unreliable—several observer-rated depression scales are available: the *Depressive Signs Scale* (Katona & Aldridge, 1985) the *Cornell Scale* for depression in dementia (Alexopoulos et al., 1988) and the Dementia Mood Assessment Scale (Sunderland et al., 1988). However, it is worth noting that in mild dementia it may be valid to use the self-report *Geriatric Depression Scale* (Ott & Fogel, 1992).

There is increasing interest in the evaluation of health related quality of life, as a means of evaluating health care interventions. A number of approaches are possible (see Bowling, 1997), including the *SF-36*, a brief questionnaire, which has been used in older populations (Hayes et al., 1995; Murray, Lefort & Ribiero, 1997).

ASSESSING BEHAVIOUR AND SELF-CARE

Often, particularly in dementia, a person's actual behaviour—level of function, excesses and deficits—is very important in finding a suitable placement or in monitoring change. Behaviour can be assessed in several ways.

Rating scales

Here those familiar with the older person's day-to-day behaviour (usually nurses, care-attendants or relatives) complete the scales from their uncontrolled, unsystematic observations of the person, perhaps over a specified time period. Many different scales are in use, differing in behavioural areas covered, range and depth of content, length and format. The purpose of the assessment should guide the choice of scale. Long scales are only likely to be completed conscientiously by busy care staff if the results are immediately relevant to patient management.

There are a number of scales indicating the person's general functional ability and degree of care needed (Little & Doherty, 1996). These scales include aspects of behaviour such as toileting, feeding, mobility and so on. Among the most frequently used are the *Crichton Geriatric Rating Scale* (Robinson, 1977); the Behaviour Rating Scale from the *Clifton Assessment Procedures for the Elderly* (CAPE; Pattie & Gilleard, 1979; Pattie, 1988); the *Brighton Clinic Adaptive Behaviour Scale* (BCABS; Ward, Murphy & Proctor, 1991); the *Behavioural Assessment Scale of Later Life* (BASOLL) (Brooker, 1998). These scales all include items relating to behaviour problems as well as to self-care. Specific brief measures of basic self-care skills are provided by the *Index of Activities of Daily Living* (ADL) (Katz et al., 1963) and the *Physical Self Maintenance Scale* (PSMS) (Lawton & Brody, 1969). Higher level self-care skills (e.g. shopping, cooking, finances) are assessed by the *Functional Activities Questionnaire* (Pfeffer et al., 1982) and the *Instrumental Activities of Daily Living Scale* (Lawton & Brody, 1969).

Scales mixing self-care and problem behaviour items vary greatly in their breadth and depth of coverage, especially of challenging behaviour. Inter-rater reliabilities tend to be much lower for items such as aggression and social disturbance than for ratings of physical functioning, suggesting they are more difficult to define and rate objectively. The Clifton is probably most useful for general screening. It gives four factor scores (physical disability, communication difficulties, apathy and social disturbance) and has extensive norms for a variety of elderly populations (Pattie, 1988). The BCABS has been designed to be particularly appropriate for rating patients with severe dementia, and has been used in comparisons of long-term care environments (Lindesay et al., 1991).

Scales specifically designed for assessing challenging behaviour are now available. Examples include the *Present Behavioural Examination* (Hope & Fairburn, 1992) and Beck et al. (1997). Scales are being developed for specific behaviours such as aggression e.g. the *Rating of Aggressive Behaviour in the Elderly* (RAGE) (Patel & Hope, 1992) and agitated behaviour (Cohen-Mansfield, Warner & Marx, 1992). RAGE has been developed with a view to increasing reliability by having the ratings made on the basis of observation over several days.

Scales developed for use by professional staff in residential units have often not seemed ideally suited for assessment of an older person being cared for at home by a relative. The emotional involvement and 24-hour commitment of a relative mean that different behaviours from those emphasized in an institutional setting may affect the ability to cope. Greene et al.'s (1982) *Behavioural and Mood Disturbance Scale* is intended for completion by relatives. It has three factors, apathy/withdrawal, active disturbance and mood change. Gilleard's (1984) *Problem Check-list* has also been widely used in this context; Agar et al. (1997) provide a factor analysis of this scale, and indicate its potential utility.

Structured observation

Here, in contrast to the rating scale assessing everyday "natural" behaviour, a person's performance is assessed in a structured situation. This method underlies the *Performance Test of Activities of Daily Living* (PADL)(Kuriansky & Gurland, 1976; Macdonald et al., 1982). It includes 17 tasks which, with props, can be administered as a standardized structured interview. It may detect adaptive behaviour not prompted or encouraged in the ward environment: conventional rating scales are inevitably affected by the extent to which independence is reinforced and allowed by the care regime. However, underfunctioning on the PADL could occur if the patient is affected by the situation's unfamiliarity, has difficulty in understanding the instructions, or has test anxiety or motivation difficulties. Little et al. (1986) consider the relationship between the different modalities of assessing behaviour in dementia.

Skurla, Rogers & Sunderland (1988) have developed the *ADL Situational Task*, which aims to focus more on tasks depending on memory and reasoning, and less on motor tasks than the PADL. It has four tasks, again with standardized equipment, materials and instructions and specified prompts. The tasks include making a cup of coffee and using money to purchase two items. Mahurin, DeBettigures & Pirozzolo (1991) have devised a longer measure on similar lines, the *Structured Assessment of Independent Living Skills* (SAILS).

Direct observation

Here, behaviour in the natural environment is systematically observed, usually using some kind of sampling procedure to keep the quantity of data collected to manageable proportions: perhaps only particular behaviours will be observed, or observations will be made at set-time intervals, although Godlove, Richard & Rodwell (1982) showed that this sampling is not always essential with older people in institutional settings. Direct observation requires considerable preparation, allowing time for adaptation to the observer's presence by both older people and staff and careful definition of behaviours and the settings in which they are to be observed.

Some studies have looked at "engagement" to assess the proportion of residents involved in some kind of activity, interacting with people or materials (Jenkins et al., 1977). The behavioural definitions can be extended to give a more detailed description of behaviour (McFadyen, 1984; Macdonald, Craig & Warner, 1985; Ward et al., 1992). Baltes, Burgess & Stewart (1980) have used direct observation to assess the important sequential relationships in residents' and staff behaviour, and Lindesay et al. (1991) report its use in comparisons of long-term care settings for people with severe dementia. Bowie & Mountain (1993) report the development of the *Patient Behaviour Observation Instrument*, where the observer uses a hand-held computer to record the occurrence of pre-defined categories of behaviour.

Increasingly there is recognition that increasing the quantity of interactions is not enough; the quality of interactions is of crucial importance; an increase in low quality or negative interactions is not likely to be helpful. This is reflected in the development of scales such as the *Quality of Interactions Schedule* (QUIS) (Dean, Proudfoot & Lindesay, 1993b), although this has not yet been reported as being applied to individual older people— rather it has been used to evaluate the overall level of quality of interactions in a particular care environment (see below). Similarly, the very detailed observational method, *Dementia Care Mapping* (DCM) (Kitwood & Bredin, 1992), may be used to indicate the individual person's level of well-being, but is more often used to give overall profiles, reflecting the quality of the care environment. Brooker (1995) provides a useful review of observational measures in dementia care.

ASSESSING NEEDS

The recent emphasis on comprehensive assessment of needs, in order to inform care-planning, has revealed a dearth of standardised instruments in this area (Hamid, Howard & Silverman, 1995). Most of the assessments previously described focus on specific areas, and do not integrate the overall picture. Barrowclough & Fleming (1986a) use a constructional approach, assessing the whole situation and identifying the person's strengths as well as needs. Strengths are used in the care-plan to seek to meet the person's needs. The use of this approach in residential care has been validated (Barrowclough & Fleming, 1986b).

More recently, the *Camberwell Assessment of Need* (Slade et al., 1996), a scale developed for use with younger people with long-term psychiatric problems, has been adapted for use with older people (Reynolds et al., 1998). The *Care Needs Assessment Pack for Dementia* (Carenap-D) (McWalter et al., 1998) has been developed specifically for people with dementia and their carers, and some reliability and validity data have been reported. These scales have the potential for identifying needs of the person or the carer that are not being met, and should assist in care-planning and, in aggregate, in service planning. However, it should be noted that the definition of "need" is determined by the professional, not by the person or carer, and typically takes into account available resources and services. It does not necessarily map directly onto the person's wants or demands. The possibility—although it perhaps seems unlikely—of over-met needs should also be considered; it may be as detrimental as an unmet need. For example, a depressed older person is provided with home help and meals on wheels; he/she becomes dependent on these services, and is reinforced in a passive role, which serves to maintain the depressed mood; or a person is admitted to a residential home because he/she feels lonely at home alone; less radical, and more specific, ways of meeting needs should be the first step.

ASSESSING THE CARE ENVIRONMENT

Methods of assessing institutional environments can assist in identifying features needing change and in monitoring intervention attempts. A comprehensive and detailed measure is the Multi-phasic Environmental Assessment Procedure (MEAP) (Moos & Lemke, 1980), designed for and standardized on settings for older people. Physical and architectural features, resident and staff characteristics, the social climate and aspects of the setting's policies and regime are all covered. An example of its use is in comparing different types of care philosophy (Benjamin& Spector, 1992).

The MEAP is rather long, and not specifically geared to environments for people with dementia. Some studies, such as Lindesay et al.'s (1991) evaluation of a new type of small, homely unit for people with severe dementia (the domus), have used selected scales from the MEAP. Others have selected and adapted items from across the various scales; thus, Willcocks, Peace & Kellaher (1987) report a national survey of residential homes on a number of environmental variables. Bowie, Mountain & Clayden (1992) have developed six scales assessing aspects of the ward environment for use specifically in long-term care facilities for people with dementia, and report reliability and validity data. There is likely to be increasing interest in such measures, with more emphasis being placed on improving the quality of long-term care. Kitwood (1992) has developed a direct observational method, *Dementia Care Mapping*, which focuses further on the quality dimension, evaluating the extent to which the environment and staff practices enhance, or detract from, the personhood of the dementia sufferer. Dean, Proudfoot & Lindesay (1993b) have developed the *Quality of Interactions Schedule*, which indicates the proportion of positive interactions in the care setting, and proved useful in the evaluation of the domus units in dementia care.

In community settings, it is of great importance to assess relatives' feelings of strain arising from, for example, looking after a person suffering from dementia. Some studies (e.g. Gilleard, 1984) have used non-specific measures of distress, such as the *General Health Questionnaire* (Goldberg, 1978) or the *Beck Depression Inventory* (see above). Other scales have been developed that more specifically assess strain arising directly from the relative's care-giving (e.g. Greene et al., 1982; Gilleard, 1984; Agar et al., 1997). Ramsay, Winget & Higginson (1995) provide a useful review of these scales.

In institutional settings, staff strain and satisfaction are also important influences on the quality of the environment. Scales such as the *Maslach Burnout Inventory*, *Minnesota Job Satisfaction Scale* and the *General Health Questionnaire* have been widely used (Dean, Briggs & Lindesay, 1993a; Baillon et al., 1996; Moniz-Cook, Millington & Silver, 1997).

PSYCHOLOGICAL ASSESSMENT

Despite this chapter being less than encyclopedic in its coverage of available tests, it would perhaps be easy to gain the impression that a scale exists for anything a psychologist might wish to assess in relation to older people. It cannot be emphasized too strongly that a mechanistic approach to assessment is not appropriate. Well developed psychological skills are needed, to identify the key questions to be addressed by any assessment, and to use appropriate tests and scales alongside other assessment skills, such as interviewing and functional analysis.

The psychologist needs to be aware of the uses to which the assessment will be put, and be prepared to explain the purpose clearly to the patient, in a manner he/she can understand. There is increasing awareness of the importance of the process of sharing the diagnosis with the patient and family—often described as "breaking the bad news". Good practice, however, demands that the process begins before any assessment, with pre-diagnostic assessment counselling. This is the time to begin to explore the patient's perception of the possible outcomes, and to ensure that the patient is aware, say, that the assessment may result in advice about competence to drive. Feedback on a neuropsychological assessment cannot simply be fitted into a five-minute slot at the end of the session; time must be allowed, and further sessions scheduled as necessary.

A mechanistic approach in terms of the interpretation of test results is also not sustainable. The complex multiple pathologies that befall older people, teasing out the differential effects of physical health changes, sensory losses and "expected" age-related decline, from a dementing process cannot be achieved by the application of cut-off scores in a one-off assessment. Uncertainty is common regarding aetiology; the psychologist is able, nonetheless, to helpfully describe functional strengths and weaknesses, and to indicate how this knowledge may inform and feed into plans of care. Assessment is not a goal in itself, but a means towards improving the quality of life for all concerned, through intervention (and sometimes inaction) that is planned and appropriate to the needs of the person and his/her supporters.

ACKNOWLEDGEMENT

Parts of this chapter are adapted from the author's chapter, "Problems in the elderly—investigation", in S. Lindsay & G. Powell (Eds), *Handbook of Clinical Adult Psychology*, Routledge, London, 1994.

REFERENCES

Agar, S., Moniz-Cook, E., Orbell, S., Elston, C. & Wang, M. (1997). Measuring the outcome of psychosocial intervention for family caregivers of dementia sufferers: a factor analytic study. *Aging & Mental Health*, **1**(2), 166–175.

Alexopoulos, G.S., Abrams, R.C., Young, R.C. & Shamoian, C.A. (1988). Cornell Scale for Depression in Dementia. *Biological Psychiatry*, **23**, 271–284.

Axelrod, B.N. & Henry, R.R. (1992). Age-related performance on the Wisconsin Card Sorting, Similarities and Controlled Oral Word Association Tests. *Clinical Neuropsychologist*, **6**, 16–26.

Baddeley, A., Emslie, H. & Nimmo-Smith, I. (1992). *Speed and Capacity of Language Processing Test (SCOLP)*. Bury St Edmunds: Thames Valley Test Company.

Baddeley, A., Emslie, H. & Nimmo-Smith, I. (1993). The Spot-the-Word test: a robust estimate of verbal intelligence based on lexical decision. *British Journal of Clinical Psychology*, **32**, 55–65.

Baddeley, A., Emslie, H. & Nimmo-Smith, I. (1994). *Doors and People: a Test of Visual and Verbal Recall and Recognition*. Bury St Edmunds: Thames Valley Test Company.

Baillon, S., Scothern, G., Neville, P. G. & Boyle, A. (1996). Factors that contribute to stress in care staff in residential homes for the elderly. *International Journal of Geriatric Psychiatry*, **11**, 219–226.

Baltes, M.M., Burgess, R.L. & Stewart, R.B. (1980). Independence and dependence in self-care behaviours in nursing home residents: an operant observational study. *International Journal of Behavioural Development*, **3**, 489–500.

Barrowclough, C. & Fleming, I. (1986a). *Goal Planning with Elderly People*. Manchester: Manchester University Press.

Barrowclough, C. & Fleming, I. (1986b). Training direct care staff in goal-planning with elderly people. *Behavioural Psychotherapy*, **14**, 192–209.

Beardsall, L. (1998). Development of the Cambridge Contextual Reading Test for improving the estimation of premorbid verbal intelligence in older persons with dementia. *British Journal of Clinical Psychology*, **37**(2), 229–240.

Beardsall, L. & Brayne, C. (1990). Estimation of verbal intelligence in an elderly community; a prediction analysis using a shortened NART. *British Journal of Clinical Psychology*, **29**, 83–90.

Beardsall, L. & Huppert, F. (1997). Short NART, CCRT and Spot-the-Word: comparisons in older and demented persons. *British Journal of Clinical Psychology*, **36**(4), 619–622.

Beardsall, L. & Huppert, F.A. (1994). Improvement in NART word reading in demented and normal older persons using the Cambridge Contextual Reading Test. *Journal of Clinical & Experimental Neuropsychology*, **16**, 232–242.

Beck, C., Heithoff, K., Baldwin, B., Cuffel, B., O'Sullivan, P. & Chumbler, N.R. (1997). Assessing disruptive behavior in older adults: the Disruptive Behavior Scale. *Aging & Mental Health*, **1**(1), 71–80.

Beech, J.R. & Harding, L. (Ed.). (1990). *Assessment of the Elderly*. Windsor: NFER–Nelson.

Benjamin, L.C. & Spector, J. (1992). Geriatric care on a ward without nurses. *International Journal of Geriatric Psychiatry*, **7**, 743–750.

Benton, A.L. (1974). *The Revised Visual Retention Test*. New York: Psychological Corporation.

Benton, A.L., Eslinger, P.J. & Damasio, A.R. (1981). Normative observations on neuropsychological test performance in old age. *Journal of Clinical Neuropsychology*, **3**, 33–42.

Bigot, A. (1974). The relevance of American life satisfaction indices for research on British subjects before and after retirement. *Age & Ageing*, **3**, 113–121.

Bird, A.S., Macdonald, A.J.D., Mann, A.H. & Philpot, M.P. (1987). Preliminary experience with the SELFCARE (D): a self-rating depression questionnaire for use in elderly, non-institutionalized subjects. *International Journal of Geriatric Psychiatry*, **2**, 31–38.

Blackburn, I.M. & Tyrer, G.M.B. (1985). The value of Luria's neuropsychological investigation for the assessment of cognitive dysfunction in Alzheimer-type dementia. *British Journal of Clinical Psychology*, **24**, 171–179.

Bourke, J., Castleden, M.C., Stephen, R. & Dennis, M. (1995). A comparison of clock and pentagon drawing in Alzheimer's disease. *International Journal of Geriatric Psychiatry*, **10**(8), 703–705.

Bowie, P. & Mountain, G. (1993). Using direct observation to record the behaviour of long-stay patients with dementia. *International Journal of Geriatric Psychiatry*, **8**, 857–864.

Bowie, P. Mountain, G. & Clayden, D. (1992). Assessing the environmental quality of long-stay wards for the confused elderly. *International Journal of Geriatric Psychiatry*, **7**, 95–104.

Bowling, A. (1997). *Measuring Health: A Review of Quality of Life Measurement Scales*, 2nd edn. Buckingham: Open University Press.

Britton, P.G. & Savage, R.D. (1966). A short form of WAIS for use with the aged. *British Journal of Psychiatry*, **112**, 417–418.

van den Broek, M.D. & Bradshaw, C.M. (1990). Intellectual decline and the assessment of premorbid intelligence. In J. R. Beech & L. Harding (Eds), *Assessment of the Elderly* (pp. 13–28). Windsor: NFER–Nelson.

Brooker, D. (1998). *BASOLL—Behavioural Assessment Scale of Later Life*. Bicester: Winslow.

Brooker, D.J.R. (1995). Looking at them, looking at me; a review of observational studies into the quality of institutional care for elderly people with dementia. *Journal of Mental Health*, **4**, 145–156.

Carr, A.C., Woods, R.T. & Moore, B.J. (1986a). Automated cognitive assessment of elderly patients: a comparison of two types of response device. *British Journal of Clinical Psychology*, **25**, 305–306.

Carr, A.C., Woods, R.T. & Moore, B.J. (1986b). Developing a microcomputer-based automated testing system for use with psychogeriatric patients. *Bulletin of the Royal College of Psychiatrists*, **10**, 309–312.

Christensen, H. & Jorm, A.F. (1992). Short report: effect of premorbid intelligence on the Mini-Mental State and IQCODE. *International Journal of Geriatric Psychiatry*, **7**, 159–160.

Church, M. & Wattis, J.P. (1988). Psychological approaches to the assessment and treatment of old people. In J. P. Wattis & I. Hindmarch (Eds), *Psychological Assessment of the Elderly* (pp. 151–179). Edinburgh: Churchill Livingstone.

Clegg, F. & Warrington, E.K. (1994). Four easy memory tests for older adults. *Memory*, **2**, 167–182.

Cockburn, J. & Smith, P.T. (1989). *The Rivermead Behavioural Memory Test; Supplement 3: Elderly People*. Titchfield: Thames Valley Test Company.

Cohen-Mansfield, J., Werner, P. & Marx, M.S. (1992). The social environment of the agitated nursing home resident. *International Journal of Geriatric Psychiatry*, **7**, 789–798.

Crawford, J.R. (1997). WAIS-R short forms: assessing the statistical significance of subtest differences. *British Journal of Clinical Psychology*, **36**(4), 601–608.

Crawford, J.R., Allan, K.M. & Jack, A.M. (1992a). Short-forms of the UK WAIS-R: regression equations and their predictive validity in a general population sample. *British Journal of Clinical Psychology*, **31**, 191–202.

Crawford, J.R., Moore, J.W. & Cameron, I.M. (1992b). Verbal fluency: a NART-based equation for the estimation of premorbid performance. *British Journal of Clinical Psychology*, **31**, 327–329.

Crawford, J.R., Allan, K.M., Stephen, D.W., Parker, D.M. & Besson, J.A.O. (1989a). The Wechsler Adult Intelligence Scale—Revised (WAIS–R): factor structure in a UK sample. *Personality & Individual Differences*, **10**, 1209–1212.

Crawford, J.R., Stewart, L.E., Cochrane, R.H.B., Foulds, J.A., Besson, J.A.O. & Parker, D.M. (1989b). Estimating premorbid IQ from demographic variables: regression equations derived from a UK sample. *British Journal of Clinical Psychology*, **28**, 275–278.

Crookes, T.B. & McDonald, K.G. (1972). Benton's visual retention test in the differentiation of depression and early dementia. *British Journal of Social and Clinical Psychology*, **11**, 66–69.

David, R.M. & Skilbeck, C.E. (1984). Raven's IQ and language recovery following stroke. *Journal of Clinical Neuropsychology*, **6**, 302–308.

Davies, S. (1996). Neuropsychological assessment of the older person. In R. T. Woods (Ed.), *Handbook of the Clinical Psychology of Ageing* (pp. 441–474). Chichester: Wiley.

Dean, R., Briggs, K. & Lindesay, J. (1993a). The domus philosophy: a prospective evaluation of two residential units for the elderly mentally ill. *International Journal of Geriatric Psychiatry*, **8**, 807–817.

Dean, R., Proudfoot, R. & Lindesay, J. (1993b). The Quality of Interactions Schedule (QUIS): development, reliability, and use in the evaluation of two domus units. *International Journal of Geriatric Psychiatry*, **8**, 819–826.

DeRenzi, E. & Faglioni, P. (1978). Normative data and screening power of a shortened version of the Token test. *Cortex*, **14**, 41–49.

DeRenzi, E. & Vignolo, L.A. (1962). The token test: a sensitive test to detect receptive disturbances in aphasias. *Brain*, **85**, 665–678.

DesRosiers, G. (1992). Primary or depressive dementia: clinical features. *International Journal of Geriatric Psychiatry*, **7**, 629–638.

Enderby, P.M., Wood, V.A., Wade, D.T. & Langton-Hewer, R. (1986). The Frenchay Aphasia Screening Test: a short, simple test for aphasia appropriate for non-specialists. *International Rehabilitation Medicine*, **8**, 166–170.

Folstein, M.F., Folstein, S.E. & McHugh, P.R. (1975). "Mini-Mental State": a practical method for grading the cognitive state of patients for the clinician. *Journal of Psychiatric Research*, **12**, 189–198.

Fuld, P. A. (1977). *Fuld Object Memory Evaluation*. Windsor: NFER–Nelson.

Gallagher, D., Nies, G. & Thompson, L.W. (1982). Reliability of the Beck Depression Inventory with older adults. *Journal of Consulting & Clinical Psychology*, **50**, 152–153.

Gibson, A.J., Moyes, I.C.A. & Kendrick, D. (1980). Cognitive assessment of the elderly long-stay patient. *British Journal of Psychiatry*, **137**, 551–557.

Gilleard, C.J. (1984). *Living with Dementia*. Beckenham: Croom Helm.

Gilleard, C.J., Willmott, M. & Vaddadik, S. (1981). Self report measures of mood and morale in elderly depressives. *British Journal of Psychiatry*, **138**, 230–235.

Godlove, C., Richard, L. & Rodwell, G. (1982). Time for action: an observation study of elderly people in four different care environments. Sheffield: Social Services Monographs.

Goldberg, D. (1978). *Manual of the General Health Questionnaire*. Windsor: NFER–Nelson.

Golding, E. (1989). *Middlesex Elderly Assessment of Mental State*. Titchfield: Thames Valley Test Company.

Greene, J.G., Smith, R., Gardiner, M. & Timbury, G.C. (1982). Measuring behavioural disturbance of elderly demented patients in the community and its effect on relatives: a factor analytic study. *Age & Ageing*, **11**, 121–126.

Grewal, B.S., Haward, L.R. & Davies, I.R. (1985). Colour and form stimulus values in a test of dementia. *IRCS Medical Science Psychology & Psychiatry*, **13**, 703–704.

Grewal, B.S., Haward, L.R. & Davies, I.R. (1986). The role of colour discriminability in the Weigl test. *IRCS Medical Science Psychology and Psychiatry*, **14**, 693–694.

Gurland, B.J. (1980). The assessment of the mental health status of older adults. In J.E. Birren & R.B. Sloane (Eds), *Handbook of Mental Health and Aging*. Englewood Cliffs, NJ: Prentice-Hall.

Hamid, W.A., Howard, R. & Silverman, M. (1995). Needs assessment in old age psychiatry—a need for standardization. *International Journal of Geriatric Psychiatry*, **10**, 533–540.

Hart, S., Smith, C.M. & Swash, M. (1988). Word fluency in patients with early dementia of Alzheimer type. *British Journal of Clinical Psychology*, **27**, 115–124.

Hayes, V., Morris, J., Wolfe, C. & Morgan, M. (1995). The SF-36 health survey questionnaire: is it suitable for use with older adults? *Age & Ageing*, **24**, 120–125.

Hodkinson, H.M. (1972). Evaluation of a mental test score for assessment of mental impairment in the elderly. *Age & Ageing*, **1**, 233–238.

Holden, U. (1995). *Ageing, Neuropsychology and the "New" Dementias: Definitions, Explanations and Practical Approaches*. London: Chapman & Hall.

Holden, U.P. & Woods, R.T. (1995). *Positive Approaches to Dementia Care*. 3rd edn. Edinburgh: Churchill Livingstone.

Holland, C.A. & Rabbitt, P. (1991). The course and causes of cognitive change with advancing age. *Reviews in Clinical Gerontology*, **1**, 81–96.

Hope, R.A. & Fairburn, C.G. (1992). The Present Behavioural Examination (PBE): the development of an interview to measure current behavioural abnormalities. *Psychological Medicine*, **22**, 223–230.

Huppert, F.A. (1991). Neuropsychological assessment of dementia. *Reviews in Clinical Gerontology*, **1**, 159–169.

Huppert, F.A., Jorm, A.F., Brayne, C. & Girling, D.M. (1996). Psychometric properties of the CAMCOG and its efficacy in the diagnosis of dementia. *Aging, Neuropsychology & Cognition*, **3**(3), 201–214.

Isaacs, B. & Akhtar, A.J. (1972). The set test: a rapid test of mental function in old people. *Age & Ageing*, **1**, 222–226.

Ivnik, R.J., Malec, J.F., Smith, G.E., Tangalos, G.E., Petersen, R.C., Kokmen, E. & Kurland, L.T. (1992a). Mayo's older American normative studies: WAIS-R norms for ages 56 to 97. *Clinical Neuropsychologist*, **6**, 1–30.

Ivnik, R.J., Malec, J.F., Smith, G.E., Tangalos, G.E., Petersen, R.C., Kokmen, E. & Kurland, L.T. (1992b). Mayo's older American normative studies: WMS-R norms for ages 56 to 94. *Clinical Neuropsychologist*, **6**, 49–82.

Jenkins, J., Felce, D., Lunt, B. & Powell, E. (1977). Increasing engagement in activity of residents in old people's homes by providing recreational materials. *Behaviour Research & Therapy*, **15**, 429–434.

Jorm, A.F., Scott, R. & Jacomb, P. (1989). Assessment of cognitive decline in dementia by informant questionnaire. *International Journal of Geriatric Psychiatry*, **4**, 35–39.

Katona, C.L.E. & Aldridge, C.R. (1985). The dexamethasone suppression test and depressive signs in dementia. *Journal of Affective Disorders*, **8**, 83–89.

Katz, S., Ford, A.B., Moskowitz, R.W., Jackson, R.A. & Jaffe, M.W. (1963). Studies of illness in the aged: the index of ADL. *Journal of American Medical Association*, **185**, 914–919.

Kendrick, D.C. (1985). *Kendrick Cognitive Tests for the Elderly*. Windsor: NFER-Nelson.

Kendrick, D.C., Gibson, A.J. & Moyes, I.C.A. (1979). The revised Kendrick battery: clinical studies. *British Journal of Social and Clinical Psychology*, **18**, 329–340.

Kenn, C., Wood, H., Kucyj, M., Wattis, J. P. & Cunane, J. (1987). Validation of the Hospital Anxiety and Depression Rating Scale (HADS) in an elderly psychiatric population. *International Journal of Geriatric Psychiatry*, **2**, 189–193.

Kirshner, H.S., Webb, W.G. & Kelly, M.P. (1984). The naming disorder of dementia. *Neuropsychologia*, **22**, 23–30.

Kitwood, T. (1992). Quality assurance in dementia care. *Geriatric Medicine*, September, 34–38.

Kitwood, T. & Bredin, K. (1992). A new approach to the evaluation of dementia care. *Journal of Advances in Health & Nursing Care*, **1**, 41–60.

Klisz, D. (1978). Neuropsychological evaluation in older persons. In M. Storandt, I.C. Siegler, & M.F. Elias (Eds), *The Clinical Psychology of Aging* (pp. 71–96). New York: Plenum.

Kuriansky, J. & Gurland, B. (1976). The performance test of activities of daily living. *International Journal of Aging & Human Development*, **7**, 343–352.

Lawton, M.P. (1975). The Philadelphia Geriatric Center Morale Scale: a revision. *Journal of Gerontology*, **30**, 85–89.

Lawton, M.P. & Brody, E. (1969). Assessment of older people: self-maintaining and instrumental activities of daily living. *Gerontologist*, **9**, 179–186.

Lindesay, J., Briggs, K., Lawes, M., Macdonald, A. & Herzberg, J. (1991). The domus philosophy: a comparative evaluation of a new approach to residential care for the demented elderly. *International Journal of Geriatric Psychiatry*, **6**, 727–736.

Little, A.G., Hemsley, D.R., Volans, P.J. & Bergmann, K. (1986). The relationship between alternative assessments of self-care ability in the elderly. *British Journal of Clinical Psychology*, **25**, 51–59.

Little, A. & Doherty, B. (1996). Going beyond cognitive assessment: assessment of adjustment, behaviour and the environment. In R. T. Woods (Ed.), *Handbook of the Clinical Psychology of Ageing* (pp. 475–506). Chichester: Wiley.

Macdonald, A.J.D., Craig, T.K.J. & Warner, L.A.R. (1985). The development of a short observational method for the study of the activity and contacts of old people in residential settings. *Psychological Medicine*, **15**, 167–172.

Macdonald, A.J.D., Mann, A.H., Jenkins, R., Richard, L., Godlove, C. & Rodwell, G. (1982). An attempt to determine the impact of four types of care upon the elderly in London by the study of matched groups. *Psychological Medicine*, **12**, 193–200.

McWalter, G., Toner, H., McWalter, A., Eastwood, J., Marshall, M. & Turvey, T. (1998). A community needs assessment: the Care Needs Assessment Pack for Dementia (Carenap-D)—its development, reliability and validity. *International Journal of Geriatric Psychiatry*, **13**(1), 16–22.

Mahurin, R.K., DeBettignies, B.H. & Pirozzolo, F.J. (1991). Structured assessment of independent living skills: preliminary report of a performance measure of functional abilities in dementia. *Journal of Gerontology*, **46**, P58–66.

McFadyen, M. (1984). The measurement of engagement in the institutionalised elderly. In I. Hanley & J. Hodge (Eds), *Psychological Approaches to the Care of the Elderly*. London: Croom Helm.

McKenna, P. & Warrington, E.K. (1983). *The Graded Naming Test*. Windsor: NFER-Nelson.

Miller, E. (1980). Cognitive assessment of the older adult. In J. E. Birren & R.B. Sloane (Eds), *Handbook of Mental Health and Aging*. Englewood-Cliffs, NJ: Prentice Hall.

Miller, E. (1984). Verbal fluency as a function of a measure of verbal intelligence and in relation to different types of cerebral pathology. *British Journal of Clinical Psychology*, **23**, 53–57.

Miller, E. & Morris, R. (1993). *The Psychology of Dementia*. Chichester: Wiley.

Moniz-Cook, E. Millington, D. & Silver, M. (1997). Residential care for older people: job satisfaction and psychological health in care staff. *Health & Social Care in the Community*, **5**, 124–133.

Moniz-Cook, E. & Woods, R.T. (1997). The role of memory clinics and psychosocial intervention in the early stages of dementia. *International Journal of Geriatric Psychiatry*, **12**, 1143–1145.

Montgomery, S.A. (1988). Measuring mood. In J. P. Wattis & I. Hindmarch (Eds), *Psychological Assessment of the Elderly* (pp. 138–150). Edinburgh: Churchill Livingstone.

Moore, V. & Wyke, M.A. (1984). Drawing disability in patients with senile dementia. *Psychological Medicine*, **14**, 97–105.

Moos, R. & Lemke, S. (1980). Assessing the physical and architectural features of sheltered care settings. *Journal of Gerontology*, **35**, 571–583.

Morris, R.G. & Kopelman, M.D. (1992). The neuropsychological assessment of dementia. In J.R. Crawford, D.M. Parker & W.W. McKinlay (Eds), *A Handbook of Neuropsychological Assessment* (pp. 295–321). Hove: Erlbaum.

Morris, R.G. & McKiernan, F. (1994). Neuropsychological investigation of dementia. In A. Burns & R. Levy (Eds), *Dementia* (pp. 327–354). London: Chapman Hall.

Murray, M., Lefort, S. & Ribeiro, V. (1997). The SF-36: reliable and valid for the institutionalized elderly? *Aging & Mental Health*, **2**(1), 24–27.

Nelson, H.E. (1982). *The National Adult Reading Test*. Windsor: NFER–Nelson.

Nelson, H.E. & McKenna, P. (1975). The use of current reading ability in the assessment of dementia. *British Journal of Social and Clinical Psychology*, **14**, 259–267.

Nelson, H.E. & Willison, J. (1991). *National Adult Reading Test: Test Manual*. Windsor: NFER–Nelson.

Nelson, H.E. (1976). A modified card sorting test sensitive to frontal lobe deficits. *Cortex*, **12**, 313–324.

O'Carroll, R.E., Baikie, E.M. & Whittick, J.E. (1987). Does the National Adult Reading Test hold in Dementia? *British Journal of Clinical Psychology*, **26**, 315–316.

O'Neill, D., Rice, I., Blake, P., Walsh, J. B. & Coakley, D. (1992). The Geriatric Depression Scale: rater-administered or self-administered. *International Journal of Geriatric Psychiatry*, **7**, 511–515.

Orrell, M., Howard, R., Payne, A., Bergmann, K., Woods, R., Everitt, B.S. & Levy, R. (1992). Differentiation between organic and functional psychiatric illness in the elderly: an evaluation of four cognitive tests. *International Journal of Geriatric Psychiatry*, **7**, 263–275.

Ott, B.R. & Fogel, B.S. (1992). Measurement of depression in dementia: self versus clinician rating. *International Journal of Geriatric Psychiatry*, **7**, 899–904.

Patel, V. & Hope, R.A. (1992). A rating scale for aggressive behaviour in the elderly. *Psychological Medicine*, **22**, 211–221.

Pattie, A.H. (1988). Measuring levels of disability—the Clifton Assessment Procedures for the Elderly. In J. P. Wattis & I. Hindmarch (Eds), *Psychological Assessment of the Elderly* (pp. 61–80). Edinburgh: Churchill Livingstone.

Pattie, A.H. & Gilleard, C.J. (1979). *Manual for the Clifton Assessment Procedures for the Elderly (CAPE)*. Sevenoaks: Hodder & Stoughton Educational.

Pfeffer, R.I., Kurosaki, T.T., Harrah, C.H., Chance, J.M. & Filos, S. (1982). Measurement of functional activities in older adults in the community. *Journal of Gerontology*, **37**, 323–329.

Powell, G.E., Bailey, S. & Clark, E. (1980). A very short version of the Minnesota Aphasia test. *British Journal of Social and Clinical Psychology*, **19**, 189–194.

Raven, C.D. (1982). *Revised Manual for Raven's Progressive Matrices and Vocabulary Scale*. Windsor: NFER–Nelson.

Ramsay, M., Winget, C. & Higginson, I. (1995). Review: measures to determine the outcome of community services for people with dementia. *Age & Ageing*, **24**, 73–83.

Reynolds, T., Thornicroft, G., Woods, R.T., Abas, M. & Orrell, M. (1998). The validity and reliability of the Camberwell Assessment of Need for the Elderly (CANE). Paper presented at Royal College of Psychiatrists' Winter Meeting.

Robinson, R. A. (1977). Differential diagnosis and assessment in brain failure. *Age & Ageing*, **6** (Supplement), 42–49.

Roth, M., Huppert, F.A., Tym, E. & Mountjoy, C.Q. (1988). *CAMDEX—Cambridge Examination for Mental Disorders of the Elderly*. Cambridge: Cambridge University Press.

Ruddle, H.V. & Bradshaw, C.M. (1982). On the estimation of premorbid intellectual functioning: validation of Nelson & McKenna's, and some new normative data. *British Journal of Clinical Psychology*, **21**, 159–165.

Ryan, J.J., Paolo, A.M. & Brungardt, T.M. (1990). Standardisation of the WAIS-R for persons 75 years and older. *Psychological Assessment: a Journal of Consulting & Clinical Psychology*, **2**, 404–411.

Sahakian, B.J. (1990). Computerized assessment of neuropsychological function in Alzheimer's disease and Parkinson's disease. *International Journal of Geriatric Psychiatry*, **5**, 211–213.

Savage, R.D., Britton, P.G., Bolton, N. & Hall, E. (1973). *Intellectual Functioning in the Aged*. London: Methuen.

Sheikh, J.I. & Yesavage, J.A. (1986). Geriatric Depression Scale (GDS): recent evidence and development of a shorter version. In T. L. Brink (Ed.), *Clinical Gerontology: A Guide to Assessment and Intervention* (pp. 165–173). New York: Haworth.

Shulman, K.L., Shedletsky, R. & Silver, I.L. (1986). The challenge of time: clock drawing and cognitive function in the elderly. *International Journal of Geriatric Psychiatry*, **1**, 135–136.

Simpson, P.M., Surmon, D.J., Wesnes, K.A. & Wilcock, G.K. (1991). The cognitive drug research computerized assessment system for demented patients: a validation study. *International Journal of Geriatric Psychiatry*, **6**, 95–102.

Skilbeck, C.E. (1996). Psychological aspects of stroke. In R. T. Woods (Ed.), *Handbook of the Clinical Psychology of Ageing* (pp. 283–301). Chichester: Wiley.

Skurla, E., Rogers, J.C. & Sunderland, T. (1988). Direct assessment of activities of daily living in Alzheimer's disease: a controlled study. *Journal of the American Geriatrics Society*, **36**, 97–103.

Slade, M., Phelan, M., Thornicroft, G. & Parkman, S. (1996). The Camberwell Assessment of Need (CAN): comparison of assessments by staff and patients of the needs of the severely mentally ill. *Social Psychiatry & Psychiatric Epidemiology*, **31**, 109–113.

Spreen, D. & Strauss, E. (1991). *A Compendium of Neuropsychological Tests*. New York: Oxford University Press.

Stephens, B.J. & Jorm, A. (1994). Validation of a short form of the Informant Questionnaire of Cognitive Decline in the Elderly (IQCODE). *International Journal of Geriatric Psychiatry*, **14**, 235–238.

Stevens, S.J., Pitt, B.M.N., Nicholl, C.G., Fletcher, A.E. & Palmer, A.J. (1992). Language assessment in a memory clinic. *International Journal of Geriatric Psychiatry*, **7**, 45–51.

Storandt, M. & VandenBos, G.R. (Eds.). (1994). *Neuropsychological Assessment of Dementia and Depression in Older Adults: A Clinician's Guide*. Washington DC: American Psychological Association.

Sunderland, T., Alterman, I. S., Yount, D., Hill, J. L., Tariot, P.N., Newhouse, P.A., Mueller, E.A., Mellow, A.M. & Cohen, R.M. (1988). A new scale for assessment of depressed mood in demented patients. *American Journal of Psychiatry*, **145**, 955–959.

Sunderland, T., Hill, J.L., Mellow, A.M., Lawlor, B.A., Gundersheimer, J., New-house, P.A. & Grafman, J.H. (1989). Clock drawing in Alzheimer's disease: a novel measure of dementia severity. *Journal of American Geriatrics Society*, **37**, 725–729.

Twining, C. (1990). Assessment of personal adjustment. In J.R. Beech & L. Harding (Eds), *Assessment of the Elderly* (pp. 87–99). Windsor: NFER–Nelson.

Walker, S. (1980). Application of a test for aphasia to normal old people. *Journal of Clinical & Experimental Gerontology*, **2**, 185–198.

Ward, T., Murphy, E. & Procter, A. (1991). Functional assessment in severely demented patients. *Age & Ageing*, **20**, 212–216.

Ward, T., Murphy, E., Procter, A. & Weinman, J. (1992). An observational study of two long-stay psychogeriatric wards. *International Journal of Geriatric Psychiatry*, **7**, 211–217.

Warrington, E.K. (1984). *Recognition Memory Test Manual*. Windsor: NFER–Nelson.

Warrington, E. & James, M. (1991). *Visual Object & Space Perception Battery (VOSP)*. Bury St Edmunds: Thames Valley Test Company.

Wechsler, D. (1981). *Manual for the Wechsler Adult Intelligence Scales—Revised*. New York: Psychological Corporation.

Wechsler, D. (1987). *Wechsler Memory Scale—Revised*. New York: Psychological Corporation.

Weeks, D.J. (1988). *The Anomalous Sentences Repetition Test*. Windsor: NFER–Nelson.

Whitehead, A. (1973). Verbal learning and memory in elderly depressives. *British Journal of Psychiatry*, **123**, 203–208.

Willcocks, D.M., Peace, S. M. & Kellaher, L.A. (1987). *Private Lives in Public Places*. London: Tavistock.

Williams, B.W., Mack, W. & Henderson, V.W. (1989). Boston naming test in Alzheimer's disease. *Neuropsychologia*, **27**, 1073–1079.

Wilson, B.A., Cockburn, J. & Baddeley, A.D. (1985). *The Rivermead Behavioural Memory Test*. Titchfield: Thames Valley Test Company.

Wilson, B.A., Cockburn, J. & Halligan, P. (1987). *Behavioural Inattention Test (BIT)*. Bury St Edmunds: Thames Valley Test Company.

Yesavage, J.A., Brink, T.L. & Rose, T.L. (1983). Development and validation of a geriatric depression scale: a preliminary report. *Journal of Psychiatric Research*, **17**, 37–49.

Chapter 10

COGNITIVE-BEHAVIOURAL THERAPY

Leah P. Dick*, Dolores Gallagher-Thompson* and Larry W. Thompson*

THE THEORY OF COGNITIVE-BEHAVIOURAL THERAPY

Depressive disorders are a substantive problem for many elderly people (see Chapter 4), and the development and implementation of cost-effective treatment programmes must be a priority. Cognitive-behavioural therapy is a form of brief therapy that is effective in treating late-life depression in some elderly populations.

The application of cognitive-behavioural therapy to individuals experiencing depression is based on the conceptualization that depression is the result of the interaction of (primarily) behaviour, cognitions, emotions and (secondarily) physiological factors (Beck, 1976; Beck et al., 1979; Lewinsohn et al., 1985, 1978). This theory explains how depressed people experience a variety of symptoms spanning several domains. For example, a depressed person with the 'flu (a physiological factor) chooses to stay home from work (a behaviour) and while in bed thinks, "I'll never be able to complete the work needed to get that promotion. I'll never get anywhere with my career" (a cognition). These thoughts, in turn, create such negative emotions as depression or anxiety. Yet this pattern is not unidirectional. For example, the depressed mood can not only affect the motivation for this person to take more control of the illness (a behaviour), but it can also affect later cognitions, such as, "I am no good at

* Geriatric Research, Education and Clinical Center, VA Palo Alto Health Care System, Palo Alto, CA, and Stanford University School of Medicine, Stanford, CA, USA

Psychological Problems of Ageing: Assessment, Treatment and Care. Edited by R.T. Woods.
© 1999 John Wiley & Sons Ltd.

my job, so why try?" and can even affect the length of recovery time from the 'flu (Lewinsohn et al., 1985, 1978). Thus, the depression is manifested as a continuous downward spiral of negative thoughts that result in negative moods and behaviours that, in turn, result in more negative thoughts and decreased pleasant events (Beck, 1976; Beck et al., 1979; Lewinsohn et al., 1978).

Cognitive-behavioural therapy provides the client with strategies to challenge and replace his/her negative thought patterns as well as teach and motivate the performance of specific behaviours in order to improve mood. Clients also learn that choices made (whether behavioural or cognitive) are facilitated by the beliefs about the event or activity and, in turn, specific behaviours (whether performed or avoided) can elicit various beliefs about themselves or others. These two models are well integrated as they share dimensions of: being short-term therapies with focused and measurable goals; viewing the therapeutic relationship as a collaborative effort between the client and the therapist; using tools that stem from educational models and inductive reasoning; and using homework as a means of practising new skills and concepts learned in session (Beck, 1976; Beck et al., 1979; Lewinsohn et al., 1978).

Cognitive-behavioural therapy teaches clients to evaluate and test hypotheses about their beliefs and their behaviour in order to learn that they can make a significant contribution to their own outcomes (Beck et al., 1979; Lewinsohn et al., 1978).

The specific contribution of cognitive therapy is based on the work of Beck (1976; Beck et al., 1979), which teaches clients to understand how they interpret their world in order to challenge and replace the pieces of this structure that result in negative emotions. Consider the example described earlier. In reality, a person may experience a negative event (i.e. the 'flu) and immediately feel sad without any awareness of the beliefs that mediate the event and the feelings. Cognitive therapists assert that there are indeed beliefs that occur immediately following an event and which are responsible for the emotional consequences, hence the term "automatic thoughts" (Beck, 1976; Beck et al., 1979). The set of automatic thoughts becomes the structure or cognitive model used by the individual to interpret experiences. Beck et al. (1979) describe the specific processes involved in thought change: identifying the unhelpful, automatic beliefs; understanding the relationship between thoughts, affect and behaviour; challenging the dysfunctional thoughts by examining the evidence for their existence; replacing the automatic, unhelpful thoughts with more realistic ones; and independently identifying and challenging the situations and beliefs that cause such distress. A comprehensive description of cognitive therapy is found in the following works: Beck (1976); Beck et al. (1979); and Burns (1979, 1980).

The principles of behavioural therapy present a strong relationship between activity and mood. Depression is seen as the result of a severe decrease in pleasant activities or the disproportionate relationship between pleasant and unpleasant activities. In either case, a depressed mood results, as well as a decrease in motivation and interest to change the situation. Interventions are designed to reintroduce pleasant activities, while concurrently monitoring mood (Lewinsohn et al., 1978). Often, this involves additional behavioural interventions to overcome the obstacles in reintroducing pleasant events, such as relaxation to combat anxiety reactions in making these changes, or communication skills to enhance the client's ability to be assertive with others about his/her needs. The reader is referred to Lewinsohn, Biglan & Zeiss (1979) and Goldfried & Davison (1976) for a comprehensive description of basic behavioural therapy.

The marriage of cognitive and behavioural therapy provides not only a more comprehensive fundamental theory to conceptualize a client's distress, but also a broader repertoire of interventions, as it supplies two domains for change. Consider Mrs K, who presented to our clinic as a widowed, depressed woman who was quite isolated and had few social contacts. One of her treatment goals was to increase her social activities, specifically to visit a senior centre that was close to her home. From a cognitive-behavioural perspective, interventions around this specific goal would require information in the following areas. What are Mrs K's thoughts and expectations about visiting the senior centre and meeting new people? What kinds of activities might she enjoy that the centre provides? Is she anxious about meeting new people? Is she anxious about trying new activities that she knows very little about, and might she benefit from relaxation exercises to help control this anxiety? How might she come across in interpersonal situations, i.e. passive or aggressive? The answers to these questions would give the therapist information about which specific cognitive and behavioural skills would be most helpful to introduce to Mrs K.

THE EFFICACY OF COGNITIVE-BEHAVIOURAL (C/B) THERAPY WITH OLDER ADULTS

Before proceeding further, we want to address the question of whether this type of therapy is effective in the treatment of late-life depression. A detailed summary of the efficacy of cognitive and behavioural therapies with clinically depressed elders is available (Teri et al., 1994). They reviewed approximately 20 studies, employing variations of cognitive or behavioural strategies, and concluded that the results support the utility of these techniques in the treatment of clinical depression in the elderly. Substantial improvement was seen in 50–75% of the patients, which compares favourably with results of studies using pharmacotherapy as the treatment modality. A meta-analysis of 17 studies meeting strict criteria for methodological rigour was recently reported by Scogin & McElreath (1994). Eleven of the 17 employed either cognitive or behavioural techniques, and the remainder used supportive, reminiscence or psychodynamic techniques. Effect sizes for comparisons of cognitive and behavioural techniques with no-treatment conditions ranged from 0.70 to more than 1.0, which were substantive and compared favourably with effect sizes seen in studies evaluating pharmacotherapy. The few attempts to compare cognitive and behavioural techniques with other forms of psychotherapy have suggested only minimal differences (Scogin & McElreath, 1994). Thompson, Gallagher & Breckenridge (1987), for example, reported that brief psychodynamic therapy was comparable to both cognitive and behavioural therapy in terms of pre- to post-treatment change in depressive symptoms. Follow-up of these same patients over a two-year period yielded similar results (Gallagher-Thompson, Hanley-Peterson & Thompson, 1990). While such results suggest that different types of psychotherapy might be equally effective in working with elderly depressed patients, other explanations for the lack of differences among treatment modalities could be advanced. For example, Beutler & Clarkin (1990) have argued that some treatments might be substantially more effective with certain types of individuals than others, and the failure to see differences in randomized outcome studies may be due to the fact that individuals who might benefit more from a specific treatment have been randomly dispersed across all conditions, thereby making inter-treatment differences minimal. Support for this position was seen in a study evaluating the effects of psychotherapy in treating middle-aged and elderly caregivers who were clinically depressed. Individuals who had been family caregivers for 44 months or less responded better to brief psychodynamic therapy, whereas people who had been family caregivers for more than 44 months responded better to cognitive-behavioural therapy (Gallagher-Thompson & Steffen, 1994). This pattern of gains was also discerned at a one-year follow-up evaluation. In general, these data suggest that continued exploration of individual difference by type of treatment interactions should be fruitful.

Finally, much has been said in the clinical lore about the combination of pharmacotherapy and psychotherapy being maximally effective in the treatment of late-life depression, but few efforts have been made to evaluate this. Results of a study in our laboratory are presented here, although they have not yet been published (Thompson & Gallagher-Thompson, August, 1994). We compared desipramine, cognitive-behavioural therapy and a combination of the two in a randomized design for a period of 16–20 sessions. Endpoint analysis (includes dropouts, n = 102) showed no difference in diagnosis of depression between c/b therapy and a combination of c/b therapy and desipramine, but both of these showed significant improvement when compared to desipramine alone. Pre–post comparisons (completers only, n = 67) showed no difference between c/b therapy and desipramine and no difference between c/b therapy and a combination of the two. However, patients receiving a combination showed greater improvement than the desipramine alone condition. Contrary to results reported in the NIMH collaborative study with young clinically depressed patients (Elkin, 1994), using a cut-off score of 20 on the Hamilton Depression Scale, there was no significant severity by treatment interaction effect in favour of medication treatment for more depressed patients. One-year follow-up (n = 89) showed no difference between the three conditions. Approximately 65% showed improvement from their initial diagnosis. Thus these results, along with those reported in the literature, suggest that cognitive-behavioural therapy is an effective treatment for some well-defined depressive disorders in the elderly. Further, what little evidence is currently available suggests that this modality compares favourably with pharmacotherapy generally, and desipramine specifically.

THE PROCESS OF COGNITIVE-BEHAVIOURAL PSYCHOTHERAPY

The model of cognitive-behavioural therapy that is described here is based on the protocol of therapy developed and used for the past 10 years at the Older Adult and Family Center at the Department of Veterans Affairs Medical Center, Palo Alto (Gallagher-Thompson & Thompson, 1992). This is a brief description of a 16–20-session model of therapy that has been used in several therapy outcome studies from this center. More detailed presentations are available (Thompson et al., 1986; Thompson et al., 1991).

A note about assessment and goals

Assessment of the severity of the client's presenting complaints, as well as the client's perception of their problems, are critical pieces of information in this therapy. They are needed, in part, to facilitate setting realistic goals, as well as to operationalize and evaluate change throughout the course of treatment. Baseline measures of these presenting issues should be obtained at the start of treatment; we also ask clients to complete brief self-report measures before each session that tap the same construct (e.g. depression). For example, at intake, clients complete the long version of the Beck Depression Inventory (BDI) (Beck et al., 1961), which has shown to be a reliable measure of depression in older adults (Gallagher, 1986; Gallagher, Nies & Thompson, 1982). The brief version is completed prior to each therapy session. A full description of issues relating to assessment of late-life depression is beyond the scope of this chapter; the interested reader is referred to Pachana, Thompson & Gallagher-Thompson (1994) and Futterman et al. (1995) for that information. Similarly, other sources should be consulted for discussion of some of the complexities surrounding the very diagnosis of depression and anxiety disorders in the elderly (such as the influence of physical health, medication usage, and cognitive functioning on the presentation of affective disorders). The reader is referred to Blazer (1994, 1993), Dick & Gallagher-Thompson (1996), and Thompson, Futterman & Gallagher (1988) for a discussion of these issues.

The articulation of specific, clear, measurable treatment goals is the core of a successful brief therapy treatment programme. Clients should be encouraged to define their target issues in concrete terms, verbalizing the indicators for successful attainment of each goal. It is often helpful to ask clients the following questions. How would you know that the therapy was a success with regard to this goal? How would you know if the therapy was a partial success? How would you know if the goal was not met at all? In order to maximize a successful outcome, goals should be reviewed periodically (for example, the midpoint of treatment) to determine whether the current interventions are helpful or whether a new direction is needed. During goal review, it is also possible for the client to realize that initial goals were met and to introduce new ones.

Mental status exam

In working with older adults, it is always helpful to get some idea of their cognitive status before designing a treatment plan. Information about an older adult's cognitive status is crucial in c/b therapy, as both the in-session and outside-session work rely heavily on the older adult comprehending, remembering and producing material in both oral and written formats. Specifically, when treating depression, a brief mental status screening can begin to differentiate between symptoms of depression that overlap with dementia and vice versa. (The reader is once again referred to Pachana, Thompson & Gallagher-Thompson (1994) and Futterman et al. (1995) for a discussion of this issue). Our evaluation process begins with the administration of the Mini-Mental State Examination (MMSE) (Folstein, Folstein & McHugh, 1975), which has been shown to be a valid and reliable screening measure to detect cognitive impairment in the elderly (Braekus, Laake & Engedal, 1992; Engedal et al., 1988). In this way clients can be referred for further neuropsychological testing if needed, and treatment planning can be done with respect to the older person's cognitive capabilities.

HOW DOES COGNITIVE-BEHAVIOURAL THERAPY PROCEED?

In our work we have found it helpful to specify three distinct phases which define the treatment process. Of course, these are not rigidly adhered to, but rather provide a structure or framework within which to work. If a given facility has a maximum policy of 10 or 12 sessions, clearly the tasks will need to be collapsed. This section will briefly outline the tasks of each phase, while the next section will focus on special modifications to this process that we have found necessary and helpful in working with older adults.

Early phase (Sessions 1–3)

The initial task for the therapist during this phase is to establish a solid rapport with the client. It cannot be stated too frequently that c/b therapy is not the mere application of a "bag of tricks" or the mechanical application of a set of techniques (Beck et al., 1979). Rather, as a form of psychotherapy, it relies heavily on the adequacy of the therapeutic relationship as a foundation for the accomplishment of its goals (Beck et al., 1979).

The second task is to explain the c/b model of psychotherapy, discuss the role of homework, elicit the client's expectations of therapy, and explain the differences between c/b therapy and prior forms of therapy experiences, if needed (e.g. psychodynamic or supportive therapies, which are based on quite a different theoretical model) (see Horowitz & Kaltreider, 1979, and Weiss, 1991 for a discussion of the clinical theory of these therapies; and see Silberschatz & Curtis, 1991 for an explanation of time-limited psychodynamic therapy with older adults). Once the model and expectations for c/b therapy are discussed, the therapist and client must contract for the length of treatment (around 16–20 sessions at our centre).

The third task for these early sessions is to determine target goals for treatment. As mentioned earlier, goals should be articulated in a clear, measurable manner to facilitate the measurement of progress, and to keep the therapy focused on here-and-now issues. Finally, the therapist models the use of the three-column dysfunctional thought record (DTR) as one of the core cognitive tools that the client will be expected to learn how to use (Beck et al., 1979). An evaluation of the client's baseline relationship between the frequency of various categories of pleasant events and the magnitude of pleasure experienced from each event can also be determined by the client's completion of such scales as the Older Person's Pleasant Event Scale (Gallagher & Thompson, 1981). The latter is particularly relevant with very depressed patients, who may not be able to examine and evaluate their thoughts too well at the outset, as well as with mildly demented and/or highly anxious individuals, who may have difficulty monitoring specific thoughts and feelings.

Middle phase (Sessions 4–16)

The two key tasks for the middle phase of therapy are: to work towards attainment of the goals specified, and to teach the client a variety of cognitive and behavioural skills that are applicable to the stated goals. These skills include the use of both the three- and five-column DTRs to identify cognitive distortions, examine the evidence "for" and "against" a particular belief, design specific behavioural "experiments" for the client to test out the validity of these beliefs, and determine the pertinent themes that cause the client distress. The goal of this process is to help the client challenge the negative thought patterns and develop more adaptive ways to think about and respond to stressful situations. For some clients (particularly those who are well-educated and fairly "psychologically minded"), therapy may also include identification of fundamental beliefs (or schemas) that the client has historically used to make sense of his/her environment.

During this phase the depressed client is also asked to introduce new pleasant events, or revisit pleasant activities that have been dropped during this depressive episode. At this time, clients will learn about the distinct relationship between activities and mood and how to include behavioural interventions in managing their depression. Clients also learn about the interaction of cognitive-behavioural processes when, for example, a client's hesitation to introduce several pleasant events into daily life can be addressed with the use of a DTR to identify the cognitions that stop them from trying these new behaviours.

Finally, the middle phase is the time for clients to learn and become proficient in any one (or more) of a variety of additional techniques as needed, such as relaxation, assertiveness training or anger management, depending on the particular contingencies that seem to be maintaining negative mood states. For example, the highly anxious and depressed client may need several sessions to master methods of inducing relaxation and using them *in vivo*; to attempt to teach these skills and the use of the DTR method simultaneously would be overwhelming. Thus, the therapist might choose to wait before focusing on cognitive skills until the relaxation techniques have been thoroughly mastered. In other instances, clients may recognize (through use of the DTRs over time) their pattern of trying too hard to please other people, at the expense of their own needs. Such clients would benefit from standard assertiveness training (Cotter & Gruerra, 1976), including frequent in-session role playing, used in conjunction with thought records to monitor the client's interpretation of these new behaviours and the reactions of others to these changes.

End phase (Sessions 17–20)

There are several goals here. First, it is necessary to prepare the client to continue these skills independently to manage future stressful situations. This goal is attained through: reviewing what was learned; identifying predictors of and solutions to potential relapse; and spacing out the final sessions so that greater independence is encouraged. In our work, we create a written document with our clients that summarizes these points. Drawing on the extensive relapse prevention literature in the substance abuse field (Marlatt & Gordon, 1985), we have named it a "maintenance guide," explaining to clients that it is meant as a resource to outline the work they accomplished. The therapist's and client's collaboration on this document is crucial here, as it can also facilitate the discussion of the meaning of the therapeutic relationship for both parties.

Second, it is important to directly discuss the feelings of the client about treatment and termination. Time is needed to explore the feelings and thoughts involved as well as to allow the therapist to express what he/she has learned from the client. We have found this to be an important aspect of the termination process which shows respect for the client and enables him/her to believe that something unique has been contributed. Finally, clients may be given referrals for other services (e.g. a support group), depending on their current needs and the extent to which future depressive episodes appear likely (Yost et al., 1986).

Components of the cognitive-behavioural session

The productivity of c/b therapy is dependent upon the adherence to a structure or an "agenda' for each session. Even though the agenda is explicitly set at the beginning of each session, it should not preclude therapists' creativity and flexibility with various interventions and homework assignments. The formation of the agenda becomes another collaborative effort between the therapist and the client to ensure that each has similar views about the work and can keep the work focused. In our work, the agenda is written out during the first few minutes, with opportunities for the client to request topics. For example a "typical" agenda comprises the following components: writing the agenda and asking for input from the client; reviewing the brief assessment instrument completed (as in our use of the brief version of the BDI); reviewing the homework; working on the first topic (either a continuation from last session, a suggestion by the therapist, or a request from the client); summarizing the work completed on the first topic; working on a second topic (if time allows); summarizing the second topic; creating and assigning new homework; having both client and therapist give and receive feedback on the work from the session; and confirming the date and the time of the next appointment. This may seem to be a lot of work to complete in the "standard" 50-minute hour, so often it is desirable to extend the session length (to a full 60 or even 75 minutes) in order to ensure that there will be time to cover all of the crucial elements.

RECOMMENDED MODIFICATIONS TO PSYCHOTHERAPY WITH OLDER ADULTS

In general, older adults respond very well to cognitive-behavioural therapy, yet alterations to the process of therapy are recommended to meet some specific needs of the older person. These suggestions can be incorporated without substantially altering either the rationale or the process of therapy (Thompson et al., 1991; Thompson et al., 1986; Zeiss & Lewinsohn, 1986).

Therapist factors

We cannot discuss adapting psychotherapy for older adults without first addressing the issue of the therapist's views about treating an older client. The most primary of these beliefs is whether or not an older person is capable of change. The existing literature is in strong support of an older adult's ability to adapt to new situations and learn new ideas (Cavanaugh, 1990), which may conflict with the therapist's personal experiences with other older people, such as his/her parents, grandparents, etc. A younger therapist must also consider whether he/she can tolerate the nature and complexity of problems that some older adults bring to treatment. Problems of late life are often interdisciplinary in nature, where one person can present with a combination of clinical depression, poor health, severe financial concerns, and changes in social relationships. This complexity often requires treatment to be coordinated with other disciplines, which in turn requires the psychotherapist to gain experience in consulting with other disciplines (Dick & Gallagher-Thompson, 1996). Furthermore, many older adults are referred to therapy as a result of receiving a severe medical diagnosis, such as cancer, Parkinson's disease or even early Alzheimer's disease. Therapists must consider whether they can tolerate working with someone whose physical difficulties may deteriorate over the course of therapy.

Therapy education/socialization

Some of today's older clients were taught to believe that psychologists dealt only with "crazy" people who became committed to "snake pits" or "loony bins". Some older adults may have the belief that psychologists are an extension of their physicians and will provide a "quick fix" or a pill to cure their distress. This second view is complicated by the fact that most older clients define their difficulties in medical terms, and they are referred to psychotherapy by their primary care physician (Rapp et al., 1988). With either perception, the psychologist is faced with the responsibility of educating the older client about psychotherapy, as well as the collaborative nature of c/b therapy. The therapist should expect that the naive client might be initially uncomfortable about interacting in this way, as it may be a direct contradiction to his/her role as a medical patient. A careful discussion of the client's expectations, as well as an explanation of the structure and the limits of therapy, can begin the collaborative process. Clients should also be given an opportunity to discuss their views about whether or not they see themselves as able to change (Emery, 1981).

Zeiss & Lewinsohn (1986) believe that there should be a discussion of how each party uniquely contributes to the relationship. The therapist should explain that he/she: (a) is an expert on the latest techniques in cognitive-behavioural therapy with older adults; (b) is experienced in working with and assessing the unique concerns of older people; and (c) will arrive on time and be prepared to continue the work from last session and introduce new insights. Therapists should explain to clients that they are expected to: (a) be an active participant in this therapy; and (b) ask questions about any difficulties with the material; and (c) practise the new skills in between sessions and be open to discussing the difficulties in completing homework. In addition, the process of goal setting can model for clients how therapy is shaped around their specific needs.

An older client meeting a younger therapist can also be concerned about the therapist's age, expertise and range of life experiences. Here, one advantage of the collaborative relationship is illustrated, as we recommend that therapists take the position of explaining to clients that they wish to learn about the client's life perspective and rich life experiences (Knight & Qualls, 1995; Zeiss & Lewinsohn, 1986). In this fashion, the client is offered a chance to "give" something positive to the relationship. We also recommend that therapists share some personal information (e.g. when and where they got their degree) in order to ease the client's concerns in this regard. Further client education is necessary in discussing the role of homework in therapy. The label of "homework" may be aversive to some older clients, who have spent a considerable time out of school. In that case, the use of another term (e.g. between-session tasks, or assignments, or projects) is recommended to get the process started. The c/b therapist should explain that homework is designed as a means for the older client to practise what is learned in therapy in order to enhance the desired changes towards goal attainment. Therefore, it is essential that the completed homework gets adequate attention in the following session in order to reinforce the work's utility, while also giving an opportunity to address any obstacles experienced in its completion. Unlike other therapies, when a client does not complete his/her homework, c/b therapy places the first level of responsibility onto the therapist, suggesting that the rationale or the homework's instructions were not adequately communicated (Meichenbaum & Gilmore, 1982). This point will be revisited when we later discuss resistance within the c/b perspective.

Incomplete homework can be due to a variety of reasons, such as the therapist's lack of ability to explain the task clearly, the older adult's cognitive and sensory changes (explained below), or the client's feeling of being overwhelmed by too great an emotional task. The key to identifying and solving these problems is to address the incomplete homework at the next session. This way, the therapist and the client can creatively adapt the task to fit both the goals and the client's level of attention and motivation, in order to create a successful experience.

Often, the c/b therapist will be required to interrupt a "storytelling" client in order to keep the session focused. This may be difficult for therapists who believe that it would be a sign of disrespect towards older people. However, the development of a specific "refocusing signal" can be done in a collaborative way. As part of educating the client about c/b therapy, the therapist can explain the importance of staying true to the agenda and enlist the client's help in obtaining permission and devising a method for interrupting and refocusing the session (Thompson et al., 1991).

Sensory changes

Psychotherapy with older adults must often accommodate to some of the natural sensory changes experienced with aging. C/b therapy is well suited to adapt to changes in information processing, memory, vision and hearing. The following discussion provides some general strategies to keep the therapeutic issues in the forefront and minimize distractions or misunderstood information. Many of these recommendations are simple adjustments to the therapy environment to aid an older client in focusing on the issues at hand instead of potentially being distracted by concerns about mishearing something or experiencing difficulty in seeing written information. Please keep in mind that individual differences in intelligence, insight and motivation will require various combinations of these recommendations for each client. First, a well-lit therapy room that is less bothered by background noises should be selected. In addition, the selection of a room with easy physical access, such as a room on the ground floor or near an elevator, can alleviate any potential anxiety for a less physically able elder regarding coming to therapy. It also may be helpful for the older client and therapist to be sitting closer together in order to maximize the older adult's ability to hear and see the information presented. In addition, the therapist can also provide the client with enlarged handouts.

Similarly, older clients with concomitant chronic physical complaints (e.g. chronic pain, respiratory disease) may not be suitable for certain behavioural interventions, such as relaxation exercises that require alternating movements of tension and relaxation or even pleasant events requiring significant physical strength (Zeiss & Lewinsohn, 1986). For relaxation, the therapist can rely more on imagery techniques that require little physical strain. To enhance pleasant events, the therapist must learn to be creative and work with the client's strengths and capabilities to devise interventions.

Most older adults also experience noticeable changes in their efficiency regarding information processing and memory (Botwinick, 1978). Creative adaptations to these losses can be small, yet important, investments in maximizing therapeutic gains for older clients. For example, therapists should plan for the use of multi-media formats to provide a very active learning environment and enhance understanding of what transpires in the session. A key ingredient is the client's use of a notebook to record all homework, handouts, and therapy notes to facilitate the memory of earlier work (as it can be reviewed prior to the session) and to enhance the learning of the in-session work. We rely heavily on the use of white boards and flip charts and different-coloured, dry-erase markers to actively illustrate the use of dysfunctional thought records, mood ratings and other c/b therapy tools. Written work on a mounted board or large paper taped to the wall or affixed to an easel serves various functions: to confirm that the client and the therapist are in agreement about the content of the discussion; to actively and visually illustrate the relationship between the client's external and internal experiences; to first model the new concept for the client before asking him/her to do it; to keep the focus in the session and keep the discussion at a pace that the client can follow; and to elevate the energy level of a session, as the therapist must change positions from sitting to standing and writing in order to capture the material on the board. At times, it may be helpful also to ask the more physically able client to contribute to the writing on the board to enhance the dimensions described earlier. This work is then followed by the client recording the work in the notebook.

The use of both audio and video taping can also be quite helpful with older people. A client's review of an audio tape can provide another opportunity to maximize his/her understanding and memory of session material. The review of an in-session videotape can be quite helpful for older clients who come to therapy with issues of assertiveness or difficulties with social situations. In addition, the review of an audio tape as homework or audio taping the explanation of the homework assignment can be a helpful format for visually impaired clients or anyone who would have difficulty in completing written work (Zeiss & Lewinsohn, 1986).

In general, many older clients will benefit more when information is covered slowly and when they are asked frequently to summarize what has been covered. Summarizing can measure the client's level of understanding and memory of the material. We recommend that older clients be asked to summarize the work several times each session, and that they conclude each session with both a summary and session notes. Finally, to enhance learning, clients should be provided with handouts that explain types of dysfunctional thought patterns, ways to challenge thought patterns, etc., to act as additional resources for the retention and incorporation of these skills into everyday living.

Relationship factors: resistance, transference and countertransference

Resistance, transference and countertransference are concepts that are often associated with more traditional and less structured talking therapies. Yet they do have a place in c/b therapy. If we consider the fact that c/b therapy is designed to challenge an individual's unhelpful set of beliefs and behaviours and replace them with more constructive ones, we are requiring that clients be willing to detach themselves from the protective structure of how they make sense of their world (Beck et al., 1979; Meichenbaum & Gilmore, 1982). Who wouldn't have hesitations about that task?

It has long been assumed that resistance, transference and countertransference are ignored processes in c/b therapy due to the (mis)perception that affect is ignored within this model (Meichenbaum & Gilmore, 1982). Although affect is considered to be the consequence (thus not under voluntary control) of one's beliefs and behaviours, it still has a central role. Consider the depressed client who presents to therapy; the presenting issue is one of affect. Similarly, the presenting issue embodies resistance, as depressed clients view their situation as hopeless or unchangeable. Furthermore, the improvement of the affective complaints becomes the standard by which the success or the failure of the therapy is judged (Beck et al., 1979). Yet, within the process of therapy, affect is not ignored at all, as clients learn about what beliefs and behaviours mediate their emotional responses.

We cannot stress enough how the success of c/b therapy hinges on the collaborative therapeutic relationship. Yet there are times when this collaboration is threatened. Threats to the collaborative process occur when either the client or the therapist maintains dysfunctional beliefs about the other or the relationship that go undiscussed (e.g. transference/countertransference), or clients exhibit beliefs or behaviours that seem to hinder their commitment to the work (resistance). Note that these processes do not function as independent concepts. Clients may ignore a homework assignment because of their concerns about how the therapist may view them if they see the completed work. With each of the concepts, the responsibility of the therapist is to stay true to the principles of collaboration and the process of hypothesis testing and immediately address the observable changes in the relationship (Beck et al., 1979; Meichenbaum & Gilmore, 1982).

Like other therapies, transference and countertransference within the c/b model can have either a positive or a negative foundation. Positive transference can occur if the client has idealized the therapist, which changes the client's expectations of therapy. For example, the client may believe that the therapist will no doubt "save" the client from his/her difficulties. These beliefs ultimately set an unrealistic standard that the therapist cannot meet, which results in the client's disappointment in the therapist. Similarly, an older client working with a younger therapist may be reminded of a child or a grandchild, which could result in either positive or negative beliefs and expectations about the therapist (Knight, 1986).

Some aspects of c/b therapy, if not executed with respect to the principles of collaboration, may induce negative reactions by the client (Beck, et al., 1979). For example, an educational intervention delivered without much input from the client can be interpreted as dogmatic and inflexible. Thus, a client can begin to react with negative thought patterns about the therapist, make assumptions about how the therapist views him/her, or hesitate to complete assignments as a result of this imbalanced intervention.

A client's lack of compliance with homework is often interpreted as resistance, yet with older adults this conclusion may be hasty. As discussed earlier, it is important for therapists of older clients to ensure that they have heard, seen, understood and remembered the homework assigned. Asking the older client to repeat back (and often write out) the assignment can enhance both understanding and compliance. Furthermore, it is recommended that the first-line strategy of handling resistance is for the therapist to take responsibility to either improve the explanation or find a more creative assignment. The therapist's willingness to immediately address resistant behaviours defines another therapeutic process, transresistance, which is the therapist's resistance to the client's resistance, resulting in the therapist's reduced motivation to work with the client (Meichenbaum & Gilmore, 1982). At this juncture, as well as at any time that the therapist has an experience of countertransference or transresistance, the therapist should apply the c/b techniques to his/her own thinking to challenge the assumptions being made about the client. If this process begins to alleviate and replace the therapist's negative thought processes, it may serve to free up the therapist to brainstorm about more creative ways to help the more reluctant client make therapeutic gains (Meichenbaum & Gilmore, 1982).

Forms of resistance, transference and countertransference are natural and often expected processes in c/b therapy. Some aspects of these concepts can be anticipated and discussed at the beginning of treatment. For example, the discussion of clients' expectations of therapy can include an explanation of the non-linear process of change. Clients should learn to expect that change occurs with a variety of speeds and magnitudes, and change in one area may negatively affect another aspect of their concerns. The threat to the collaborative relationship occurs when the client is not adequately prepared for this process and becomes disillusioned with c/b therapy and the therapist. The therapist, however, is not immune to these reactions either. Naive therapists may mistake the normal ebb and flow of therapy as statements about their efficacy as a psychotherapist or even about the client. Damage to the collaborative relationship may be rectified by the head-on discussion of what is happening at the moment in the session. Therapists and clients can collaborate on strategies to understand and manage this process, which often include identifying the skills that the client has mastered to be used during these difficult times.

CASE EXAMPLES

Below is a comprehensive presentation of a client who was quite motivated for and responded well to the c/b framework.

CASE EXAMPLE: MR B
Intake evaluation

Mr B was a 74 year-old male who was caring for his wife of 50 years who had been diagnosed with emphysema seven years before. Mr B was a retired architect with a Master's Degree in architectural design. He and his wife had two sons, who were both married and lived out of state. Mr B was referred to therapy by his physician, who believed that he was experiencing some significant anxiety and depression as a result of being responsible for the care of both his wife and their household. During the intake, he reported with great sadness that he was quite committed to caring for his wife. He also described becoming anxious when she was demanding and hostile to him. Mr B described an event where she refused to eat breakfast, and was critical of him when he said he had run out of her favourite bread for her toast. Mr B reported that these difficulties had been ongoing for the past year, since his wife's health began to decline.

Mr B reported no prior episodes of depression or any prior experience with psychotherapy. At intake, Mr B exhibited a significant depression, scoring 20 on the Beck Depression Inventory and 18 on the Hamilton

Rating Scale for Depression (Hamilton, 1967). Mr B expressed a desire to contract for the standard course of 20 sessions of cognitive-behavioural therapy offered at the Older Adult Center at the Department of Veterans Affairs Medical Center, Palo Alto, but he was quite concerned about his wife's reaction to his involvement in therapy.

Early phase

Initially, it was very difficult for him comfortably to attend the therapy sessions. At first, he told his wife that he was going to his physician, but later "confessed" to her that he was seeing a psychologist. Consequently, Mr B would often come in quite anxious because his wife became increasingly demanding moments before he had to leave for his appointment. In order to keep Mr B focused on the agenda, a brief relaxation exercise was introduced at the beginning of each session. Mr B was immediately satisfied with this exercise, as he noticed that his physical tension eased, his laboured breathing subsided, and his racing thoughts decreased. The therapist provided Mr B with an audio-taped version of the relaxation exercises, suggesting that he practise them whenever he felt the physical symptoms of anxiety emerging, but he doubted that he could get a moment away from his wife to try it.

Mr B was able to articulate and define clear goals for therapy: to reduce his depression by understanding and challenging the stressful beliefs that accompanied his caregiving duties; to increase his pleasant, social activities; and to reduce his anxiety during situations with his wife where he needed to be assertive.

Mr B completed an Older Person's Pleasant Events Schedule, which revealed that he still maintained strong interests in social activities and some leisure activities, but did so infrequently or almost not at all (see Figure 10.1). This measure also demonstrated that Mr B enjoyed recognition from others, but experienced so few times when someone (particularly his wife) complimented or thanked him for a job well done.

Mr B explained that he rarely socialized with friends, because he believed that he could not leave his wife alone or with any other paid caregiver, as it would "upset her". He also believed he was the only person who could competently take care of her. These beliefs were further complicated by the fact that he reported many situations where his wife would be critical of his care, as well as asking him not to leave the house even to run household errands. Thus Mr B started to believe that his desire to find time for himself made him "a bad caregiver".

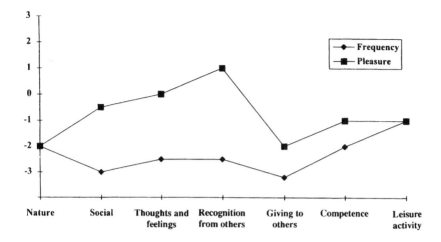

Figure 10.1 Mr B's Older Person's Pleasant Events Scale: the relationship between the frequency and the pleasure of his pleasant events

Middle phase

Behavioral interventions

The sessions in this phase often began with a relaxation exercise in order to calm Mr B's anxiety as a result of his wife's objection to his participation in therapy. Mr B inconsistently practised this exercise at home, as his only attempts were when his wife napped during the day, or when he hid in the bathroom. Even though his work with relaxation was intermittent, he reported a significant change in his level of tension immediately following the exercise.

Interventions were made to help Mr B increase his pleasant events, but this too was met with initial resistance. Mr B was, however, quite able to generate a list of pleasant activities that he once enjoyed and would like to "eventually" pursue. This list included golf, lunch with old friends from his company, reading, walking outside, and watching a movie with his wife. He displayed a strong interest in reintroducing these activities into his daily life, but he had several negative cognitions about leaving his wife for his own needs, and had fears that she would become increasingly agitated and irritable when he returned, which would ultimately "ruin" the time he had for himself. At this point, the therapy focused on challenging Mr B's dysfunctional thought patterns in order to help him replace his "rules" about not allowing time for himself. It was the therapist's hope that, as Mr B saw that there was little evidence to support these restrictions he placed upon himself, he would be more motivated to experiment with new activities.

Cognitive interventions

Mr B quickly mastered the use of the dysfunctional thought records by skilfully identifying his unhelpful thoughts and recognizing the types of thoughts he reported (see Table 10.1). For example, Mr B began to notice that he would often use "should" statements to create rules about being a good caregiver. He believed that he "should be responsible for her quality of life", and "I should forgive her anything because her life is so difficult". Many of Mr B's dysfunctional thought patterns flourished when he was faced with a situation where he chose not to assert his own needs and wishes.

Table 10.1 Mr B's three-column dysfunctional thought record illustrating his common thought patterns

Describe the event that led to your unpleasant emotions	What are your negative thoughts? Identify your unhelpful thought patterns	What are you feeling? (sad, angry, anxious, etc.)
During breakfast, I served my wife the wrong milk and she screamed at me, "Take it away!"	She always rejects me. In order for things to come out nicely, I will go along with her wishes. I should do a better job taking care of her because she deserves a good quality of life. *Dysfunctional thought patterns:* over-generalization, fortune telling, "should" statements	Angry Hurt Guilty

Having noticed this theme, Mr B was presented with the option to learn assertiveness skills. As expected, Mr B hesitated, believing that his needs were still unimportant as long as he was a caregiver. The therapist challenged this belief by pointing out that his level of depression and anxiety was a clear indication that his current strategies were not providing him with positive outcomes. He was in strong agreement with this assessment, and decided to learn these new skills.

Assertiveness training

Mr B responded very well to the educational intervention regarding the difference between assertive, aggressive and passive communication and behaviours. He was open to role-play exercises to help him choose the actual words that he could use in difficult situations with his wife. He also practised stating his needs in a clear, decisive manner, using brief statements and not trying to "over-justify" his needs. Mr B was amazed that he was able to clearly tell his wife that he wanted "one hour alone in his study", and although she initially protested, he was able to "stick to his guns". Mr B reported that he was quite uncomfortable the first time he "hid" in the study, but after practising the relaxation exercise, he noticed how pleased he was to have one whole hour to himself!

Mr B was also able to discuss his beliefs surrounding his acceptance of his assertive rights through the use of a DTR (see Table 10.2). Mr B explained that it was most difficult for him to assert himself in the evenings when he wished to spend time alone. He reported that once his wife stated that she felt lonely, he would sacrifice his own plans to "keep her happy". Mr B was quite motivated to be more assertive with her during these times, hoping that both of them could get some of what they want.

Final phase

By the final phase of therapy, Mr B was able to spend one hour in his study each morning, 30 minutes in his study after lunch, and one hour each evening. He was also able to plan outings with old friends, as well as schedule a weekly golf game. Mr B introduced each of these activities by stating helpful cognitions, such as, "In order for me to be a good caregiver, I must take care of myself" and "I deserve to enjoy my retirement and keep up with things and people that I enjoy". Mr B also demonstrated a significant decrease in his anxiety around asserting his needs to his wife. He also hired a paid caregiver to come to the house for four hours each day to give him a break from the household chores and in order to make plans with his wife.

Mr B was also quite collaborative in the creation of a "maintenance guide", which was his summary of all of the changes he made, skills he learned, and how he would handle future difficult situations (see below). Mr B completed therapy with a BDI of three, and a score of four on the Hamilton Anxiety Scale. The therapist asked Mr B if he would be interested in a "booster session" which could serve as a check to see how he

Table 10.2 Mr B's five-column dysfunctional thought record demonstrating his beliefs about his assertive rights

Describe the event that led to your unpleasant emotions	What are your negative thoughts? Identify your unhelpful thought patterns	What are you feeling (sad, angry, anxious, etc.)?	Challenge your negative thoughts and replace them with more helpful ones	What emotions are you feeling now?
In the evening, I plan to go into my study to listen to music, but my wife calls me to sit with her while she watches TV	I can't to anything for myself; I have to make sure that she is happy. If I don't do what she asks, her life will be more miserable than it is. If I keep my plans, then I am ignoring her and being a bad caregiver. *Dysfunctional thought patterns:* over-generalization "should" statements, "fortune telling"	Sad Anxious	I must find time for myself, or else I will be in poor shape to take care of her. I am not completely responsible for her quality of life; she is able to make decisions too. I am a good caregiver, and wanting some time alone does not make me a bad caregiver	Less sad Still anxious (about communicating this to my wife) Hopeful

was handling these new skills independently. Mr B agreed and a booster session was scheduled for one month later.

Maintenance guide

Part I: Were my goals met? What skills did I learn?

Goals:
1. To change my beliefs that I am a bad caregiver.
2. To increase my pleasant activities and time for myself.
3. To reduce my anxiety about asserting myself with my wife as well as learning better ways to be assertive.

Changes I have made:
1. I am certain that I am a good caregiver, and I cannot take complete responsibility for my wife's displeasure.
2. Although physically frail, my wife can make decisions, and she is responsible for her own reactions and moods.

3. I now have a standing golf game each Wednesday with two friends I used to play with when my wife was well.
4. I have hired a paid caregiver to come in four hours each day and six hours on Wednesdays.
5. I am able to use my study for time alone in the house.
6. I know that I must take good care of myself in order to be a good caregiver, so asserting my rights and not sacrificing my needs will help me accomplish that goal.

Skills:
1. Relaxation. I am quite comfortable with the relaxation skills I learned. I use them frequently, often preceding an event where I must be assertive.
2. Dysfunctional thought records. After an upsetting event, I will often go into the study and complete a DTR to change my negative thought patterns and reduce my tension. I am also becoming quite skilled at thinking through DTRs in my head when I cannot get to my study.
3. Assertiveness skills. I clearly understand how assertiveness can help me. I have found that the more I try these skills, the easier it gets. I also combine these with relaxation before I need to be assertive.
4. Scheduling time for myself. I make sure I get to do several pleasant events each day. I use my study to read or listen to music, I take a walk each day and I have recontacted my friends for golf and lunch.

Part II: Future stressful events
What stressful events might I anticipate in the future?
1. My wife's continued health decline.
2. My wife's disagreement with me when I am trying to be assertive.

What will I do about these events?
1. I will support my belief that I must maintain my mental well-being. This means that I will keep up the skills that I have learned, and realize that during times of extreme stress, these skills are more necessary than ever.
2. I will also make arrangements for additional paid help when my wife's needs become too difficult for me. I will not think of this help as a criticism of my caregiving abilities, but rather an opportunity to spend time with her without straining all of my resources.

What additional supports can I use?
I can join a men's caregiver's support group.

Part III: Signs of relapse
How will I know that my depression has returned?
1. I will experience an increase in the negative thoughts I have about myself.

2. I will start cancelling plans with my friends, or stop seeing them altogether.
3. My anxiety will increase.
4. I will probably give up the time in my study to make sure that my wife's needs are met.

If I become depressed again, what will I do?

1. I will reread all of my notes from therapy.
2. I will recontact my therapist for a "booster" or to restart therapy, if needed.

Booster session

During this session, Mr B reported that his use of his new skills has become "quite routine". He explained that he did an abbreviated version of the relaxation exercise immediately before difficult situations with his wife. He also reported that, due to his new-found assertiveness, many of these situations were less problematic than they had been prior to therapy. In fact, Mr B stated that he was now finding times when he enjoyed his wife's company, and they had agreed to have "movie dates" three times a week, where they would sit together and watch video rentals. Mr B stated great confidence in his new skills and beliefs, finally asserting that he was a good caregiver.

COGNITIVE BEHAVIOURAL THERAPY AND CHRONIC ILLNESS

The prevalence of chronic illness with age increases to the point where 50–86% of adults aged 65 and over report at least one chronic illness (Boczkowski & Zeichner, 1985; Rybarczyk et al., 1992). Chronic illness demands that patients develop long-term strategies to cope as well as independently manage many physical and psychological stressors. In general, it has been reported that most people cope well (Cassileth et al., 1984). However, high rates of depression have been reported by patients with several medical problems, such as stroke (Robinson & Price, 1982), arthritis (Gregg, Robertus & Stone, 1989), and Parkinson's disease (Mayeaux et al., 1984), among others. Older adults with chronic illnesses were twice as likely to be depressed as those without (Rybarczyk et al., 1992).

Given the fact that depressed older adults with chronic illnesses are asked to cope with a variety of stressors from the following domains— behavioural (loss of independence, disability), cognitive (uncertainty about the future, thoughts about "usefulness"), physiological (pain) and emotional (depression, anxiety, anger)—the c/b therapy approach seems to be exceptionally appropriate (Rybarczyk et al., 1992). This group described several treatment issues commonly found in this kind of client. First, these clients may have several realistic barriers to the initiation or the continuation of treatment, which may include fitting therapy into heavily scheduled medical appointments, acute flare-ups of their illness that interrupt the flow of therapy, limited tolerance to sit for a full session, or transportation problems. C/b therapy can teach clients to become more assertive in stating their needs and more comfortable regarding their "right" to consider their needs first. Second, clients with chronic illnesses may interpret their depression as a side-effect of their physical illness and feel resigned to endure it rather than believing that it can be controlled and reversed. This therapy can work towards educating and challenging clients on this very belief before providing interventions to treat the depression itself. Third, when introduced to a new challenge, the depressed older client with a chronic condition may be more apt to state "I can't", without any valid evidence of their inability. Cognitive interventions can challenge these perceptions with concurrent behavioural assignments to collect data to immediately dispel these misperceptions. Fourth, the decline of social roles is a significant symptom of depression for these people and can be improved by allowing the client to explore alternative strategies to maintain independence and giving to others. Finally, perceptions that this type of client is a burden to others can be directly challenged with cognitive strategies and behavioural interventions designed to promote maximal functional independence.

Consider the following case example of how cognitive-behavioural therapy is a good fit for someone with a chronic health problem.

EXAMPLE: MR M

Mr M is an 80 year-old male with a 20-year history of arthritis and a 30-year history of diabetes. He lives with his wife in the home they have shared for 40 years. He reports good relationships with his four grown children and 18 grandchildren, who all live in the area. Mr M is a retired teacher, spending most of his time writing short stories, gardening, and at exercise classes. Mr M was referred to therapy by his physician, who was concerned about his coping with a recent flare-up of the arthritis in his left hip. At intake, Mr M's long-form BDI score was 21, and it was noted that several endorsements were due to his concomitant physical complaints.

Mr M was initially hesitant about trying cognitive-behavioural therapy. His many reasons included: difficulty of travelling and a belief that "nothing can be done, I have lived with this for so long". The therapist explained that, while she could not intervene on his medical status, she was convinced that his accompanying sad mood had the potential to improve. Mr M finally agreed to come, stating that he "promised the doctor".

The initial interview with Mr M did demonstrate that he was significantly depressed and somewhat anxious. Mr M's depression was evident in his beliefs that his physical decline had made him less important to the family, and his anxiety was captured in his concerns about how much of the family's resources and time he "uses". Therefore Mr M was not convinced that the commitment to therapy would be easy for him or his wife. During the intake interview, Mr M stated many cognitive distortions regarding his wife's beliefs about taking him to therapy, as driving was especially difficult for him. At this point, the therapist asked him if he wanted to invite his wife in to ask her what she thought about his participation in therapy. He was agreeable to this, convinced that she would confirm his suspicions. To his surprise, she clearly stated that she had quite an investment in his feeling better and she would be willing to take him to therapy. Mr M's discovery of his wife's true beliefs enabled him to consider contracting for therapy. Mr M's perception of the unchangeable nature of his depression was less quickly altered. He was willing to contract for 10 of the 20 sessions, with the understanding that after an evaluation of his progress, he would consider contracting for the rest of the therapy. He was able to identify two goals for therapy: to feel less depressed and hopeless; and to increase his enjoyment in his leisure activities.

Sessions 1–9

Behavioural interventions

Mr M reported that he had little energy for engaging in his leisure activities, and thus his enjoyment of them had greatly decreased. He described that it was painful for him to be in his garden, and he no longer had the desire to take his walk around the neighbourhood in the afternoon. Mr M was immediately introduced to relaxation exercises to help his perception of pain, which, after much in-session practice, he agreed to try at home. The therapist also asked Mr M to make a daily schedule of his activities in order for her to learn how he planned his day. It was immediately noticed that Mr M expected to spend three hours in the garden each morning, thus feeling frustrated and "useless" when he could not complete the task. This strategy of overestimating his expectations was present in all daily activities.

Mr M seemed to respond well to the educational interventions around the topic of pacing (Widner & Zeichner, 1993). The therapist explained that pacing was the interaction of the expectations of the task with the available energy to perform it. In order to help Mr M improve the pacing of his activities, she obtained information about when his "high-functioning" times of the day were, how long he could sit/stand/walk without discomfort, and the types of activities that helped him refuel his energy. This information helped the therapist and Mr M devise a more realistic plan to maximize his energy and his pleasure in his daily activities.

Yet, despite these efforts, Mr M still maintained the belief that he was "no good" unless he could function at his "old level". The therapist urged Mr M to begin to investigate how his way of thinking was hindering the changes in his behaviour.

Cognitive interventions

Although Mr M demonstrated immediate acceptance that his way of thinking was contributing to his mood, he saw few (or no) options to improve it. The therapist asked Mr M if he would try to monitor his thoughts for a while in order for them to learn what kinds of cognitions he was using. The therapist modelled the use of the DTR and Mr M successfully completed one in the session. As a result, Mr M became quite compliant with the completion of the DTRs as homework, and a theme to Mr M's beliefs began to emerge. Mr M believed: that he was no longer a good role model for his family as a result of his disabilities; that he was a burden to the family; and that he saw no use in continuing the activities that he once enjoyed.

The therapist began to challenge these beliefs using techniques such as examining the evidence (Burns, 1979, 1980), which encouraged Mr M to consider the overt "proof" that his family believed these thoughts about him. This technique also pointed out that Mr M engaged in mind reading to perceive what others were thinking, but not saying, about him. Despite these challenges, Mr M still maintained a fundamental belief that he was not providing anything of "value" to his family. When asked to define his meaning of "value", he replied, "something to give my family that will have eternal meaning".

The therapist asked Mr M to brainstorm ways (or things) that he could give to his family that would state his importance to the family. Among Mr M's material objects listed was an entry that stated "family history":

THERAPIST: I see "family history" written here. What does it mean?

MR M: I am trying to find a way to tell my family about their ancestry. It was very hard for my parents to come to this country, and my life during the Depression was so different from my own children's and grandchildren's. I think knowing your roots is an essential part of life.

THERAPIST: How could you give them this history?

MR M: Well, when I tell them stories, or compare their life to my own at their age, they seem so disinterested.

THERAPIST: What evidence do you have of that?

MR M: They haven't exactly said it out loud, if that's what you mean.

THERAPIST: I do. Would you like to find out if they're interested?

MR M: I guess so. It's just that I have so many of my mother's journals. I'd like them to know about her.

THERAPIST: How else could you share them?

MR M: I have wanted to return to creative writing. I guess I could start by recording my family's history for my children and grandchildren.

THERAPIST: That would make a beautiful, everlasting gift.

Mr M's decision to create a document of his family history was a turning point in the therapy, as it gave him a realistic way to demonstrate that he still had an important role in his family. This turnabout in his attitude was reached by Session 9, when it became time for Mr M and the therapist to negotiate for more sessions. Mr M asked if therapy could also help him with his pacing of his writing at the computer as he worked on his family history. The therapist agreed to this new goal.

Sessions 10–20

During the second half of therapy, Mr M became skilled at completing five-column DTRs to challenge his tendencies to jump to conclusions about his family's reactions to him, as well as his habit of labelling himself based on his (loss of) abilities. Mr M's attempts to pace his daily activities better were met with initial protests and beliefs that he was regressing. Once he spent less time in the garden or at the computer, taking more breaks and doing relaxation exercises, he began to report many benefits: he was able to get more accomplished with less discomfort; he had more energy throughout the day; his mood improved dramatically; he required less assistance from his family, but also felt less guilt about asking for help; and he had fewer negative thoughts about himself and even praised himself for new accomplishments.

Eventually, Mr M's flare-up subsided and he was encouraged by the therapist to realize that these skills were not merely ways of coping with a flare-up, but they could be considered preventative steps as well. With this in mind, the therapist and Mr M created a very detailed maintenance guide to ensure that Mr M had a record of his work in therapy. Mr M's BDI score at termination was four, and he was considered no longer depressed.

Mr M returned for a booster session five weeks later. He brought with him the proofs of part of his family history that contained prose, a family tree and several photographs. Mr M proudly reported that when he finally shared his soon-to-be-gift with his family, their reaction was one of great joy, which was a clear statement to him that he was still a revered member of his family, despite his many physical limitations. He reported that he asked his grandchildren if they would draw pictures of their families to be included in this work. Mr M demonstrated no symptoms of depression and no increase in the discomfort of any of his physical symptoms.

Working with depressed clients who also have a personality disorder or features

One of the few documented outcome studies demonstrating the efficacy of cognitive-behavioural therapy with older adults with concomitant personality disorders has been reported in Thompson, Gallagher & Czirr (1987). Clinical impressions about working with such clients reveal that a helpful strategy in working with these clients is using the information they present within the context of the therapeutic relationship to make interventions. In general, one would expect that the duration of therapy with an older client with strong Axis II features (DSM-IV) (American Psychiatric Association, 1994) would be longer, with smaller gains during treatment. Thus, it becomes the c/b therapist's responsibility to revise the measurable expectations for success while focusing a significant amount of the initial work on fostering the therapeutic relationship. This strategy may be particularly tricky in c/b therapy due to the fact that the nature of the work involves challenging the client's core beliefs about him/herself and others. Challenging the interpretive structure of someone with strong personality features may be initially quite threatening and prevent the client from "buying into" the framework. Here, the c/b therapist must rely on rapport-building skills common to all therapists, such as being non-judgemental, showing empathy and having patience. The flexibility and creativity to work with the issues and experiences the client brings (while still maintaining the c/b in-session agenda) are an additional skill that seems to be required for the c/b therapist who would be successful in these instances.

CASE EXAMPLE: MS H

Ms H is a 68-year-old retired bookkeeper who never married or had children. Her major social contacts had been with local chapters of women's organizations, but for the past year she had isolated herself from many of her old friends. Ms H came to therapy experiencing a substantial depression, although she was interested in reconnecting with her former group of friends. Ms H presented her goals in a very all-or-nothing manner, declaring that she wanted to be "forever free of her depression". She also explained that she was quite disappointed in her old friends, who had been declining her invitations to visit. She reported that she felt rejected and consequently wanted to retreat from them altogether.

Ms H was quite resistant in completing any of the initial homework assigned. Instead, she would re-organize the assignment, ultimately doing something that was not related to the issue at hand. At first, the therapist offered the explanation that she was not clear about the assignment, but it was soon revealed that Ms H's core beliefs about criticism and rejection made confrontations about her resistance a fragile issue. Thus, Ms H's gains were smaller and slower to achieve through the process of building this relationship.

Ultimately, the relationship between Ms H and the therapist became the vehicle to challenge Ms H's perceptions about others. Dysfunctional thought records and role plays were designed around the following questions. What was it like for Ms H to be "assigned" homework? What was it like for Ms H to have her understanding of the homework "corrected" by the therapist? What did she expect from the therapist? How could Ms H explain what she wanted to do in a calm, assertive manner?

Ms H was quite open to working on these issues in the context of the relationship. As a result, her participation, as well as her co-operation, increased. She was willing to complete DTRs addressing her perceptions of what the therapist thought of her (see Table 10.3). She also became more open to feedback from the therapist about her communication style and unrealistic expectations of others. Eventually, Ms H was willing to experiment with her assertiveness skills (as opposed to her previous aggressive patterns) and was able to develop more realistic expectations about others outside of therapy.

Ms H's initial trials at asking others to make plans and compromising to meet some of her friends' needs were marginally successful. Ms H continued to evaluate herself in comparison to others, demonstrating schemas of "I am no good" and "I have no value". At this point, Ms H

Table 10.3 Ms H's core beliefs illustrated in a five-column dysfunctional thought record

Describe the event that led to your unpleasant emotions	What are your negative thoughts? Identify your unhelpful thought patterns	What are you feeling (sad, angry, anxious, etc.)?	Challenge your negative thoughts and replace them with more helpful ones	What emotions are you feeling now?
My therapist started to talk about the homework I did not do	She thinks I am not a good person. I should be a better client. She will not want to see me any more. I'll just quit now! *Dysfunctional thought patterns:* jumping to conclusions, "should" statements, catastrophizing	Shame Depressed Anxious	She doesn't look angry, and she's never said I was a bad person. I also do not know what she thinks of me—I could ask! If I quit, I will be further isolating myself and I could get more depressed	Less anxious Relieved Less depressed

was willing to complete homework as assigned, which allowed the therapy to be more focused as it shifted to this issue. Ms H was open to writing a cost–benefit analysis (Burns, 1980) around her beliefs, which indicated that she saw the costs of this schema as isolating herself from others, feelings of depression, and missing out on trying new things. Ms H's benefit from this schema was that she felt a sense of security by not putting herself at risk to be rejected by others because she would continue to be a loner.

Although she made moderate gains in her goals to alleviate her depression and renew social contacts, she still experienced distress during social situations where she believed that she was being compared to others. It was revealed that she held a constellation of schemas that reflected her isolation, such as "I have never been accepted", "I have always been alone and unloved" and "I will never be good enough". Ms H explained that her belief of having always been alone was the most painful of this set of beliefs. Before termination began, Ms H was offered an opportunity to work further in therapy to understand the development of this belief and to learn tools for modifying it. However, she explained that she was quite satisfied with her progress and would rather work on the maintenance of her gains independently. During the creation of the maintenance guide, the therapist wanted Ms H to have a clear understanding of the "danger signals" that might bring her back to therapy. Ms H was able to identify that if she were to begin to spend more and more time isolated from her rediscovered friends, then that would be a clear signal to her that her depressive thoughts and behaviours were returning.

SCHEMA CHANGE THERAPY

Ms H ended therapy having identified a painful core belief. Had she been willing to continue, she would have engaged in a process to understand, challenge and replace this core schema. This process is an advanced form of cognitive therapy called schema change therapy, which was developed in response to working with clients with personality disorders or strong personality features (Beck, Freeman & Associates, 1990; Young, 1990; 1994). Beck, Freeman & Associates (1990) describe those with personality disorders as people who maintain a rigid, long-standing belief system that functions as the person's interpretive model. Young (1990, 1994) describes this process as the development of a set of stable negative themes that are seen as early as childhood as a result of negative interactions with peers or family. This set is referred to as "early maladaptive schemas" (EMS). Both theories do agree, however, that these schemas become quite active during experiences of high affect, and are highly resistant to change.

The process of schema therapy differs from the standard course of cognitive-behavioural therapy on several counts. First, this part of therapy is longer and more affectively driven. The relationship between client and therapist is still quite active, with increased activity on the part of the therapist to be more confrontational with the client. Furthermore, the therapeutic relationship becomes a core vehicle for changing the schema, as clients are able to demonstrate their long-standing constellation of schemas within the context of the relationship, as well as experiment with the new set of schemas. Schema change therapy is also longer than the standard course of cognitive-behavioural therapy (e.g. an additional 20 or more sessions may be required), and change occurs at a slower rate. A key element in this approach is the introduction and development of new schemas that are more adaptive and which can gradually replace the dysfunctional beliefs. Often therapy is ended when progress has been made in this regard, with full recognition that the job isn't over at the end of the formal treatment. Rather, a process has begun that the client needs to continue on his/her own, so that the more functional schemas really become operative in the client's daily life. It is only by the continued challenging of dysfunctional beliefs and their replacement with more moderate and adaptive ones that the client will solidify gains made. One of the schema change methods that we frequently use is called the historical test of schemas. It is a modified version of one developed by Young (1990, 1994; Padesky & Beck, 1990; Young, Beck & Weinberger, 1993). The goal of this method is to help the client understand the development and the maintenance of the schema during the significant periods in the client's life. This understanding will hopefully initiate an alternative and more adaptive schema to replace the more harmful one. The steps in this process include: the identification of the schema; the client's creation of a time-line of his/her life marked by pivotal events (e.g. birth of siblings, school graduations, marriages, children, or any other emotionally laden event); the therapist and the client discussing each time period, charting events and memories that either contradict or support the schema, with careful attention to formulating conclusions about the activity of the schema at each time period; and the reformulation of a new schema based on the consolidation of evidence from the details of the client's history. A recent detailed description of schema change therapy can be found in Coon (1994) and Dick & Gallagher-Thompson (1995); the latter specifically applies these methods to an older depressed person with a dependent personality style. Other methods for schema change with older adults are being explored at our centre, including extensive use of imagery and rescripting techniques, which have been very helpful in the treatment of PTSD victims (Smucker et al., 1995). This work is relatively new and the interested reader is encouraged to follow this literature closely as new techniques are developed and evaluated for the treatment of older adults with such complex presenting problems.

CONCLUDING REMARKS

Besides using c/b approaches to treat late-life depression (either alone or in the medically ill elderly, or in combination with various anxiety disorders), and to treat depressogenic schemas in older adults with deeply ingrained dysfunctional beliefs, variants of c/b therapy have been used by persons affiliated with our center to treat many common psychological problems of later life. Detailed descriptions of all of these applications is beyond the scope of this chapter; however, the interested reader is referred to the following publications for more information. Many are case reports dealing with, for example, the facilitation of inhibited grief (Florsheim & Gallagher-Thompson, 1990; Gantz, Gallagher-Thompson &

Rodman, 1992) and the use of crisis intervention with suicidal elders (DeVries & Gallagher-Thompson, 1994). Others focus on general topics such as handling resistance (Silven & Gallagher, 1987) and increasing the use of interpersonal data to challenge negative thoughts (Florsheim et al., 1991). Still others focus on specific subgroups of elders, such as family caregivers (Baum & Gallagher, 1985–1986; DeVries & Gallagher-Thompson, 1993; Kaplan & Gallagher-Thompson, 1995), the medically ill elderly (Czirr & Gallagher, 1983) and those with very severe depression requiring both pharmacotherapy and psychotherapy (Rodman et al., 1991). Review of these papers will give the reader an even clearer sense of the range of problems that can be successfully treated with c/b approaches, as well as other modifications that can be made to "tailor" the basic treatment approach to the needs of the individual client.

RECOMMENDATIONS FOR FUTURE TRENDS IN RESEARCH AND PRACTICE

In our opinion, the vigorous treatment of depression in late life using psychotherapeutic interventions (either alone or in combination with appropriate pharmacotherapy) should be strongly encouraged. This is necessary in order to improve elders' quality of life and increase their ability to cope adaptively with the common stressful events associated with aging in our society. However, for maximum impact, the field of clinical gerontology needs to become more creative and flexible in several ways. First, we must recognize that most depressed older adults suffer from at least one co-morbid condition (e.g. a significant chronic medical problem) which should not be used to exclude them from major outcome studies (as had commonly been the case in many research projects). Continued use of this practice can make it difficult to generalize research findings to the "real world" of ageing. Second, in order to really understand the effectiveness of c/b therapy and other forms of psychotherapeutic treatments with distressed elders, we need to do therapy with clients who represent the full socioeconomic and sociocultural spectrums. Much research and many published clinical reports have described therapy with middle- to upper-class Caucasians; very little data exists on the application of psychotherapy to low-income elders or to those from various racial and ethnic minority groups. Clearly, a more concerted effort is needed to recruit such elders into both clinical and research settings. Although this can be a difficult enterprise, guidelines are beginning to appear to assist in this process (Arean & Gallagher-Thompson, 1996). Third, we recommend that more research and clinical care be provided in non-traditional ways and in non-traditional settings, such as using telephone counselling with older adults who are homebound, and providing treatment in the nursing home or at the bedside, or even in the patients' home setting, whenever circumstances warrant this type of special consideration. Finally, we believe that the development of a "core battery" of individual and outcome measures would facilitate comparisons of research results across centres in different locations. This would also enable the application of more powerful design and analytic tools to evaluate outcome and to identify psychosocial factors associated with therapeutic efficacy. By instituting these practices we are confident that the next decade will foster a true expansion of geriatric psychosocial intervention research; this can only be of benefit to the elderly individuals whom we wish to serve.

ACKNOWLEDGMENT

This project was supported in part by the National Institute of Mental Health, by Grants MH19104 and MH37196 to Larry W. Thompson PhD, Principal Investigator.

REFERENCES

American Psychiatric Association (1994). *Diagnostic and Statistical Manual of Mental Disorders*, 4th edn. Washington DC: American Psychiatric Association.
Arean, P. & Gallagher-Thompson, D. (1996). Issues and recommendations for the recruitment and retention of older ethnic minority adults into clinical research. *Journal of Consulting and Clinical Psychology*, **64**, 875–880. (Invited paper.)
Baum, D. & Gallagher, D. (1985–1986). Case studies of psychotherapy with depressed caregivers. *Clinical Gerontologist*, **4**, 19–29.
Beck, A.T. (1976). *Cognitive Therapy and the Emotional Disorders*. New York: International Universities Press.
Beck, A.T., Freeman, A. & Associates (1990). *Cognitive Therapy of Personality Disorders*. New York: Guilford.
Beck, A.T., Rush, J., Shaw, B. & Emery, G. (1979). *Cognitive Therapy of Depression*. New York: Guilford.
Beck, A.T., Ward, C.H., Mendelson, M., Mock, J. & Erbaugh, J. (1961). An inventory for measuring depression. *Archives of General Psychiatry*, **4**, 561–571.
Beutler, L.E. & Clarkin, J.F. (1990). *Systematic Treatment Selection: Towards Targeted Therapeutic Interventions*. New York: Brunner/Mazel.
Blazer, D.G. (1993). *Depression in Late Life*, 2nd ed. St Louis, MO: Mosby.
Blazer, D. (1994). Epidemiology of late-life depression. In L. Schneider, C.F. Reynolds, B. Lebowitz & A. Friedhoff (Eds), *Diagnosis and Treatment of Depression in Late Life* (pp. 9–19). Washington, DC: American Psychiatric Press.
Boczkowski, J. & Zeichner, A. (1985). Medication compliance and the elderly, *Clinical Gerontologist*, **4**(1), 3–15.
Botwinick, J. (1978). Aging and Behavior, 2nd edn. New York: Springer.

Braekhus, A., Laake, K. & Engedal, K. (1992). The mini-mental state examination: identifying the most efficient variables for detecting cognitive impairment in the elderly. *Journal of the American Geriatrics Society*, **40**, 1139–1145.

Burns, D.D. (1979). *Feeling Good: The New Mood Therapy*. New York: Signet.

Burns, D.D. (1980). *The Feeling Good Handbook: Using the New Mood Therapy in Everyday Life*. New York: William Morrow.

Cassileth, B.R., Lusk, E.J., Strouse, T.B., Miller, D.S. & Brown, L. (1984). Psychosocial status in chronic illness—a comparative analysis of six diagnostic groups. *New England Journal of Medicine*, **311**, 506–511.

Cavanaugh, J.C. (1990). *Adult Development and Aging*. Belmont: Wadsworth Publishing Co.

Coon, D.W. (1994). Cognitive-behavioral interventions with avoidant personality: a single case study. *Journal of Cognitive Psychotherapy: An International Quarterly*, **8**(3), 243–253.

Cotter, S.B. & Gruerra, J.J. (1976). *Assertion Training*. Illinois: Research Press.

Czirr, R. & Gallagher, D. (1983). Case report: behavioral treatment of depression and somatic complaints in rheumatoid arthritis. *Clinical Gerontologist*, **2**(1), 63–66.

DeVries, H. & Gallagher-Thompson, D. (1993). Cognitive-behavioral therapy and the angry caregiver. *Clinical Gerontologist*, **13**(4), 53–57.

DeVries, H. & Gallagher-Thompson, D. (1994). Crises with geriatric patients. In F. Dattilio & A. Freeman (Eds), *Cognitive-Behavior Therapy and Crisis Intervention* (pp. 200–218). New York: Guilford.

Dick, L.P. & Gallagher-Thompson, D. (1995). Cognitive therapy to change the core beliefs of a distressed, lonely caregiver. *Journal of Cognitive Psychotherapy: An International Quarterly*, **9**, 215–227.

Dick, L.P. & Gallagher-Thompson, D. (1996) Assessment and treatment of late-life depression. In M. Hersen & V.B. Van Hesselt (Eds), *Psychological Treatment of Older Adults: An Introductory Textbook* (pp. 181–208). New York: Plenum.

Elkin, I. (1994). The NIMH treatment of depression collaborative research programme: where we began and where we are. In A.E. Bergin & S.L. Garfield (Eds) *Handbook of Psychotherapy and Behavior Change*, 4th edn. (pp. 114–139). New York: Wiley.

Emery, G. (1981). Cognitive therapy with the elderly. In G. Emery, S.D. Holton & R.C. Bedrosian (Eds), *New Directions in Cognitive Therapy* (pp. 84–98). New York: Guilford.

Engedal, K., Haugen, P.K., Gilje, K. & Laake, P. (1988). Efficacy of short mental tests in the detection of mental impairment in old age. *Comprehensive Gerontology A*, **2**, 87–93.

Florsheim, M.J. & Gallagher-Thompson, D. (1990). Cognitive-behavioral treatment of atypical bereavement: a case study. *Clinical Gerontologist*, **10**(2), 73–76.

Florsheim, M.J., Leavesley, G., Hanley-Petersen, P. & Gallagher-Thompson, D. (1991). An expansion of the A–B–C approach to cognitive-behavioral therapy. *Clinical Gerontologist*, **10**(4), 65–69.

Folstein, M., Folstein, S. & McHugh, P. (1975). ''Mini-Mental State''—a practical method for grading the cognitive status of patients for the clinician. *Journal of Psychiatric Research*, **12**, 189–198.

Futterman, A., Thompson, L.W., Gallagher-Thompson, D. & Ferris, R. (1995). Depression in later life: epidemiology, assessment, etiology and treatment. In E. Beckham & R. Leber (Eds), *Handbook of Depression*, 2nd edn (pp. 494–525). New York: Guilford Press.

Gallagher, D. (1986). The Beck Depression Inventory and older adults: review of its development and utility. *Clinical Gerontologist*, **5**, 149–163.

Gallagher, D., Nies, G. & Thompson, L.W. (1982). Reliability of the Beck Depression Inventory with older adults. *Journal of Consulting and Clinical Psychology*, **50**(1), 152–153.

Gallagher D. & Thompson, L.W. (1981). *Depression in the Elderly: A Behavioral Treatment Manual*. Los Angeles: University of Southern California Press.

Gallagher-Thompson, D., Hanley-Peterson, P. & Thompson, L.W. (1990). Maintenance of gains versus relapse following brief psychotherapy for depression. *Journal of Counseling and Clinical Psychology*, **58**, 371–374.

Gallagher-Thompson, D. & Steffen, A. (1994). Comparative effects of cognitive-behavioral and brief psychodynamic psychotherapies for depressed family caregivers. *Journal of Counseling and Clinical Psychology*, **62**, 543–549.

Gallagher-Thompson, D. & Thompson, L.W. (1992). *Cognitive-Behavioral Therapy for Late-life Depression: A Treatment Manual*. Palo Alto, CA: Department of Veterans Affairs Medical Center.

Gantz, F., Gallagher-Thompson, D. & Rodman, J. (1992). Cognitive-behavioral facilitation of inhibited grief. In A. Freeman & F. Dattilio (Eds), *Comprehensive Casebook of Cognitive-Behavioral Therapy* (pp. 359–379). London: Oxford University Press.

Goldfried, M. & Davison, G.C. (1976). *Clinical Behavior Therapy*. New York: Wiley.

Gregg, C.H., Robertus, J.L. & Stone, J. (1989). *The Psychological Aspects of Chronic Illness*. Springfield, IL: Charles C. Thomas.

Hamilton, M. (1967). Development of a rating scale for primary depressive illness. *British Journal of Social and Clinical Psychology*, **6**, 278–296.

Horowitz, M. & Kaltreider, N. (1979). Brief therapy of the stress response syndrome. *Psychiatric Clinics of North America*, **2**, 365–377.

Kaplan, C. & Gallagher-Thompson, D. (1995). The treatment of clinical depression in caregivers of spouses with dementia. *Journal of Cognitive Psychotherapy: An International Quarterly*, **9**, 35–44.

Knight, B.G. (1986). *Psychotherapy with Older Adults*. Beverly Hills, CA: Sage.

Knight, B.G. & Qualls, S.H. (1995). The older client in developmental context: life course and family systems perspectives. *Clinical Psychologist*, **48**(2), 11–16.

Lewinsohn, P.M., Biglan, A. & Zeiss, A. (1979). Behavioral treatment of depression. In P. Davidson (Ed.), *Behavioral Management of Anxiety, Depression, and Pain* (pp. 91–146). New York: Brunner/Mazel.

Lewinsohn, P.M., Hoberman, H., Teri, L. & Hautzinger, M. (1985). An integrative theory of depression. In S. Reiss & R.R. Bootzin (Eds), *Theoretical Issues in Behavior Therapy* (pp 331–359). New York: Academic Press.

Lewinsohn, P.M., Munoz, R.F., Youngren, M.A. & Zeiss, A.M. (1978). *Control Your Depression*. New Jersey: Prentice Hall.

Marlatt, G.A. & Gordon, J.R. (Eds) (1985) *Relapse Prevention: Maintenance Strategies in the Treatment of Addictive Behaviors*. New York: Guilford.

Mayeaux, R., Williams, J.B.W., Stern, Y. & Cote, L. (1984). Depression and Parkinson's disease. *Advances in Neurology*, **40**, 241–251.

Meichenbaum, D. & Gilmore, J.B. (1982). Resistance from a cognitive-behavioral perspective. In P. Wachtel (Ed.), *Resistance: Psychodynamic and Behavioral Approaches* (pp. 133–155). New York: Plenum.

National Institutes of Health Consensus Development Conference Consensus Statement (1992). Diagnosis and treatment of depression in late-life. *Journal of the American Medical Association*, **268**(8), 1018–1024.

Pachana, N., Thompson, L.W. & Gallagher-Thompson, D. (1994). Measurement of depression. In M.P. Lawton & J. Teresi (Eds), *Annual Review of Gerontology and Geriatrics*, Vol. 14 (pp. 234–256). New York: Springer.

Padesky, C.A. & Beck, A.T. (1990). Cognitive therapy of personality disorders, complex marital cases, and inpatient depression. Paper presented at the Cognitive Therapy Conference, 2–4 February, 1990, Newport Beach, CA.

Rapp, S.R., Parisi, S.A., Walsh, D.A. & Wallace, C.E. (1988) Detecting depression in elderly medical patients. *Journal of Consulting and Clinical Psychology*, **56**(4), 509–513.

Robinson, R.G. & Price, T.R. (1982). Post-stroke depressive disorders: a follow-up study of 103 patients. *Stroke*, **13**(5), 635–640.

Rodman, J., Gantz, F., Schneider, J. & Gallagher-Thompson, D. (1991). Short term treatment of endogenous depression using cognitive-behavioral therapy and pharmacotherapy. *Clinical Gerontologist*, **10**(3), 81–84.

Rybarczyk, B., Gallagher-Thompson, D., Rodman, J., Zeiss, A., Gantz, F. & Yesavage, J. (1992). Applying cognitive-behavioral psychotherapy to the chronically ill elderly: treatment issues and case illustration. *International Psychogeriatrics*, **4**(1), 127–140.

Scogin, F. & McElreath, L. (1994). Efficacy of psychosocial treatments for geriatric depression: a quantitative review. *Journal of Counseling and Clinical Psychology*, **62**, 69–74.

Silberschatz, G. & Curtis, J.T. (1991). Time-limited psychodynamic therapy with older adults. In W. Myers (Ed.), *New Techniques in the Psychotherapy of Older Patients* (pp. 95–108). Washington, DC: American Psychiatric Press.

Silven, D. & Gallagher, D. (1987). Resistance in cognitive-behavioral therapy: a case study. *Clinical Gerontologist*, **6**, 75–78.

Smucker, M.R., Dancu, C., Foa, E.B. & Nideree, J.L. (1995). Imagery rescripting: a new treatment for survivors of childhood sexual abuse suffering from post-traumatic stress. *Journal of Cognitive Psychotherapy: An International Quarterly*, **9**(1), 3–18.

Teri, L., Curtis, J., Gallagher-Thompson, D., Thompson, L. (1994). Cognitive-behavioral therapy with depressed older adults. In L.S. Schneider, C.F. Reynolds, B.D. Lebowitz & A.J. Friedhoff (Eds), *Diagnosis and Treatment of Depression in Late Life: Results of the NIH Consensus Development Conference* (pp. 279–291). Washington, DC: American Psychiatric Press.

Thompson, L.W., Davies, R., Gallagher, D. & Krantz, S.E. (1986). Cognitive therapy with older adults. *Clinical Gerontologist*, **5**(3/4), 245–279.

Thompson, L.W., Futterman, A. & Gallagher, D. (1988). Assessment of late life depression. *Psychopharmacology Bulletin*, **24**(4), 577–585.

Thompson, L.W., Gallagher, D. & Breckenridge, J. (1987). Comparative effectiveness of psychotherapies for depressed elders. *Journal of Consulting and Clinical Psychology*, **55**, 385–390.

Thompson, L.W., Gallagher, D. & Czirr, R. (1987). Personality disorder and outcome in the treatment of late-life depression. *Journal of Geriatric Psychiatry*, **21**(2), 133–146.

Thompson, L.W. & Gallagher-Thompson, D. (1994) Comparison of desipramine and cognitive/behavioral therapy for the treatment of late-life depression: a progress report. Paper presented at the Annual Meeting of the American Psychological Association, Los Angeles, CA, August.

Thompson, L.W., Gantz, F., Florsheim, M., DelMaestro, A., Rodman, J., Gallagher-Thompson, D. & Bryan, H. (1991). Cognitive-behavioral therapy for affective disorders in the elderly. In W. Myers (Ed.), *New Techniques in the Psychotherapy of Older Patients* (pp. 3–19). Washington, DC: American Psychiatric Association Press.

Weiss, J. (1991). Part I: Theory and clinical observations. In J. Weiss & H. Sampson (Eds), *The Psychoanalytic Process: Theory, Clinical Observation and Empirical Research* (pp. 3–138). New York: Guilford.

Widner, S. & Zeichner, A. (1993). Psychological interventions for the elderly chronic pain patient. *Clinical Gerontologist*, **13**(4), 3–18.

Yost, E., Beutler, L., Corbishley, M.A. & Allender, J.R. (1986). *Group Cognitive Therapy: A Treatment Approach for Depressed Older Adults*. New York: Pergamon.

Young, J.E. (1990). *Cognitive Therapy for Personality Disorders: A Schema-focused Approach*. Sarasota, FL: Professional Resource Press.

Young, J.E. (1994). *Cognitive Therapy for Personality Disorders: A Schema-focused Approach*, revised edn. Sarasota, FL: Professional Resource Press.

Young, J.E., Beck, A.T. & Weinberger, A. (1993). Depression. In D. Barlow (Ed.), *Clinical Handbook of Psychological Disorders* (pp. 240–277). New York: Guilford..

Zeiss, A.M. & Lewinsohn, P.M. (1986). Adapting behavioral treatment for depression to meet the needs of the elderly. *Clinical Psychologist*, 98–100.

Chapter 11

PSYCHODYNAMIC THERAPY AND SCIENTIFIC GERONTOLOGY

Bob G. Knight*

INTRODUCTION

In this overview of issues of psychodynamic therapy with older adults, several themes in psychodynamic therapy with the elderly are considered within the context of empirical research and of concepts from scientific gerontology. The chapter begins with a brief history of psychodynamic approaches and then describes a recent model which integrates psychotherapeutic observations with research and theory drawn from social gerontology. The empirical literature evaluating psychodynamic therapy with older adults is reviewed. Finally, several topics related to psychodynamic concepts are examined: life review therapy, griefwork, character disorders in late life, and transference and countertransference.

EARLY HISTORY OF PSYCHODYNAMIC THERAPY WITH "OLDER" ADULTS

The first mention of age as a factor in psychotherapy was in a speech by Freud to the faculty of the Medical College in Vienna in 1904 (Freud, 1905/1953). In this early phase of the development of his thinking, and in speaking to what he seemed to regard as a hostile audience, Freud addressed the indications and contra-indications for psychotherapy. He first states that they can "... scarcely be definitely laid down as yet, because of the many practical limitations to which my activities have been

* University of Southern California Andrus Gerontology Center, Los Angeles, CA: USA

Psychological Problems of Ageing: Assessment, Treatment and Care. Edited by R.T. Woods.
© 1999 John Wiley & Sons Ltd.

subjected." (p. 263). He goes on to state several limitations, including seeing therapy as unsuitable for persons with "neuropathic degeneracy"; persons with psychoses, confusional states and "deeply rooted" depression are also ruled out. "A reasonable degree of education and a fairly reliable character" are required for successful therapy. In this context, he said the following about age:

> The age of patients has this much importance in determining their fitness for psycho-analytic treatment, that, on the one hand, near or above the age of 50 the elasticity of the mental processes, on which the treatment depends, is as a rule lacking—old people are no longer educable—and, on the other hand, the mass of material to be dealt with would prolong the duration of the treatment indefinitely (p. 264).

Freud was 48 at the time of this address.

An early response to Freud came from Abraham (1919/1977) as he cautioned against preconceived notions of treatment with older adults. He stated that it was the task of psychoanalysis to ask whether and under what conditions it could be effective with older patients. Abraham wrote about successful treatment with some older neurotic patients (referring to patients who were around 50 years of age), stating that the prognosis was good if the neurosis became severe long after puberty, if the individual had several years of normal sexual functioning, and a period of social productivity. In short, "the age of the neurosis is more important than the age of the patient" (p. 317).

Freud's early dictum is often cited as a basis of therapeutic pessimism about working with the older adult, although few modern therapists would seriously consider people of around 50 years of age to be no longer educable. Meerloo (1955) observed that the approach of death leads the older adult to life review, the evaluation of accomplishments, and decreased defensiveness, allowing easier access to the patient's unconscious.

The early years were largely, but not entirely, psychoanalytic. Cutner (1950) reported on a successful Jungian analysis. The Jungian approach was argued to be more appropriate to the older adult, since Jung (1933) saw the second half of life as having its own tasks and as involving the development of previously neglected aspects of the personality.

In the first integrative review of psychotherapy with older adults, Rechtschaffen (1959) presented a generally optimistic portrayal, although he left open the question of whether psychotherapy with older adults requires modification. His case summaries encompassed subgroups that have become more salient and distinctive in the years since 1959. For example, he did not separate residents of institutions, including those with organic brain disorders, from other elderly when surveying types of interventions.

The positive experiences of clinicians doing therapy with older adults, as reported in case histories, are an encouraging first step in demonstrating the effectiveness of this approach. More rigorous proof of the effectiveness of psychodynamic therapy can only come from evaluation research with sound experimental design. Since 1980, such studies have been reported in the literature and are reviewed in the next section.

DOES PSYCHODYNAMIC THERAPY WORK WITH OLDER ADULTS?

A small number of randomized studies of the effectiveness of brief psychodynamic therapy with depressed older adults (Gallagher & Thompson, 1982; Steuer et al., 1984; Sloane, Staples & Schneider, 1985; Thompson, Gallagher & Breckenridge, 1987) and one study with caregivers (Gallagher-Thompson & Steffen 1994) support the efficacy of psychodynamic therapy as compared with delayed treatment controls and with other types of therapy, including behavioural therapy, cognitive therapy and psychotropic medication. In passing, it can be noted that Thompson, Gallagher & Breckenridge (1987) report that there was no spontaneous remission of depression in their delayed treatment group, a clear contrast to studies with younger clients. In summary, psychodynamic therapy has been found to be superior to no treatment and roughly equal in effectiveness to other types of treatment.

These results are generally obtained in brief periods of time; the Thompson/Gallagher-Thompson group. uses 16–20 sessions of therapy. Steuer et al. (1984) used nine months of group therapy sessions and noted that most change in both conditions occurred after 26 weeks. In the only known finding of a therapy type by patient characteristic interaction in older adults, Gallagher-Thompson & Steffen (1994) reported the finding, contrary to hypothesis, that psychodynamic therapy worked better with those caregivers who were new to caregiving (less than 44 months) rather than with those who had been on the job longer. Perhaps the focus on past conflicts over dependency issues and individuation is more salient in the first years of caregiving.

As we have seen, psychotherapy with older adults has been done, discussed and studied for about eight decades. In general, both the case studies and the controlled research on outcomes have been positive

(Knight, Kelly & Gatz, 1992). For the most part, people who have experience in doing psychotherapy with older adults have described it as valuable for clients and rewarding for the therapist, whereas those who have not worked with older adults have argued that the aged cannot benefit from psychotherapy. Since the 1970s, writing about therapy with older adults has increasingly drawn upon scientific gerontology (Knight, Kelly & Gatz, 1992). In the next section, a model is presented which can serve as a framework for applying gerontological knowledge to thinking about older adults in therapy.

THE CONTEXTUAL, COHORT-BASED, MATURITY/ SPECIFIC CHALLENGE MODEL: INTEGRATING PSYCHOTHERAPY AND GERONTOLOGY

The early history of gerontology as a discipline was characterized by a split between researchers, who were discovering that ageing was a more positive experience than society believed, and practitioners, who were struggling with the problems of selected elderly and who generalized the real problems of frail older adults to all ageing people. The loss-deficit model of ageing, which portrays the normative course of later life as a series of losses and the typical response as depression, has been an integral part of the practitioner heritage. More recently, Knight (1992, 1993) has proposed a contextual, cohort-based, maturity/specific challenge model to integrate scientific concepts from gerontology with psychotherapy experience to guide our thinking about the need to adapt psychotherapy for work with older adults.

Maturation in adult development and ageing

There are trends in gerontological thinking that suggest a potential for continual growth toward maturity throughout the adult life span. In this sense, maturity means: increasing cognitive complexity, possibly including post-formal reasoning; development of expertise in areas of experiential competence, including work, family and relationships; androgyny, at least in the sense of acquiring role competencies and interests stereotypically associated with the opposite gender; and a greater emotional complexity, with better comprehension and control of emotional reactions.

Cognitive maturation throughout adulthood and into later life may also be characterized by the development of expert systems, dependent on the individual's experiences in adult life (Rybash, Hoyer & Roodin, 1986) and by movement to a stage of post-formal reasoning with an appreciation of the dialectical nature of argument and social change, and a greater appreciation that people hold differing points of view (Rybash, Hoyer & Roodin, 1986). On the emotional side, older adults have been seen as becoming less impulsive and driven by anxiety (Gynther, 1979) and more emotionally complex, with more complex reactions to events (Schulz, 1982) and more complex experience of, and ability to control, emotional states (Labouvie-Vief, DeVoe & Bulka, 1989). The mechanism for such improvement can be as simple (and as complex) as the accumulation of life experiences, which can be understood as an increasingly complex database of human interaction.

The specificity of late-life problems

Many elderly clients seeking help in therapy are struggling with problems that threaten psychological homeostasis at any point in the life span: chronic illness, disability and the loss of loved ones to death. These problems are not unique to late life, but are more likely in the latter third of life. In addition, late life is not immune to the usual vicissitudes of all of life: disappointment in love, arguments with family members, and failing at the tasks we set ourselves. Finally, many people who have struggled with depression, anxiety, substance abuse or psychosis all of their lives eventually become older adults and are still struggling with these problems.

The specific nature of these problems is important to the practice of psychotherapy with individual older people. These specific problems require specific knowledge on the part of the psychologist working with older adults: knowledge about the way in which diseases and their treatments affect and are affected by emotion and behaviour in later life, and an ability to recognize and work with grief when it occurs.

Cohort differences as a source of client/therapist difference

Another contribution to understanding older adults from scientific gerontology comes from methodologies used to study life-span development, which separate the effects of maturation from the effects of cohort membership and social change. Much of social gerontology could be summarized as the discovery that many of the differences between the old and the young that society has attributed to the ageing process are due, in fact, to cohort effects. Cohort differences are explained by membership of a birth-year-defined group that is socialized into certain beliefs, attitudes and personality dimensions that will stay constant as it ages and which distinguish that cohort from those born earlier and later.

For example, later-born cohorts in the twentieth century in the USA have more years of formal schooling than earlier-born groups. Research on cognitive abilities shows that later-born cohorts may be superior on spatial abilities and reasoning, whereas earlier-born cohorts may have the advantage on numerical abilities. Cohort comparisons are not always linear: some cognitive abilities (e.g. word fluency) have both improved and declined across successive cohorts (Schaie, 1990). Memory research has shown that earlier-born cohorts use "old words", and some differences between older people and younger people in learning word lists are eliminated if cohort-appropriate lists are used (see Barrett & Wright, 1981). In other domains, social change that occurs before or during our childhood years may be taken for granted; that which occurs during our adult years will be truly experienced as change.

These differences, while not developmental, are real. Working with older adults involves learning something of the folkways of members of earlier-born cohorts, just as working with adolescents or young adults demands staying current in their folkways and world view. During times of rapid social and technological change (the twentieth century comes to mind), cohort effects may overwhelm advantages of developmental maturation. Preparation to do therapy with older people has to include learning what it was like to grow up before we were born.

The separate social world of the elderly

A final consideration for understanding older adults in psychotherapy is the need to understand the distinctive social milieu of older adults. In the USA of the late twentieth century, this context includes specific environments (age-segregated housing, age-segregated social and recreational centers, the ageing services network, age-segregated long-term care, and so on) as well as specific rules for older adults (healthcare regulations, laws regarding competency and substitute decision-making, and so forth). The network of ageing services is yet another element of this context. An understanding of this social context that is based on both knowledge of what is supposed to be and experience of actual operations is important to the understanding of what clients say. A danger of selective exposure of professionals to these environments for older adults is that many people who are expert about a given context (e.g. skilled nursing facilities) imagine that they are expert about older adults in general.

Experience in training new therapists suggests that those student therapists without other contact with the social world of the elderly find the clients' descriptions of this different world inordinately confusing. The social worlds of older and younger adults in our culture are sufficiently different that an accurate description of what goes on at a typical meal site can sound neurotic or even delusional to the uninitiated younger therapist. For example, an older client once described being anxious about being watched whenever she entered or left her elderly-only apartment building. I wondered about her suspiciousness until I went to the same building to visit a different client and was scrutinized by two residents sitting by the elevator.

Implications for psychodynamic theories

Gerontology, and especially the life-span developmental approach to the study of ageing, tends to emphasize normal development. Psychodynamic theory is rooted in the practice of psychotherapy and so generalizes from experience with (usually small numbers of) older people in trouble. This generalization becomes a problem when concepts about older adults who are clinically depressed, have personality disorders, and so on, are used to theorize about universal developmental processes of adulthood and old age. A second error in generalization occurs when the specificity of illness is not recognized; for example, cognitive loss due to Alzheimer's disease poses different problems in later life from the physical limitations of heart disease, which are in turn different from the psychological issues posed by cancer.

For example, as noted by Newton et al. (1986), self-psychology theories about ageing are concerned with the threats that developmental ageing pose to the self-esteem of the older adult. First, it can be noted that gerontological research does not show a general decline in self-esteem with ageing; Bengtson, Reedy & Gordon (1985) reported that existing studies were equally divided between equal and greater self-esteem among older adults as compared to younger ones. As noted above, maturation perspectives suggest a strengthening of self-concept in normal ageing. In fact, Newton et al. (1986) cite an example from Kohut (1972) of an older adult with a brain injury as an example of threats to self-esteem. The maturity/specific challenge model would argue that the older client should be expected to have a stronger self; when this is not the case, the reason should be sought in specific challenges, such as brain injury or other disease, or in the individual's failure to mature normally (e.g. character disorder).

With regard to more classic psychoanalytic theories, as reviewed by Newton et al., the current model would also question whether alterations in libido or psychological regression are related to developmental ageing. For the older woman at least, there is no compelling scientific evidence of decline in libido; the usual problem for the older woman is finding an appropriate partner (Adams & Turner, 1985). This issue is part of the social context of ageing, not a part of developmental ageing. With regard to regression, Newton et al. (1986, p. 214) note that this phenomenon is observed primarily in the psychologically and physically frail older adult. This observation would make regression part of an expectable response to illness and frailty at any age, not an expected aspect of late life.

The third theoretical trend in psychodynamic therapy discussed by Newton et al. (1986) is the advent of developmental approaches, including Erikson's stage models and Gutmann's concept of re-emerging powers (see Gutmann, 1987). The maturation component of the model described here is closely linked to this trend, although rooted more in scientific gerontology than in psychodynamic theory and practice. The developmental concept leads naturally to a discussion of Erikson and of life review as a model of therapy in later life.

LIFE REVIEW AS THERAPY

Outside of gerontology and mental health and ageing, Erikson (1950/1963, 1968) is best known for his work in ego psychology as a re-interpreter of childhood developmental stages into less sexual terms, and for extending stage theory into adolescence and early adulthood. In later years, he wrote more about old age and suggested the need for a ninth stage, given that people routinely live a decade and more after the usual age of integrity/despair (Erikson, Erikson & Kivnick, 1986).

A strong view of stage theory would argue that one cannot move on to the next stage until the current one is resolved in a positive manner. Erikson himself clearly argued for a weaker interpretation in which people move on to later stages and revisit earlier ones that are still conflictual (Erikson, Erikson & Kivnick, 1986). As a guide to therapy, especially with clients who have personality disorders, the image that clients are stuck at earlier stages and therefore earlier ages can be very helpful. Realizing that a 75 year-old client may still be six years old (or 15 or 20) is a potent insight that can re-orientate the therapist to the appropriate developmental issues and to appropriate ways of relating to the client's intrapsychic age. The model also suggests that there are important developmental conflicts in adulthood and late life; therefore, the sources of problems in later life may be in the adult years and adult family contexts, not always in the childhood years and the family of origin. There is also the clear implication that later life should move on from the middle-age years, and the therapist should not be hampered by a middle-age view of life.

This developmental stage view can run into several problems. One which is acknowledged by most therapists working with older adults is that working with clients who are further along the life cycle requires us to move beyond our personal experience of life's stages. This movement is not, in principle, different from moving outside of our experience to work with clients of a different gender, social class, sexual orientation, work experience, and so forth. Second, the task of reviewing a life which is six or more decades long is overwhelming (Freud's second, and usually forgotten, caution about psychoanalysis with older clients) and requires considerable editing and an awareness of not having the full story. This is, of course, likely to be true of shorter lives as well, since no-one does day-by-day reviews, but it is highly salient in work with older adults.

The third is the prevalent error of confusing development with socially defined age-graded roles (Neugarten & Hagestad, 1976). Much of change in adulthood and old age is not so much an ontogenetic unfolding of personality development as it is the assumption and discarding of social roles which are roughly age linked, although less so in the 1990s than in earlier decades. Retirement, for example, is often presented as a developmental milestone (see Newton et al., 1986, p. 209, for example). Retirement is a socially created role, quite rare prior to the Great Depression, which is being redefined continually. While the post-retirement lifestyle is clearly different from the working middle-age years, the difference is one of adapting to, or breaking out of, social roles rather than of coping with ontogenetic change.

The contextual and cohort-based portions of the current model are important checks on this tendency to overgeneralize the importance of developmental influence in late life. The social context of older adulthood is quite different from that of earlier years because society creates a different role for older people. An important part of helping older adults understand what they are up against is interpreting this world and finding their individual responses to it. This interpretation and response is in turn determined in part by the client's cohort, that is, older clients matured in a different cultural context, with its own expectations of what later life would be like and its own evaluation of the current circumstances of later life. For example, people who grew up with a sense of self that was embedded in a family with history and who had the expectation of an unending succession of generations may be dismayed by children or grandchildren who decide not to have children. The therapist must be able to take on alternative viewpoints based on development, current social context and an understanding of the context of earlier-born cohorts.

Does life review therapy work?

Life review and reminiscence therapies have developed parallel to stage theories and other psychodynamic theory rather than directly out of them. Butler's (1963) seminal article on recognizing reminiscence as a normal and healthful activity of ageing led to both unstructured encouragement of this reminiscence and more structured life review therapy (e.g. Lewis & Butler, 1974). Early admonitions that the process could have a negative outcome (Butler, 1963; Erikson, 1950/1963) were largely ignored for several years, but are re-emerging in more careful modern theoretical formulations (e.g. Fry, 1994).

The range of what is meant by reminiscence and life review therapy, and the variety of outcomes, is apparent from the systematic attempts to evaluate these interventions. In their meta-analysis of psychosocial treatments for depression in the elderly, Scogin & McElreath (1994) report effect sizes for reminiscence vs. no-treatment controls in the studies which they reviewed that ranged from d = 0 (no effect) to d = 3.23 (a very large effect and the largest in the review).

A closer look at a few available studies may suggest possible influences. Reminiscence in nursing homes raises the interesting possibility, confirmed by Goldwasser, Auerbach & Harkins (1987), that one is reminiscing with dementing older adults with substantial memory impairment. While there would seem to be obvious reasons to be troubled by this practice, no one seems to find it unusual. It is more troubling since the article, as published, shows the facilitators guiding reminiscence by failing to distinguish between the First and Second World Wars and by asserting that the Second World War (sic) occurred in 1912, making the client about 10. Since the USA entered the First World War in 1917 (client about age 15), the client is likely to find this guidance baffling rather than facilitating. The gains in depression reported in this small study (nine patients per group) result from high mean pre-test scores in the treatment group dropping to the level of the comparison groups (p. 216). quite possibly due to random variation. Rattenbury & Stones (1989), also reporting on a nursing-home sample, found no difference between reminiscence and current events discussion groups.

Haight (1988, 1992) reported on structured life review with homebound frail older adults and found no significant change in depression, although life satisfaction scores improved. Fry (1983) obtained much stronger results, the largest effect size in the Scogin & McElreath meta-analysis. Fry's subjects were community-dwelling older adults with professional or managerial pre-retirement jobs who were pre-screened for high levels of depressed mood, thus eliminating possible floor effects. The reminiscence training is highly structured and contains elements and principles of psychodynamic therapy: a focus on negative life events, a concern with intrusive thoughts and avoidance, expression of strong affect, descriptions of images and compulsive thoughts, telling of dreams, focus on unresolved feelings, and more. The other studies described here rely on loosely guided, non-emotionally charged recollections about the past. With both a more appropriate sample and stronger intervention techniques, the stronger results are not surprising.

Many of the same techniques used in Fry's structured reminiscence training are also part of classic approaches to griefwork (Rando, 1984; Worden, 1992). In the next section, we turn to investigations of grief in older adults to see what science offers to practice in helping older adults with this common challenge of later life.

GRIEF

Wortman & Silver (1989) describe several myths about the grieving process which are not supported by available scientific evidence. Distress is generally thought to be both inevitable and necessary. In fact, based on evidence in their review and a study of bereaved older adults by Gilewski et al. (1991), many bereaved people, including the elderly, do not experience depression after the loss, and the initial reaction tends to be fairly stable over the next few years, that is, those with initial psychological distress tend to remain relatively highly distressed. This evidence also bears on two other myths: the expectation of recovery and the attainment of a state of resolved feelings. In general, the evidence suggests that affective and cognitive effects of bereavement continue for at least two to seven years after the loss (Wortman & Silver, 1989; Thompson et al., 1991).

The importance of "working through" the loss is perhaps more equivocal. Wortman & Silver argued that the existing evidence does not support a connection between active processing of the death and lower emotional distress 18 months to four years after the death. Stroebe & Stroebe (1991) reported that among younger-adult bereaved spouses, avoidance coping impaired adjustment for widowers but not for widows, whose depression was so stable over time (78% of variance in Time 2 scores predicted by Time 1 scores) that there was little additional variance to predict. One could also question, based on psychodynamic concepts of defence strategies, whether people who report not thinking much about the death would not also be likely to fail to self-report emotional distress on research question-naires; however, this line of thought needs further empirical study in order to avoid intellectual sophistry. The empirical evaluation of interventions based on different models of helping could clarify these issues.

The finding that the emotional response to the death of a loved one is stable, but not universal, challenges the concept that depression in response to grief is a normative reaction with a naturally occurring recovery. These observations could lead to more questioning about the severe depression reaction when it occurs. It is likely to be of clinical and scientific importance to understand why some bereaved people become depressed and others do not. It is possible that depressed mourners were depressed prior to the death (Gilewski et al., 1991), had specific types of dependent or conflictual relationships with the deceased, or have long-standing difficulty in coping with stressful life events, perhaps due to character disorders or dysfunctional personality traits. In any case, it seems that there is reason to question the policy of both public and private insurers who (at least in the USA) disallow bereavement counselling on the grounds of the normality of bereavement and expected recovery from grieving without intervention.

CHARACTER DISORDERS IN LATE LIFE

To the extent that the focus of psychodynamic approaches to therapy emphasizes the individual's lifelong ego development and coping patterns (Newton et al, 1986; Newton & Lazarus, 1992), psychodynamic therapy focuses on character analysis more than, or at least in addition, to current problem analysis. Given this emphasis, a frequent clinical focus of psychodynamic approaches is personality disorder rather than transient situational distress.

Personality disorders in the elderly have only recently become a focus for research and clinical writing (Sadavoy & Fogel, 1992). The course of personality disorders over the life span is not clear at present. Cluster B disorders (antisocial, borderline, histrionic and narcissistic) are often thought to show some improvement, possibly due to maturation with increased development of the self, to decreased impulsiveness or to decades of life experience. The other clusters (which include paranoid, schizoid, schizotypal, avoidant, dependent, obsessive-compulsive, and passive–aggressive disorders) appear to stay stable or perhaps worsen (Sadavoy & Fogel, 1992). In theoretical terms, while maturity concepts would lead one to expect improvement in personality disorders with ageing, personality disorders can also be conceptualized as the consequence of being stuck in earlier stages of development and so unable to mature naturally or to incorporate new experiences in the way a more mature individual could.

Sadavoy & Fogel (1992) also argue that institutional environments and other circumstances of later life that enforce high levels of intimacy and prevent regulation of distress and conflict by distancing (e.g. long-term caregiving) may lead to apparent worsening of personality disorders in later life in those who had found ways to cope at earlier stages. They also argue that older adults with residual personality disorder (e.g. cluster B disorders that have improved with age) may present greater, or at least different, problems in psychotherapy than older adults who have never had a personality disorder.

Personality disorders are known to have negative effects on treatment outcomes in later life for all types of interventions studied (Thompson, Gallagher & Czirr, 1988). Intriguingly, the same study found that depression makes the diagnosis of personality disorder more likely by influencing the client's presentation of typical personality functioning.

Controlled evaluations of attempts to ameliorate personality disorders in late life have not been done. Decades of clinical case reports of psychodynamic therapy with older adults would appear to provide grounds for optimism, although many clinicians clearly set goals that do not include personality change (for reviews, see Newton & Lazarus, 1992; Knight, Kelly & Gatz, 1992).

While popular wisdom seems to argue that character is less changeable in later life, the evidence for stability or maturation of personality would seem to argue that personality change would be no more difficult than in earlier years. In an early review of psychotherapy with older adults, Rechtschaffen (1959) cautioned about how easily older adults incorporate therapeutic interpretations. Knight (1992, 1996) has argued that late life is free of some of the pressures that militate against change (expectations from work and family) and provides sufficient leisure time to work on change. Nemiroff & Colarusso (1985), among others, have argued that the nearing of death is a powerful motivation for change.

The role of psychodynamic therapy in the treatment of personality disorders in later life clearly needs more exploration in clinical work, scholarship and controlled evaluation studies. It would seem appropriate for heuristic reasons to explore the potential strengths of psychodynamic approaches in this area rather than to attribute so much differentness to the older adult that psychodynamic therapy of character disorders is never attempted.

TRANSFERENCE AND COUNTERTRANSFERENCE

The role of the therapeutic relationship is central in psychodynamic therapy and the potential for changes from the more typical relationship when the client is older has been recognized for some time (Rechtschaffen, 1959). In these early writings, the usual change described is the possibility of the therapist being seen as child rather than as parent. Knight (1996) suggested the possibility of grandchild transferences and being identified with the spouse at an earlier age, as well as noting the continuing possibility of parental transference and erotic transference. Others have described transference and its use in psychotherapy in greater detail (Hinze, 1987; Semel's chapters in Brody & Semel, 1992). Hinze (1987) notes the possibility of several changes in the transference during one client's psychotherapy.

Countertransference has often been cited as an obstacle to older adults receiving therapy (Knight, 1996; Newton et al., 1986) and has often been defined too broadly so that it includes ageist prejudice, misinformation about the elderly, failures to take another cohort's perspective, and the stress of working with such problems as grief and adjustment to chronic illness without appropriate preparation or adequate ongoing support. Hinze (1987) notes the importance of having a specific technical definition, and Semel (1992) argued for separation of social prejudice from individual clinician countertransference. Both offer excellent and incisive case descriptions that clarify the importance of monitoring specific countertransferential issues arising from the therapist's past history and their impact on the misperception of the individual client.

While the clinical reports attest to the importance of the phenomenon, wider-scale attention to these issues in training, in scholarship and in research is needed in order to further clarify what remains a somewhat murky picture. Global descriptions of transference and countertransference do little to clarify what is a quintessentially idiosyncratic phenomenon. Detailed case history accounts and exploration in clinical supervision do more to clarify the issue at this level.

Systematic research would probably lead to better conceptual analysis and to results that would contradict what is now believed. To take examples from related areas of research, it was long believed that therapists' ageist biases were a major barrier to older adults receiving treatment. Research has generally proved this to be incorrect and pointed to systemic factors as more important (Gatz & Pearson, 1988; Smyer, Zarit & Qualls, 1990). Research on the therapeutic alliance in therapy with older adults has shown independence of therapist and client ratings of the alliance (Marmar et al., 1989) and stronger association of alliance with outcome in cognitive therapy (Marmar et al., 1989) and of patient defensiveness with patient commitment to treatment in cognitive therapy than in psychodynamic therapy (Gaston et al., 1988). The researchers speculate that cognitive therapy requires a stronger commitment from the patient and that cognitive therapists may not handle defensiveness well. While these studies have changed our understanding of other aspects of the relationship between therapists and their older clients, research on transference and countertransference is needed in order to subject concepts based on observation to potential falsification in research settings.

SUMMARY

Psychodynamic therapy has a long history of case studies reporting success with older clients. More recently, these case studies have been confirmed by randomized clinical outcome studies of brief psychodynamic therapy and by the success of Fry's structured reminiscence approach. A contextual, cohort-based maturity/specific challenge model is presented that applies gerontological theory and data to psychotherapy. This approach suggests modifications in some traditional psychodynamic conceptions of ageing, with more attention to maturation with age, to social context factors, to the change of context over successive cohorts, and to the distinction between disease and other stressors associated with later life from the developmental process itself. A summary of existing empirical research supported the effectiveness of psychodynamic therapy with older adults. Recent trends in understanding griefwork, character disorders and transference are summarized. The interplay between gerontology and psychodynamic theory can strengthen both fields and contribute to the ability of therapists to help older adults cope with the challenges of the final third of life.

REFERENCES

Abraham, K. (1919/1977). The applicability of psychoanalytic treatment to patients at an advanced age. In S. Steury & M.L. Blank (Eds), *Readings in Psychotherapy with Older People* (pp. 18–20). Washington, DC: Department of Health, Education, and Welfare.

Adams, C.G. & Turner, B.F. (1985). Reported change in sexuality from young adulthood to old age. *Journal of Sex Research*, **21**, 126–141.

Barrett, T.R. & Wright, M. (1981). Age-related facilitation in recall following semantic processing. *Journal of Gerontology*, **36**, 194–199.

Bengtson, V.L., Reedy, M.N. & Gordon, C. (1985). Aging and self-conceptions: personality processes and social contexts. In J.E. Birren & K.W. Schaie (Eds), *Handbook of the Psychology of Aging*, 2nd edn. (pp. 544–593). New York: Van Nostrand Reinhold.

Brody, C.M. & Semel, V.G. (eds) (1992). *Strategies for Therapy with the Elderly: Living with Hope and Meaning*. New York: Springer.

Butler, R.N. (1963). The life review: an interpretation of reminiscence in the aged. *Psychiatry*, **119**, 712–728.

Cutner, M. (1950). Analysis in later life. *British Journal of Medical Psychology*, **23**, 75–86.

Erikson, E. (1950/1963). *Childhood and Society*, 2nd edn. New York: W.W. Norton.

Erikson, E. (1968). *Identity: Youth and Crisis*. New York: W.W. Norton.

Erikson, E.H., Erikson, J. & Kivnick, H.Q. (1986). *Vital Involvements in Old Age*. New York: W.W. Norton.

Freud, S. (1905/1953). On psychotherapy (J. Strachey, trans.). In *The Complete Psychological Works of Sigmund Freud*, Vol. 6. London: Hogarth.

Fry, P.S. (1983). Structured and unstructured reminiscence training and depression among the elderly. *Clinical Gerontologist*, **1**, 15–37.

Fry, P.S. (1994). A conceptual model of reminiscence. In J.D. Webster (Chair), State of the Art: Life Review and Reminiscing. A symposium at the Meeting of the Gerontological Society of America, Atlanta, GA.

Gallagher, D. & Thompson, L.W. (1982). Treatment of major depressive disorder in older adult outpatients with brief psychotherapies. *Psychotherapy: Theory, Research and Practice*, **19**, 482–489.

Gallagher-Thompson, D. & Steffen A.M. (1994). Comparative effects of cognitive-behavioral and brief psychodynamic psychotherapies for depressed family caregivers. *Journal of Consulting and Clinical Psychology*, **62**, 543–549.

Gaston, L., Marmar, C.R., Thompson, L.W. & Gallagher, D. (1988). Relation of patient pretreatment characteristics to the therapeutic alliance in diverse psychotherapies. *Journal of Consulting and Clinical Psychology*, **56**, 483–489.

Gatz, M. & Pearson, C.G. (1988). Ageism revisited and the provision of psychological services. *American Psychologist*, **43**, 184–188.

Gilewski, M.J., Farberow, N.L., Gallagher, D. & Thompson, L.W. (1991). Interaction of depression and bereavement on mental health in the elderly. *Psychology and Aging*, **6**, 67–75.

Goldwasser, A.N., Auerbach, S.M. & Harkins, S.W. (1987). Cognitive, affective, and behavioral effects of reminiscence group therapy on demented elderly. *International Journal of Aging and Human Development*, **25**, 209–222.

Gutmann, D. (1987). *Reclaimed Powers: Toward New Psychology of Men and Women in Later Life*. New York: Basic Books.

Gynther, M.D. (1979). Aging and personality. In J.N. Butcher (Ed.), *New Developments in the Use of the MMPI* (pp. 39–68). Minneapolis, MN: University of Minnesota Press.

Haight, B. (1988). The therapeutic role of a structured life review process in homebound elderly subjects. *Journal of Gerontology*, **43**, 40–44.

Haight, B.K. (1992). Long term effects of a structured life review process. *Journals of Gerontology: Psychological Sciences*, **47**, P312–315.

Hinze, E. (1987). Transference and countertransference in the psychoanalytic treatment of older patients. *International Review of Psycho-analysis*, **14**, 465–473.

Jung, C.J. (1933). *Modern Man in Search of a Soul.* New York: Harcourt Brace Jovanovich.

Knight, B.G. (1996). *Psychotherapy with the Older Adult*, 2nd edn. Thousand Oaks, CA: Sage.

Knight, B. (1992). *Older Adults in Psychotherapy: Case Histories.* Newbury Park, CA: Sage.

Knight, B.G. (1993). Psychotherapy as applied gerontology: a contextual, cohort-based, maturity-specific challenge model. In M. Smyer (Ed.), *Mental Health and Aging.* New York: Springer.

Knight, B., Kelly, M. & Gatz, M. (1992). Psychotherapy with the elderly. In D.K. Freedheim (ed.), *The History of Psychotherapy.* Washington, DC: American Psychological Association.

Kohut, H. (1972). Thoughts on narcissism and narcissistic rage. *Psychoanalytic Study of the Child*, **27**, 360–400.

Labouvie-Vief, G., DeVoe, M. & Bulka, D. (1989). Speaking about feelings: conceptions of emotion across the life span. *Psychology and Aging*, **4**, 425–437.

Lewis M.I. & Butler, R.N. (1974). Life review therapy: putting memories to work in individual and group psychotherapy. *Geriatrics*, **29**, 165–172.

Marmar, C.R., Gaston, L., Gallagher, D. & Thompson, L.W. (1989). Alliance and outcome in late life depression. *Journal of Nervous and Mental Disease*, **177**, 464–472.

Meerloo, J.A.M. (1955). Psychotherapy with elderly people. *Geriatrics*, **10**, 583–587.

Nemiroff, R.A. & Colarusso, C.A. (1985). Adult development and transference. In R.A. Nemiroff & C.A. Colarusso (Eds), *The Race Against Time: Psychotherapy and Psychoanalysis in the Second Half of Life.* New York: Plenum Press.

Neugarten, B.L. & Hagestad, G.O. (1976). Age and the life course. In R.H. Binstock & E. Shanas (Eds), *Handbook of Aging and the Social Sciences.* New York: Van Nostrand.

Newton, N.A., Brauer, D., Gutmann, D.L. & Grunes, J. (1986). Psychodynamic therapy with the aged: a review. *Clinical Gerontologist*, **5**, 205–229.

Newton, N.A. & Lazarus, L.W. (1992). Behavioral and psychotherapeutic interventions. In J.E. Birren, R.B. Sloane & G.D. Cohen (Eds), *Handbook of Mental Health and Aging*, 2nd edn. (pp. 699–719). San Diego: Academic Press.

Rando, T.A. (1984). *Grief, Dying, and Death.* Campaign, IL: Research Press.

Rattenbury, C. & Stones, M.J. (1989). A controlled evaluation of reminiscence and current topics discussion groups in a nursing home context. *The Gerontologist*, **29**, 768–771.

Rechtschaffen, A. (1959). Psychotherapy with geriatric patients: a review of the literature. *Journal of Gerontology*, **14**, 73–84.

Rybash, J.M., Hoyer, W.J. & Roodin, P.A. (1986). *Adult Cognition and Aging.* New York: Pergamon.

Sadavoy, J. & Fogel, B. (1992). Personality disorders in old age. In J.E. Birren, R.B. Sloane & G.D. Cohen (Eds), *Handbook of Mental Health and Aging*, 2nd edn. (pp. 433–462). San Diego, CA: Academic Press.

Schaie, K.W. (1990). Intellectual development in adulthood. In J.E. Birren & K.W. Schaie (Eds), *Handbook of Psychology and Aging*, 3rd edn. (pp. 291–310). San Diego: Academic Press.

Schulz, R. (1982). Emotionality and aging: a theoretical and empirical analysis. *Journal of Gerontology*, **37**, 42–51.

Scogin, F. & McElreath, L. (1994). Efficacy of psychosocial treatments for geriatric depression: a quantitative review. *Journal of Consulting and Clinical Psychology*, **62**, 69–74.

Semel, V.G. (1992). Private practice. In C.M. Brody & V.G. Semel (Eds), *Strategies for Therapy with the Elderly: Living with Hope and Meaning* (pp. 93–14). New York: Springer.

Sloane, R.B., Staples, F.R. & Schneider, L.S. (1985). Interpersonal therapy versus nortriptyline for depression in the elderly. In G.D. Burrows, T.R. Norman & L. Dennerstein (Eds), *Clinical and Pharmacological Studies in Psychiatric Disorders* (pp. 344–346). London: John Libbey and Co.

Smyer, M.A., Zarit, S.H. & Qualls, S.H. (1990). Psychological intervention with the aging individual. In J.E. Birren & K.W. Schaie (Eds), *Handbook of Psychology and Aging*, 3rd edn. (pp. 375–404). San Diego: Academic Press.

Steuer, J.L., Mintz, J., Hammen, C.L., Hill, M.A., Jarvik L.F., McCarley, T., Motoike, P. & Rosen, R. (1984). Cognitive-behavioral and psychodynamic group psychotherapy in treatment of geriatric depression. *Journal of Consulting and Clinical Psychology*, **52**, 180–189.

Stroebe, M. & Stroebe, W. (1991). Does "grief work" work? *Journal of Consulting and Clinical Psychology*, **59**, 479–482.

Thompson, L.W., Gallagher, D. & Breckenridge, J.S. (1987). Comparative effectiveness of psychotherapies for depressed elders. *Journal of Consulting and Clinical Psychology*, **55**, 385–390.

Thompson, L.W., Gallagher, D. & Czirr, R. (1988). Personality disorder and outcome in the treatment of late life depression. *Journal of Geriatric Psychiatry*, **21**, 133–153.

Thompson, L.W., Gallagher-Thompson, D., Futterman, A., Gilewski, M.J. & Peterson, J. (1991). The effects of late life spousal bereavement over a 30 month period. *Psychology and Aging*, **6**, 434–441.

Worden, W. (1992). *Grief Counseling and Grief Therapy*, 2nd edn. New York: Springer.

Wortman, C.B. & Silver, R.C. (1989). The myths of coping with loss. *Journal of Consulting and Clinical Psychology*, **57**, 349–357.

Chapter 12

PSYCHOLOGICAL "THERAPIES" IN DEMENTIA

*Robert T. Woods**

INTRODUCTION

This chapter is concerned with psychological approaches to working with older people with dementia. The development of such approaches can be traced back over at least 35 years; Miller (1977) and Woods & Britton (1977) are good sources for much of the earlier work in this field. Are these approaches"therapies"? Certainly they have usually implicitly assumed that improvements in aspects of the function of the person with dementia are feasible and attainable; however, connotations of a curative model have often been avoided by describing these approaches as "management techniques". In fact, in terms of efficacy, it is not at all clear that the pharmacological therapies currently available are appreciably superior to the best of the psychological approaches (Orrell & Woods, 1996).

These are not merely issues of semantics. Caregivers' expectations and the provision of resources are strongly influenced by how the various interventions available are viewed. Raising false hopes that cannot be fulfilled, leading to disappointment and disillusionment, damages the movement towards more positive approaches in dementia care (Woods, 1995a, b). There must be realism as to what may be achieved; but emphasis must also be given to the value, to the person with dementia and to those who provide care, of those changes, however limited, in state and function that are achievable. Only then will the necessary resources of staff time, support and training be made available. We have come a long way from the days when the view that nothing could be done for people

* University of Wales, Bangor, UK

Psychological Problems of Ageing: Assessment, Treatment and Care. Edited by R.T. Woods.
© 1999 John Wiley & Sons Ltd.

with dementia held sway. Now the priority is to define more clearly what can be achieved, and the most effective methods to bring about change.

PSYCHOLOGICAL APPROACHES: A FRAMEWORK

Before presenting information on some of the specific "therapies" that have been described over the years, it is worth discussing their place in the overall scheme of dementia care. Holden & Woods (1995) present an integrated approach which is of use in recognizing some of the general issues that are relevant to most approaches.

Attitudes, values and principles

The attitudes, values and principles underlying the implementation of any approach are of prime importance. Psychological and emotional needs must be addressed as much as the physical needs, which often appear paramount. Attitudes which encourage individuality as an adult, dignity, self-respect, choice and independence are seen as providing the basis for any positive approach. Similar considerations emerge from the application of social role valorization principles to dementia care (see Stirling, 1996; King's Fund, 1986). Kitwood has described a "malignant social psychology" (MSP) around the person with dementia, which comprises negative attitudes and practices (see Kitwood, 1990, 1996, 1997). Kitwood argues that this MSP leads to reduced function in people with dementia, and perhaps even increases the rate of decline and neurological impairment. Dehumanization, objectification and invalidation form the core of the MSP and unfortunately are pervasive throughout dementia care. They detract from the personhood of the individual with dementia and distort and corrupt the therapies used. They need to be dealt with before any approach can be applied appropriately.

A number of examples are to be found in the literature of dubious practices being carried out in the name of one "therapy" or another (e.g. Buckholdt & Gubrium, 1983). Several of these relate to reality orientation (RO), which seems particularly prone to being applied mechanically, in a depersonalized manner. Why are negative attitudes so prevalent? The vast majority of care-staff are well-meaning and do not act maliciously. Common sense and good intentions are not enough, however; understanding, empathy and imagination are required to acquire the insight needed to view the world from the perspective of the person with dementia. Reducing the pace of caregiving is not easy when other pressures compete. Possibly some features of dementia particularly make it difficult to recognize the person with dementia as being the same person as previously, and deserving of the same respect. Fears of developing dementia may lead some to maintain a distance, avoiding the empathy and closeness that would come from fully recognizing the personhood of the dementia sufferer. Aspects of attitudes and attitude change in dementia care are discussed elsewhere in this volume (Chapter 8); the key point here is that an explicit set of values and principles emphasizing the value and worth of the person with dementia is an essential prerequisite to the application of any psychological approach.

Individualization

Individualization is the second component of the integrated framework. It is important as a basic principle of personhood, with each person being unique, and in addition has strong pragmatic support. There are differences in neurological impairment: many different types and subtypes of dementia; many different stages in the progress of these disorders; a random element in some disorders as to which parts of the brain are particularly affected. Even greater are the differences in the person's interests, preferences, priorities, personality traits, lifestyle, ways of coping, health and life experiences, which have influenced and shaped the person's life over many years to the present, leading to an enormous range of variation. Simply knowing that the person has dementia is remarkably uninformative in the face of such diversity, which demands an individualized response. Lawton's model of "environmental docility" (Parmelee & Lawton, 1990) suggests that the lower the person's competence and level of function, the more likely he/she are to be shaped by and vulnerable to environmental contingencies. People with dementia are less able to modify and adjust the environment themselves; they therefore require input geared to their individual needs and abilities. They may show a lowered tolerance to variations from their uniquely ideal "person-environment fit", simply because they do not have the reserve capacity to adapt and accommodate. Those who work with the person with dementia must then "fine tune" their approach so that it is as close as possible to being spot-on for that individual.

Learning is possible

The third key aspect of this integrated framework is the contention that learning is possible. Clearly, new learning is a primary deficit in most forms of dementia (see, for example, Chapter 5 in this volume); however, a great deal of experimental evidence has now accumulated to indicate that under the right conditions, some limited, but potentially valuable, ability to learn is identifiable (see Miller & Morris, 1993, pp. 113–115). This is apparent in at least four areas of learning:

1. *Classical conditioning*. For example, the eye-blink response that is elicited by a puff of air into the eye will in time be produced by a buzzer that was initially paired with the puff of air on a number of learning trials.
2. *Operant conditioning*. Patients with dementia have been trained to make a response (such as pressing a lever) contingent on a "reward"; thus four out of five patients with dementia learned to press a lever to obtain music (Burgess et al., 1992).
3. *Procedural and implicit memory*. There are many examples of skills learning being preserved in dementia. In addition, there is evidence of certain aspects of implicit memory remaining relatively unimpaired. This is shown in situations where performance is enhanced without conscious or explicit recall of material, such as priming, where prior exposure to an item facilitates later processing of that, or a related, item.
4. *Verbal learning and retention*. Perhaps surprisingly, when information is adequately registered, rates of forgetting after the first 10 minutes or so may be relatively normal in many people with dementia. For example, Little et al. (1986) showed retention of information over a one- or two-month period by patients with a moderate degree of dementia. Bäckman (1992) concludes that support must be given at both the time of learning and the point of retrieval to maximize learning in dementia; the person with dementia may then need more learning trials, with fewer items at a time, and more guidance in encoding the material, as well as more retrieval cues.

These experimental findings provide some indications for cognitive rehabilitation (see below) and more generally refute the notion that no change is possible in the fundamental cognitive deficits of dementia.

Selection of targets

The careful and creative selection of targets is essential; approaches such as RO have been criticized for emphasizing verbal orientation, which may be of limited clinical relevance. Does the person really need to know the day of the week or the name of the prime minister? When changes are inevitably fairly limited in size, and require considerable input for their achievement, it is essential that they address the key issues which will make a real difference for the person concerned. Learning to find the toilet on the ward might be important for one patient; for another, improving dressing skills may be the priority; for others, increasing social contact may be important. For some patients in the community who receive different services on different days, learning to keep touch with days and dates may be vital. In view of the often noted specificity of learning in dementia, with improvements not readily generalizing from one goal to another, targets have to be very carefully selected to be precisely and individually relevant and appropriate.

Maintenance of benefits

Maintaining any positive changes is a further major concern. There is a sense that the assumed natural history of decline in the dementias results in an uphill struggle to hold onto function against a backdrop of progressive deterioration. In reality, the clinical picture is considerably more complex, with great variation in rates of change, and some patients showing remarkable stability. Expecting any "therapy", psychological or pharmacological, to have lasting effects without any further maintenance input is simply unrealistic; interventions need to be ongoing, with targets regularly reviewed as the person's condition changes.

Effects on staff and carers

The attitudes, well-being and behaviour of staff and carers will have a major impact on the quality of life of the person with dementia. The consequences of any approach for those caregiving day by day must then be considered. If positive, staff or carers may be assisted in their difficult and demanding task—a worthy aim. Improved morale and less strain and burden are likely to lead to more positive interactions between caregivers and patients, and so will be of benefit for all concerned. The improvement in carers' mood reported by Greene et al. (1983), coincident with their relative with dementia attending RO sessions at a day hospital, is one of the most interesting positive indications. The increase in staff knowledge of individual patients related to reminiscence and RO reported by Baines, Saxby & Ehlert (1987), is also important. Salmon (1993) reports an increase in positive staff–patient interactions during formal RO and suggests that it provides a structure for positive interaction. An integrated approach must take into account the needs, strengths, perceptions, commitment and abilities of caregivers if practicable, realistic care plans are to be developed. Simply to produce positive change in the patient's behaviour is not enough. As Tarrier & Larner (1983) report, staff may not perceive objectively measured change.

Realistic expectations

Realistic expectations are important if caregivers are not to become disappointed when the latest "therapy" turns out to be no more of a cure-all than those that have preceded it. Changes are generally likely to be small and probably quite specific. Individualized targets for the achievement of change and development should be established, and set at a level where small successes may readily be achieved, so that staff do not become disappointed and the patient is not over-pressured. Even when function does not improve, there can be valuable achievements in involving the person in a positive experience—a feeling of success, a moment of contact with another human being, a smile of appreciation. Kitwood & Bredin (1992) argue that it is possible to recognize indications of (relative) well-being in people with dementia when personhood is being maintained. These indicators are thought to be expressions of four "global sentient states": (a) a sense of personal worth—a deep self-esteem; (b) a sense of agency—to have some control over their personal life, to achieve something; (c) a sense of social confidence—of being at ease with others; and finally (d) a sense of hope—feeling secure, trusting that all will be well. The expression of such states, however fleeting, is a worthy aim of dementia care.

Individual programme planning

These considerations lead naturally to an approach that has been described as "individual programme planning" (Woods & Britton, 1985) or "goal planning" (Barrowclough & Fleming, 1986). At the centre of this approach is the individual plan, covering all aspects of the person's life. Developing an individual plan begins with careful and thorough assessment of the person's strengths and needs, including any medical conditions and sensory deficits. As far as possible, the person with dementia and his/her family should be involved in this planning process. Discovering the wishes of the person with dementia may not be easy, especially when communication is poor. Information from relatives, friends of long standing and so on regarding the person's past life and experiences will be invaluable. Placing the dementing person in the context of his/her whole life is vital. Reminiscence-based activities may be a great help;

preparing a life chart of the important events, people and experiences in the person's life is a good starting point (Woods et al., 1992).

The assessment stage will include attempts to understand, as well as to define, the person's behaviour. The reasons for difficulties must be examined, including consideration of specific neuropsychological deficits. Generalized descriptions of behaviour, such as "attention-seeking", "confused", "incontinent" and so on must be replaced by detailed descriptions of the person's behaviour, the exact circumstances, its frequency and intensity. Where particular specific neuropsychological deficits are identified, efforts should be made to find ways of overcoming the effects of the problems and ways of compensating for the disability.

Once the initial assessment phase is complete, the plan is drawn up. The strengths and needs that have been identified are used to form the plan. The person's strengths and resources are used to help meet particular needs selected for intervention. These are not selected simply for the convenience of staff, but in relation to the quality of life of the person. It may be that where a particular problem behaviour has been identified, the targets will include the encouragement of activities that are incompatible with, or will reduce the frequency of, the "problem". For instance, the target for a person who is frequently incontinent might be for the person to learn where the toilet is on the ward. This process in relation to challenging behaviour is discussed more fully by Stokes (1996).

The various "therapies" contribute to the individual plan as possible approaches to some of the very common—almost universal—needs of people with dementia. Achieving success in valued activities, engaging in person-to-person contact and communication, finding important places and making sense of what is happening may all emerge in many patients' individual plans, and may all be addressed by one therapy or another. These approaches are then seen as subordinate to the individual planning process, but contributing significantly to the developing repertoire of methods of meeting individual patients' identified needs available to caregivers.

PSYCHOLOGICAL THERAPIES

Stimulation and activity

These approaches arose from the notion that people with dementia are under-stimulated, receiving inadequate sensory input. Reduced sensory input may be experienced for several reasons; first, normal decline in sensory acuity; second, the monotonous environments in which some older people live; and third, some patients withdraw and reject stimulation, cutting off from the environment, perhaps as a way of coping with perplexing, almost alien, surroundings. Support came from sensory deprivation experiments, showing that even young people suffered from confusion when deprived of sensory stimulation for a period of time (see Holden & Woods, 1995). Sensory deprivation results as much from monotony as from lack of stimulation.

A number of early studies reported positive effects from a range of social, physical and psychological stimulation, including occupational therapy and domestic and recreational activities (see Woods & Britton, 1977). Such activities have become a widely accepted aspect of good practice and are now offered in many care settings. More recently, different types of stimulation or activity have been evaluated, and ways of increasing the response of people with dementia, including those most severely impaired, to activity and stimulation have been explored.

For example, Norberg, Melin & Asplund (1986) evaluated the effects of music, touch and objects expected to stimulate the person's senses of taste, touch and smell (e.g. fur, hay, bread, camphor). Two severely impaired patients with dementia, who showed little, if any, verbal communication, were carefully observed whilst receiving the various forms of stimulation. A definite positive response to music was identified, but no differences in reaction to different objects or to touch were detected. Similarly, Gaebler & Hemsley (1991) identified a response to music in the majority of a group of six patients whose dementia was very advanced and with whom verbal communication was impossible. These studies are particularly important in their focus on severely impaired patients and their painstaking use of observational methods to reliably detect a response that would be perhaps imperceptible to the untrained eye.

The effects of music have also been evaluated on a less impaired group of "Alzheimer patients" by Lord & Garner (1993). Groups of 20 nursing-home residents had either "big band" music from the 1920s and 1930s, or puzzle exercises, or the "standard" recreational activities of drawing, painting and TV, over a six-month period in daily half-hour recreational sessions. The music group showed better recall of personal information, and their mood and social interaction also improved compared with the other two groups: "The subjects in the music therapy sessions always smiled, laughed, sang, danced and whistled while listening to the music". The other activities did not elicit the same degree of anticipation, enjoyment and pleasure, and were less effective as triggers of social interaction.

Pet animals are another popular source of stimulation. Several evaluative studies have been reported. Elliott & Milne (1991) and Haughie, Milne &

Elliott (1992) evaluated the impact of a visitor with a dog in a psychiatric hospital ward where most patients had a diagnosis of dementia. In both studies interaction levels increased markedly when the dog and visitor were present. In the latter study, to control for novelty, photographs of the dog and visitor were also used as stimuli; they were associated with smaller, but still significant, increases in interaction. A number of aspects of the patients' behaviour, including mobility and dependency, were rated by nurses as improved when the dog was present. The improvements were not maintained on days subsequent to the visits of the dog. The presence of a stimulus is needed to elicit the higher level of interaction and other changes. Other sources of stimulation yet to be formally evaluated include visits by carefully prepared school-age children (Langford, 1993).

Most activity programmes have included some form of physical exercise, usually highly structured—light bending and stretching exercises whilst sitting in a chair, throwing a ball, knocking down skittles, brisk walking, rhythmical movements, movement to music, etc., all demanding task attention. Morgan (1991) reviews several studies on the effects of exercise in dementia. While there are some indications of limited benefits on aspects of cognitive function (e.g. Molloy, Richardson & Crilly, 1988), overall the studies have not been well controlled, so any benefits cannot be linked with certainty to the physical exercise component of the intervention. Also, diagnostic criteria have been weak in these studies.

There is much interest in "Snoezelen", an approach originating in Holland which seeks to increase the amount of sensory stimulation through changing coloured lights and visual effects, relaxing armchairs and cushions, pleasant smells and even a vibrating cushion and a soap bubble machine. The word "Snoezelen" is a contraction of two Dutch words meaning "sniffing and dozing". A positive evaluation has appeared (Benson, 1994), which suggests increased relaxation, improved mood and decreased agitation during Snoezelen sessions, although with little carry-over beyond the session. This article also suggests that conventional relaxation techniques—gentle music and one-to-one encouragement of slow, deep breathing—were equally effective in calming patients with dementia. A randomized controlled trial is reported by Baker et al. (1997), contrasting eight Snoezelen sessions with eight sessions of other activities. Both groups showed short-term improvements in mood and behaviour immediately after the sessions, but in the longer term, patients participating in Snoezelen showed significant reductions in disturbed behaviour at home. Spaull, Leach & Frampton (1998) have evaluated the effects of individual sensory stimulation sessions on four dementing patients. Interaction and interest increased during the sessions, and disturbed behaviour was rated as having reduced following the sessions.

Methods of providing tactile and sensory stimulation—hand or foot massage, aromatherapy, etc.—are also suggested as relaxing, enjoyable activities (e.g. West & Brockman, 1994). However, Brooker et al. (1997) reported a limited response to massage and aromatherapy in four severely impaired patients, suggesting it may not be beneficial in all cases. One of the four patients showed a significant improvement in agitation in the hour following massage or aromatherapy. Two patients appeared to be more agitated following the interventions, possibly feeling confined by the intervention.

Some support for the usefulness of relaxation techniques is provided by Welden & Yesavage (1982). Twenty-four matched pairs of patients with dementia attended either a relaxation training group or a current affairs discussion group for an hour three times a week over a three-month period. Relaxation instructions included progressive muscle reduction and a self-hypnosis technique. Subjects attending relaxation sessions showed improvement on ratings of behavioural function compared with the control group. In addition just over 40% of those taught relaxation techniques no longer required sleeping medication; none of the control group was able to discontinue.

It has been argued that too much stimulation is unhelpful for people with dementia, and "reduced stimulation units" have been described (Cleary et al., 1988). Clearly stimulus overload is to be avoided; many care environments are too noisy, and too much happening around the person can be perplexing and can add to confusion. The emphasis in practice has been to devise stimulation and activity that will engage the person with dementia, that will be enjoyed and valued and not act as an irritant. There will be individual differences, of course; some will not want dogs or children, and individuals' musical preferences must be respected. The growing interest in calming forms of stimulation suggests that some people with dementia are seen as over-aroused, having high levels of internal stimulation, emerging as feelings of anxiety and agitation. The sensory deprivation hypothesis is too simplistic to encompass all these strands, but has been a useful starting point.

Reality orientation

This long-established psychosocial approach has been used with older people with dementia for over 30 years, and an extensive literature, both evaluative and descriptive, is available (see Holden & Woods (1995) and Woods (1992) for full reviews).

Two major components of reality orientation (RO) are described. Twenty-four-hour RO (or informal RO) involves a number of changes to the environment, with clear signposting of locations around the ward or home, extensive use of notices and other memory aids, and a consistent approach by all staff in interacting with the person with dementia. In its original form, staff undertaking 24-hour RO were intended to offer orientating information in each and every interaction; more recently, a modification has been described where staff are trained to take a more reactive stance, orientating the person only in response to his/her requests (Reeve & Ivison, 1985; Williams, Reeve et al., 1987). RO sessions (or RO classes) are structured group sessions, involving a small number of patients and staff, meeting regularly, often several times a week for half an hour or so. A wide variety of activities and materials are used to engage the patients with their surroundings, to maintain contact with the wider world and to provide cognitive stimulation. A typical session would go over basic information (such as names of those in the group, day, date, time and place), discuss a current relevant theme of interest, perhaps play a number or naming game, and finish with refreshments. Throughout there would be a tangible focus: a white-board for the current information; pictures or objects appropriate to the theme; personal diaries and notebooks for those able to record information for later use.

Holden & Woods (1995) identified 21 studies, meeting the criterion of reporting an evaluation of the effects of RO in comparison with either no treatment or an alternative intervention. There are many differences between the studies:

1. In the type of RO evaluated. Only a third of studies included 24-hour RO; just two of these evaluated the extent to which this intensive approach was actually being implemented.
2. In location. Hospital wards, residential and nursing homes, day centres and out-patients have all been the setting for one or more projects.
3. In the specificity of the diagnosis of dementia. Diagnostic criteria have not always been well described.
4. In measures used. A wide variety of brief cognitive scales (mainly orientation tests) and behaviour rating scales have been adopted.
5. In duration of the intervention period. The briefest period was three weeks, the longest a year. Frequency of RO sessions varied from twice daily to once a week; most studies had sessions five times a week.
6. In design and methodological adequacy. Whilst some studies have randomly allocated patients to groups, others have had comparison

groups in different wards/homes/units. Each approach has its problems, the former especially where 24-hour RO is included, with inevitable "contamination" across the groups. Few studies have employed raters "blind" to group membership, and few have followed patients up after the end of the intervention.

7. In comparison groups included. "No treatment" has been most commonly used, but about a third of studies have offered an alternative group activity, sometimes as a placebo to control for the effects of attention, at times as a viable alternative to RO sessions.

Despite these variations between studies, some remarkably consistent conclusions have emerged. First, there is strong support for RO sessions being associated with increased scores on measures of verbal orientation, as compared with no-treatment control groups. Only one study to date (Williams et al., 1987) has reported cognitive changes that could be attributed specifically to 24-hour RO, but, as mentioned above, few studies have actually demonstrated its implementation. With the emphasis in RO on verbal orientation, these findings may not seem so surprising, although given the severity of the learning problems in dementia, any indications of improvements are welcome. More controversial are suggestions that more general cognitive improvements may occur. Some studies suggest that only those orientation items specifically taught are learned; others that from a battery of cognitive tests, only the orientation items show improvement. More recent reports (e.g. Breuil et al., 1994; Zanetti et al, 1995) have tended to support the notion that more wide-ranging improvements in cognition may follow cognitive stimulation of this type.

The second main conclusion is that changes in function and behaviour are much more elusive than cognitive changes; in general they have been the exception rather than the rule. There are many possible factors in this difference between the change in cognitive test performance and real-life function: behaviour rating scales used have often been less sensitive to the small changes envisaged; an environment encouraging dependence (as many have been shown to do) may counteract any benefits from group sessions; it is doubtful whether verbal orientation has any influence on many of the areas of function, such as feeding and dressing, which comprise much of the content of the behaviour rating scales typically used. It may be argued that direct training of a particular skill will be required for behavioural change; several workers have shown this in relation to ward orientation—the person finding his/her way around the ward or home. Improvements in this domain have been shown in relation to specific training by Hanley, McGuire & Boyd (1981) and associated with 24-hour RO by Reeve & Ivison (1985) and Williams et al. (1987). These studies have in common a demonstrable intervention in the person's living environment, the former through direct training, the latter two through the monitored evaluation of 24-hour RO. The greatest range of behavioural improvement reported was evident in these studies.

The RO literature raises many questions, but does indicate that scope for cognitive management in dementia does exist. Further work from a more specifically cognitive standpoint is described below. RO has been much criticized in relation to its mechanical, inflexible, insensitive, confrontational application and its over-emphasis on cognitive aspects. Used appropriately, within an individualized framework, it still has an important part to play in dementia care.

Reminiscence

The use of past memories to establish a point of interest and contact has been often used in RO sessions, and has attracted much interest as an approach in its own right (Woods & McKiernan, 1995; Gibson, 1994). Reminiscence work with older people more generally developed from psychotherapeutic considerations, emphasizing the place of life review in adaptation (Coleman, 1986; Bornat, 1994). Reminiscence has been used extensively with patients who are depressed, as well as those with dementia; it should be recognized that the aims and techniques may need to be different in each case. Norris (1986) provides an excellent description of the practical application of a variety of reminiscence techniques. There is an accumulation of evidence for the effectiveness of various types of reminiscence work in reducing depressive symptoms in older people (Scogin & McElreath, 1994).

Haight & Burnside (1993) draw attention to the way in which this psychotherapeutic use of life review has been confused with other reminiscence work, such as that with people with dementia. Whilst the terms "reminiscence" and "life review" have often been used interchangeably, they suggest that life review be used solely to describe an intervention where the therapist is seeking to assist the person in achieving a sense of integrity. This involves the older person recalling and evaluating events and experiences throughout his/her life, usually in a one-to-one setting with the therapist, who acts as a therapeutic listener. Garland (1994) provides a useful account of life review therapy. Life review therapy, as described here, is much more likely to involve working through difficult and painful memories and experiences; it should be undertaken, like any other personal therapy, with the person's consent, with a clear aim, by properly trained and supervised workers. Generally speaking, it is a more appropriate approach for older people without cognitive impairment. "Reminiscence", on the other hand, is seen as having a variety of goals, including increased communication and socialization, and providing pleasure and entertainment. It may be individual or group-based; may be structured or free-flowing; may include more general memories than specific events or experiences; themes and prompts are frequently used; evaluation of memories is not specifically encouraged; and the focus is on a relaxed, positive atmosphere. Sad memories may emerge, but support is available from the group leader and other members, or from the worker in individual work, to contain any distress or pain associated with such memories. Reminiscence work is appropriate for people with dementia, but some caution is still required, taking into account Coleman's (1986) report of large individual differences in attitudes to reminiscence amongst older people and the need to avoid an intrusive approach that invades individuals' privacy. Particularly in a group setting, awareness of participants' life histories is important to ensure that appropriate support can be given if events that have traumatic connotations for certain individuals are being raised by other members.

The cognitive roots of using this approach arise from the apparent preservation of remote memory in dementia; the person appears to remember events from his/her childhood whilst unable to recall what he/she had for lunch. Of course, when this area has been systematically tested, recall for specific events from many years ago is not relatively preserved (Morris, 1994); performance across the life span is depressed compared with age-matched controls. People with dementia, like normal older people, recall more memories from early life; such memories are often over-learned or well rehearsed, or have particular personal and/or emotional significance for the person concerned. Morris points out that studies of autobiographical memory indicate that there is typically virtually no recall from the person's middle years; this disconnection must add greatly to the difficulty of regaining orientation to the present time.

Reminiscence therapy has been used with individuals and in small groups (Norris, 1986; Thornton & Brotchie, 1987; Woods et al., 1992; Gibson, 1994). Photographs, music and archive recordings, video tapes of newsreels and items from the past are used to stimulate a variety of personal memories.

Despite a number of positive anecdotal reports, empirical research on reminiscence with people with dementia remains in its infancy. Thornton & Brotchie (1987) and Woods & McKiernan (1995) provide detailed reviews. No changes in cognitive or behavioural function were reported by

Goldwasser, Auerbach & Harkins (1987), who compared twice-weekly reminiscence and support groups with a no-treatment control over a five-week period. The reminiscence group showed an improvement in depression, but this was lost at a follow-up six weeks post-intervention. It appeared that the less impaired patients showed most response.

Baines, Saxby & Ehlert (1987) compared reminiscence and RO groups in a residential-home setting, with residents having a moderate to severe degree of cognitive impairment. Staff involved in a reminiscence group acquired much more individual knowledge of the residents in the group than they did of residents in a control group who received no additional treatment. Residents were rated as deriving a great deal of enjoyment from the groups, both by staff taking part in the groups and by staff who saw the residents only outside the groups. Attendance at the reminiscence groups was consistently high. Some effects on cognitive and behavioural function following reminiscence sessions were apparent in a group of five residents who had previously responded well to a month of RO sessions. They showed a reduction in scores on a problem behaviour rating scale, as well as an increase in verbal orientation. A group who had a month of reminiscence sessions before going on to RO sessions showed far fewer positive changes in relation to the untreated controls.

Other studies have looked at changes within the group session. Head, Portnoy & Woods (1990) contrasted reminiscence work with alternative group activities in two day centres. In only one centre was there a clear increase in the contributions made by group members during reminiscence as opposed to other activities. The lack of difference in the second centre appeared to be related to it having a much more stimulating range of alternative activities, rather than any failure on the part of the reminiscence work to elicit communication. In an initially unstimulating environment, the results of any intervention will appear much more dramatic. Woods & McKiernan (1995) report the results of work by McKiernan, Yardley & Bender indicating increased engagement of patients with a moderate to severe degree of dementia during reminiscence groups in three different units, confirming "that it provides a meaningful, appropriate and stimulating activity for people with even a very severe impairment".

A larger-scale evaluation of a number of "general" reminiscence groups is reported by Gibson (1994), with a sample of four residential homes and two day centres. Some groups were specifically for people with dementia, whilst others had a mixed membership. People with dementia showed pleasure and enjoyment in mixed groups and rarely exhibited any behavioural disturbance within the group; outside the group some individuals were reported by staff to be less agitated and restless. In the dementia-specific groups interactions tended to be between leaders and members, rather than between members, as had more commonly been the case in the mixed groups. Small, structured groups seemed to be most effective for people with dementia.

Gibson (1994) has also been developing individual reminiscence work with people with dementia. Five cases were selected as the most "troubled or troubling" residents of nursing homes. For each person, a detailed life history was compiled, from which a care plan was evolved, including "special" reminiscence-type work. The aim was to use "life-history as a working tool to enrich the quality of social exchange in the present". Trips and activities that related to the person's interests and experiences were planned, and the environment personalized and indi-vidualized according to the person's own style and preferences. Res-idents were reported to have shown increased sociability, decreased aggression and less demanding behaviour following the implementation of this individualized approach. Staff also responded positively, recogniz-ing more of the "personhood" of each individual. This study illustrates the value of life histories as a major influence in care planning (see also Woods et al., 1992; note that what they describe as "life reviews" are better regarded as life histories). The aim is to help the care staff see the person in the context of his/her life span, and so assist in improving the quality of their interactions with the person with dementia.

Outcome research on reminiscence in dementia is inconclusive; there are clear benefits within group sessions, but the impact outside is less certain. Changes in staff perceptions are promising. Many questions remain re-garding how best to run reminiscence groups and how to use one-to-one work most effectively. Reminiscence continues to offer exciting pos-sibilities in dementia care. There is a pressing need for more sophisticated research which focuses less on overall outcome and more on how best reminiscence may be adapted to individual needs and circumstances.

Validation therapy

Validation grew out of the dissatisfaction felt by Naomi Feil, a social worker in the USA, with approaches such as RO, which appeared over-confrontational. Feil found that insisting upon the person being orien-tated to the present reality often led to the person withdrawing and even becoming hostile (Feil, 1992a). Jones (1985) sums up the approach as "communicating with disoriented elderly persons by validating and sup-porting their feelings in whatever time or location is real to them, even though this may not correspond to our 'here and now' reality". Although Feil has been developing the approach since the 1960s, it was in the 1980s that the approach began to attract wider interest, initially in the USA and then further afield. Several publications describe aspects of the approach (Feil, 1992a, b, 1993). Feil (1993) gives the most detailed description of the techniques involved.

At the core of the approach lies a recognition of the individuality of the person with dementia and respect for his/her value as a person, which fits well with the explicit values discussed above. There is an emphasis on what has gone on previously in the person's life, influencing his/her current state; specifically, the person with dementia is seen as endeavouring to resolve "unfinished business" before the end of his/her life. Four stages of this "resolution" phase of life are identified: malorientation, time confusion, repetitive motion and vegetation. People with dementia are viewed as progressing through these stages, showing increased physical deterioration and withdrawal inwards. The aim of validation is to restore dignity and prevent the deterioration into vegetation, through the provision of an empathic, non-judgemental listener who accepts the person's view of reality. Painful feelings from the past that are expressed, acknowledged and validated in this way are thought to decrease in strength, whereas if ignored or not expressed they are said to heighten.

Feil (1993, p. 31) acknowledges that people do not remain neatly in one stage or another, and that there is considerable fluctuation. However, by detailing different techniques for different stages she is offering some insights into what may be more or less helpful in particular types of situation. The specific techniques include many aspects of non-verbal communication—use of touch, eye contact, tone of voice—as well as using music and reminiscence. The loss of recent memory, combined with sensory losses, is seen as leading to the retrieval of earlier memories and familiar faces, and "the need to go back to mend torn relationships" (Feil, 1993, p. 30). There is thought to be a reason behind all behaviour, and an important technique is to link the person's behaviour with the unmet human need underlying it. Three needs are seen as universal: the need to be loved and nurtured; the need to be active and usefully engaged; and the need to be able to express deep, raw emotions to an empathic listener.

The core technique is to recognize the person's communication of feelings and emotions, and to acknowledge and validate these, verbally and non-verbally. Whatever the person's current reality, whatever the facts of the matter, their feelings have their own validity. To respond to emotions at a cognitive level alone is to ignore an entire (and probably the most important) dimension of communication. For example, many people with dementia speak often about their parents as if they were still alive. To respond at a cognitive level, to correct the person, may well miss a key issue for the person with dementia. Miesen (1992, 1993) has shown the importance of attachment for many people with dementia, reflecting a need for security and safety in a perplexing and at times frightening environment; this need for attachment returns to the parents, the original attachment figures, in the person with dementia, who develops a "parent fixation". This should, then, be seen as an expression of need, not simply as a sign of confusion.

Validation techniques are often applied in a group setting, but can be used effectively on a one-to-one basis. Even a few minutes several times a week is thought to be a worthwhile input; as with other communication-based approaches, much can be achieved during routine caregiving, although it may well be demanding work in its own right. More severely impaired patients, in particular, will require an individual approach. In group settings, there is an emphasis on comfort, and of the time together being "special". Music is used as a uniting activity, and every effort is made to minimize communication difficulties. Group members are encouraged to take on responsibilities within the group—song-leader, welcomer, giving out refreshments, and so on. The wisdom of group members is drawn upon, placing them in the position of having something to give from their extensive experience of life, e.g. "What advice would you give a young couple thinking of getting married?". Issues for discussion are chosen to reflect real concerns and issues: there is no avoidance of controversial topics.

There are very few published studies documenting the efficacy of validation, although numerous anecdotal reports are referred to by Feil (1992b, 1993). Morton & Bleathman (1991) report an evaluation of a validation group which ran over a 20-week period in a residential home. Five residents with dementia participated; for 10 weeks beforehand, their behaviour, mood and interaction levels in the day-room of the home were monitored. These measurements continued during the period of the group and for 10 weeks afterwards, when reminiscence techniques were used in the group. The group sessions were held for one hour, once a week. Three of the residents completed the study; the individual results suggested that for two residents verbal interactions increased during the validation therapy period, with a decline during the reminiscence period, while the remaining resident showed the opposite pattern, with an increase apparent during the reminiscence phase. It should be emphasized that these interaction measures were taken outside the group setting, in the home's day-room. There was a remarkable contrast between how little these residents interacted during any phase and the depth of interaction apparent during the group sessions (see Bleathman & Morton, 1992, for an illuminating selection of transcripts from the sessions). It is unclear whether this is attributable to the specific validation techniques, rather than to the more general influence of the carefully structured small-group setting.

Cognitive psychology is beginning to recognize the importance of emotional aspects alongside the cognitive components of models of human function. Williams (1995) suggests that the interacting cognitive subsystems model, developed by Teasdale & Barnard (1993), may be helpful in conceptualizing validation. The model proposes two meaning subsystems, propositional and implicational, reflecting cognitive and emotional representations respectively. If the implicational subsystem is intact, the propositional subsystem will not be able to make sense of its output in relation to recent events, as propositional event memory is clearly impaired in dementia. Instead, it will use material relating to events perhaps many years previously to complete the fragmented description emerging from the implicational subsystem. For example, the person's emotion of feeling lonely and abandoned, generated in the implicational subsystem, may be only interpretable propositionally, as "Where is my mother?". The task for the caregiver is to respond at a level that connects with the implicational content. Reframing validation in this way may assist in developing the approach from a theoretical foundation.

Validation has been subject to some criticism. Confusion has arisen as to whether or not it was intended to be used with people with dementia (Stokes & Goudie, 1990). This has resulted in part from the idiosyncratic and changing terminology adopted by Feil. Feil (1993) makes it clear that people with dementia are the focus. Younger people (i.e. under 70) with Alzheimer's disease are identified as generally continuing to deteriorate despite the use of validation, unlike older people with dementia (Feil, 1993, p. 24). However, the techniques are still recommended as having some transitory effect.

Kitwood (1992) cautions that the emphasis on past life, on unresolved conflicts and difficulties, means that current sources of devaluation and impoverishment may be overlooked. Each behaviour may well have a reason behind it, but it may be in the "here and now", rather than buried in the mists of time. Many people with dementia daily experience all manner of unhelpful, unsupportive interactions which may have as great an impact as past conflicts. By emphasizing the role of "unfinished business", an implicit assumption arises that if one could learn to cope with life's problems adaptively, dementia could be avoided. This implies that people with dementia have in a sense inflicted it upon themselves, by their lifestyle and ways of coping. There is no evidence to suggest that this is in fact the case, and there is a real danger of accentuating further the "them and us" divide between cared-for and caregivers, if dementia is attributed to the person's own actions.

Resolution therapy

Resolution therapy is described by Stokes & Goudie (1990). It is similar to validation in that the aim is to tune in to the emotional communication of the person with dementia, adopting empathic listening skills. However, there is less emphasis on unresolved issues from the past, and more on the need for careful listening to identify feelings relating to making sense of the current situation, or expressing a current need. What the person says may, on the surface, not make "sense", but using counselling skills— warmth, acceptance, reflective listening, etc.—the concealed meaning may become apparent, reflecting the underlying feelings. The focus is on what the feeling is, not on why the person feels it; demanding explanations is seldom helpful in any context. Having identified the feelings, the next stage is to acknowledge them, verbally and non-verbally, and to modify the environment and the pattern of care to respond to unmet needs.

As well as counselling approaches such as this, there have also been exciting developments in the application of dynamic psychotherapy (Hausman, 1992; Sinason, 1992) and cognitive–behavioural therapy (Thompson et al., 1990) to older people with dementia. These developments reflect the earlier recognition and diagnosis of dementing conditions, resulting in a growing number of individuals with a much clearer awareness of what is happening to them. As yet, detailed studies of these approaches with these patients are not available; the application of a range of therapeutic listening techniques to people with dementia is long overdue. An important issue will be to consider to what extent such approaches have an impact on the overall process of dementia, or whether they are better seen as ways of enhancing communication with the person with dementia. The latter would itself be a very useful objective, and might facilitate short-term changes in function and well-being. As interest increases in this area, it may be that more attention will be given to what the person with dementia should be told about his/her diagnosis and prognosis: current practice is usually to inform the relative rather than the patient, unless the dementia is mild (Rice & Warner, 1994).

Cognitive management

From an analysis of cognitive deficits in dementia (Bäckman, 1992), it is clear that problems are more likely where performance depends on episodic memory or even semantic memory. Accordingly, to enhance function, cognitive load must be kept to a minimum, strong support provided for encoding and retrieval, with the use of retrieval cues where appropriate, and procedural memory and implicit memory utilized. So far little attention has been given to cognitive deficits other than memory and learning, and so the applications described largely emerge from this domain.

Reducing cognitive load

Alberoni et al. (1992) suggested that working with people with dementia individually, rather than in groups would reduce their cognitive load. They demonstrated that in group conversations people with dementia have difficulty in remembering who said what, particularly when the group size was larger. Patients tended to use spatial location as a cue, and performance was particularly disrupted when group members changed places. It should be noted that these difficulties were elicited in relation to patients watching a video tape of a group conversation, rather than participating themselves. In an actual conversation, with familiar people, the problems might not be so marked. Morris (1994) suggests that these deficits mean that group therapies "can degenerate into a monologue between individual staff members and patients". This is borne out by the finding of Woods et al. (1992) that in reminiscence sessions the majority of interactions taking place were between staff and patients; as would be predicted, they occurred more often between patients in a smaller group. Gibson (1994) similarly recommends small groups for people with dementia. In choosing whether to work with individuals or a small group, the advantages of working in groups—peer support, a social atmosphere, shared experiences—need to be weighed against their undoubted cognitive demands. Where groups are used, they should be as small as possible, with members retaining the same seating position from session to session; background noise and distractions should be kept to a minimum, and care taken to ensure that only one person speaks at a time.

External memory aids

External memory aids reduce the level of demand on effortful, self-initiated cognitive processes and provide support for the person in cuing and prompting retrieval of information—key features of effective cognitive training approaches (Bäckman, 1992). Retrieval cues in dementia generally require a high degree of specificity in order to be effective. Nonspecific external aids, such as an alarm clock or a kitchen timer, serve only to remind the person that something is to be remembered, leaving them with the frustration of not recalling what it was that had to be done. The effects of more specific aids have mainly been demonstrated through single-case studies. For example, a 68-year-old patient with a severe memory impairment successfully used a diary to prompt continuing awareness of personal information taught to her in daily individual sessions (Woods, 1983). Hanley & Lusty (1984) report a single-case study where an 84-year-old patient with dementia was able to achieve a higher level of orientation, using a watch and a diary as retrieval cues. Specific training was required in the use of the cues; without this, the patient did not spontaneously make use of them. During the training phase, the patient kept a far greater proportion of her "appointments" than previously, demonstrating an impact on everyday behaviour as well as on testing.

In a series of studies, Bourgeois (1990, 1992) has evaluated the effects of a prosthetic memory aid on conversational skills in people with dementia. The aid consisted of photographs and pictures of past and more recent events, important people in the person's life, and so on, in a convenient, robust wallet or book format. The person's spouse and other visitors were encouraged to use the aid when talking with the person. The results suggest that its use was associated with fewer ambiguous utterances and more statements of fact. The quality of conversation was assessed by independent raters as being significantly improved with the use of the aid as a focus for conversation. The aid is also reported to have proved useful in improving the quality of interaction between pairs of people with dementia. Although the aid is described as a prosthesis, it appears to be effective in prompting a number of memories related to each item, rather than simply acting as a replacement memory store for the specific information contained therein.

External memory aids have been explicitly used to reduce the load on the person's own memory and to support retrieval in daily living tasks by Josephsson et al. (1993). Four patients with dementia were evaluated on tasks such as preparing and consuming a drink or snack. Signs on drawers and cupboards indicated the location of required items. Physical demonstrations of task components were provided, for the patient to repeat. Verbal prompts and cues were also given. Improvements in task performance were shown by three patients; for two of these, continued environmental support and guidance were needed to maintain these gains. The remaining patient's lack of improvement was attributed to a high level of anxiety interfering with the learning process.

The need for staff input, at least initially, in reinforcing the use of the external aids is seen in the RO literature on signposting. Signs are usually more effective when combined with staff involvement, pointing out the signs and using them to orientate the person in training sessions (Hanley, 1981; Gilleard, Mitchell & Riordan, 1981; Lam & Woods, 1986). Such signposts may be viewed as retrieval cues; certainly some people with dementia are capable of benefiting from them, with practice in their use, even though not using them spontaneously.

Enhancing new learning

As discussed above, it is thought that once information is adequately registered, the rate of forgetting after the first 10 minutes or so may be virtually normal. Several techniques to achieve this initial learning have been described.

In spaced retrieval or expanded rehearsal (see, for example, Moffat, 1989; Camp & Schaller, 1989; McKitrick, Camp & Black, 1992) only one item at a time is learned. On each trial the retrieval period is adjusted according to whether the item was successfully recalled on the preceding trial; if it was, it is doubled; if not, it is halved. In this way, the item becomes fully registered, and subject to a relatively normal rate of forgetting, rather than the immediate decay of the memory trace usually associated with dementia. The next item is taught only when the first is fully established. Although this seems (and is) a laborious process, there is some evidence that learning may generalize to items not specifically taught in some situations. For example, Moffat (1989) indicated some generalization in retrieving the names of pictures of objects in a younger patient with Alzheimer's disease. Camp et al. (1996) showed that patients with dementia could be taught to make use of a memory aid (a calendar listing activities) using the spaced retrieval procedure. Errorless learning, where the conditions of learning shape and prompt the correct response, is thought to be an important component of this approach. Where the person makes errors during learning, these interfere with the memory for the correct response, and so hinder performance.

Several studies (see Bäckman, 1992; Martin et al., 1985) suggest that encoding information in the form of a motor act (such as acting out a movement associated with the word to be learned) is helpful, even where the degree of dementia is severe. Bird & Kinsella (1996) have combined spaced retrieval and motor learning, and have shown both to make a useful contribution to learning. Sandman (1993) provides an interesting example of giving support at both encoding and retrieval. He showed that people with dementia improved their recall of a TV programme when they worked with their relatives on creating their own test question on it, i.e. they established their own retrieval cues at the time of learning. Self-generated cues are likely to be the most effective.

From the same study comes a further example of how support at the time of encoding might be given, by making the event more distinctive and memorable. A significant event was planned by the caregiver with the patient. It was chosen to stand out from the usual routine, and might be a picnic, a trip out or a meal at a special restaurant. Patients were subsequently asked about details of the day not directly related to the event, such as what they were wearing, who they met that day, and so on. Patients showed normal recall for items from these special days, whilst being significantly impaired on items from ordinary days. Caregivers are often encouraged to develop a routine, as this may reduce memory load; this should not, however, be at the cost of having nothing worth remembering. These findings suggest that to "de-emphasize memorization as a goal" (Sandman, 1993) may itself be helpful. By making the experience as rich and meaningful as possible, memories associated with it will be enhanced. Helping the person to work on the material (but not asking them to remember it) and using retrieval cues are probably the best ways of enhancing performance.

Implicit and procedural memory

An application of procedural memory is reported by Zanetti et al. (1994). Employing the time taken to perform various basic and instrumental acts of daily living tasks as the outcome measure, four patients were reported to have shown improvements after three weeks of daily one-hour training sessions. Improvements were noted on both the specific activities trained and control tasks not included in the programme.

An example of implicit memory is "priming", where exposure to an item enhances later processing of that, or a related, item. Morris, Wheatley & Britton (1983) report a study where the person was shown a list of words, then given the initial letters of the words to be recalled. Word-stem completion occurred more readily where the person had had prior exposure to the word; the effect in patients with dementia was near normal. Priming has had some practical application, for example in the use of word-stem cues to aid verbal orientation.

Making use of preserved implicit memory, by reducing reliance on effortful processing and building on more automatic, well preserved skills, is an approach with much to commend it. These processes could be seen as underlying several approaches described previously, e.g. spaced retrieval (Bäckman, 1992), retrieval cues (Josephsson et al., 1993) and ward orientation training (e.g. Lam & Woods, 1986). However, two caveats should be noted. First, the various forms of implicit memory may not all be affected in the same way by the person's dementia. Thus Heindel et al. (1989) indicate that people with Huntington's disease show an impairment on procedural memory, but not on lexical priming, whereas people with Alzheimer-type dementia show the opposite pattern. Parkinson's disease patients with dementia were impaired on both types of implicit memory. Secondly, it should not be assumed that such techniques help the person to achieve "normal" memory. The person in fact may have little or no conscious memory of the event (as is suggested by the definition); what is being accessed are more automatic processes, achieving the goal by a different pathway. Indeed, the person may feel he/she is guessing the answer (Downes, 1987). However, to achieve a goal by a different route is a perfectly reasonable rehabilitation goal, but it is not "normal function" that is being restored.

Behavioural management

Whilst it is the cognitive aspects of dementia which often seem to attract most attention from researchers, it is the behavioural changes and disturbances which have most impact on care-givers and on decisions regarding placement and pattern of care. Responding appropriately to them may be of great significance to the person with dementia. Stokes (1996, p. 620) suggests that:

> challenging behaviour in dementia may . . . represent the communication of a need that is not anchored in time, for example, to be pain-free, to be loved, to be clean, to be safe, to "know".

Examples of behavioural difficulties may include wandering, verbal and physical aggression, urinary and faecal incontinence, sexual difficulties, excessive noise-making (e.g. shouting and screaming), eating difficulties, restlessness and lack of attention to personal hygiene. The individualized focus described above is especially important here; two patients may show, say, aggression in quite different ways, or in different circumstances (Ware, Fairburn & Hope, 1990; Patel & Hope, 1993). Similarly, a number of different types of wandering may be identified (Hope &

Fairburn, 1990). The label by itself is uninformative, and a full description of the behaviour and its context are required before a management plan can be considered.

The assessment process in such cases needs to be thorough and wide-ranging. A number of possible contributing factors must be considered including:

- *Physical health*—e.g. is the person in pain? What are the effects of medication being taken? What sensory problems does he/she have?
- *Neuropsychological deficits*—e.g. does the person recognize the toilet as a toilet? Does he/she have a dressing dyspraxia (rather than being simply uncooperative)? Does the person misidentify people and events on the TV as being real and occurring in his/her living room?
- *Environmental factors*—e.g. does the person find the day-room too noisy? Is the residential home layout unfamiliar, confusing and poorly signposted?
- *Emotional factors*—e.g. is the person feeling anxious and insecure or threatened?
- *Abnormal experiences*—e.g. is the person hallucinating or does he/she have delusions that he/she will be harmed?
- *Interpersonal*—does the person respond differently to different staff, to different approaches? Is he/she provoked by the behaviour of other residents?

Identifying the needs underlying the behavioural difficulty and seeking to meet them, using where possible the person's strengths and resources, is the essence of the goal-planning approach described by Barrowclough & Fleming (1986). As Stokes (1996) points out, the difficulty in dementia can arise because it becomes difficult for the person to communicate clearly his/her needs, which may lead to the person's behaviour being misinterpreted.

There are very few studies demonstrating the effectiveness of behavioural management in dementia. Bird, Alexopoulos & Adamowicz (1995) report a series of single-case studies where a highly individualized approach was adopted to a variety of challenging behaviours. Using spaced-retrieval learning methods (see above), the person is taught to respond to cues that aim to prompt appropriate behaviour, such as going into his/her own bedroom rather than those of other residents, or urinating in the toilet rather than the corner of the room. Cues were faded when the person's learning of the association was established. Examples of cues included signs indicating "no-go" areas and a sign indicating the location of the toilet. A portable alarm device, set to beep at certain intervals, was used to reduce the frequency of demands to go to the toilet by one patient. He learned to associate the alarm going off with being taken to the toilet, and his demands—based on a fear of being incontinent—reduced dramatically. This use of cues to prompt particular behaviours has similarities with the approach described some years previously by Hussian (1981).

Improved self-care has been reported by Rinke et al. (1978) in six nursing home residents and by Pinkston & Linsk (1984) in a family setting. In the latter case-study, differential reinforcement alone was effective, whereas in the nursing home prompting was also important. Prompting has formed the basis for a highly effective programme to reduce incontinence—prompted voiding (Schnelle et al., 1989; 1993; Burgio et al., 1988). The aim here is not full independence in toileting, but to reduce the number of episodes of incontinence. Residents are asked on a regular basis (usually two-hourly) whether they would like to go to the toilet, and are assisted with toileting if they respond positively. Positive results from the approach have been so rapid that it seems unlikely that re-learning could have taken place; rather, the procedure encourages staff to attend to residents' toileting needs in a structured way.

Given the multi-factorial nature of challenging behaviour in dementia, multi-disciplinary management approaches, encompassing a number of modalities, have much to recommend them. For example, in a community study, Hinchliffe et al. (1995) reported improvements in behavioural disturbance and carer well-being in response to an individualized care package, including medication, simple psychological techniques (mainly memory aids) and social interventions. Successfully treating care-giver depression directly, where it was present, led to some behaviours previously viewed as intolerable no longer being regarded as problems. This should serve as a reminder that the care-giver's perspective of the problem is an important part of the assessment, and often of the intervention, in challenging behaviour. Effective psychological therapies for depression in care-givers are discussed in Chapter 10. Care-givers' coping and management strategies are likely to be much more effective when they are able to emerge from the negative thought patterns and reduced problem-solving ability associated with depressed mood.

CONCLUSION

The emphasis in this chapter has been on working directly with people with dementia on goals largely related to orientation, communication and achievement. A number of approaches have something to contribute to this work, within the framework of individual assessment and care planning that has been outlined.

Training family caregivers to implement these approaches has not yet been given much attention (see Brodaty, 1992, for a review). Some examples exist in the behavioural literature (e.g. Green, Linsk & Pinkston, 1986) and in the use of a prosthetic memory aid (Bourgeois, 1990) to enhance conversation. It is noteworthy that in the latter study, whilst independent raters confirmed improvements in conversational quality, the relatives involved did not perceive these changes. More attention needs to be given to developing approaches that family caregivers can make use of, without adding to their sense of strain, and which will target areas of value to both caregiver and care recipient. The added dimension of the existing pattern of relationship may well complicate the application of approaches such as RO, reminiscence, validation, etc., and a good deal of creative work is needed to find ways of implementing useful techniques in the family home.

Developing further cognitive models for rehabilitation and management may be particularly helpful, particularly when emotional and behavioural aspects are considered in the overall model, but these need to be extended beyond memory and learning to reflect the wide range of cognitive deficits to be found in dementia. As with all the approaches, the application of cognitive techniques must recognize the individuality of the person with dementia, and ensure that his/her perspective is recognized and respected. The increasing use of psychotherapeutic approaches in dementia is to be welcomed, and special issues arising in working with the person with a mild cognitive impairment need to be identified. Therapeutic listening may hold the key to relating to the person's implicational cognitive subsystem (Teasdale & Barnard, 1993). This affective subsystem perhaps increases its influence on the person's quality of life whilst the cognitive subsystem's integrity declines.

REFERENCES

Alberoni, M., Baddeley, A., Della Sala, S., Logie, R. & Spinnler, H. (1992). Keeping track of a conversation: impairments in Alzheimer's disease. *International Journal of Geriatric Psychiatry*, **7**, 639–646.

Bäckman, L. (1992). Memory training and memory improvement in Alzheimer's disease: rules and exceptions. *Acta Neurologica Scandinavica*, Supplement 139, 84–89.

Baines, S., Saxby, P. & Ehlert, K. (1987). Reality orientation and reminiscence therapy: a controlled cross-over study of elderly confused people. *British Journal of Psychiatry*, **151**, 222–231.

Baker, R., Dowling, Z., Wareing, L. A., Dawson, J. & Assey, J. (1997). Snoezelen: its long-term and short-term effects on older people with dementia. *British Journal of Occupational Therapy*, **60**(5), 213–218.

Barrowclough, C. & Fleming, I. (1986). Training direct care staff in goal-planning with elderly people. *Behavioural Psychotherapy*, **14**, 192–209.

Benson, S. (1994). Sniff and doze therapy. *Journal of Dementia Care*, **2**(1), 12–14.

Bird, M., Alexopoulos, P. & Adamowicz, J. (1995). Success and failure in five case studies: use of cued recall to ameliorate behaviour problems in senile dementia. *International Journal of Geriatric Psychiatry*, **10**, 305–311.

Bird, M. & Kinsella, G. (1996). Long-term cued recall of tasks in senile dementia. *Psychology & Aging*, **11**, 45–56.

Bleathman, C. & Morton, I. (1992). Validation therapy: extracts from 20 groups with dementia sufferers. *Journal of Advanced Nursing*, **17**, 658–666.

Bornat, J. (ed.) (1994). *Reminiscence Reviewed: Perspectives, Evaluations, Achievements*. Buckingham: Open University Press.

Bourgeois, M.S. (1990). Enhancing conversation skills in patients with Alzheimer's disease using a prosthetic memory aid. *Journal of Applied Behavior Analysis*, **23**, 29–42.

Bourgeois, M.S. (1992). *Conversing with Memory Impaired Individuals Using Memory Aids: A Memory Aid Workbook*. Bicester: Winslow Press.

Breuil, V., Rotrou, J.D., Forette, F., Tortrat, D., Ganansia-Ganem, A., Frambourt, A., Moulin, F. & Boller, F. (1994). Cognitive stimulation of patients with dementia: preliminary results. *International Journal of Geriatric Psychiatry*, **9**, 211–217.

Brodaty, H. (1992). Carers: training informal carers. In T. Arie (Ed.), *Recent Advances in Psychogeriatrics*, Vol. 2. (pp. 163–171). Edinburgh: Churchill Livingstone.

Brooker, D.J.R., Snape, M., Johnson, E., Ward, D. & Payne, M. (1997). Single case evaluation of the effects of aromatherapy and massage on disturbed behaviour in severe dementia. *British Journal of Clinical Psychology*, **36**(2), 287–296.

Buckholdt, D.R. & Gubrium, J.F. (1983). Therapeutic pretence in reality orientation. *International Journal of Aging and Human Development*, **16**, 167–181.

Burgess, I.S., Wearden, J.H., Cox, T. & Rae, M. (1992). Operant conditioning with subjects suffering from dementia. *Behavioural Psychotherapy*, **20**, 219–237.

Burgio, L., Engel, B. T., McCormick, K., Hawkins, A. & Scheve, A. (1988). Behavioral treatment for urinary incontinence in elderly inpatients: initial attempts to modify prompting and toileting procedures. *Behavior Therapy*, **19**, 345–357.

Camp, C.J. & Schaller, J.R. (1989). Epilogue: spaced-retrieval memory training in an adult day-care center. *Educational Gerontology*, **15**, 641–648.

Camp, C.J., Foss, J.W., O'Hanlon, A.M. & Stevens, A.B. (1996). Memory interventions for persons with dementia. *Applied Cognitive Psychology*, **10**, 193–210.

Cleary, T.A., Clamon, C., Price, M. & Shullaw, G. (1988). A reduced stimulation unit: effects on patients with Alzheimer's disease and related disorders. *Gerontologist*, **28**, 511–514.

Coleman, P.G. (1986). *Ageing and Reminiscence Processes: Social and Clinical Implications*. Chichester: Wiley.

Downes, J. (1987). Classroom RO and the enhancement of orientation—a critical note. *British Journal of Clinical Psychology*, **26**, 147–148.

Elliott, V. & Milne, D. (1991). Patients' best friend? *Nursing Times*, **87**(6), 34–35.

Feil, N. (1992a). Validation therapy with late-onset dementia populations. In G. Jones & B. Miesen (Eds), *Care-giving in Dementia: Research and Applications* (pp. 199–218). London: Routledge.

Feil, N. (1992b). *Validation: The Feil Method. How to Help Disoriented Old-old*, 2nd edn. Cleveland, OH: Edward Feil Productions/Winslow Press.

Feil, N. (1993). *The Validation Breakthrough: Simple Techniques for Communicating with People with "Alzheimer's Type Dementia".* Baltimore: Health Professions Press.

Gaebler, H.C. & Hemsley, D.R. (1991). The assessment and short-term manipulation of affect in the severely demented. *Behavioural Psychotherapy*, **19**, 145–156.

Garland, J. (1994). What splendour, it all coheres: life-review therapy with older people. In J. Bornat (Ed.), *Reminiscence Reviewed: Evaluations, Achievements, Perspectives* (pp. 21–31). Buckingham: Open University Press.

Gibson, F. (1994). What can reminiscence contribute to people with dementia? In J. Bornat (Ed.), *Reminiscence Reviewed: Evaluations, Achievements, Perspectives* (pp. 46–60). Buckingham: Open University Press.

Gilleard, C., Mitchell, R.G. & Riordan, J. (1981). Ward orientation training with psychogeriatric patients. *Journal of Advanced Nursing*, **6**, 95–98.

Goldwasser, A.N., Auerbach, S.M. & Harkins, S.W. (1987). Cognitive, affective and behavioral effects of reminiscence group therapy on demented elderly. *International Journal of Aging and Human Development*, **25**, 209–222.

Green, G.R., Linsk, N.L. & Pinkston, E.M. (1986). Modification of verbal behavior of the mentally impaired elderly by their spouses. *Journal of Applied Behavior Analysis*, **19**, 329–336.

Greene, J.G., Timbury, G.C., Smith, R. & Gardiner, M. (1983). Reality orientation with elderly patients in the community: an empirical evaluation. *Age and Ageing*, **12**, 38–43.

Haight, B.K. & Burnside, I. (1993). Reminiscence and life review: explaining the differences. *Archives of Psychiatric Nursing*, **7**, 91–98.

Hanley, I.G. (1981). The use of signposts and active training to modify ward disorientation in elderly patients. *Journal of Behaviour Therapy and Experimental Psychiatry*, **12**, 241–247.

Hanley, I.G. & Lusty, K. (1984). Memory aids in reality orientation: a single-case study. *Behaviour Research and Therapy*, **22**, 709–712.

Hanley, I.G., McGuire, R.J. & Boyd, W.D. (1981). Reality orientation and dementia: a controlled trial of two approaches. *British Journal of Psychiatry*, **138**, 10–14.

Haughie, E., Milne, D. & Elliott, V. (1992). An evaluation of companion dogs with elderly psychiatric patients. *Behavioural Psychotherapy*, **20**, 367–372.

Hausman, C. (1992). Dynamic psychotherapy with elderly demented patients. In G. Jones & B.M.L. Miesen (Eds), *Care-giving in Dementia: Research and Applications* (pp. 181–198). London: Routledge.

Head, D., Portnoy, S. & Woods, R.T. (1990). The impact of reminiscence groups in two different settings. *International Journal of Geriatric Psychiatry*, **5**, 295–302.

Heindel, W.C., Salmon, D.P., Shults, C.W., Walicke, P.A. & Butters, N. (1989). Neuropsychological evidence for multiple implicit memory systems: a comparison of Alzheimer's, Huntington's and Parkinson's disease patients. *Journal of Neuroscience*, **9**, 582–587.

Hinchliffe, A.C., Hyman, I.L., Blizard, B. & Livingston, G. (1995). Behavioural complications of dementia—can they be treated? *International Journal of Geriatric Psychiatry*, **10**, 839–847.

Holden, U.P. & Woods, R.T. (1995). *Positive Approaches to Dementia Care*, 3rd edn. Edinburgh: Churchill Livingstone.

Hope, R.A. & Fairburn, C.G. (1990). The nature of wandering in dementia: a community-based study. *International Journal of Geriatric Psychiatry*, **5**, 239–245.

Hussian, R. A. (1981). *Geriatric Psychology: A Behavioral Perspective*. New York: Van Nostrand Reinhold.

Jones, G. (1985). Validation therapy: a companion to reality orientation. *Canadian Nurse*, March, 20–23.

Josephsson, S., Bäckman, L., Borell, L., Bernspang, B., Nygard, L. & Ronnberg, L. (1993). Supporting everyday activities in dementia: an intervention study. *International Journal of Geriatric Psychiatry*, **8**, 395–400.

King's Fund (1986). Living Well into Old Age: Applying Principles of Good Practice to Services for People with Dementia. Project Paper 63. London: King's Fund.

Kitwood, T. (1990). The dialectics of dementia: with particular reference to Alzheimer's disease. *Ageing and Society*, **10**, 177–196.

Kitwood, T. (1992). How valid is validation therapy. Geriatric Medicine, April, 23.

Kitwood, T. & Bredin, K. (1992). Towards a theory of dementia care: personhood and well-being. *Ageing and Society*, **12**, 269–287.

Kitwood, T. (1996). A dialectical framework for dementia. In R. T. Woods (Ed.), *Handbook of the Clinical Psychology of Ageing* (pp. 267–282). Chichester: Wiley.

Kitwood, T. (1997). *Dementia Reconsidered: The Person Comes First*. Buckingham: Open University Press.

Lam, D.H. & Woods, R.T. (1986). Ward orientation training in dementia: a single-case study. *International Journal of Geriatric Psychiatry*, **1**, 145–147.

Langford, S. (1993). A shared vision. *Nursing Times*, 89(44), 66–69.

Little, A.G., Volans, P.J., Hemsley, D.R. & Levy, R. (1986). The retention of new information in senile dementia. *British Journal of Clinical Psychology*, **25**, 71–72.

Lord, T.R. & Garner, J.E. (1993). Effects of music on Alzheimer patients. *Perceptual and Motor Skills*, **76**, 451–455.

Martin, A., Browers, P., Cox, C. & Fedio. P. (1985). On the nature of the verbal memory deficits in Alzheimer's disease. *Brain and Language*, **25**, 323–341.

McKitrick, L.A., Camp, C.J. & Black, F.W. (1992). Prospective memory intervention in Alzheimer's disease. *Journal of Gerontology*, **47**, P337–P343.

Miesen, B.M.L. (1992). Attachment theory and dementia. In G. Jones & B.M.L. Miesen (Eds), *Care-giving in Dementia* (pp. 38–56). London: Routledge.

Miesen, B.M.L. (1993). Alzheimer's disease, the phenomenon of parent fixation and Bowlby's attachment theory. *International Journal of Geriatric Psychiatry*, **8**, 147–153.

Miller, E. (1977). The management of dementia: a review of some possibilities. *British Journal of Social and Clinical Psychology*, **16**, 77–83.

Miller, E. & Morris, R. (1993). *The Psychology of Dementia*. Chichester: Wiley.

Moffat, N.J. (1989). Home-based cognitive rehabilitation with the elderly. In L.W. Poon, D.C. Rubin & B.A. Wilson (Eds), *Everday Cognition in Adulthood and Late Life* (pp. 659–680). Cambridge: Cambridge University Press.

Molloy, D.W., Richardson, L.D. & Crilly, R.G. (1988). The effects of a three-month exercise programme on neuropsychological function in elderly institutionalized women: a randomized controlled trial. *Age and Ageing*, **17**, 303–310.

Morgan, K. (1991). Trial and error: evaluating the psychological benefits of physical activity. *International Journal of Geriatric Psychiatry*, **4**, 125–127.

Morris, R.G. (1994). Recent developments in the neuropsychology of dementia. *International Review of Psychiatry*, **6**, 85–107.

Morris, R.G., Wheatley, J. & Britton, P.G. (1983). Retrieval from long-term memory in senile dementia—cued recall revisited. *British Journal of Clinical Psychology*, **22**, 141–142.

Morton, I. & Bleathman, C. (1991). The effectiveness of validation therapy in dementia: a pilot study. *International Journal of Geriatric Psychiatry*, **6**, 327–330.

Norberg, A., Melin, E. & Asplund, K. (1986). Reactions to music, touch and object presentation in the final stage of dementia: an exploratory study. *International Journal of Nursing Studies*, **23**, 315–323.

Norris, A. (1986). *Reminiscence*. London: Winslow Press.

Orrell, M., & Woods, R. T. (1996). Tacrine and psychological therapies in dementia—no contest? *International Journal of Geriatric Psychiatry*, **11**, 189–192.

Parmelee, P.A. & Lawton, M.P. (1990). The design of special environments for the aged. In J.E. Birren & K.W. Schaie (Eds), *Handbook of the Psychology of Aging* (pp. 464–488). San Diego, CA: Academic Press.

Patel, V. & Hope, T. (1993). Aggressive behaviour in elderly people with dementia: a review. *International Journal of Geriatric Psychiatry*, **8**, 457–472.

Pinkston, E.M. & Linsk, N.L. (1984). *Care of the Elderly—A Family Approach*. New York: Pergamon.

Reeve, W. & Ivison, D. (1985). Use of environmental manipulation and classroom and modified informal reality orientation with institutionalized, confused elderly patients. *Age and Ageing*, **14**, 119–121.

Rice, K. & Warner, N. (1994). Breaking the bad news: what do psychiatrists tell patients with dementia about their illness? *International Journal of Geriatric Psychiatry*, **9**, 467–471.

Rinke, C.L., Williams, J.J., Lloyd, K.E. & Smith-Scott, W. (1978). The effects of prompting and reinforcement on self-bathing by elderly residents of a nursing home. *Behavior Therapy*, **9**, 873–881.

Salmon, P. (1993). Interactions of nurses with elderly patients: relationships to nurses' attitudes and to formal activity periods. *Journal of Advanced Nursing*, **18**, 14–19.

Sandman, C.A. (1993). Memory rehabilitation in Alzheimer's disease: preliminary findings. *Clinical Gerontologist*, **13**, 19–33.

Schnelle, J.F., Newman, D., White, M., Abbey, J., Wallston, K.A., Fogarty, T. & Ory, M.G. (1993). Maintaining continence in nursing home residents through the application of industrial quality control. *Gerontologist*, **33**, 114–121.

Schnelle, J.F., Traughber, B., Sowell, V.A., Newman, D.R., Petrilli, C.O. & Ory, M. (1989). Prompted voiding treatment of urinary incontinence in nursing home patients: a behavior management approach for nursing home staff. *Journal of American Geriatrics Society*, **37**, 1051–1057.

Scogin, F. & McElreath, L. (1994). Efficacy of psychosocial treatments for geriatric depression: a quantitative review. *Journal of Consulting and Clinical Psychology*, **62**, 69–74.

Sinason, V. (1992). The man who was losing his brain. In V. Sinason (Ed.), *Mental Handicap and the Human Condition: New Approaches from the Tavistock* (pp. 87—110). London: Free Association Books, London.

Spaull, D., Leach, C. & Frampton, I. (1998). An evaluation of the effects of sensory stimulation with people who have dementia. *Behavioural & Cognitive Psychotherapy*, **26**, 77–86.

Stirling, E. (1996). Social role valorization: making a difference to the lives of older people? In R. T. Woods (Ed.), *Handbook of the Clinical Psychology of Ageing* (pp. 389–422). Chichester: Wiley.

Stokes, G. (1996). Challenging behaviour in dementia: a psychological approach. In R. T. Woods (Ed.), *Handbook of the Clinical Psychology of Ageing* (pp. 601–628). Chichester: Wiley.

Stokes, G. & Goudie, F. (ed.) (1990). *Working with Dementia*. Bicester: Winslow Press.

Tarrier, N. & Larner, S. (1983). The effects of manipulation of social reinforcement on toilet requests on a geriatric ward. *Age and Ageing*, **12**, 234–239.

Teasdale, J.D. & Barnard, P.J. (1993). *Affect, Cognition and Change: Re-modelling Depressive Thought*. Hove: Erlbaum.

Thompson, L.W., Wagner, B., Zeiss, A. & Gallagher, D. (1990). Cognitive/behavioural therapy with early stage Alzheimer's patients: an exploratory view of the utility of this approach. In E. Light & B.D. Lebowitz (Eds), *Alzheimer's Disease: Treatment and Family Stress* (pp. 383–397). New York: Hemisphere.

Thornton, S. & Brotchie, J. (1987). Reminiscence: a critical review of the empirical literature. *British Journal of Clinical Psychology*, **26**, 93–111.

Ware, C.J.G., Fairburn, C.G. & Hope, R. A. (1990). A community based study of aggressive behaviour in dementia. *International Journal of Geriatric Psychiatry*, **5**, 337–342.

Welden, S. & Yesavage, J.A. (1982). Behavioral improvement with relaxation training in senile dementia. *Clinical Gerontologist*, **1**, 45–49.

West, B. & Brockman, S. (1994). The calming power of aromatherapy. *Journal of Dementia Care*, **2**(2), 20–22.

Williams, J.M.G. (1995). Interacting cognitive subsystems and unvoiced murmurs: a review of "Affect, cognition and change" by John Teasdale and Philip Barnard. *Cognition and Emotion*, **8**, 571–574.

Williams, R., Reeve, W., Ivison, D. & Kavanagh, D. (1987). Use of environmental manipulation and modified informal reality orientation with institutionalized confused elderly subjects: a replication. *Age and Ageing*, **16**, 315–318.

Woods, R.T. (1983). Specificity of learning in reality orientation sessions; a single-case study. *Behaviour Research and Therapy*, **21**, 173–175.

Woods, R.T. (1992). What can be learned from studies on reality orientation? In G. Jones & B. Miesen (Eds), *Care-giving in Dementia* (pp.121–136). London: Routledge.

Woods, R.T. (1995a). The beginnings of a new culture in care. In T. Kitwood & S. Benson (Eds), *The New Culture of Dementia Care* (pp. 19–23). London: Hawker Publications.

Woods, R.T. (1995b). Dementia care: progress and prospects. *Journal of Mental Health*, **4**, 115–124.

Woods, R.T. & Britton, P.G. (1977). Psychological approaches to the treatment of the elderly. *Age and Ageing*, **6**, 104–112.

Woods, R.T. & Britton, P.G. (1985). *Clinical Psychology with the Elderly*. London: Croom Helm/Chapman and Hall.

Woods, R.T. & McKiernan, F. (1995). Evaluating the impact of reminiscence on older people with dementia. In B.K. Haight & J. Webster (Eds), *The Art and Science of Reminiscing: Theory, Research, Methods and Applications* (pp. 233–242). Washington, DC: Taylor & Francis.

Woods, R.T., Portnoy, S., Head, D. & Jones, G. (1992). Reminiscence and life-review with persons with dementia: which way forward? In G. Jones & B. Miesen (Eds), *Care-giving in Dementia* (pp. 137–161). London: Routledge.

Zanetti, O., Magni, E., Binetti, G., Bianchetti, A. & Trabucchi, M. (1994). Is procedural memory stimulation effective in Alzheimer's disease? *International Journal of Geriatric Psychiatry*, **9**, 1006–1007.

Zanetti, O., Frisoni, G. B., DeLeo, D., Buono, M. D., Bianchetti, A. & Trabucchi, M. (1995). Reality orientation therapy in Alzheimer's disease: useful or not? a controlled study. *Alzheimer Disease and Associated Disorders*, **9**, 132 – 138.

INDEX

The Wiley Series in

CLINICAL PSYCHOLOGY

Paul Dickens	Quality and Excellence in Human Services
Edgar Miller and Robin Morris	The Psychology of Dementia
Ronald Blackburn	The Psychology of Criminal Conduct: Theory, Research and Practice
Ian H. Gotlib and Constance L. Hammen	Psychological Aspects of Depression: Toward a Cognitive-Interpersonal Integration
Max Birchwood and Nicholas Tarrier (Editors)	Innovations in the Psychological Management of Schizophrenia: Assessment, Treatment and Services
Robert J. Edelmann	Anxiety: Theory, Research and Intervention in Clinical and Health Psychology
Alastair Agar (Editor)	Microcomputers and Clinical Psychology: Issues, Applications and Future Developments
Bob Remington (Editor)	The Challenge of Severe Mental Handicap: A Behaviour Analytic Approach
Colin A. Espie	The Psychological Treatment of Insomnia
Martin Herbert	Clinical Child Psychology: Social Learning, Development and Behaviour
David Peck and C.M. Shapiro (Editors)	Measuring Human Problems: A Practical Guide
Roger Baker (Editor)	Panic Disorder: Theory, Research and Therapy
Friedrich Försterling	Attribution Theory in Clinical Psychology
Anthony Lavender and Frank Holloway (Editors)	Community Care in Practice: Services for the Continuing Care Client
John Clements	Severe Learning Disability and Psychological Handicap

Related titles of interest...

Handbook of the Clinical Psychology of Ageing
Edited by ROBERT T. WOODS
This handbook focuses on the key areas in the psychology of ageing:
- Problems associated with later life development and change, including neuropsychological and cognitive difficulties arising from conditions such as the dementias
- Emotional problems and depression associated with loss of physical health and with losses and changes in the areas of social relationship and personal identity
- The important clinical context of service delivery is examined, including community care, family care-giving and institutional aspects
- Discusses a broad range of therapeutic orientations, including cognitive-behavioural, psychodynamic, and family therapy approaches.

0471 96136 1 694pp 1996 Hardback

Life-Span Developmental Psychology
Edited by ANDREAS DEMETRIOU, WILLEM DOISE and CORNELIS F. M. VAN LIESHOUT

Offers a broad coverage of all sub-fields of developmental psychology, including chapters on:
- the biological bases of development
- perceptual and motor development
- cognitive development
- communication and language development
- social development
- personality and emotional development
- moral development and wisdom
- developmental psychopathology

0471 97078 6 536pp July 1998 Paperback

618.97   Psychological
Psy   problems of ageing.

DATE			
DEC 1 3 2000			
4/7/a			
11/21/02			
12/4/0			

BAKER & TAYLOR